Get the eBooks FREE!

(PDF, ePub, Kindle, and liveBook all included)

We believe that once you buy a book from us, you should be able to read it in any format we have available. To get electronic versions of this book at no additional cost to you, purchase and then register this book at the Manning website.

Go to https://www.manning.com/freebook and follow the instructions to complete your pBook registration.

That's it!
Thanks from Manning!

Rust in Action

Rust in Action

SYSTEMS PROGRAMMING
CONCEPTS AND TECHNIQUES

TIM MCNAMARA

MANNING

SHELTER ISLAND

Manning Publications Co.
20 Baldwin Road
PO Box 761
Shelter Island, NY 11964

Development editor:	Elesha Hyde
Technical development editor:	René van den Berg
Review editor:	Mihaela Batinic
Production editor:	Deirdre S. Hiam
Copy editor:	Frances Buran
Proofreader:	Melody Dolab
Technical proofreader:	Jerry Kuch
Typesetter:	Dennis Dalinnik
Cover designer:	Marija Tudor

ISBN: 9781617294556
Printed in the United States of America

To everyone aspiring to write safer software.

contents

10 Processes, threads, and containers 328

11 Kernel 365

preface

No one knows whether reading a technical book is going to be worth the effort. These books can be expensive, dull, and poorly written. Even worse, there's a good chance that you won't learn anything. Luckily, this book is written by someone who understands that.

This book's first aim is to teach you Rust. *Rust in Action* presents large, working projects to promote your learning. Over the course of the book, you'll write a database, a CPU emulator, an operating system kernel, and several other interesting projects. You'll even dabble with generative art. Each project is designed to enable you to explore the Rust programming language at your own pace. For those readers who know little Rust, there are many opportunities to expand the projects in whatever direction you choose.

There is more to learning a programming language than studying its syntax and semantics, however. You are also joining a community. Unfortunately, established communities can create invisible barriers for new entrants because of their shared knowledge, jargon, and practices.

One such barrier for many new Rust programmers is the concept of systems programming. Lots of programmers come to Rust without a background in that area. To compensate for this, *Rust in Action* has a second aim—to teach you systems programming. And, among other topics, you'll learn about how memory, digital timekeeping, and device drivers work in the book's 12 chapters. I hope this enables you to feel more comfortable when becoming a member of the Rust community. And we need you!

Our societies depend on software, yet critical security holes are accepted as normal and, perhaps, inevitable. Rust demonstrates that these are neither. Moreover, our computers are filled with bloated, energy-intensive applications. Rust provides a viable alternative for developing software that is less demanding on these finite resources.

Rust in Action is about empowerment. This book's ultimate objective is to convince you of that. Rust is not reserved for a select group of experts. It is a tool that's available for everyone. Well done for making it this far through your learning journey; it's my pleasure to take you a few more steps.

acknowledgments

Thank you to Katie for preventing me from collapsing and for picking me up when I fell down anyway. Thanks also to Florence and Octavia for your hugs and smiles, even when Dad was unable to play because he was writing.

I'm indebted to so many that it feels unfair to list only a select few. There are many members of the Rust community who have supported the book's development. Thousands of readers submitted corrections, questions, and suggestions via the liveBook during the book's development. Every contribution has helped me refine the text. Thank you.

I'm especially grateful to a small number of readers, many of whom have become friends. To Aï Maiga, Ana Hobden, Andrew Meredith, Andréy Lesnikóv, Andy Grove, Arturo J. Pérez, Bruce Mitchener, Cecile Tonglet, Daniel Carosone, Eric Ridge, Esteban Kuber, Florian Gilcher, Ian Battersby, Jane Lusby, Javier Viola, Jonathan Turner, Lachezar Lechev, Luciano Mammino, Luke Jones, Natalie Bloomfield, Oleksandr Kaleniuk, Olivia Ifrim, Paul Faria, Paul J. Symonds, Philipp Gniewosz, Rod Elias, Stephen Oates, Steve Klabnik, Tannr Allard, Thomas Lockney, and William Brown; interacting with you over the last four years has been a special privilege.

To the book's reviewers, I extend my warm thanks to Afshin Mehrabani, Alastair Smith, Bryce Darling, Christoffer Fink, Christopher Haupt, Damian Esteban, Federico Hernandez, Geert Van Laethem, Jeff Lim, Johan Liseborn, Josh Cohen, Konark Modi, Marc Cooper, Morgan Nelson, Ramnivas Laddad, Riccardo Moschetti, Sanket Naik, Sumant Tambe, Tim van Deurzen, Tom Barber, Wade Johnson, William Brown, William Wheeler, and Yves Dorfsman. All of your comments were read. Many of the improvements in the latter stages of the book's development are owed to your thoughtful feedback.

Two team members at Manning deserve special credit for their patience, professionalism, and positivity: Elesha Hyde and Frances Buran have skillfully guided the book through many, many drafts.

Thank you also to the rest of the development editors, including Bert Bates, Jerry Kuch, Mihaela Batinić, Rebecca Rinehart, René van den Berg, and Tim van Deurzen. My thanks also extends to the production editors, including Benjamin Berg, Deirdre Hiam, Jennifer Houle, and Paul Wells.

Rust in Action had 16 releases during its MEAP process, and these would have been impossible without the support of many. Thank you to Aleksandar Dragosavljević, Ana Romac, Eleonor Gardner, Ivan Martinović, Lori Weidert, Marko Rajkovic, Matko Hrvatin, Mehmed Pasic, Melissa Ice, Mihaela Batinic, Owen Roberts, Radmila Ercegovac, and Rejhana Markanovic.

Thanks also to the members of the marketing team, including Branko Latincic, Candace Gillhoolley, Cody Tankersley, Lucas Weber, and Stjepan Jureković. You've been a tremendous source of encouragement for me.

The wider Manning team has also been very responsive and helpful. To Aira Dučić, Andrew Waldron, Barbara Mirecki, Branko Latincic, Breckyn Ely, Christopher Kaufmann, Dennis Dalinnik, Erin Twohey, Ian Hough, Josip Maras, Julia Quinn, Lana Klasic, Linda Kotlyarsky, Lori Kehrwald, and Melody Dolab, thank you for your assistance during the book's development. And to Mike Stephens, thanks for kicking this whole life-changing process off. You warned me that it would be hard. You were right.

about this book

Rust in Action is primarily intended for people who may have explored Rust's free material online, but who then have asked themselves, "What's next?" This book contains dozens of examples that are interesting and can be extended as creativity and time allow. Those examples allow the book's 12 chapters to cover a productive subset of Rust and many of the ecosystem's most important third-party libraries.

The code examples emphasize accessiblity to beginners over elegant, idiomatic Rust. If you are already a knowledgeable Rust programmer, you may find yourself disagreeing with some style decisions in the examples. I hope that you will tolerate this for the sake of learners.

Rust in Action is not intended as a comprehensive reference text book. There are parts of the languages and standard library that have been omitted. Typically, these are highly specialized and deserve specific treatment. Instead, this book aims to provide readers with enough basic knowledge and confidence to learn specialized topics when necessary. *Rust in Action* is also unique from the point of view of systems programming books as almost every example works on Microsoft Windows.

Who should read this book

Anyone who is interested in Rust, who learns by applying practical examples, or who is intimidated by the fact that Rust is a systems programming language will enjoy *Rust in Action*. Readers with prior programming experience will benefit most as some computer programming concepts are assumed.

How this book is organized: A roadmap

Rust in Action has two parts. The first introduces Rust's syntax and some of its distinctive characteristics. The second part applies the knowledge gained in part one to several projects. In each chapter, one or two new Rust concepts are introduced. That said, part 1 provides a quick-fire introduction to Rust:

- Chapter 1, "Introducing Rust," explains why Rust exists and how to get started programming with it.
- Chapter 2, "Language foundations," provides a solid base of Rust syntax. Examples include a Mandelbrot set renderer and a grep clone.
- Chapter 3, "Compound data types," explains how to compose Rust data types and its error-handling facilities.
- Chapter 4, "Lifetimes, ownership, and borrowing," discusses the mechanisms for ensuring that accessing data is always valid.

Part 2 applies Rust to introductory systems programming areas:

- Chapter 5, "Data in Depth," covers how information is represented in digital computers with a special emphasis on how numbers are approximated. Examples include a bespoke number format and a CPU emulator.
- Chapter 6, "Memory," explains the terms references, pointers, virtual memory, stack, and heap. Examples include a memory scanner and a generative art project.
- Chapter 7, "Files and storage," explains the process for storing data structures into storage devices. Examples include a hex dump clone and a working database.
- Chapter 8, "Networking," provides an explanation of how computers communicate by reimplementing HTTP multiple times, stripping away a layer of abstraction each time.
- Chapter 9, "Time and timekeeping," explores the process for keeping track of time within a digital computer. Examples include a working NTP client.
- Chapter 10, "Processes, threads, and containers," explains processes, threads, and related abstractions. Examples include a turtle graphics application and a parallel parser.
- Chapter 11, "Kernel," describes the role of the operating system and how computers boot up. Examples include compiling your own bootloader and an operating system kernel.
- Chapter 12, "Signals, interrupts, and exceptions," explains how the external world communicates with the CPU and operating systems.

The book is intended to be read linearly. Latter chapters assume knowledge taught in earlier ones. However, projects from each chapter are standalone. Therefore, you are welcome to jump backward and forward if there are topics that you would like to cover.

About the code

The code examples in *Rust in Action* are written with the 2018 edition of Rust and have been tested with Windows and Ubuntu Linux. No special software is required outside of a working Rust installation. Installation instructions are provided in chapter 2.

This book contains many examples of source code both in numbered listings and inline with normal text. In both cases, source code is formatted in a `fixed-width font, like this`, to separate it from ordinary text. Sometimes code is also in **bold** to highlight code that has changed from the previous steps in the chapter, such as when a new feature is added to an existing line of code.

In many cases, the original source code has been reformatted; we've added line breaks and reworked indentation to accommodate the available page space in the book. In rare cases, even this was not enough, and listings include line-continuation markers (➥). Additionally, comments in the source code have often been removed from the listings when the code is described in the text. Code annotations accompany many of the listings, highlighting important concepts.

liveBook discussion forum

Purchase of *Rust in Action* includes free access to a private web forum run by Manning Publications where you can make comments about the book, ask technical questions, and receive help from the author and from other users:

- To access the forum, go to https://livebook.manning.com/book/rust-in-action/welcome/v-16/.
- You can also learn more about Manning's forums and the rules of conduct at this location: https://livebook.manning.com/#!/discussion.

Manning's commitment to our readers is to provide a venue where a meaningful dialogue between individual readers and between readers and the author can take place. It is not a commitment to any specific amount of participation on the part of the author, whose contribution to the forum remains voluntary (and unpaid). We suggest you try asking the author some challenging questions lest his interest stray! The forum and the archives of previous discussions will be accessible from the publisher's website as long as the book is in print.

Other online resources

Tim can be found on social media as @timClicks. His primary channels are Twitter (https://twitter.com/timclicks), YouTube (https://youtube.com/c/timclicks), and Twitch (https://twitch.tv/timclicks). You are also welcome to join his Discord server at https://discord.gg/vZBX2bDa7W.

about the author

TIM MCNAMARA learned programming to assist with humanitarian relief projects around the world from his home in New Zealand. Over the last 15 years, Tim has become an expert in text mining, natural language processing, and data engineering. He is the organizer of Rust Wellington and hosts regular Rust programming tutorials in person and online via Twitch and YouTube.

about the cover illustration

The figure on the cover of *Rust in Action* is captioned "Le maitre de chausson" or "The boxer." The illustration is taken from a collection of works by many artists, edited by Louis Curmer and published in Paris in 1841. The title of the collection is *LesFrançais peints par eux-mêmes*, which translates as *The French People Painted by Themselves.* Each illustration is finely drawn and colored by hand, and the rich variety of drawing in the collection reminds us vividly of how culturally apart the world's regions, towns, villages, and neighborhoods were just 200 years ago. Isolated from each other, people spoke different dialects and languages. In the streets or in the countryside, it was easy to identify where they lived and what their trade or station in life was just by their dress.

Dress codes have changed since then and the diversity by region, so rich at the time, has faded away. It is now hard to tell apart the inhabitants of different continents, let alone different towns or regions. Perhaps we have traded cultural diversity for a more varied personal life—certainly for a more varied and fast-paced technological life.

At a time when it is hard to tell one computer book from another, Manning celebrates the inventiveness and initiative of the computer business with book covers based on the rich diversity of regional life of two centuries ago, brought back to life by pictures from collections such as this one.

Introducing Rust 1

This chapter covers

- Introducing Rust's features and goals
- Exposing Rust's syntax
- Discussing where to use Rust and when to avoid it
- Building your first Rust program
- Explaining how Rust compares to object-oriented and wider languages

Welcome to Rust—the empowering programming language. Once you scratch its surface, you will not only find a programming language with unparalleled speed and safety, but one that is enjoyable enough to use every day.

When you begin to program in Rust, it's likely that you will want to continue to do so. And this book, *Rust in Action*, will build your confidence as a Rust programmer. But it will not teach you how to program from the beginning. This book is intended to be read by people who are considering Rust as their next language and for those who enjoy implementing practical working examples. Here is a list of some of the larger examples this book includes:

- Mandelbrot set renderer
- A grep clone

1

- CPU emulator
- Generative art
- A database
- HTTP, NTP, and hexdump clients
- LOGO language interpreter
- Operating system kernel

As you may gather from scanning through that list, reading this book will teach you more than just Rust. It also introduces you to *systems programming* and *low-level programming*. As you work through *Rust in Action*, you'll learn about the role of an operating system (OS), how a CPU works, how computers keep time, what pointers are, and what a data type is. You will gain an understanding of how the computer's internal systems interoperate. Learning more than syntax, you will also see why Rust was created and the challenges that it addresses.

1.1   *Where is Rust used?*

Rust has won the "most loved programming language" award in Stack Overflow's annual developer survey every year in 2016-2020. Perhaps that's why large technology leaders such as the following have adopted Rust:

- Amazon Web Services (AWS) has used Rust since 2017 for its serverless computing offerings, AWS Lambda and AWS Fargate. With that, Rust has gained further inroads. The company has written the Bottlerocket OS and the AWS Nitro System to deliver its Elastic Compute Cloud (EC2) service.[1]
- Cloudflare develops many of its services, including its public DNS, serverless computing, and packet inspection offerings with Rust.[2]
- Dropbox rebuilt its backend warehouse, which manages exabytes of storage, with Rust.[3]
- Google develops parts of Android, such as its Bluetooth module, with Rust. Rust is also used for the crosvm component of Chrome OS and plays an important role in Google's new operating system, Fuchsia.[4]
- Facebook uses Rust to power Facebook's web, mobile, and API services, as well as parts of HHVM, the HipHop virtual machine used by the Hack programming language.[5]
- Microsoft writes components of its Azure platform including a security daemon for its Internet of Things (IoT) service in Rust.[6]

---

[1] See "How our AWS Rust team will contribute to Rust's future successes," http://mng.bz/BR4J.

[2] See "Rust at Cloudflare," https://news.ycombinator.com/item?id=17077358.

[3] See "The Epic Story of Dropbox's Exodus From the Amazon Cloud Empire," http://mng.bz/d45Q.

[4] See "Google joins the Rust Foundation," http://mng.bz/ryOX.

[5] See "HHVM 4.20.0 and 4.20.1," https://hhvm.com/blog/2019/08/27/hhvm-4.20.0.html.

[6] See https://github.com/Azure/iotedge/tree/master/edgelet.

- Mozilla uses Rust to enhance the Firefox web browser, which contains 15 million lines of code. Mozilla's first two Rust-in-Firefox projects, its MP4 metadata parser and text encoder/decoder, led to overall performance and stability improvements.
- GitHub's npm, Inc., uses Rust to deliver "upwards of 1.3 billion package downloads per day."[7]
- Oracle developed a container runtime with Rust to overcome problems with the Go reference implementation.[8]
- Samsung, via its subsidiary SmartThings, uses Rust in its *Hub*, which is the firmware backend for its Internet of Things (IoT) service.

Rust is also productive enough for fast-moving startups to deploy it. Here are a few examples:

- Sourcegraph uses Rust to serve syntax highlighting across all of its languages.[9]
- Figma employs Rust in the performance-critical components of its multi-player server.[10]
- Parity develops its client to the Ethereum blockchain with Rust.[11]

1.2 Advocating for Rust at work

What is it like to advocate for Rust at work? After overcoming the initial hurdle, it tends to go well. A 2017 discussion, reprinted below, provides a nice anecdote. One member of Google's Chrome OS team discusses what it was like to introduce the language to the project:[12]

```
indy on Sept 27, 2017
Is Rust an officially sanctioned language at Google?

  zaxcellent on Sept 27, 2017
  Author here: Rust is not officially sanctioned at Google, but there are
  pockets of folks using it here. The trick with using Rust in this
  component was convincing my coworkers that no other language was right
  for job, which I believe to be the case in this instance.

  That being said, there was a ton of work getting Rust to play nice
  within the Chrome OS build environment. The Rust folks have been super
  helpful in answering my questions though.

    ekidd on Sept 27, 2017
    > The trick with using Rust in this component was convincing my
```

---

[7] See "Rust Case Study: Community makes Rust an easy choice for npm," http://mng.bz/xm9B.

[8] See "Building a Container Runtime in Rust," http://mng.bz/d40Q.

[9] See "HTTP code syntax highlighting server written in Rust," https://github.com/sourcegraph/syntect_server.

[10] See "Rust in Production at Figma," https://www.figma.com/blog/rust-in-production-at-figma/.

[11] See "The fast, light, and robust EVM and WASM client," https://github.com/paritytech/parity-ethereum.

[12] See "Chrome OS KVM—A component written in Rust," https://news.ycombinator.com/item?id=15346557.

```
> coworkers that no other language was right for job, which I believe
> to be the case in this instance.

I ran into a similar use case in one of my own projects—a vobsub
subtitle decoder, which parses complicated binary data, and which I
someday want to run as web service.  So obviously, I want to ensure
that there are no vulnerabilities in my code.

I wrote the code in Rust, and then I used 'cargo fuzz' to try and
find vulnerabilities. After running a billion(!) fuzz iterations, I
found 5 bugs (see the 'vobsub' section of the trophy case for a list
https://github.com/rust-fuzz/trophy-case).

Happily, not _one_ of those bugs could actually be escalated into an
actual exploit. In each case, Rust's various runtime checks
successfully caught the problem and turned it into a controlled panic.
(In practice, this would restart the web server cleanly.)

So my takeaway from this was that whenever I want a language (1) with
no GC, but (2) which I can trust in a security-critical context, Rust
is an excellent choice. The fact that I can statically link Linux
binaries (like with Go) is a nice plus.

    Manishearth on Sept 27, 2017
    > Happily, not one of those bugs could actually be escalated into
    > an actual exploit. In each case, Rust's various runtime checks
    > successfully caught the problem and turned it into a controlled
    > panic.

    This has been more or less our experience with fuzzing rust code in
    firefox too, fwiw. Fuzzing found a lot of panics (and debug
    assertions / "safe" overflow assertions). In one case it actually
    found a bug that had been under the radar in the analogous Gecko
    code for around a decade.
```

From this excerpt, we can see that language adoption has been "bottom up" by engineers looking to overcome technical challenges in relatively small projects. Experience gained from these successes is then used as evidence to justify undertaking more ambitious work.

In the time since late 2017, Rust has continued to mature and strengthen. It has become an accepted part of Google's technology landscape, and is now an officially sanctioned language within the Android and Fuchsia operating systems.

1.3   *A taste of the language*

This section gives you a chance to experience Rust firsthand. It demonstrates how to use the compiler and then moves on to writing a quick program. We tackle full projects in later chapters.

NOTE   To install Rust, use the official installers provided at https://rustup.rs/.

1.3.1 Cheating your way to "Hello, world!"

The first thing that most programmers do when they reach for a new programming language is to learn how to print "Hello, world!" to the console. You'll do that too, but with flair. You'll verify that everything is in working order *before* you encounter annoying syntax errors.

If you use Windows, open the Rust command prompt that is available in the Start menu after installing Rust. Then execute this command:

```
C:\> cd %TMP%
```

If you are running Linux or macOS, open a Terminal window. Once open, enter the following:

```
$ cd $TMP
```

From this point forward, the commands for all operating systems should be the same. If you installed Rust correctly, the following three commands will display "Hello, world!" on the screen (as well as a bunch of other output):

```
$ cargo new hello
$ cd hello
$ cargo run
```

Here is an example of what the entire session looks like when running cmd.exe on MS Windows:

```
C:\> cd %TMP%

C:\Users\Tim\AppData\Local\Temp\> cargo new hello
     Created binary (application) `hello` project

C:\Users\Tim\AppData\Local\Temp\> cd hello

C:\Users\Tim\AppData\Local\Temp\hello\> cargo run
   Compiling hello v0.1.0 (file:///C:/Users/Tim/AppData/Local/Temp/hello)
    Finished dev [unoptimized + debuginfo] target(s) in 0.32s
     Running `target\debug\hello.exe`
Hello, world!
```

And on Linux or macOS, your console would look like this:

```
$ cd $TMP

$ cargo new hello
     Created binary (application) `hello` package

$ cd hello

$ cargo run
   Compiling hello v0.1.0 (/tmp/hello)
```

```
   Finished dev [unoptimized + debuginfo] target(s) in 0.26s
    Running `target/debug/hello`
Hello, world!
```

If you have made it this far, fantastic! You have run your first Rust code without needing to write any Rust. Let's take a look at what just happened.

Rust's cargo tool provides both a build system and a package manager. That means cargo knows how to convert your Rust code into executable binaries and also can manage the process of downloading and compiling the project's dependencies.

cargo new creates a project for you that follows a standard template. The tree command can reveal the default project structure and the files that are created after issuing cargo new:

```
$ tree hello
hello
├── Cargo.toml
└── src
    └── main.rs

1 directory, 2 files
```

All Rust projects created with cargo have the same structure. In the base directory, a file called Cargo.toml describes the project's metadata, such as the project's name, its version, and its dependencies. Source code appears in the src directory. Rust source code files use the .rs filename extension. To view the files that cargo new creates, use the tree command.

The next command that you executed was cargo run. This line is much simpler to grasp, but cargo actually did much more work than you realized. You asked cargo to run the project. As there was nothing to actually run when you invoked the command, it decided to compile the code in debug mode on your behalf to provide maximal error information. As it happens, the src/main.rs file always includes a "Hello, world!" stub. The result of that compilation was a file called hello (or hello.exe). The hello file was executed, and the result printed to your screen.

Executing cargo run has also added new files to the project. We now have a Cargo.lock file in the base of our project and a target/ directory. Both that file and the directory are managed by cargo. Because these are artifacts of the compilation process, we won't need to touch these. Cargo.lock is a file that specifies the exact version numbers of all the dependencies so that future builds are reliably built the same way until Cargo.toml is modified.

Running tree again reveals the new structure created by invoking cargo run to compile the hello project:

```
$ tree --dirsfirst hello
hello
├── src
│   └── main.rs
```

```
├── target
│   └── debug
│       ├── build
│       ├── deps
│       ├── examples
│       ├── native
│       └── hello
├── Cargo.lock
└── Cargo.toml
```

For getting things up and running, well done! Now that we've cheated our way to "Hello, World!", let's get there via the long way.

1.3.2 Your first Rust program

For our first program, we want to write something that outputs the following text in multiple languages:

```
Hello, world!
Grüß Gott!
ハロー・ワールド
```

You have probably seen the first line in your travels. The other two are there to highlight a few of Rust's features: easy iteration and built-in support for Unicode. For this program, we'll use cargo to create it as before. Here are the steps to follow:

1 Open a console prompt.
2 Run `cd %TMP%` on MS Windows; otherwise `cd $TMP`.
3 Run `cargo new hello2` to create a new project.
4 Run `cd hello2` to move into the project's root directory.
5 Open the file src/main.rs in a text editor.
6 Replace the text in that file with the text in listing 1.1.

The code for the following listing is in the source code repository. Open ch1/ch1-hello2/src/hello2.rs.

Listing 1.1 "Hello World!" in three languages

Array literals use square brackets.

The exclamation mark indicates the use of a macro, which we'll discuss shortly.

Assignment in Rust, more properly called variable binding, uses the let keyword.

Unicode support is provided out of the box.

Many types can have an iter() method to return an iterator.

The ampersand "borrows" region for read-only access.

```
1 fn greet_world() {
2     println!("Hello, world!");
3     let southern_germany = "Grüß Gott!";
4     let japan = "ハロー・ワールド";
5     let regions = [southern_germany, japan];
6     for region in regions.iter() {
7             println!("{}", &region);
8     }
9 }
```

```
10
11 fn main() {
12     greet_world();              ◄───┤  Calls a function. Note
13 }                                    │  that parentheses follow
                                        │  the function name.
```

Now that src/main.rs is updated, execute cargo run from the hello2/ directory. You should see three greetings appear after some output generated from cargo itself:

```
$ cargo run
   Compiling hello2 v0.1.0 (/path/to/ch1/ch1-hello2)
    Finished dev [unoptimized + debuginfo] target(s) in 0.95s
     Running `target/debug/hello2`
Hello, world!
Grüß Gott!
ハロー・ワールド
```

Let's take a few moments to touch on some of the interesting elements of Rust from listing 1.1.

One of the first things that you are likely to notice is that strings in Rust are able to include a wide range of characters. Strings are guaranteed to be encoded as UTF-8. This means that you can use non-English languages with relative ease.

The one character that might look out of place is the exclamation mark after println. If you have programmed in Ruby, you may be used to thinking that it is used to signal a destructive operation. In Rust, it signals the use of a *macro*. Macros can be thought of as fancy functions for now. These offer the ability to avoid boilerplate code. In the case of println!, there is a lot of type detection going on under the hood so that arbitrary data types can be printed to the screen.

1.4   *Downloading the book's source code*

In order to follow along with the examples in this book, you might want to access the source code for the listings. For your convenience, source code for every example is available from two sources:

- https://manning.com/books/rust-in-action
- https://github.com/rust-in-action/code

1.5   *What does Rust look and feel like?*

Rust is the programming language that allows Haskell and Java programmers to get along. Rust comes close to the high-level, expressive feel of dynamic languages like Haskell and Java while achieving low-level, bare-metal performance.

We looked at a few "Hello, world!" examples in section 1.3, so let's try something slightly more complex to get a better feel for Rust's features. Listing 1.2 provides a quick look at what Rust can do for basic text processing. The source code for this listing is in the ch1/ch1-penguins/src/main.rs file. Some features to notice include

- *Common control flow mechanisms*—This includes for loops and the continue keyword.
- *Method syntax*—Although Rust is not object-oriented as it does not support inheritance, it carries over this feature of object-oriented languages.
- *Higher-order programming*—Functions can both accept and return functions. For example, line 19 (.map(|field| field.trim())) includes a *closure*, also known as an *anonymous function* or *lambda function*.
- *Type annotations*—Although relatively rare, these are occasionally required as a hint to the compiler (for example, see line 27 beginning with if let Ok(length)).
- *Conditional compilation*—In the listing, lines 21–24 (if cfg!(…);) are not included in release builds of the program.
- *Implicit return*—Rust provides a return keyword, but it's usually omitted. Rust is an *expression-based language.*

Listing 1.2 Example of Rust code showing some basic processing of CSV data

```
1  fn main() {
2      let penguin_data = "\
3  common name,length (cm)
4  Little penguin,33
5  Yellow-eyed penguin,65
6  Fiordland penguin,60
7  Invalid,data
8  ";
9
10     let records = penguin_data.lines();
11
12     for (i, record) in records.enumerate() {
13         if i == 0 || record.trim().len() == 0 {
14             continue;
15         }
16
17         let fields: Vec<_> = record
18             .split(',')
19             .map(|field| field.trim())
20             .collect();
21         if cfg!(debug_assertions) {
22             eprintln!("debug: {:?} -> {:?}",
23                     record, fields);
24         }
25
26         let name = fields[0];
27         if let Ok(length) = fields[1].parse::<f32>() {
28             println!("{}, {}cm", name, length);
29         }
30     }
31 }
```

Executable projects require a main() function.

Escapes the trailing newline character

Skips header row and lines with only whitespace

Starts with a line of text

Splits record into fields

Trims whitespace of each field

Builds a collection of fields

cfg! checks configuration at compile time.

eprintln! prints to standard error (stderr).

Attempts to parse field as a floating-point number

println! prints to standard out (stdout).

Listing 1.2 might be confusing to some readers, especially those who have never seen Rust before. Here are some brief notes before moving on:

- On line 17, the `fields` variable is annotated with the type `Vec<_>`. `Vec` is shorthand for _vector_, a collection type that can expand dynamically. The underscore (_) instructs Rust to infer the type of the elements.

- On lines 22 and 28, we instruct Rust to print information to the console. The `println!` macro prints its arguments to standard out (stdout), whereas `eprintln!` prints to standard error (stderr).

   Macros are similar to functions except that instead of returning data, these return code. Macros are often used to simplify common patterns.

   `eprintln!` and `println!` both use a string literal with an embedded minilanguage in their first argument to control their output. The `{}` placeholder tells Rust to use a programmer-defined method to represent the value as a string rather than the default representation available with `{:?}`.

- Line 27 contains some novel features. `if let Ok(length) = fields[1].parse ::<f32>()` reads as "attempt to parse `fields[1]` as a 32-bit floating-point number and, if that is successful, then assign the number to the length variable."

   The `if let` construct is a concise method of conditionally processing data that also provides a local variable assigned to that data. The `parse()` method returns `Ok(T)` (where `T` stands for any type) when it can successfully parse the string; otherwise, it returns `Err(E)` (where `E` stands for an error type). The effect of `if let Ok(T)` is to skip any error cases like the one that's encountered while processing the line `Invalid,data`.

   When Rust is unable to infer the types from the surrounding context, it will ask for you to specify those. The call to `parse()` includes an inline type annotation as `parse::<f32>()`.

Converting source code into an executable file is called *compiling*. To compile Rust code, we need to install the Rust compiler and run it against the source code. To compile listing 1.2, follow these steps:

1 Open a console prompt (such as cmd.exe, PowerShell, Terminal, or Alacritty).
2 Move to the ch1/ch1-penguins directory (not ch1/ch1-penguins/src) of the source code you downloaded in section 1.4.
3 Execute `cargo run`. Its output is shown in the following code snippet:

```
$ cargo run
   Compiling ch1-penguins v0.1.0 (../code/ch1/ch1-penguins)
    Finished dev [unoptimized + debuginfo] target(s) in 0.40s
     Running `target/debug/ch1-penguins`
dbg: " Little penguin,33" -> ["Little penguin", "33"]
Little penguin, 33cm
dbg: " Yellow-eyed penguin,65" -> ["Yellow-eyed penguin", "65"]
Yellow-eyed penguin, 65cm
dbg: " Fiordland penguin,60" -> ["Fiordland penguin", "60"]
Fiordland penguin, 60cm
dbg: " Invalid,data" -> ["Invalid", "data"]
```

You probably noticed the distracting lines starting with dbg:. We can eliminate these by compiling a *release build* using cargo's --release flag. This conditional compilation functionality is provided by the cfg!(debug_assertions) { … } block within lines 22–24 of listing 1.2. Release builds are much faster at runtime, but incur longer compilation times:

```
$ cargo run --release
    Compiling ch1-penguins v0.1.0 (.../code/ch1/ch1-penguins)
    Finished release [optimized] target(s) in 0.34s
     Running `target/release/ch1-penguins`
Little penguin, 33cm
Yellow-eyed penguin, 65cm
Fiordland penguin, 60cm
```

It's possible to further reduce the output by adding the -q flag to cargo commands. -q is shorthand for *quiet*. The following snippet shows what that looks like:

```
$ cargo run -q --release
Little penguin, 33cm
Yellow-eyed penguin, 65cm
Fiordland penguin, 60cm
```

Listing 1.1 and listing 1.2 were chosen to pack as many representative features of Rust into examples that are easy to understand. Hopefully these demonstrated that Rust programs have a high-level feel, paired with low-level performance. Let's take a step back from specific language features now and consider some of the thinking behind the language and where it fits within the programming language ecosystem.

1.6 *What is Rust?*

Rust's distinguishing feature as a programming language is its ability to prevent invalid data access at compile time. Research projects by Microsoft's Security Response Center and the Chromium browser project both suggest that issues relating to invalid data access account for approximately 70% of serious security bugs.[13] Rust eliminates that class of bugs. It guarantees that your program is *memory-safe* without imposing any runtime costs.

Other languages can provide this level of safety, but these require adding checks that execute while your program is running, thus slowing it down. Rust manages to break out of this continuum, creating its own space as illustrated by figure 1.1.

Rust's distinguishing feature as a professional community is its willingness to explicitly include values into its decision-making process. This ethos of inclusion is pervasive. Public messaging is welcoming. All interactions within the Rust community are governed by its code of conduct. Even the Rust compiler's error messages are ridiculously helpful.

---

[13] See the articles "We need a safer systems programming language," http://mng.bz/VdN5 and "Memory safety," http://mng.bz/xm7B for more information.

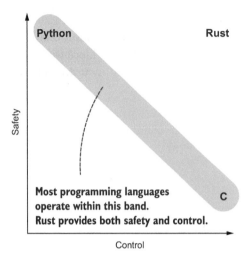

Figure 1.1   **Rust provides both safety and control. Other languages have tended to trade one against the other.**

Until late 2018, visitors to the Rust home page were greeted with the (technically heavy) message, "Rust is a systems programming language that runs blazingly fast, prevents segfaults, and guarantees thread safety." At that point, the community implemented a change to its wording to put its users (and its potential users) at the center (table 1.1).

Table 1.1   **Rust slogans over time. As Rust has developed its confidence, it has increasingly embraced the idea of acting as a facilitator and supporter of everyone wanting to achieve their programming aspirations.**

Until late 2018	From that point onward
"Rust is a systems programming language that runs blazingly fast, prevents segfaults, and guarantees thread safety."	"Empowering everyone to build reliable and efficient software."

Rust is labelled as a *systems programming language*, which tends to be seen as quite a specialized, almost esoteric branch of programming. However, many Rust programmers have discovered that the language is applicable to many other domains. Safety, productivity, and control are useful in all software engineering projects. Moreover, the Rust community's inclusiveness means that the language benefits from a steady stream of new voices with diverse interests.

Let's flesh out those three goals: safety, productivity, and control. What are these and why do these matter?

1.6.1   *Goal of Rust: Safety*

Rust programs are free from

- *Dangling pointers*—Live references to data that has become invalid over the course of the program (see listing 1.3)

- *Data races*—The inability to determine how a program will behave from run to run because external factors change (see listing 1.4)
- *Buffer overflow*—An attempt to access the 12th element of an array with only 6 elements (see listing 1.5)
- *Iterator invalidation*—An issue caused by something that is iterated over after being altered midway through (see listing 1.6)

When programs are compiled in debug mode, Rust also protects against *integer overflow*. What is integer overflow? Well, integers can only represent a finite set of numbers; these have a fixed-width in memory. Integer overflow is what happens when the integers hit their limit and flow over to the beginning again.

The following listing shows a dangling pointer. Note that you'll find this source code in the ch1/ch1-cereals/src/main.rs file.

Listing 1.3 Attempting to create a dangling pointer

```
 1 #[derive(Debug)]                          Allows the println! macro
 2 enum Cereal {                             to print the Cereal enum
 3     Barley, Millet, Rice,
 4     Rye, Spelt, Wheat,          An enum (enumeration) is
 5 }                               a type with a fixed number
 6                                 of legal variants.
 7 fn main() {                                Initializes an empty
 8     let mut grains: Vec<Cereal> = vec![];  vector of Cereal
 9     grains.push(Cereal::Rye);
10     drop(grains);                          Adds one item to
11     println!("{:?}", grains);              the grains vector
12 }
         Attempts to access        Deletes grains
         the deleted value         and its contents
```

Listing 1.3 contains a pointer within `grains`, which is created on line 8. `Vec<Cereal>` is implemented with an internal pointer to an underlying array. But the listing does not compile. An attempt to do so triggers an error message that complains about attempting to "borrow" a "moved" value. Learning how to interpret that error message and to fix the underlying error are topics for the pages to come. Here's the output from attempting to compile the code for listing 1.3:

```
$ cargo run
   Compiling ch1-cereals v0.1.0 (/rust-in-action/code/ch1/ch1-cereals)
error[E0382]: borrow of moved value: `grains`
  --> src/main.rs:12:22
   |
8  |     let mut grains: Vec<Cereal> = vec![];
   |         ------- move occurs because `grains` has type
   |                 `std::vec::Vec<Cereal>`, which does not implement
   |                 the `Copy` trait
9  |     grains.push(Cereal::Rye);
10 |     drop(grains);
   |          ------ value moved here
11 |
```

```
12 |       println!("{:?}", grains);
   |                        ^^^^^^ value borrowed here after move

error: aborting due to previous error

For more information about this error, try `rustc --explain E0382`.
error: could not compile `ch1-cereals`.
```

Listing 1.4 shows an example of a data race condition. If you remember, this condition results from the inability to determine how a program behaves from run to run due to changing external factors. You'll find this code in the ch1/ch1-race/src/main.rs file.

Listing 1.4   Example of Rust preventing a race condition

```
1 use std::thread;          ◄──┐  Brings multi-threading
2 fn main() {                   │  into local scope
3     let mut data = 100;
4
5     thread::spawn(|| { data = 500; });      │  thread::spawn() takes a
6     thread::spawn(|| { data = 1000; });     │  closure as an argument.
7     println!("{}", data);
8 }
```

If you are unfamiliar with the term *thread*, the upshot is that this code is not deterministic. It's impossible to know what value data will hold when main() exits. On lines 6 and 7 of the listing, two threads are created by calls to thread::spawn(). Each call takes a closure as an argument, denoted by vertical bars and curly braces (e.g., || {...}). The thread spawned on line 5 is attempting to set the data variable to 500, whereas the thread spawned on line 6 is attempting to set it to 1,000. Because the scheduling of threads is determined by the OS rather than the program, it's impossible to know if the thread defined first will be the one that runs first.

Attempting to compile listing 1.5 results in a stampede of error messages. Rust does not allow multiple places in an application to have write access to data. The code attempts to allow this in three places: once within the main thread running main() and once in each child thread created by thread::spawn(). Here's the compiler message:

```
$ cargo run
   Compiling ch1-race v0.1.0 (rust-in-action/code/ch1/ch1-race)
error[E0373]: closure may outlive the current function, but it
              borrows `data`, which is owned by the current function
  --> src/main.rs:6:19
   |
6  |     thread::spawn(|| { data = 500; });
   |                   ^^   ---- `data` is borrowed here
   |                   |
   |                   may outlive borrowed value `data`
   |
note: function requires argument type to outlive `'static`
  --> src/main.rs:6:5
```

```
6 |        thread::spawn(|| { data = 500; });
  |        ^^^^^^^^^^^^^^^^^^^^^^^^^^^^^^^^^^^^
help: to force the closure to take ownership of `data`
      (and any other referenced variables), use the `move` keyword
  |
6 |        thread::spawn(move || { data = 500; });
  |                      ^^^^^^^
```

                                    Three other errors omitted.
...   ◄┘
error: aborting due to 4 previous errors

```
Some errors have detailed explanations: E0373, E0499, E0502.
For more information about an error, try `rustc --explain E0373`.
error: could not compile `ch1-race`.
```

Listing 1.5 provides an example of a buffer overflow. A buffer overflow describes situations where an attempt is made to access items in memory that do not exist or that are illegal. In our case, an attempt to access `fruit[4]` results in the program crashing, as the `fruit` variable only contains three fruit. The source code for this listing is in the file ch1/ch1-fruit/src/main.rs.

Listing 1.5   Example of invoking a panic via a buffer overflow

```
1 fn main() {
2     let fruit = vec!['🍎', '🍌', '🍑'];          Rust will cause a crash rather
3                                                  than assign an invalid memory
4     let buffer_overflow = fruit[4];      ◄───┘   location to a variable.
5     assert_eq!(buffer_overflow, '🍑')    ◄───┐
6 }                                             assert_eq!() tests that
                                                arguments are equal.
```

When listing 1.5 is compiled and executed, you'll encounter this error message:

```
$ cargo run
   Compiling ch1-fruit v0.1.0 (/rust-in-action/code/ch1/ch1-fruit)
   Finished dev [unoptimized + debuginfo] target(s) in 0.31s
    Running `target/debug/ch1-fruit`
thread 'main' panicked at 'index out of bounds:
   the len is 3 but the index is 4', src/main.rs:3:25
note: run with `RUST_BACKTRACE=1` environment variable
   to display a backtrace
```

The next listing shows an example of iterator invalidation, where an issue is caused by something that's iterated over after being altered midway through. The source code for this listing is in ch1/ch1-letters/src/main.rs.

Listing 1.6   Attempting to modify an iterator while iterating over it

```
1 fn main() {
2     let mut letters = vec![       ◄───┐   Creates a mutable
3         "a", "b", "c"                     vector letters
4     ];
```

```
 5
 6      for letter in letters {                    Copies each letter
 7          println!("{}", letter);                and appends it to the
 8          letters.push(letter.clone());  ◁─┐     end of letters
 9      }
10  }
```

Listing 1.6 fails to compile because Rust does not allow the `letters` variable to be modified within the iteration block. Here's the error message:

```
$ cargo run
   Compiling ch1-letters v0.1.0 (/rust-in-action/code/ch1/ch1-letters)
error[E0382]: borrow of moved value: `letters`
 --> src/main.rs:8:7
  |
2 |   let mut letters = vec![
  |           ---------- move occurs because `letters` has type
  |                      `std::vec::Vec<&str>`, which does not
  |                      implement the `Copy` trait
...
6 |   for letter in letters {
  |                 -------
  |                    |
  |                 `letters` moved due to this implicit call
  |                 to `.into_iter()`
  |                 help: consider borrowing to avoid moving
  |                 into the for loop: `&letters`
7 |       println!("{}", letter);
8 |       letters.push(letter.clone());
  |       ^^^^^^^ value borrowed here after move

error: aborting due to previous error

For more information about this error, try `rustc --explain E0382`.
error: could not compile `ch1-letters`.

To learn more, run the command again with --verbose.
```

While the language of the error message is filled with jargon (*borrow, move, trait,* and so on), Rust has protected the programmer from stepping into a trap that many others fall into. And fear not—that jargon will become easier to understand as you work through the first few chapters of this book.

Knowing that a language is safe provides programmers with a degree of liberty. Because they know their program won't implode, they become much more willing to experiment. Within the Rust community, this liberty has spawned the expression *fearless concurrency.*

1.6.2 Goal of Rust: Productivity

When given a choice, Rust prefers the option that is easiest for the developer. Many of its more subtle features are productivity boosts. But programmer productivity is a difficult concept to demonstrate through an example in a book. Let's start with something that can snag beginners—using assignment (=) within an expression that should use an equality (==) test:

```
1 fn main() {
2     let a = 10;
3
4     if a = 10 {
5         println!("a equals ten");
6     }
7 }
```

In Rust, the preceding code fails to compile. The Rust compiler generates the following message:

```
error[E0308]: mismatched types
  --> src/main.rs:4:8
   |
4 |     if a = 10 {
   |        ^^^^^^
   |        |
   |        expected `bool`, found `()`
   |        help: try comparing for equality: `a == 10`

error: aborting due to previous error

For more information about this error, try `rustc --explain E0308`.
error: could not compile `playground`.

To learn more, run the command again with --verbose.
```

At first, "mismatched types" might feel like a strange error message to encounter. Surely we can test variables for equality against integers.

After some thought, it becomes apparent why the if test receives the wrong type. The if is not receiving an integer. It's receiving the result of an assignment. In Rust, this is the blank type: (). () is pronounced *unit*.[14]

When there is no other meaningful return value, expressions return (). As the following shows, adding a second equals sign on line 4 results in a working program that prints a equals ten:

```
1 fn main() {
2     let a = 10;
3
4     if a == 10 {
5         println!("a equals ten");
6     }
7 }
```

Using a valid assignment operator (==) allows the program to compile.

---

[14] The name *unit* reveals some of Rust's heritage as a descendant of the ML family of programming languages that includes OCaml and F#. The term stems from mathematics. Theoretically, a unit type only has a single value. Compare this with Boolean types that have two values, true or false, or strings that have an infinite number of valid values.

Rust has many ergonomic features. It offers generics, sophisticated data types, pattern matching, and closures.[15] Those who have worked with other ahead-of-time compilation languages are likely to appreciate Rust's build system and its comprehensive package manager: cargo.

At first glance, we see that cargo is a front end for rustc, the Rust compiler, but cargo provides several additional utilities including the following:

- cargo new creates a skeleton Rust project in a new directory (cargo init uses the current directory).
- cargo build downloads dependencies and compiles the code.
- cargo run executes cargo build and then also runs the resulting executable file.
- cargo doc builds HTML documentation for every dependency in the current project.

1.6.3 *Goal of Rust: Control*

Rust offers programmers fine-grained control over how data structures are laid out in memory and their access patterns. While Rust uses sensible defaults that align with its "zero cost abstractions" philosophy, those defaults do not suit all situations.

At times, it is imperative to manage your application's performance. It might matter to you that data is stored in the *stack* rather than on the *heap*. Perhaps, it might make sense to add *reference counting* to create a shared reference to a value. Occasionally, it might be useful to create one's own type of *pointer* for a particular access pattern. The design space is large and Rust provides the tools to allow you to implement your preferred solution.

> **NOTE** If terms such as *stack, heap,* and *reference counting* are new, don't put the book down! We'll spend lots of time explaining these and how they work together throughout the rest of the book.

Listing 1.7 prints the line a: 10, b: 20, c: 30, d: Mutex { data: 40 }. Each representation is another way to store an integer. As we progress through the next few chapters, the trade-offs related to each level become apparent. For the moment, the important thing to remember is that the menu of types is comprehensive. You are welcome to choose exactly what's right for your specific use case.

Listing 1.7 also demonstrates multiple ways to create integers. Each form provides differing semantics and runtime characteristics. But programmers retain full control of the trade-offs that they want to make.

---

[15] If these terms are unfamiliar, do keep reading. These are explained throughout the book. They are language features that you will miss in other languages.

Listing 1.7   Multiple ways to create integer values

```
 1 use std::rc::Rc;
 2 use std::sync::{Arc, Mutex};
 3
 4 fn main() {
 5     let a = 10;
 6     let b = Box::new(20);
 7     let c = Rc::new(Box::new(30));
 8     let d = Arc::new(Mutex::new(40));
 9     println!("a: {:?}, b: {:?}, c: {:?}, d: {:?}", a, b, c, d);
10 }
```

Integer on the stack

Integer on the heap, also known as a boxed integer

Boxed integer wrapped within a reference counter

Integer wrapped in an atomic reference counter and protected by a mutual exclusion lock

To understand why Rust is doing something the way it is, it can be helpful to refer back to these three principles:

- The language's first priority is safety.
- Data within Rust is immutable by default.
- Compile-time checks are strongly preferred. Safety should be a "zero-cost abstraction."

1.7   Rust's big features

Our tools shape what we believe we can create. Rust enables you to build the software that you want to make, but were too scared to try. What kind of tool is Rust? Flowing from the three principles discussed in the last section are three overarching features of the language:

- Performance
- Concurrency
- Memory efficiency

1.7.1   Performance

Rust offers all of your computer's available performance. Famously, Rust does not rely on a garbage collector to provide its memory safety.

There is, unfortunately, a problem with promising you faster programs: the speed of your CPU is fixed. Thus, for software to run faster, it needs to do less. Yet, the language is large. To resolve this conflict, Rust pushes the burden onto the compiler.

The Rust community prefers a bigger language with a compiler that does more, rather than a simpler language where the compiler does less. The Rust compiler aggressively optimizes both the size and speed of your program. Rust also has some less obvious tricks:

- *Cache-friendly data structures are provided by default.* Arrays usually hold data within Rust programs rather than deeply nested tree structures that are created by pointers. This is referred to as *data-oriented programming.*

- *The availability of a modern package manager (cargo) makes it trivial to benefit from tens of thousands of open source packages.* C and C++ have much less consistency here, and building large projects with many dependencies is typically difficult.
- *Methods are always dispatched statically unless you explicitly request dynamic dispatch.* This enables the compiler to heavily optimize code, sometimes to the point of eliminating the cost of a function call entirely.

1.7.2   Concurrency

Asking a computer to do more than one thing at the same time has proven difficult for software engineers. As far as an OS is concerned, two independent threads of execution are at liberty to destroy each other if a programmer makes a serious mistake. Yet Rust has spawned the expression *fearless concurrency.* Its emphasis on safety crosses the bounds of independent threads. There is no global interpreter lock (GIL) to constrain a thread's speed. We explore some of the implications of this in part 2.

1.7.3   Memory efficiency

Rust enables you to create programs that require minimal memory. When needed, you can use fixed-size structures and know exactly how every byte is managed. High-level constructs, such as iteration and generic types, incur minimal runtime overhead.

1.8   Downsides of Rust

It's easy to talk about this language as if it is the panacea for all software engineering. For example

- "A high-level syntax with low-level performance!"
- "Concurrency without crashes!"
- "C with perfect safety!"

These slogans (sometimes overstated) are great. But for all of its merits, Rust does have some disadvantages.

1.8.1   Cyclic data structures

In Rust, it is difficult to model cyclic data like an arbitrary graph structure. Implementing a doubly-linked list is an undergraduate-level computer science problem. Yet Rust's safety checks do hamper progress here. If you're new to the language, avoid implementing these sorts of data structures until you're more familiar with Rust.

1.8.2   Compile times

Rust is slower at compiling code than its peer languages. It has a complex compiler toolchain that receives multiple intermediate representations and sends lots of code to the LLVM compiler. The unit of compilation for a Rust program is not an individual file but a whole package (known affectionately as a *crate*). As crates can include multiple modules, these can be exceedingly large units to compile. Although this enables whole-of-crate optimization, it requires whole-of-crate compilation as well.

1.8.3 *Strictness*

It's impossible—well, difficult—to be lazy when programming with Rust. Programs won't compile until everything is just right. The compiler is strict, but helpful.

Over time, it's likely that you'll come to appreciate this feature. If you've ever programmed in a dynamic language, then you may have encountered the frustration of your program crashing because of a misnamed variable. Rust brings that frustration forward so that your users don't have to experience the frustration of things crashing.

1.8.4 *Size of the language*

Rust is large! It has a rich type system, several dozen keywords, and includes some features that are unavailable in other languages. These factors all combine to create a steep learning curve. To make this manageable, I encourage learning Rust gradually. Start with a minimal subset of the language and give yourself time to learn the details when you need these. That is the approach taken in this book. Advanced concepts are deferred until much later.

1.8.5 *Hype*

The Rust community is wary of growing too quickly and being consumed by hype. Yet, a number of software projects have encountered this question in their Inbox: "Have you considered rewriting this in Rust?" Unfortunately, software written in Rust is still software. It not immune to security problems and does not offer a panacea to all of software engineering's ills.

1.9 *TLS security case studies*

To demonstrate that Rust will not alleviate all errors, let's examine two serious exploits that threatened almost all internet-facing devices and consider whether Rust would have prevented those.

By 2015, as Rust gained prominence, implementations of SSL/TLS (namely, OpenSSL and Apple's own fork) were found to have serious security holes. Known informally as *Heartbleed* and *goto fail;*, both exploits provide opportunities to test Rust's claims of memory safety. Rust is likely to have helped in both cases, but it is still possible to write Rust code that suffers from similar issues.

1.9.1 *Heartbleed*

Heartbleed, officially designated as CVE-2014-0160,[16] was caused by re-using a buffer incorrectly. A *buffer* is a space set aside in memory for receiving input. Data can leak from one read to the next if the buffer's contents are not cleared between writes.

---

[16] See "CVE-2014-0160 Detail," https://nvd.nist.gov/vuln/detail/CVE-2014-0160.

Why does this situation occur? Programmers hunt for performance. Buffers are reused to minimize how often memory applications ask for memory from the OS.

Imagine that we want to process some secret information from multiple users. We decide, for whatever reason, to reuse a single buffer through the course of the program. If we don't reset this buffer once we use it, information from earlier calls will leak to the latter ones. Here is a précis of a program that would encounter this error:

Binds a reference (&) to a mutable (mut) array ([...]) that contains 1,024 unsigned 8-bit integers (u8) initialized to 0 to the variable buffer

Fills buffer with bytes from the data from user1

```
let buffer = &mut[0u8; 1024];
read_secrets(&user1, buffer);
store_secrets(buffer);

read_secrets(&user2, buffer);
store_secrets(buffer);
```

The buffer still contains data from user1 that may or may not be overwritten by user2.

Rust does not protect you from logical errors. It ensures that your data is never able to be written in two places at the same time. It does not ensure that your program is free from all security issues.

1.9.2   *Goto fail;*

The goto fail; bug, officially designated as CVE-2014-1266,[17] was caused by programmer error coupled with C design issues (and potentially by its compiler not pointing out the flaw). A function that was designed to verify a cryptographic key pair ended up skipping all checks. Here is a selected extract from the original SSLVerifySigned-ServerKeyExchange function with a fair amount of obfuscatory syntax retained:[18]

```
1 static OSStatus
2 SSLVerifySignedServerKeyExchange(SSLContext *ctx,
3                                  bool isRsa,
4                                  SSLBuffer signedParams,
5                                  uint8_t *signature,
6                                  UInt16 signatureLen)
7 {
8     OSStatus        err;
9     ...
10
11    if ((err = SSLHashSHA1.update(
12        &hashCtx, &serverRandom)) != 0)
13        goto fail;
14
15    if ((err = SSLHashSHA1.update(&hashCtx, &signedParams)) != 0)
```

Initializes OSStatus with a pass value (e.g., 0)

A series of defensive programming checks

---

[17] See "CVE-2014-1266 Detail," https://nvd.nist.gov/vuln/detail/CVE-2014-1266.
[18] Original available at http://mng.bz/RKGj.

```
16          goto fail;              ┌─ Unconditional goto skips SSLHashSHAI.final()
17          goto fail;           ◄──┘  and the (significant) call to sslRawVerify().
18      if ((err = SSLHashSHA1.final(&hashCtx, &hashOut)) != 0)
19          goto fail;
20
21      err = sslRawVerify(ctx,
22                          ctx->peerPubKey,
23                          dataToSign,             /* plaintext \*/
24                          dataToSignLen,          /* plaintext length \*/
25                          signature,
26                          signatureLen);
27      if(err) {
28          sslErrorLog("SSLDecodeSignedServerKeyExchange: sslRawVerify "
29                      "returned %d\n", (int)err);
30          goto fail;
31      }
32
33 fail:
34      SSLFreeBuffer(&signedHashes);      ┌─ Returns the pass value of 0, even for inputs
35      SSLFreeBuffer(&hashCtx);         ◄─┘  that should have failed the verification test
36      return err;
37 }
```

In the example code, the issue lies between lines 15 and 17. In C, logical tests do not require curly braces. C compilers interpret those three lines like this:

```
    if ((err = SSLHashSHA1.update(&hashCtx, &signedParams)) != 0) {
        goto fail;
    }
    goto fail;
```

Would Rust have helped? Probably. In this specific case, Rust's grammar would have caught the bug. It does not allow logical tests without curly braces. Rust also issues a warning when code is unreachable. But that doesn't mean the error is made impossible in Rust. Stressed programmers under tight deadlines make mistakes. In general, similar code would compile and run.

TIP   Code with caution.

1.10   *Where does Rust fit best?*

Although it was designed as a systems programming language, Rust is a general-purpose language. It has been successfully deployed in many areas, which we discuss next.

1.10.1   *Command-line utilities*

Rust offers three main advantages for programmers creating command-line utilities: minimal startup time, low memory use, and easy deployment. Programs start their work quickly because Rust does not need to initialize an interpreter (Python, Ruby, etc.) or virtual machine (Java, C#, etc.).

As a bare metal language, Rust produces memory-efficient programs.[19] As you'll see throughout the book, many types are zero-sized. That is, these only exist as hints to the compiler and take up no memory at all in the running program.

Utilities written in Rust are compiled as *static binaries* by default. This compilation method avoids depending on shared libraries that you must install before the program can run. Creating programs that can run without installation steps makes these easy to distribute.

1.10.2 Data processing

Rust excels at text processing and other forms of data wrangling. Programmers benefit from control over memory use and fast startup times. As of mid-2017, Rust touts the world's fastest regular expression engine. In 2019, the Apache Arrow data-processing project—foundational to the Python and R data science ecosystems—accepted the Rust-based DataFusion project.

Rust also underlies the implementation of multiple search engines, data-processing engines, and log-parsing systems. Its type system and memory control provide you with the ability to create high throughput data pipelines with a low and stable memory footprint. Small filter programs can be easily embedded into the larger framework via Apache Storm, Apache Kafka, or Apache Hadoop streaming.

1.10.3 Extending applications

Rust is well suited for extending programs written in a dynamic language. This enables JNI (Java Native Interface) extensions, C extensions, or Erlang/Elixir NIFs (native implemented functions) in Rust. C extensions are typically a scary proposition. These tend to be quite tightly integrated with the runtime. Make a mistake and you could be looking at runaway memory consumption due to a memory leak or a complete crash. Rust takes away a lot of this anxiety.

- Sentry, a company that processes application errors, finds that Rust is an excellent candidate for rewriting CPU-intensive components of their Python system.[20]
- Dropbox used Rust to rewrite the file synchronization engine of its client-side application: "More than performance, [Rust's] ergonomics and focus on correctness have helped us tame sync's complexity."[21]

1.10.4 Resource-constrained environments

C has occupied the domain of microcontrollers for decades. Yet, the Internet of Things (IoT) is coming. That could mean many billions of insecure devices exposed to the network. Any input parsing code will be routinely probed for weaknesses. Given how infrequently firmware updates for these devices occur, it's critical that these are as

---

[19] The joke goes that Rust is as close to bare metal as possible.
[20] See "Fixing Python Performance with Rust," http://mng.bz/ryxX.
[21] See "Rewriting the heart of our sync engine," http://mng.bz/Vdv5.

secure as possible from the outset. Rust can play an important role here by adding a layer of safety without imposing runtime costs.

1.10.5 Server-side applications

Most applications written in Rust live on the server. These could be serving web traffic or supporting businesses running their operations. There is also a tier of services that sit between the OS and your application. Rust is used to write databases, monitoring systems, search appliances, and messaging systems. For example

- The npm package registry for the JavaScript and node.js communities is written in Rust.[22]
- sled (https://github.com/spacejam/sled), an embedded database, can process a workload of 1 billion operations that includes 5% writes in less than a minute on a 16-core machine.
- Tantivy, a full text search engine, can index 8 GB of English Wikipedia in approximately 100 s on a 4-core desktop machine.[23]

1.10.6 Desktop applications

There is nothing inherent in Rust's design that prevents it from being deployed to develop user-facing software. Servo, the web browser engine that acted as an incubator for Rust's early development, is a user-facing application. Naturally, so are games.

1.10.7 Desktop

There is still a significant need to write applications that live on people's computers. Desktop applications are often complex, difficult to engineer, and hard to support. With Rust's ergonomic approach to deployment and its rigor, it is likely to become the secret sauce for many applications. To start, these will be built by small, independent developers. As Rust matures, so will the ecosystem.

1.10.8 Mobile

Android, iOS, and other smartphone operating systems generally provide a blessed path for developers. In the case of Android, that path is Java. In the case of macOS, developers generally program in Swift. There is, however, another way.

Both platforms provide the ability for native applications to run on them. This is generally intended for applications written in C++, such as games, to be able to be deployed to people's phones. Rust is able to talk to the phone via the same interface with no additional runtime cost.

---

[22] See "Community makes Rust an easy choice for npm: The npm Registry uses Rust for its CPU-bound bottlenecks," http://mng.bz/xm9B.

[23] See "Of tantivy's indexing," https://fulmicoton.com/posts/behold-tantivy-part2/.

1.10.9 Web

As you are probably aware, JavaScript is the language of the web. Over time though, this will change. Browser vendors are developing a standard called WebAssembly (Wasm) that promises to be a compiler target for many languages. Rust is one of the first. Porting a Rust project to the browser requires only two additional command-line commands. Several companies are exploring the use of Rust in the browser via Wasm, notably CloudFlare and Fastly.

1.10.10 Systems programming

In some sense, systems programming is Rust's raison d'être. Many large programs have been implemented in Rust, including compilers (Rust itself), video game engines, and operating systems. The Rust community includes writers of parser generators, databases, and file formats.

Rust has proven to be a productive environment for programmers who share Rust's goals. Three standout projects in this area include the following:

- Google is sponsoring the development of Fuchsia OS, an operating system for devices.[24]
- Microsoft is actively exploring writing low-level components in Rust for Windows.[25]
- Amazon Web Services (AWS) is building Bottlerocket, a bespoke OS for hosting containers in the cloud.[26]

1.11 Rust's hidden feature: Its community

It takes more than software to grow a programming language. One of the things that the Rust team has done extraordinarily well is to foster a positive and welcoming community around the language. Everywhere you go within the Rust world, you'll find that you'll be treated with courtesy and respect.

1.12 Rust phrase book

When you interact with members of the Rust community, you'll soon encounter a few terms that have special meaning. Understanding the following terms makes it easier to understand why Rust has evolved the way that it has and the problems that it attempts to solve:

- *Empowering everyone*—All programmers regardless of ability or background are welcome to participate. Programming, and particularly systems programming, should not be restricted to a blessed few.

---

[24] See "Welcome to Fuchsia!," https://fuchsia.dev/.
[25] See "Using Rust in Windows," http://mng.bz/A0vW.
[26] See "Bottlerocket: Linux-based operating system purpose-built to run containers," https://aws.amazon.com/bottlerocket/.

- *Blazingly fast*—Rust is a fast programming language. You'll be able to write programs that match or exceed the performance of its peer languages, but you will have more safety guarantees.
- *Fearless concurrency*—Concurrent and parallel programming have always been seen as difficult. Rust frees you from whole classes of errors that have plagued its peer languages.
- *No Rust 2.0*—Rust code written today will always compile with a future Rust compiler. Rust is intended to be a reliable programming language that can be depended upon for decades to come. In accordance with *semantic versioning*, Rust is never backward-incompatible, so it will never release a new major version.
- *Zero-cost abstractions*—The features you gain from Rust impose no runtime cost. When you program in Rust, safety does not sacrifice speed.

Summary

- Many companies have successfully built large software projects in Rust.
- Software written in Rust can be compiled for the PC, the browser, and the server, as well as mobile and IoT devices.
- The Rust language is well loved by software developers. It has repeatedly won Stack Overflow's "most loved programming language" title.
- Rust allows you to experiment without fear. It provides correctness guarantees that other tools are unable to provide without imposing runtime costs.
- With Rust, there are three main command_line tools to learn:
  - cargo, which manages a whole crate
  - rustup, which manages Rust installations
  - rustc, which manages compilation of Rust source code
- Rust projects are not immune from all bugs.
- Rust code is stable, fast, and light on resources.

Part 1

Rust language distinctives

Part 1 of the book is a quick-fire introduction to the Rust programming language. By the end of the chapters in this part, you will have a good understanding of Rust syntax and know what motivates people to choose Rust. You will also understand some fundamental differences between Rust and its peer languages.

Language foundations 2

This chapter covers

- Coming to grips with the Rust syntax
- Learning fundamental types and data structures
- Building command-line utilities
- Compiling programs

This chapter introduces you to the fundamentals of Rust programming. By the end of the chapter, you will be able to create command-line utilities and should be able to get the gist of most Rust programs. We'll work through most of the language's syntax, but defer much of the detail about *why* things are *how* they are for later in the book.

> **NOTE** Programmers who have experience with another programming language will benefit the most from this chapter. If you are an experienced Rust programmer, feel free to skim through it.

Beginners are welcomed. Rust's community strives to be responsive to newcomers. At times, you may strike a mental pothole when you encounter terms such as *lifetime elision*, *hygienic macros*, *move semantics*, and *algebraic data types* without context. Don't be afraid to ask for help. The community is much more welcoming than these helpful, yet opaque, terms might suggest.

In this chapter, we will build grep-lite, a greatly stripped-down version of the ubiquitous grep utility. Our grep-lite program looks for patterns within text and prints lines that match. This simple program allows us to focus on the unique features of Rust.

The chapter takes a spiral approach to learning. A few concepts will be discussed multiple times. With each iteration, you will find yourself learning more. Figure 2.1 shows a completely unscientific map of the chapter.

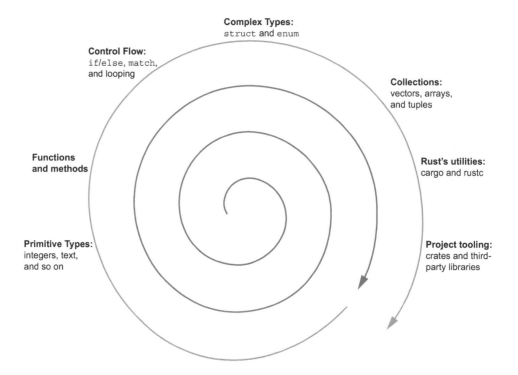

Figure 2.1   Chapter topic outline. Starting with primitive types, the chapter progresses through several concepts with increasing levels of depth.

It's highly recommended that you follow along with the examples in this book. As a reminder, to access or download the source code for the listings, use either of these two sources:

- https://manning.com/books/rust-in-action
- https://github.com/rust-in-action/code

2.1 Creating a running program

Every plain text file has a hidden superpower: when it includes the right symbols, it can be converted into something that can be interpreted by a CPU. That is the magic of a programming language. This chapter's aim is to allow you to become familiar with the process of converting Rust source code into a running program.

Understanding this process is more fun than it sounds! And it sets you up for an exciting learning journey. By the end of chapter 4, you will have implemented a virtual CPU that can also interpret programs that you create.

2.1.1 Compiling single files with rustc

Listing 2.1 is a short, yet complete Rust program. To translate it into a working program, we use software called a *compiler*. The compiler's role is to translate the source code into machine code, as well as take care of lots of bookkeeping to satisfy the operating system (OS) and CPU that it is a runnable program. The Rust compiler is called *rustc*. You'll find the source code for listing 2.1 in the file ch2/ok.rs.

> **Listing 2.1 Almost the shortest valid Rust program**

```
1 fn main() {
2   println!("OK")
3 }
```

To compile a single file written in Rust into a working program

1 Save your source code to a file. In our case, we'll use the filename ok.rs.
2 Make sure that the source code includes a main() function.
3 Open a shell window such as Terminal, cmd.exe, Powershell, bash, zsh, or any other.
4 Execute the command rustc <file>, where <file> is the file you want to compile.

When compilation succeeds, rustc sends no output to the console. Behind the scenes, rustc has dutifully created an executable, using the input filename to choose the output filename.

Assuming that you've saved listing 2.1 to a file called ok.rs, let's see what that looks like. The following snippet provides a short demonstration of the process:

```
$ rustc ok.rs
$ ./ok          ⟵─┤  For Windows, include the .exe filename
OK                    extension (for example, ok.exe).
```

2.1.2 Compiling Rust projects with cargo

Most Rust projects are larger than a single file. These typically include dependencies. To prepare ourselves for that, we'll use a higher-level tool than rustc, called cargo. cargo understands how to drive rustc (and much more).

Migrating from a single file workflow managed by rustc to one managed by cargo is a two-stage process. The first is to move that original file into an empty directory. Then execute the `cargo init` command.

Here is a detailed overview of that process, assuming that you are starting from a file called ok.rs generated by following the steps in the previous section:

1 Run `mkdir <project>` to create an empty directory (e.g., `mkdir ok`).
2 Move your source code into the <project> directory (e.g., `mv ok.rs ok`).
3 Change to the <project> directory (e.g., `cd ok`).
4 Run `cargo init`.

From this point on, you can issue `cargo run` to execute your project's source code. One difference from rustc is that compiled executables are found in a <project>/ target subdirectory. Another is that cargo provides much more output by default:

```
$ cargo run
    Finished dev [unoptimized + debuginfo] target(s) in 0.03s
    Running `target/debug/ok`
OK
```

If you're ever curious about what cargo is doing under the hood to drive rustc, add the verbose flag (-v) to your command:

```
$ rm -rf target/                    ◁──────────    Added here to provoke
$ cargo run -v                                     cargo into compiling
   Compiling ok v0.1.0 (/tmp/ok)                   the project from
     Running `rustc                                scratch
    --crate-name ok
    --edition=2018
    ok.rs
    --error-format=json
    --json=diagnostic-rendered-ansi
    --crate-type bin
    --emit=dep-info,link
    -C embed-bitcode=no
    -C debuginfo=2
    -C metadata=55485250d3e77978
    -C extra-filename=-55485250d3e77978
    --out-dir /tmp/ok/target/debug/deps
    -C incremental=/tmp/target/debug/incremental
    -L dependency=/tmp/ok/target/debug/deps
    -C link-arg=-fuse-ld=lld`
   Finished dev [unoptimized + debuginfo] target(s) in 0.31s
     Running `target/debug/ok`
OK
```

2.2   *A glance at Rust's syntax*

Rust is boring and predictable where possible. It has variables, numbers, functions, and other familiar things that you have seen in other languages. For example, it delimits blocks with curly brackets ({ and }), it uses a single equals sign as its assignment operator (=), and it is whitespace-agnostic.

2.2.1 Defining variables and calling functions

Let's look at another short listing to introduce some fundamentals: defining variables with type annotations and calling functions. Listing 2.2 prints (a + b) + (c + d) = 90 to the console. As you can see from lines 2–5 in the listing, there are multiple syntactic choices for annotating data types to integers. Use whichever feels most natural for the situation at hand. The source code for this listing is in ch2/ch2-first-steps.rs.

Listing 2.2 Adding integers using variables and declaring types

Rust is flexible with the location of the main() function.

Types can be inferred by the compiler...

...or declared by the programmer when creating variables.

Numeric types can include a type annotation in their literal form.

Numbers can include underscores, which are intended to increase readability and have no functional impact.

```
1  fn main() {
2      let a = 10;
3      let b: i32 = 20;
4      let c = 30i32;
5      let d = 30_i32;
6      let e = add(add(a, b), add(c, d));
7
8      println!("( a + b ) + ( c + d ) = {}", e);
9  }
10
11 fn add(i: i32, j: i32) -> i32 {
12     i + j
13 }
```

Type declarations are required when defining functions.

Functions return the last expression's result so that return is not required.

NOTE In the listing, be careful about adding a semicolon to the add() function declaration. This changes the semantics, returning () (unit) rather than i32.

Although there are only 13 lines of code, there is quite a lot packed into listing 2.2. Here's a brief description that should provide the gist of what's going on. We will cover the details in the rest of the chapter.

In line 1 (fn main() {), the fn keyword begins a function definition. The entry point to all Rust programs is main(). It takes no arguments and returns no value.[1] Code blocks, also known as *lexical scopes,* are defined with curly braces: { and }.

In line 2 (let a = 10;), we use let to declare *variable bindings*. Variables are *immutable* by default, meaning that they are read-only rather than read-write. And finally, statements are delimited with semicolons (;).

In line 3 (let b: i32 = 20;), you can designate a specific data type for the compiler. At times, this will be required as the compiler will be unable to deduce a unique type on your behalf.

In line 4 (let c = 30i32;), you'll note that Rust's numeric literals can include types annotations. This can be helpful when navigating complex numerical expressions. And

---

[1] This isn't technically correct, but is accurate enough for now. If you're an experienced Rust programmer skimming through this chapter, you'll know that main() returns () (unit) by default and can also return a Result.

in line 5 (`let c = 30_i32;`), you'll see that Rust permits the use of underscores within numeric literals. These increase readability but are insignificant to the compiler. In line 6 (`let e = add(add(a, b), add(c, d));`), it should be easy to see that calling functions looks like what you've experienced in most other programming languages.

In line 8 (`println!("( a + b ) + ( c + d ) = {}", e);`), `println!()` is a *macro*, which is function-like but returns code rather than values. When printing to the console, every input data type has its own way of being represented as a text string. `println!()` takes care of figuring out the exact methods to call on its arguments.

Strings use double quotes (`"`) rather than single quotes (`'`). Rust uses single quotes for single characters, which are a distinct type, `char`. And with Rust, string formatting uses `{}` as a placeholder, rather than the C-like `printf` style of `%s` or other variants.

Finally, in line 10 (`fn add(…) -> i32 {`), you can see that Rust's syntax for defining functions is similar to those programming languages that use explicit type declarations. Commas delimit parameters, and type declarations follow variable names. The dagger (`->`) or thin arrow syntax indicates the return type.

2.3   Numbers

Computers have been associated with numbers for longer than you have been able to say "formula translator." This section discusses how to create numeric types in Rust and how to perform operations on these.

2.3.1   Integers and decimal (floating-point) numbers

Rust uses a relatively conventional syntax for creating integers (1, 2, ...) and floating-point numbers (1.0, 1.1, ...). Operations on numbers use *infix notation*, meaning that numeric expressions look like those that you're used to seeing in most programming languages. To operate on multiple types, Rust also allows the same token (+) for addition. This is called *operator overloading*. Some notable differences from other languages follow:

- *Rust includes a large number of numeric types.* You will become used to declaring the size in bytes, which affects how many numbers the type can represent and whether your type is able to represent negative numbers.
- *Conversions between types are always explicit.* Rust does not automatically convert your 16-bit integer into a 32-bit integer.
- *Rust's numbers can have methods.* For example, to round 24.5 to the nearest integer, Rust programmers use `24.5_f32.round()` rather than (`round(24.5_f32)`). Here, the type suffix is required because a concrete type is necessary.

To start, let's consider a small example. You'll find the code in ch2/ch2-intro-to-numbers.rs in the examples for this book. Listing 2.3 prints these few lines to the console:

```
20 + 21 + 22 = 63
1000000000000
42
```

Listing 2.3   Numeric literals and basic operations on numbers in Rust

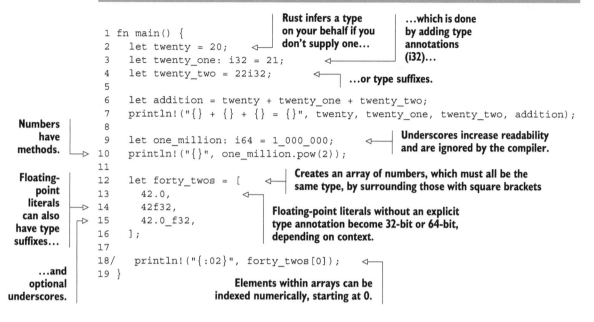

Numbers have methods.

Floating-point literals can also have type suffixes...

...and optional underscores.

```
1 fn main() {
2   let twenty = 20;
3   let twenty_one: i32 = 21;
4   let twenty_two = 22i32;
5
6   let addition = twenty + twenty_one + twenty_two;
7   println!("{} + {} + {} = {}", twenty, twenty_one, twenty_two, addition);
8
9   let one_million: i64 = 1_000_000;
10  println!("{}", one_million.pow(2));
11
12  let forty_twos = [
13    42.0,
14    42f32,
15    42.0_f32,
16  ];
17
18/   println!("{:02}", forty_twos[0]);
19 }
```

Rust infers a type on your behalf if you don't supply one...

...which is done by adding type annotations (i32)...

...or type suffixes.

Underscores increase readability and are ignored by the compiler.

Creates an array of numbers, which must all be the same type, by surrounding those with square brackets

Floating-point literals without an explicit type annotation become 32-bit or 64-bit, depending on context.

Elements within arrays can be indexed numerically, starting at 0.

2.3.2   Integers with base 2, base 8, and base 16 notation

Rust also has built-in support for numeric literals that allow you to define integers in base 2 (binary), base 8 (octal), and base 16 (hexadecimal). This notation is also available within the formatting macros like println!. Listing 2.4 demonstrates the three styles. You can find the source code for this listing in ch2/ch2-non-base2.rs. It produces the following output:

```
base 10: 3 30 300
base 2:  11 11110 100101100
base 8:  3 36 454
base 16: 3 1e 12c
```

Listing 2.4   Using base 2, base 8, and base 16 numeric literals

```
1 fn main() {
2   let three = 0b11;
3   let thirty = 0o36;
4   let three_hundred = 0x12C;
5
6   println!("base 10: {} {} {}", three, thirty, three_hundred);
7   println!("base 2:  {:b} {:b} {:b}", three, thirty, three_hundred);
8   println!("base 8:  {:o} {:o} {:o}", three, thirty, three_hundred);
9   println!("base 16: {:x} {:x} {:x}", three, thirty, three_hundred);
10 }
```

The 0b prefix indicates binary (base 2) numerals.

The 0o prefix indicates octal (base 8) numerals.

The 0x prefix indicates hexadecimal (base 16) numerals.

In binary (base 2) numerals, 0b11 equals 3 because $3 = 2 \times 1 + 1 \times 1$. With octal (base 8) numerals, 0o36 equals 30 because $30 = 8 \times 3 + 1 \times 6$. And with hexadecimal (base 16) numerals, 0x12C equals 300 because $300 = 256 \times 1 + 16 \times 2 + 1 \times 12$. Table 2.1 shows the types that represent scalar numbers.

Table 2.1   **Rust types for representing scalar (single) numbers**

i8, i16, i32, i64	Signed integers ranging from 8 bit to 64 bit.
u8, u16, u32, u64	Unsigned integers ranging from 8 bit to 64 bit.
f32, f64	Floating-point numbers in 32-bit and 64-bit variants.
isize, usize	Integers that assume the CPU's "native" width. For example, in 64-bit CPUs, usize and isize will be 64-bits wide.

Rust contains a full complement of numeric types. The types are grouped into a few families:

- Signed integers (i) represent negative as well as positive integers.
- Unsigned integers (u) only represent positive integers but can go twice as high as their signed counterparts.
- Floating-point types (f) represent real numbers with special bit patterns to represent infinity, negative infinity, and "not a number" values.

Integer width is the number of bits that the type uses in RAM and in the CPU. Types that take up more space, such as u32 vs. i8, can represent a wider range of numbers. But this incurs the expense of needing to store extra zeros for smaller numbers, as table 2.2 shows.

Table 2.2   **Multiple bit patterns can represent the same number.**

Number	Type	Bit pattern in memory
20	u32	00000000000000000000000000010100
20	i8	00010100
20	f32	01000001101000000000000000000000

Although we've only touched on numbers, we nearly have enough exposure to Rust to create a prototype of our pattern-matching program. But let's look at comparing numbers before we create our program.

2.3.3 *Comparing numbers*

Rust's numeric types support a large suite of comparisons that you're probably familiar with. Enabling support for these comparisons is provided by a feature that you have not encountered yet. It is called *traits*.[2] Table 2.3 summarizes the comparison operators available to you.

---

[2] For the curious and eager, the traits involved here are std::cmp::PartialOrd and std::cmp::PartialEq.

Table 2.3 Mathematical operators supported by Rust's numeric types

Operator	Rust syntax	Example
Less than (<)	<	1.0 < 2.0
Greater than (>)	>	2.0 > 1.0
Equal to (=)	==	1.0 == 1.0
Unequal to (≠)	!=	1.0 != 2.0
Equal to or less than (≤)	<=	1.0 <= 2.0
Equal to greater than or (≥)	>=	2.0 >= 1.0

That support does include a few caveats. We'll look at these conditions in the rest of this section.

IMPOSSIBLE TO COMPARE DIFFERENT TYPES

Rust's type safety requirements prevent comparisons between types. For example, this code does not compile:

```
fn main() {
  let a: i32 = 10;
  let b: u16 = 100;

  if a < b {
    println!("Ten is less than one hundred.");
  }
}
```

To appease the compiler, we need to use an as operator to cast one of the operands to the other's type. The following code shows this type cast: b as i32:

```
fn main() {
  let a: i32 = 10;
  let b: u16 = 100;

  if a < (b as i32) {
    println!("Ten is less than one hundred.");
  }
}
```

It is safest to cast the smaller type to a larger one (for example, a 16-bit type to a 32-bit type). This is sometimes referred to as *promotion*. In this case, we could have demoted a down to a u16, but such a move is generally more risky.

> **WARNING** Using type casts carelessly will cause your program to behave unexpectedly. For example, the expression 300_i32 as i8 returns 44.

In some cases, using the as keyword is too restrictive. It's possible to regain fuller control over the type conversion process at the cost of introducing some bureaucracy. The following listing shows a Rust method to use instead of the as keyword when the conversion might fail.

Listing 2.5   The `try_into()` method converts between types

```
 1 use std::convert::TryInto;      ◄────   Enables try_into() to be
 2                                          called on those types that have
 3 fn main() {                              implemented it (such as u16)
 4    let a: i32 = 10;
 5    let b: u16 = 100;
 6                                          try_into() returns a Result
 7    let b_ = b.try_into()                 type that provides access to
 8              .unwrap();        ◄────     the conversion attempt.
 9
10    if a < b_ {
11      println!("Ten is less than one hundred.");
12    }
13 }
```

Listing 2.5 introduces two new Rust concepts: traits and error handling. On line 1, the use keyword brings the std::convert::TryInto trait into local scope. This unlocks the try_into() method of the b variable. We'll bypass a full explanation of why this occurs for now. In the meantime, consider a *trait* as a collection of methods. If you are from an object-oriented background, traits can be thought of as *abstract classes* or *interfaces*. If your programming experience is in functional languages, you can think of traits as *type classes*.

Line 7 provides a glimpse of error handling in Rust. b.try_into() returns an i32 value wrapped within a Result. Result is introduced properly in chapter 3. It can contain either a success value or an error value. The unwrap() method can handle the success value and returns the value of b as an i32 here. If the conversion between u16 and i32 were to fail, then calling unsafe() would crash the program. As the book progresses, you will learn safer ways of dealing with Result rather than risking the program's stability!

A distinguishing characteristic of Rust is that it only allows a type's methods to be called when the trait is within local scope. An implicit prelude enables common operations such as addition and assignment to be used without explicit imports.

TIP   To understand what is included in local scope by default, you should investigate the std::prelude module. Its documentation is available online at https://doc.rust-lang.org/std/prelude/index.html.

Floating-point hazards

Floating-point types (f32 and f64, for example) can cause serious errors for the unwary. There are (at least) two reasons for this:

- *These often approximate the numbers that they're representing.* Floating-point types are implemented in base 2, but we often want to calculate numbers in base 10. This mismatch creates ambiguity. Moreover, although often described as representing the real numbers, floating point values have a limited precision. Representing all of the reals would require infinite precision.

- *These can represent values that have unintuitive semantics.* Unlike integers, floating-point types have some values that do not play well together (by design). Formally, these only have a *partial equivalence relation*. This is encoded in Rust's type system. `f32` and `f64` types only implement the `std::cmp::PartialEq` trait, whereas other numeric types also implement `std::cmp::Eq`.

To prevent these hazards, here are two guidelines to follow:

- Avoid testing floating-point numbers for equality.
- Be wary when results may be mathematically undefined.

Using equality to compare floating-point numbers can be highly problematic. Floating-point numbers are implemented by computing systems that use binary (base 2) mathematics, but are often asked to perform operations on decimal (base 10) numbers. This poses a problem because many values we care about, such as 0.1, have no exact representation in binary.[a]

To illustrate the problem, consider the following snippet. Should it run successfully, or should it crash? Although the expression that is being evaluated (0.1 + 0.2 = 0.3) is a mathematical tautology, it crashes on most systems that run it:

```
fn main() {
    assert!(0.1 + 0.2 == 0.3);
}
```

◁— **assert! crashes the program unless its argument evaluates to true.**

But not all. It turns out that the data type can affect whether the program succeeds or fails. The following code, available at ch2/ch2-add-floats.rs, interrogates the internal bit patterns of each value to find where the differences lie. It then performs the test in the previous example against both `f32` and `f64` types. Only one test passes:

```
 1 fn main() {
 2     let abc: (f32, f32, f32) = (0.1, 0.2, 0.3);
 3     let xyz: (f64, f64, f64) = (0.1, 0.2, 0.3);
 4
 5     println!("abc (f32)");
 6     println!("   0.1 + 0.2: {:x}", (abc.0 + abc.1).to_bits());
 7     println!("        0.3: {:x}", (abc.2).to_bits());
 8     println!();
 9
10     println!("xyz (f64)");
11     println!("   0.1 + 0.2: {:x}", (xyz.0 + xyz.1).to_bits());
12     println!("        0.3: {:x}", (xyz.2).to_bits());
13     println!();
14
15     assert!(abc.0 + abc.1 == abc.2);      ◁—| **Runs successfully**
16     assert!(xyz.0 + xyz.1 == xyz.2);      ◁—| **Triggers a crash**
17 }
```

(continued)

When executed, the program successfully generates the short report that follows, which reveals the error. After that, it crashes. Significantly, it crashes on line 14, when it compares the result of the f64 values:

```
abc (f32)
   0.1 + 0.2: 3e99999a
         0.3: 3e99999a

xyz (f64)
   0.1 + 0.2: 3fd3333333333334
         0.3: 3fd3333333333333

thread 'main' panicked at 'assertion failed: xyz.0 + xyz.1 == xyz.2',
ch2-add-floats.rs.rs:14:5
note: run with `RUST_BACKTRACE=1` environment variable to display
a backtrace
```

Generally speaking, it is safer to test whether mathematical operations fall within an acceptable margin of their true mathematical result. This margin is often referred to as the *epsilon*.

Rust includes some tolerances to allow comparisons between floating-point values. These tolerances are defined as f32::EPSILON and f64::EPSILON. To be more precise, it's possible to get closer to how Rust is behaving under the hood, as the following small example shows:

```
fn main() {
  let result: f32 = 0.1 + 0.1;
  let desired: f32 = 0.2;
  let absolute_difference = (desired - result).abs();
  assert!(absolute_difference <= f32::EPSILON);
}
```

In the example, what actually happens is interesting, but mostly irrelevant. The Rust compiler actually delegates the comparison to the CPU. Floating-point operations are implemented using bespoke hardware within the chip.[b]

Operations that produce mathematically undefined results, such as taking the square root of a negative number (-42.0.sqrt()), present particular problems. Floating-point types include "not a number" values (represented in Rust syntax as NAN values) to handle these cases.

NAN values poison other numbers. Almost all operations interacting with NAN return NAN. Another thing to be mindful of is that, by definition, NAN values are never equal. This small program will always crash:

```
fn main() {
  let x = (-42.0_f32).sqrt();
  assert_eq!(x, x);
}
```

To program defensively, make use of the `is_nan()` and `is_finite()` methods. Inducing a crash, rather than silently proceeding with a mathematical error, allows you to debug close to what has caused the problem. The following illustrates using the `is_finite()` method to bring about this condition:

```
fn main() {
  let x: f32 = 1.0 / 0.0;
  assert!(x.is_finite());
}
```

---

[a] If this is confusing to think about, consider that many values, such as 1/3 (one third), have no exact representation within the decimal number system.

[b] Illegal or undefined operations trigger a CPU exception. You will read about those in chapter 12.

2.3.4   *Rational, complex numbers, and other numeric types*

Rust's standard library is comparatively slim. It excludes numeric types that are often available within other languages. These include

- Many mathematical objects for working with rational numbers and complex numbers
- Arbitrary size integers and arbitrary precision floating-point numbers for working with very large or very small numbers
- Fixed-point decimal numbers for working with currencies

To access these specialized numeric types, you can use the num crate. *Crates* are Rust's name for packages. Open source crates are shared at the https://crates.io repository, which is where cargo downloads num from.

Listing 2.6 demonstrates adding two complex numbers together. If you're unfamiliar with the term *complex numbers*, these are two-dimensional, whereas numbers that you deal with day to day are one-dimensional. Complex numbers have "real" and "imaginary" parts and are denoted as `<real>` + `<imaginary>`i.[3] For example, $2.1 + -1.2i$ is a single complex number. That's enough mathematics. Let's look at the code.

Here is the recommended workflow to compile and run listing 2.6:

1 Execute the following commands in a terminal:

```
git clone --depth=1 https://github.com/rust-in-action/code rust-in-action
cd rust-in-action/ch2/ch2-complex
cargo run
```

2 For those readers who prefer to learn by doing everything by hand, the following instructions will achieve the same end result:

a Execute the following commands in a terminal:

```
cargo new ch2-complex
cd ch2-complex
```

---

[3] Mechanical engineers use *j* rather than *i*.

b Add version 0.4 of the num crate into the [dependencies] section of Cargo.toml. That section will look like this:

```
[dependencies]
num = "0.4"
```

c Replace src/main.rs with the source code from listing 2.6 (available at ch2/ch2-complex/src/main.rs).

d Execute cargo run.

After several lines of intermediate output, cargo run should produce the following output:

```
13.2 + 21.02i
```

Listing 2.6 Calculating values with complex numbers

```
1 use num::complex::Complex;          ◁──┐  The use keyword brings the
2                                         │  Complex type into local scope.
3 fn main() {
4     let a = Complex { re: 2.1, im: -1.2 };   ◁──┐  Every Rust type
5     let b = Complex::new(11.1, 22.2);        ◁──┤  has a literal syntax.
6     let result = a + b;
7                                                  Most types implement
8     println!("{} + {}i", result.re, result.im)  ◁──┐ a new() static method.
9 }
                   Accesses fields with the dot operator
```

Some points from the listing are worth pausing to consider:

- *The* use *keyword pulls crates into local scope, and the namespace operator (::) restricts what's imported.* In our case, only a single type is required: Complex.
- *Rust does not have constructors; instead, every type has a literal form.* You can initialize types by using the type name (Complex) and assigning their fields (re, im) values (such as 2.1 or -1.2) within curly braces ({ }).
- *Many types implement a* new() *method for simplicity.* This convention, however, is not part of the Rust language.
- *To access fields, Rust programmers use the dot operator (.).* For example, the num::complex::Complex type has two fields: re represents the real part, and im represents the imaginary part. Both are accessible with the dot operator.

Listing 2.6 also introduces some new commands. It demonstrates two forms of initializing non-primitive data types.

One is a *literal* syntax available as part of the Rust language (line 4). The other is the new() static method, which is implemented by convention only and isn't defined as part of the language (line 5). A *static method* is a function that's available for a type, but it's not an instance of that type.[4]

---

[4] Although Rust is not object-oriented (it's impossible to create a subclass, for example), Rust makes use of some terminology from that domain. It's common to hear of Rust programmers discussing instances, methods, and objects.

The second form is often preferred in real-world code because library authors use a type's `new()` method to set defaults. It also involves less clutter.

Shortcut for adding a third-party dependency to a project

I recommend that you install the cargo-edit crate to enable the `cargo add` subcommand. You can do this with the following code:

```
$ cargo install cargo-edit
    Updating crates.io index
  Installing cargo-edit v0.6.0
  ...
  Installed package `cargo-edit v0.6.0` (executables `cargo-add`,
    `cargo-rm`, `cargo-upgrade`)
```

Up to this point, we have manually added dependencies to Cargo.toml. The `cargo add` command simplifies this process by editing the file correctly on your behalf:

```
$ cargo add num
    Updating 'https://github.com/rust-lang/crates.io-index' index
      Adding num v0.4.0 to dependencies
```

We've now addressed how to access built-in numeric types and types available from third-party libraries. We'll move on to discussing some more of Rust's features.

2.4 Flow control

Programs execute from top to bottom, except when you don't want that. Rust has a useful set of *flow control* mechanisms to facilitate this. This section provides a brief tour of the fundamentals.

2.4.1 For: The central pillar of iteration

The `for` loop is the workhorse of iteration in Rust. Iterating through collections of things, including iterating over collections that may have infinitely many values, is easy. The basic form is

```
for item in container {
  // ...
}
```

This basic form makes each successive element in `container` available as `item`. In this way, Rust emulates many dynamic languages with an easy-to-use, high-level syntax. However, it does have some pitfalls.

Counterintuitively, once the block ends, accessing the container another time becomes invalid. Even though the `container` variable remains within local scope, its *lifetime* has ended. For reasons that are explained in chapter 4, Rust assumes that `container` is no longer needed once the block finishes.

When you want to reuse `container` later in your program, use a reference. Again, for reasons that are explained in chapter 4, when a reference is omitted, Rust assumes that `container` is no longer needed. To add a reference to the container, prefix it with an ampersand (&) as this example shows:

```
for item in &container {
  // ...
}
```

If you need to modify each `item` during the loop, you can use a *mutable reference* by including the `mut` keyword:

```
for item in &mut collection {
  // ...
}
```

As an implementation detail, Rust's `for` loop construct is expanded to method calls by the compiler. As the following table shows, these three forms of `for` each map to a different method.

Shorthand	Equivalent to	Access
`for item in collection`	`for item in IntoIterator::into_iter(collection)`	Ownership
`for item in &collection`	`for item in collection.iter()`	Read-only
`for item in &mut collection`	`for item in collection.iter_mut()`	Read-write

ANONYMOUS LOOPS

When a local variable is not used within a block, by convention, you'll use an underscore (_). Using this pattern in conjunction with the _exclusive range syntax_ (n..m) and the *inclusive range syntax* (n..=m) makes it clear that the intent is to perform a loop for a fixed number of times. Here's an example:

```
for _ in 0..10 {
  // ...
}
```

AVOID MANAGING AN INDEX VARIABLE

In many programming languages, it's common to loop through things by using a temporary variable that's incremented at the end of each iteration. Conventionally, this variable is named `i` (for index). A Rust version of that pattern is

```
let collection = [1, 2, 3, 4, 5];
for i in 0..collection.len() {
  let item = collection[i];
  // ...
}
```

This is legal Rust. It's also essential in cases when iterating directly over collection via for item in collection is impossible. However, it is generally discouraged. The manual approach introduces two problems with this:

- *Performance*—Indexing values with the collection[index] syntax incurs runtime costs for *bounds checking*. That is, Rust checks that index currently exists within collection as valid data. Those checks are not necessary when iterating directly over collection. The compiler can use compile-time analysis to prove that illegal access is impossible.
- *Safety*—Periodically accessing collection over time introduces the possibility that it has changed. Using a for loop over collection directly allows Rust to guarantee that the collection remains untouched by other parts of the program.

2.4.2 *Continue: Skipping the rest of the current iteration*

The continue keyword operates as you would expect. Here's an example:

```
for n in 0..10 {
  if n % 2 == 0 {
    continue;
  }
  // ...
}
```

2.4.3 *While: Looping until a condition changes its state*

The while loop proceeds as long as a condition holds. The condition, formally known as a *predicate*, can be any expression that evaluates to true or false. This (non-functioning) snippet takes air quality samples, checking to avoid anomalies:

```
let mut samples = vec![];

while samples.len() < 10 {
  let sample = take_sample();
  if is_outlier(sample) {
    continue;
  }

  samples.push(sample);
}
```

USING WHILE TO STOP ITERATING ONCE A DURATION IS REACHED
Listing 2.7 (source code available at ch2/ch2-while-true-incr-count.rs) provides a working example of while. It isn't an ideal method for implementing benchmarks, but can be a useful tool to have in your toolbox. In the listing, while continues to execute a block when a time limit is not reached.

Listing 2.7   Testing how fast your computer can increment a counter

```
 1 use std::time::{Duration, Instant};          ◄─────  This form of an import hasn't been seen
 2                                                       before. It brings the Duration and Instant
 3 fn main() {                                           types from std::time into local scope.
 4     let mut count = 0;
 5     let time_limit = Duration::new(1,0);      ◄─────  Creates a Duration that
 6     let start = Instant::now();               ◄─────  represents 1 second
 7
 8     while (Instant::now() - start) < time_limit {  ◄──  Accesses time from
 9         count += 1;                                     the system's clock
10     }                                    An Instant minus an Instant
11     println!("{}", count);                   returns a Duration.
12 }
```

AVOID WHILE WHEN ENDLESSLY LOOPING

Most Rust programmers avoid the following idiom to express looping forever. The preferred alternative is to use the `loop` keyword, explained in the next section.

```
while true {
  println!("Are we there yet?");
}
```

2.4.4   *Loop: The basis for Rust's looping constructs*

Rust contains a `loop` keyword for providing more control than `for` and `while`. `loop` executes a code block again and again, never stopping for a tea (or coffee) break. `loop` continues to execute until a `break` keyword is encountered or the program is terminated from the outside. Here's an example showing the `loop` syntax:

```
loop {
  // ...
}
```

`loop` is often seen when implementing long-running servers, as the following example shows:

```
loop {
  let requester, request = accept_request();
  let result = process_request(request);
  send_response(requester, result);
}
```

2.4.5   *Break: Aborting a loop*

The `break` keyword breaks out of a loop. In this regard, Rust's generally operates as you are used to:

```
for (x, y) in (0..).zip(0..) {
  if x + y > 100 {
    break;
  }
```

```
  // ...
}
```

BREAK FROM NESTED LOOPS

You can break out of a nested loop with loop labels.[5] A *loop label* is an identifier prefixed with an apostrophe (`'`), like this example shows:

```
'outer: for x in 0.. {
  for y in 0.. {
    for z in 0.. {
      if x + y + z > 1000 {
        break 'outer;
      }

      // ...
    }
  }
}
```

Rust does not include the `goto` keyword, which provides the ability to jump to other parts of the program. The `goto` keyword can make control flow confusing, and its use is generally discouraged. One place where it is still commonly used, though, is to jump to and clean up a section of a function when an error condition is detected. Use loop labels to enable that pattern.

2.4.6 *If, if else, and else: Conditional branching*

So far, we've indulged in the exciting pursuit of looking for numbers within lists of numbers. Our tests have involved utilizing the `if` keyword. Here's an example:

```
if item == 42 {
  // ...
}
```

`if` accepts any expression that evaluates to a Boolean value (e.g., `true` or `false`). When you want to test multiple expressions, it's possible to add a chain of `if else` blocks. The `else` block matches anything that has not already been matched. For example

```
if item == 42 {
  // ...
} else if item == 132 {
  // ...
} else {
  // ...
}
```

---

[5] This functionality is also available with `continue`, but it's less common.

Rust has no concept of "truthy" or "falsey" types. Other languages allow special values such as 0 or an empty string to stand in for false and for other values to represent true, but Rust doesn't allow this. The only value that can be used for true is true, and for false, use false.

Rust is an expression-based language

In programming languages from this heritage, all expressions return values and almost everything is an expression. This heritage reveals itself through some constructs that are not legal in other languages. In idiomatic Rust, the return keyword is omitted from functions as shown in the following snippet:

```
fn is_even(n: i32) -> bool {
  n % 2 == 0
}
```

For example, Rust programmers assign variables from conditional expressions:

```
fn main() {
  let n = 123456;
  let description = if is_even(n) {
    "even"
  } else {
    "odd"
  };
  println!("{} is {}", n, description);     ⟵⎯ Prints "123456
}                                                   is even"
```

This can be extended to other blocks including match like this:

```
fn main() {
  let n = 654321;
  let description = match is_even(n) {
    true => "even",
    false => "odd",
  };
  println!("{} is {}", n, description);     ⟵⎯ Prints "654321
}                                                   is odd"
```

Perhaps most surprisingly, the break keyword also returns a value. This can be used to allow "infinite" loops to return values:

```
fn main() {
  let n = loop {
      break 123;
  };

  println!("{}", n);     ⟵⎯ Prints "123"
}
```

You may wonder what parts of Rust are *not* expressions and, thus, do not return values. Statements are not expressions. These appear in Rust in three places:

- Expressions delimited by the semicolon (`;`)
- Binding a name to a value with the assignment operator (`=`)
- Type declarations, which include functions (`fn`) and data types created with the `struct` and `enum` keywords

Formally, the first form is referred to as an *expression statement*. The last two are both called *declaration statements*. In Rust, no value is represented as `()` (the "unit" type).

2.4.7 Match: Type-aware pattern matching

While it's possible to use `if`/`else` blocks in Rust, `match` provides a safer alternative. `match` warns you if you haven't considered a relevant alternative. It is also elegant and concise:

```
match item {
    0            => {},
    10 ..= 20    => {},
    40 |  80     => {},
                 => {},
    _
}
```

To match a single value, provide the value. No operator is required.

The `..=` syntax matches an inclusive range.

The vertical bar (`|`) matches values on either side of it.

The underscore (`_`) matches every value.

`match` offers a sophisticated and concise syntax for testing multiple possible values. Some examples are

- Inclusive ranges (`10 ..= 20`) to match any value within the range.
- A Boolean OR (`|`) will match when either side matches.
- The underscore (`_`) to match everything.

`match` is analogous to the `switch` keyword in other languages. Unlike C's `switch`, however, `match` guarantees that all possible options for a type are explicitly handled. Failing to provide a branch for every possible value triggers a compiler error. Additionally, a match does not "fall through" to the next option by default. Instead, `match` returns immediately when a match is found.

Listing 2.8 demonstrates a larger example of `match`. The source code for this listing is in ch2/ch2-match-needles.rs. The code prints these two lines to the screen:

```
42: hit!
132: hit!
```

Listing 2.8   Using `match` to match multiple values

```
1 fn main() {                              The variable needle
2   let needle = 42;                       is now redundant.
3   let haystack = [1, 1, 2, 5, 14, 42, 132, 429, 1430, 4862];
4
5   for item in &haystack {                This match expression returns a value
6     let result = match item {            that can be bound to a variable.
7       42 | 132 => "hit!",                Success! 42 | 132 matches
8       _ => "miss",                       both 42 and 132.
9     };
10                                         A wildcard pattern that
11     if result == "hit!" {               matches everything
12       println!("{}: {}", item, result);
13     }
14   }
15 }
```

The `match` keyword plays an important role within the Rust language. Many control structures (like looping) are defined in terms of `match` under the hood. These really shine when combined with the `Option` type that's discussed in depth in the next chapter.

Now that we have taken a good look at defining numbers and working with some of Rust's flow control mechanisms, let's move on to adding structure to programs with functions.

2.5   *Defining functions*

Looking back to where the chapter begins, the snippet in listing 2.2 contained a small function, `add()`. `add` takes two `i32` values and returns their sum. The following listing repeats the function.

Listing 2.9   Defining a function (extract of listing 2.2)

```
10 fn add(i: i32, j: i32) -> i32 {         add() takes two integer parameters and
11   i + j                                 returns an integer. The two arguments
12 }                                       are bound to the local variables i and j.
```

For the moment, let's concentrate on the syntax of each of the elements in listing 2.9. Figure 2.2 provides a visual picture of each of the pieces. Anyone who has programmed in a strongly-typed programming language should be able to squint their way through the diagram.

Rust's functions require that you specify your parameter's types and the function's return type. This is the foundational knowledge that we'll need for the majority of our work with Rust. Let's put it to use with our first non-trivial program.

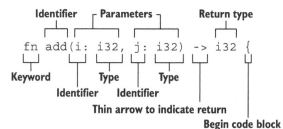

Figure 2.2   Rust's function definition syntax

2.6   *Using references*

If you have only used a dynamic programming language so far in your career, the syntax and semantics of references can be frustrating. It can be difficult to form a mental picture of what is happening. That makes it difficult to understand which symbols to put where. Thankfully, the Rust compiler is a good coach.

A *reference* is a value that stands in place for another value. For example, imagine that variable a is a large array that is costly to duplicate. In some sense, a reference r is a cheap copy of a. But instead of creating a duplicate, the program stores a's address in memory. When the data from a is required, r can be *dereferenced* to make a available. The following listing shows the code for this.

Listing 2.10   Creating a reference to a large array

```
fn main() {
  let a = 42;
  let r = &a;
  let b = a + *r;

  println!("a + a = {}", b);
}
```

r is a reference to a.

Adds a to a (via dereferencing r) and assigns it to b

Prints "a + a = 84"

References are created with the *reference operator* (&) and dereferencing occurs with the *dereference operator* (*). These operators act as *unary operators*, meaning that these only take one operand. One of the limitations of source code written in ASCII text is that multiplication and dereferencing use the same symbol. Let's see these in use as part of a larger example.

Listing 2.11 searches for a number (the needle defined on line 2) within an array of numbers (the haystack defined on line 3). The code then prints 42 to the console when compiled. The code for this listing is in ch2/ch2-needle-in-haystack.rs.

Listing 2.11   Searching for an integer in an array of integers

```
1 fn main() {
2   let needle = 0o204;
3   let haystack = [1, 1, 2, 5, 15, 52, 203, 877, 4140, 21147];
4
5   for item in &haystack {
```

Iterates over references to elements within haystack

```
 6      if *item == needle {
 7          println!("{}", item);
 8      }
 9  }
10 }
```

⊲ ┤ **The syntax *item returns the item's referent.**

Each iteration changes the value of item to refer to the next item within haystack. On the first iteration, *item returns 1, and on the last, it returns 21147.

2.7   *Project: Rendering the Mandelbrot set*

So far, we haven't learned much Rust, but we already have the tools to create some interesting pictures of fractals. So let's do that now with listing 2.12. To begin

1 In a terminal window, execute the following commands to create a project that can render the Mandelbrot set:

   a cd $TMP (or cd %TMP% on MS Windows) to move to a directory that's not critical.

   b cargo new mandelbrot --vcs none creates a new blank project.

   c cd mandelbrot moves into the new project root.

   d cargo add num to edit Cargo.toml, adding the num crate as a dependency (see the sidebar entitled "2.2" in section 2.3.4 for instructions to enable this cargo feature).

2 Replace src/main.rs with the code in listing 2.12, which you'll also find in ch2/ch2-mandelbrot/src/main.rs.

3 Execute cargo run. You should see the Mandelbrot set rendered in the terminal:

```
                                       .................................●●●*●**●.............
                                    .................................●●●***●●●..............
                                 ...............................●●●***+%+***●.................
                              .............................●●●●●●●●●*$%%%%%*●●●●●●.............
                           .........................●●**+*●●*******%%%*****+●●●●●*●...........
                        .....................●●●●●*%%+*%%%%%%%%%%%%%%%x*+*+*●●...........
                     ...................●●●●●**++%%%%%%%%%%%%%%%%%%%%%%%**●●...........
              .*●●●●●●●●●●●●●●●*+%%%%%%%%%%%%%%%%%%%%%%%%%%%%%%%*●●●.............
           ●●●***●●●●●**●●●●●●*+%%%%%%%%%%%%%%%%%%%%%%%%%%%%%%%%%%+●.............
        ●●●●●*+%*%#xx%****x%%%%%%%%%%%%%%%%%%%%%%%%%%%%%%%%%%%%**●..............
      ●●●●*++%%%%%%%%%%%+*%%%%%%%%%%%%%%%%%%%%%%%%%%%%%%%%%%%%**●...............
    ●●●●●●●●●●**+**+%%%%%%%%%%%%+%%%%%%%%%%%%%%%%%%%%%%%%%%%%%%%*●●...............
%%%%%%%%%%%%%%%%%%%%%%%%%%%%%%%%%%%%%%%%%%%%%%%%%%%%%%%%%%%%%%%%%%%*●●●●............
    ●●●●●●●●●●**+**+%%%%%%%%%%%%+%%%%%%%%%%%%%%%%%%%%%%%%%%%%%%%*●●...............
      ●●●●*++%%%%%%%%%%%+*%%%%%%%%%%%%%%%%%%%%%%%%%%%%%%%%%%%%**●...............
        ●●●●●*+%*%#xx%****x%%%%%%%%%%%%%%%%%%%%%%%%%%%%%%%%%%%%**●..............
           ●●●***●●●●●**●●●●●●*+%%%%%%%%%%%%%%%%%%%%%%%%%%%%%%%%%%+●.............
              .*●●●●●●●●●●●●●●●*+%%%%%%%%%%%%%%%%%%%%%%%%%%%%%%%*●●●.............
                     ...................●●●●●**++%%%%%%%%%%%%%%%%%%%%%%%**●●...........
                        .....................●●●●●*%%+*%%%%%%%%%%%%%%%x*+*+*●●...........
                           .........................●●**+*●●*******%%%*****+●●●●●*●...........
                              .............................●●●●●●●●●*$%%%%%*●●●●●●.............
                                 ...............................●●●***+%+***●.................
                                    .................................●●●***●●●..............
                                       .................................●●●*●**●.............
```

Listing 2.12   Rendering the Mandelbrot set

Imports the Complex number type from
num crate and its complex submodule

Converts between the output space (a grid of rows
and columns) and a range that surrounds the
Mandelbrot set (a continuous region near (0,0))

If a value has not escaped before reaching
the maximum number of iterations, it's
considered to be within the Mandelbrot set.

Parameters that specify the space
we're searching for to look for
members of the set

Parameters that represent the
size of the output in pixels

Creates a container
to house the data
from each row

Iterates row by row,
allowing us to print
the output line by line

Calculates the
proportion of the
space covered in
our output and
converts that to
points within the
search space

Called at every pixel
(e.g., every row and column
that's printed to stdout)

Initializes a complex
number at the origin with
real (re) and imaginary
(im) parts at 0.0

Initializes a complex number from the
coordinates provided as function arguments

Checks the escape condition and calculates
the distance from the origin (0, 0), an
absolute value of a complex number

Repeatedly mutates z to check whether
c lies within the Mandelbrot set

As i is no longer in scope, we fall back to max_iters.

```rust
1  use num::complex::Complex;
2
3  fn calculate_mandelbrot(
4
5    max_iters: usize,
6    x_min: f64,
7    x_max: f64,
8    y_min: f64,
9    y_max: f64,
10   width: usize,
11   height: usize,
12 ) -> Vec<Vec<usize>> {
13
14   let mut rows: Vec<_> = Vec::with_capacity(width);
15   for img_y in 0..height {
16
17     let mut row: Vec<usize> = Vec::with_capacity(height);
18     for img_x in 0..width {
19
20       let x_percent = (img_x as f64 / width as f64);
21       let y_percent = (img_y as f64 / height as f64);
22       let cx = x_min + (x_max - x_min) * x_percent;
23       let cy = y_min + (y_max - y_min) * y_percent;
24       let escaped_at = mandelbrot_at_point(cx, cy, max_iters);
25       row.push(escaped_at);
26     }
27
28     all_rows.push(row);
29   }
30   rows
31 }
32
33 fn mandelbrot_at_point(
34   cx: f64,
35   cy: f64,
36   max_iters: usize,
37 ) -> usize {
38   let mut z = Complex { re: 0.0, im: 0.0 };
39   let c = Complex::new(cx, cy);
40
41   for i in 0..=max_iters {
42     if z.norm() > 2.0 {
43       return i;
44     }
45     z = z * z + c;
46   }
47   max_iters
48 }
49
```

```
50 fn render_mandelbrot(escape_vals: Vec<Vec<usize>>) {
51   for row in escape_vals {
52     let mut line = String::with_capacity(row.len());
53     for column in row {
54       let val = match column {
55         0..=2 => ' ',
56         2..=5 => '.',
57         5..=10 => '•',
58         11..=30 => '*',
59         30..=100 => '+',
60         100..=200 => 'x',
61         200..=400 => '$',
62         400..=700 => '#',
63         _ => '%',
64       };
65
66       line.push(val);
67     }
68     println!("{}", line);
69   }
70 }
71
72 fn main() {
73   let mandelbrot = calculate_mandelbrot(1000, 2.0, 1.0, -1.0,
74                                          1.0, 100, 24);
75
76   render_mandelbrot(mandelbrot);
77 }
```

So far in this section, we've put the basics of Rust into practice. Let's continue our exploration by learning how to define functions and types.

2.8   *Advanced function definitions*

Rust's functions can get somewhat scarier than the add(i: i32, j: i32) -> i32 from listing 2.2. To assist those who are reading more Rust source code than writing it, the following sections provide some extra content.

2.8.1   *Explicit lifetime annotations*

As a bit of forewarning, allow me to introduce some more complicated notation. As you read through Rust code, you might encounter definitions that are hard to decipher because those look like hieroglyphs from an ancient civilizations. Listing 2.13 provides an extract from listing 2.14 that shows one such example.

> **Listing 2.13   A function signature with explicit lifetime annotations**

```
1 fn add_with_lifetimes<'a, 'b>(i: &'a i32, j: &'b i32) -> i32 {
2   *i + *j
3 }
```

Like all unfamiliar syntax, it can be difficult to know what's happening at first. This improves with time. Let's start by explaining *what* is happening, and then go on to discuss *why* it is happening. The following bullet points break line 1 of the previous snippet into its parts:

- `fn add_with_lifetimes(...)` `-> i32` should be familiar to you already. From this we can infer that `add_with_lifetimes()` is a function that returns an `i32` value.
- `<'a, 'b>` declares two lifetime variables, `'a` and `'b`, within the scope of `add_with_lifetimes()`. These are normally spoken as *lifetime a* and *lifetime b*.
- `i: &'a i32` binds lifetime variable `'a` to the lifetime of `i`. The syntax reads as "parameter `i` is a reference to an `i32` with lifetime a."
- `j: &'b i32` binds the lifetime variable `'b` to the lifetime of `j`. The syntax reads as "parameter `j` is a reference to an `i32` with lifetime b."

The significance of binding a lifetime variable to a value probably isn't obvious. Underpinning Rust's safety checks is a lifetime system that verifies that all attempts to access data are valid. Lifetime annotations allow programmers to declare their intent. All values bound to a given lifetime must live as long as the last access to any value bound to that lifetime.

The lifetime system usually works unaided. Although every parameter has a lifetime, these checks are typically invisible as the compiler can infer most lifetimes by itself.[6] But the compiler needs assistance in difficult cases. Functions that accept multiple references as arguments or return a reference are often when the compiler will request assistance via an error message.

No lifetime annotations are required when calling a function. When used in a complete example as in the next listing, you can see lifetime annotations at the function definition (line 1), but not when it's used (line 8). The source code for the listing is in ch2-add-with-lifetimes.rs.

Listing 2.14 Type signature of a function with lifetime explicit annotations

```
1 fn add_with_lifetimes<'a, 'b>(i: &'a i32, j: &'b i32) -> i32 {
2    *i + *j
3 }
4
5 fn main() {
6    let a = 10;
7    let b = 20;
8    let res = add_with_lifetimes(&a, &b);
9
10   println!("{}", res);
11 }
```

Adds the values referred to by i and j rather than adding the references directly

&10 and &20 mean reference 10 and 20, respectively. No lifetime notation is required when calling a function.

On line 2, `*i + *j` adds together the referent values held by the `i` and `j` variables. It's common to see lifetime parameters when using references. While Rust can infer lifetimes

---

[6] Omitting lifetime annotations is formally referred to as *lifetime elision*.

in other cases, references require the programmer to specify the intent. Using two lifetime parameters (a and b) indicates that the lifetimes of i and j are decoupled.

> **NOTE**   Lifetime parameters are a way of providing control to the programmer while maintaining high-level code.

2.8.2   *Generic functions*

Another special case of function syntax appears when programmers write Rust functions to handle many possible input types. So far, we have seen functions that accept 32-bit integers (i32). The following listing shows a function signature that can be called by many input types as long as these are all the same.

Listing 2.15   Type signature of a generic function

```
fn add<T>(i: T, j: T) -> T {           The type variable T is introduced with angle brackets
    i + j                              (<T>). This function takes two arguments of the
                                       same type and returns a value of that type.
}
```

Capital letters in place of a type indicate a *generic type*. Conventionally, the variables T, U, and V are used as placeholder values, but this is arbitrary. E is often used to denote an error type. We'll look at error handling in detail in chapter 3.

Generics enable significant code reuse and can greatly increase the usability of a strongly-typed language. Unfortunately, listing 2.15 doesn't compile as is. The Rust compiler complains that it cannot add two values of any type T together. The following shows the output produced when attempting to compile listing 2.15:

```
error[E0369]: cannot add `T` to `T`
  --> add.rs:2:5
   |
2  |     i + j
   |     - ^ - T
   |     |
   |     T
   |
help: consider restricting type parameter `T`
   |
1  | fn add<T: std::ops::Add<Output = T>>(i: T, j: T) -> T {
   |         ^^^^^^^^^^^^^^^^^^^^^^^^^^^^

error: aborting due to previous error

For more information about this error, try `rustc --explain E0369`.
```

This issue arises because T really means any type at all, even types where addition is not supported. Figure 2.3 provides a visual representation of the problem. Listing 2.15 attempts to refer to the outer ring, whereas addition is only supported by types within the inner ring.

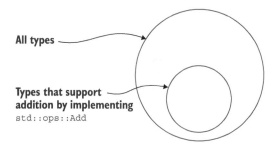

All types

Types that support
addition by implementing
`std::ops::Add`

Figure 2.3 Only a subset of types have implement operators. When creating generic functions that include such an operator, that operation's trait must be included as a trait bound.

How do we specify that type T must implement addition? Answering this requires introducing some new terminology.

All of Rust's operators, including addition, are defined within *traits*. To require that type T must support addition, we include a trait bound alongside the type variable in the function's definition. The following listing gives an example of this syntax.

Listing 2.16 Type signature of a generic function with trait bounds

```
fn add<T: std::ops::Add<Output = T>>(i: T, j: T) -> T {
  i + j
}
```

The fragment `<T: std::ops::Add<Output = T>>` says that T must implement `std::ops::Add`. Using a single type variable T with the trait bound ensures that arguments i and j, as well as the result type, are the same type and that their type supports addition.

What is a trait? A *trait* is a language feature that is analogous to an interface, protocol, or contract. If you have a background in object-oriented programming, consider a trait to be an abstract base class. If you have a background in functional programming, Rust's traits are close to Haskell's type classes. For now, it's enough to say that traits enable types to advertise that they are using common behavior.

All of Rust's operations are defined with traits. For example, the addition operator (+) is defined as the `std::ops::Add` trait. Traits are properly introduced in chapter 3 and are progressively explained in depth during the course of the book.

To reiterate: all of Rust's operators are syntactic sugar for a trait's methods. Rust supports operator overloading this way. During the compilation process, a + b is converted to `a.add(b)`.

Listing 2.17 is a full example that demonstrates that generic functions can be called by multiple types. The listing prints these three lines to the console:

```
4.6
30
15s
```

Listing 2.17   A generic function with a type variable and trait bounds

Brings the Add trait from
std::ops into local scope

Brings the Duration
type from std::time
into local scope

The arguments to add()
can accept any type
that implements
std::ops::Add.

```
1 use std::ops::{Add};
2 use std::time::{Duration};
3
4 fn add<T: Add<Output = T>>(i: T, j: T) -> T {
5   i + j
6 }
7
8 fn main() {
9   let floats = add(1.2, 3.4);
10  let ints = add(10, 20);
11  let durations = add(
12    Duration::new(5, 0),
13    Duration::new(10, 0)
14  );
15
16  println!("{}", floats);
17  println!("{}", ints);
18  println!("{:?}", durations);
19
20 }
```

Calls add() with
floating-point values

Calls add() with
integer values

Calls add() with Duration values, representing
a duration between two points in time

Because std::time::Duration does
not implement the std::fmt::Display
trait, we can fall back to requesting
std::fmt::Debug.

As you can see, function signatures can become somewhat convoluted. Interpreting these can take some patience. Hopefully, you now have the tools to break the pieces apart in case you get stuck down the track. Here are a few principles that should assist you when reading Rust code:

- Terms in lowercase (i, j) denote variables.
- Single uppercase letters (T) denote generic type variables.
- Terms beginning with uppercase (Add) are either traits or concrete types, such as String or Duration.
- Labels ('a) denote lifetime parameters.

2.9   *Creating grep-lite*

We've spent most of the chapter discussing numbers. It's time for another practical example. We'll use it to learn a little bit about how Rust handles text.

Listing 2.18 is our first iteration of grep-lite. The code for this program is in the ch2-str-simple-pattern.rs file. Its hard-coded parameters restrict flexibility somewhat, but these are useful illustrations of string literals. The code prints a line to the console:

```
dark square is a picture feverishly turned--in search of what?
```

Listing 2.18   Searching for a simple pattern within lines of a string

```
1 fn main() {
2   let search_term = "picture";
```

```
 3   let quote = "\
 4 Every face, every shop, bedroom window, public-house, and
 5 dark square is a picture feverishly turned--in search of what?
 6 It is the same with books.
 7 What do we seek through millions of pages?";
 8
 9   for line in quote.lines() {
10     if line.contains(search_term) {
11       println!("{}", line);
12     }
13   }
14 }
```

Multilined strings do not require special syntax. The \ character on line 3 escapes the new line.

lines() returns an iterator over quote where each iteration is a line of text. Rust uses each operating system's conventions on what constitutes a new line.

As you can see, Rust's strings can do quite a lot by themselves. Some features of listing 2.18 that are worth highlighting include the following. From here, we'll expand the functionality of our proto-application:

- Line 9 (`quote.lines()`) demonstrates iterating line-by-line in a platform-independent manner.
- Line 10 (`line.contains()`) demonstrates searching for text using the method syntax.

Navigating Rust's rich collection of string types

Strings are complicated for newcomers to Rust. Implementation details tend to bubble up from below and make comprehension difficult. How computers represent text is complicated, and Rust chooses to expose some of that complexity. This enables programmers to have full control but does place a burden on those learning the language.

`String` and `&str` both represent text, yet are distinct types. Interacting with values from both types can be an annoying exercise at first as different methods are required to perform similar actions. Prepare yourself for irritating type errors as your intuition develops. Until that intuition develops, however, you will usually have fewer issues if you convert your data to the `String` type.

A `String` is (probably) closest to what you know as a string type from other languages. It supports familiar operations such as concatenation (joining two strings together), appending new text onto an existing string, and trimming whitespace.

`str` is a high-performance, relatively feature-poor type. Once created, `str` values cannot expand or shrink. In this sense, these are similar to interacting with a raw memory array. Unlike a raw memory array, though, `str` values are guaranteed to be valid UTF-8 characters.

`str` is usually seen in this form: `&str`. A `&str` (pronounced *string slice*) is a small type that contains a reference to `str` data and a length. Attempting to assign a variable to type `str` will fail. The Rust compiler wants to create fixed-sized variables within a function's stack frame. As `str` values can be of arbitrary length, these can only be stored as local variables by reference.

(continued)

For those readers that have prior experience with systems programming, `String` uses dynamic memory allocation to store the text that it represents. Creating `&str` values avoids a memory allocation.

`String` is an *owned* type. Ownership has a particular meaning within Rust. An *owner* is able to make any changes to the data and is responsible for deleting values that it owns when it leaves scope (this is fully explained in chapter 3). A `&str` is a *borrowed* type. In practical terms, this means that `&str` can be thought of as read-only data, whereas `String` is read-write.

String literals (e.g., `"Rust in Action"`) have the type `&str`. The full type signature including the lifetime parameter is `&'static str`. The `'static` lifetime is somewhat special. It too owes its name to implementation details. Executable programs can contain a section of memory that is hard-coded with values. That section is known as *static memory* because it is read-only during execution.

Some other types may be encountered in your travels. Here's a short list:[a]

- `char`—A single character encoded as 4 bytes. The internal representation of `char` is equivalent to UCS-4/UTF-32. This differs from `&str` and `String`, which encodes single characters as UTF-8. Conversion does impose a penalty, but it means that `char` values are of fixed-width and are, therefore, easier for the compiler to reason about. Characters encoded as UTF-8 can span 1 to 4 bytes.
- `[u8]`—A slice of raw bytes, usually found when dealing with streams of binary data.
- `Vec<u8>`—A vector of raw bytes, usually created when consuming `[u8]` data. `String` is to `Vec<u8>` as `str` is to `[u8]`.
- `std::ffi::OSString`—A platform-native string. It's behavior is close to `String` but without a guarantee that it's encoded as UTF-8 and that it won't contain the zero byte (`0x00`).
- `std::path::Path`—A string-like type that is dedicated to handling filesystem paths.

Fully understanding the distinction between `String` and `&str` requires knowledge of arrays and vectors. Textual data is similar to these two types with added convenience methods applied over the top.

---

[a] Unfortunately, this is not an exhaustive list. Specific use cases sometimes require special handling.

Let's start adding functionality to grep-lite by printing the line number along with the match. This is equivalent to the -n option within the POSIX.1-2008 standard for the grep utility (http://mng.bz/ZPdZ).

Adding a few lines to our previous example, we now see the following line printed to the screen. Listing 2.19 shows the code that adds this functionality, which you'll find in ch2/ch2-simple-with-linenums.rs:

```
2: dark square is a picture feverishly turned--in search of what?
```

Listing 2.19 Manually incrementing an index variable

```
1  fn main() {
2    let search_term = "picture";
3    let quote = "\
4  Every face, every shop, bedroom window, public-house, and
5  dark square is a picture feverishly turned--in search of what?
6  It is the same with books. What do we seek through millions of pages?";
7    let mut line_num: usize = 1;
8
9    for line in quote.lines() {
10     if line.contains(search_term) {
11       println!("{}: {}", line_num, line);
12     }
13     line_num += 1;
14   }
15 }
```

A backslash escapes the newline character in the string literal.

Declares line_num as mutable via let mut and initializes it with 1

Increments line_num in place

Updates the println! macro to allow for both values to be printed

Listing 2.20 shows a more ergonomic approach to incrementing i. The output is the same, but here the code makes use of the enumerate() method and method chaining. enumerate() takes an iterator I, returning another (N, I), where N is a number that starts at 0 and increments by 1 each iteration. The source code for this listing can be found in ch2/ch2-simple-with-enumerate.rs.

Listing 2.20 Automatically incrementing an index variable

```
1  fn main() {
2    let search_term = "picture";
3    let quote = "\
4  Every face, every shop, bedroom window, public-house, and
5  dark square is a picture feverishly turned--in search of what?
6  It is the same with books. What do we seek through millions of pages?";
7
8    for (i, line) in quote.lines().enumerate() {
9      if line.contains(search_term) {
10       let line_num = i + 1;
11       println!("{}: {}", line_num, line);
12     }
13   }
14 }
```

Because lines() returns an iterator, it can be chained with enumerate().

Performs addition to calculate the line number, avoiding calculations at every step

Another feature of grep that is extremely useful is to print some context before and after the line that matches. In the GNU grep implementation, this is the -C NUM switch. To add support for that feature in grep-lite, we need to be able to create lists.

2.10   *Making lists of things with arrays, slices, and vectors*

Lists of things are incredibly common. The two types that you will work with most often are *arrays* and *vectors*. Arrays are fixed-width and extremely lightweight. Vectors are growable but incur a small runtime penalty because of the extra bookkeeping that these do. To understand the underlying mechanisms with text data in Rust, it helps to have a cursory understanding of what is happening.

The goal of this section is to support printing out *n* lines of context that surround a match. To get there, we need to segue somewhat and explain more fully arrays, slices, and vectors. The most useful type for this exercise is the vector. To learn about vectors, though, we need to start by learning about its two simpler cousins: arrays and slices.

2.10.1   Arrays

An *array*, at least as far as Rust is concerned, is a tightly-packed collection of the same thing. It's possible to replace items within an array, but its size cannot change. Because variable-length types like `String` add a degree of complication, we'll revert back to discussing numbers for a little while.

Creating arrays takes two forms. We can provide a comma-delimited list within square brackets (for example, `[1, 2, 3]`) or a *repeat expression*, where you furnish two values delimited by a semicolon (for example, `[0; 100]`). The value on the left (`0`) is repeated by the number of times on the right (`100`). Listing 2.21 shows each variation on lines 2–5. The source code for this listing is in the ch2-3arrays.rs file. It prints these four lines to the console:

```
[1, 2, 3]:     1 + 10 = 11     2 + 10 = 12     3 + 10 = 13     (Σ[1, 2, 3] = 6)
[1, 2, 3]:     1 + 10 = 11     2 + 10 = 12     3 + 10 = 13     (Σ[1, 2, 3] = 6)
[0, 0, 0]:     0 + 10 = 10     0 + 10 = 10     0 + 10 = 10     (Σ[0, 0, 0] = 0)
[0, 0, 0]:     0 + 10 = 10     0 + 10 = 10     0 + 10 = 10     (Σ[0, 0, 0] = 0)
```

Listing 2.21   Defining arrays and iterating over their elements

```
 1 fn main() {
 2   let one              = [1, 2, 3];
 3   let two: [u8; 3]     = [1, 2, 3];
 4   let blank1           = [0; 3];
 5   let blank2: [u8; 3] = [0; 3];
 6
 7   let arrays = [one, two, blank1, blank2];
 8
 9   for a in &arrays {
10     print!("{:?}: ", a);
11     for n in a.iter() {
12       print!("\t{} + 10 = {}", n, n+10);
13     }
14
15     let mut sum = 0;
16     for i in 0..a.len() {
17       sum += a[i];
18     }
19     println!("\t(Σ{:?} = {})", a, sum);
20   }
21 }
```

Arrays are a simple data structure from the machine's point of view. These are a contiguous block of memory with elements of a uniform type. The simplicity is still somewhat deceptive. Arrays can cause a few learning difficulties for newcomers:

- *The notation can be confusing.* [T; n] describes an array's type, where T is the elements' type and *n* is a non-negative integer. [f32; 12] denotes an array of 12 32-bit floating-point numbers. It's easy to get confused with slices [T], which do not have a compile-time length.
- *[u8; 3] is a different type than [u8; 4].* The size of the array matters to the type system.
- *In practice, most interaction with arrays occurs via another type called a slice ([T]).* The slice is itself interacted with by reference (&[T]). And to add some linguistic confusion into the mix, both slices and references to slices are called *slices*.

Rust maintains its focus on safety. Array indexing is bounds checked. Requesting an item that's out of bounds crashes (*panics* in Rust terminology) the program rather than returning erroneous data.

2.10.2 Slices

Slices are dynamically sized array-like objects. The term *dynamically sized* means that their size is not known at compile time. Yet, like arrays, these don't expand or contract. The use of the word *dynamic* in dynamically sized is closer in meaning to *dynamic typing* rather than movement. The lack of compile-time knowledge explains the distinction in the type signature between an array ([T; n]) and a slice ([T]).

Slices are important because it's easier to implement traits for slices than arrays. Traits are how Rust programmers add methods to objects. As [T; 1], [T; 2], ..., [T; n] are all different types, implementing traits for arrays can become unwieldy. Creating a slice from an array is easy and cheap because it doesn't need to be tied to any specific size.

Another important use for slices is their ability to act as a view on arrays (and other slices). The term *view* here is taken from database technology and means that slices can gain fast, read-only access to data without needing to copy anything around.

The problem with slices is that Rust wants to know the size of every object in your program, and slices are defined as not having a compile-time size. References to the rescue. As mentioned in the discussion about the use of the term dynamically sized, slice size is fixed in memory. These are made up of two usize components (a pointer and a length). That's why you typically see slices referred to in their referenced form, &[T] (like string slices that take the notation &str).

> **NOTE** Don't worry too much about the distinctions between arrays and slices yet. In practice, it's not material. Each term is an artifact of implementation details. Those implementation details are important when dealing with performance-critical code but not when learning the basics of the language.

2.10.3 *Vectors*

Vectors (Vec<T>) are growable lists of T. Using vectors is extremely common in Rust code. These incur a small runtime penalty compared to arrays because of the extra bookkeeping that must be done to enable their size to change over time. But vectors almost always make up for this with their added flexibility.

The task at hand is to expand the feature set of the grep-lite utility. Specifically, we want the ability to store *n* lines of context around a match. Naturally, there are many ways to implement such a feature.

To minimize code complexity, we'll use a two-pass strategy. In the first pass, we'll tag lines that match. During the second pass, we'll collect lines that are within *n* lines of each of the tags.

The code in listing 2.22 (available at ch2/ch2-introducing-vec.rs) is the longest you've seen so far. Take your time to digest it.

The most confusing syntax in the listing is probably Vec<Vec<(usize, String)>>, which appears on line 15. Vec<Vec<(usize, String)>> is a vector of vectors (e.g., Vec<Vec<T>>), where T is a pair of values of type (usize, String). (usize, String) is a tuple that we'll use to store line numbers along with the text that's a near match. When the needle variable on line 3 is set to "oo", the following text is printed to the console:

```
1: Every face, every shop,
2: bedroom window, public-house, and
3: dark square is a picture
4: feverishly turned--in search of what?
3: dark square is a picture
4: feverishly turned--in search of what?
5: It is the same with books.
6: What do we seek
7: through millions of pages?
```

Listing 2.22 Enabling context lines to be printed out with a Vec<Vec<T>>

```
 1 fn main() {
 2   let ctx_lines = 2;
 3   let needle = "oo";
 4   let haystack = "\
 5 Every face, every shop,
 6 bedroom window, public-house, and
 7 dark square is a picture
 8 feverishly turned--in search of what?
 9 It is the same with books.
10 What do we seek
11 through millions of pages?";
12
13   let mut tags: Vec<usize> = vec![];
14   let mut ctx: Vec<Vec<(
15            usize, String)>> = vec![];
16
17   for (i, line) in haystack.lines().enumerate() {
```

tags holds line numbers where matches occur.

ctx contains a vector per match to hold the context lines.

Iterates through the lines, recording line numbers where matches are encountered

```
18        if line.contains(needle) {
19          tags.push(i);
20
21          let v = Vec::with_capacity(2*ctx_lines + 1);      <─┤  Vec::with_capacity(n)
22          ctx.push(v);                                          reserves space for n
23        }                                                       items. No explicit type
24      }                                                         signature is required
25                                                                as it can be inferred
26      if tags.is_empty() {   <─┐  When there are no             via the definition of
27        return;                 matches, exits early           ctx on line 15.
28      }
29
30      for (i, line) in haystack.lines().enumerate() {   <─┐  For each tag, at every
31        for (j, tag) in tags.iter().enumerate() {            line, checks to see if
32          let lower_bound =                                  we are near a match.
33              tag.saturating_sub(ctx_lines);   <─┐          When we are, adds
34          let upper_bound =                                 that line to the
35              tag + ctx_lines;                              relevant Vec<T>
36                                                            within ctx.
37          if (i >= lower_bound) && (i <= upper_bound) {
38            let line_as_string = String::from(line);   <─┐  saturating_sub() is
39            let local_ctx = (i, line_as_string);            subtraction that returns
40            ctx[j].push(local_ctx);                          0 on integer underflow
41          }                                                  rather than crashing the
42        }                                                    program (CPUs don't like
43      }                                                      attempting to send usize
44                                                             below zero).
45      for local_ctx in ctx.iter() {
46        for &(i, ref line) in local_ctx.iter() {   <─┐  Copies line into a new
47          let line_num = i + 1;                          String and stores that
48          println!("{}: {}", line_num, line);            locally for each match
49        }
50      }                                                 ref line informs the compiler
51    }                                                   that we want to borrow this
                                                          value rather than move it.
                                                          These two terms are explained
                                                          fully in later chapters.
```

Vec<T> performs best when you can provide it with a size hint via Vec::with_capacity(). Providing an estimate minimizes the number of times memory will need to be allocated from the OS.

NOTE When considering this approach in real text files, encodings can cause issues. String is guaranteed to be UTF-8. Naively reading in a text file to a String causes errors if invalid bytes are detected. A more robust approach is to read in data as [u8] (a slice of u8 values), then decode those bytes with help from your domain knowledge.

2.11 *Including third-party code*

Incorporating third-party code is essential to productive Rust programming. Rust's standard library tends to lack many things that other languages provide, like random number generators and regular expression support. That means it's common to incorporate third-party crates into your project. To get your feet wet, let's start with the regex crate.

Crates are the name the Rust community uses where others use terms such as package, distribution, or library. The regex crate provides the ability to match regular expressions rather than simply looking for exact matches.

To use third-party code, we'll rely on the cargo command-line tool. Follow these instructions:

1   Open a command prompt.
2   Move to a scratch directory with cd /tmp (cd %TMP% on MS Windows).
3   Run cargo new grep-lite --vcs none. It produces a short confirmation message:

```
Created binary (application) `grep-lite` package
```

4   Run cd grep-lite to move into the project directory.
5   Execute cargo add regex@1 to add version 1 of the regex crate as a dependency. This alters the file /tmp/grep-lite/Cargo.toml. If cargo add is unavailable for you, see the sidebar, "2.2," in section 2.3.4.
6   Run cargo build. You should see output fairly similar to the following begin to appear:

```
  Updating crates.io index
Downloaded regex v1.3.6
 Compiling lazy_static v1.4.0
 Compiling regex-syntax v0.6.17
 Compiling thread_local v1.0.1
 Compiling aho-corasick v0.7.10
 Compiling regex v1.3.6
 Compiling grep-lite v0.1.0 (/tmp/grep-lite)
  Finished dev [unoptimized + debuginfo] target(s) in 4.47s
```

Now that you have the crate installed and compiled, let's put it into action. First, we'll support searching for exact matches in listing 2.23. Later, in listing 2.26, the project grows to support regular expressions.

2.11.1 *Adding support for regular expressions*

Regular expressions add great flexibility to the patterns that we are able to search for. The following listing is a copy of an early example that we'll modify.

Listing 2.23   Matching on exact strings with the `contains()` method

```
fn main() {
  let search_term = "picture";
  let quote = "Every face, every shop, bedroom window, public-house, and
dark square is a picture feverishly turned--in search of what?
It is the same with books. What do we seek through millions of pages?";

  for line in quote.lines() {          ⟵─┤  Implements a contains()
    if line.contains(search_term) {         method that searches for
      println!("{}", line);                 a substring
```

```
      }
    }
  }
}
```

Make sure that you have updated grep-lite/Cargo.toml to include regex as a dependency as described in the previous section. Now, open grep-lite/src/main.rs in a text editor and fill it in with the code in the following listing. The source code for this listing is available in ch2/ch2-with-regex.rs.

```
use regex::Regex;
                                    Brings the Regex type from the            unwrap() unwraps a Result,
                                    regex crate into local scope              crashing if an error occurs.
fn main() {                                                                   Handling errors more robustly
  let re = Regex::new("picture").unwrap();                                    is discussed in depth later in
                                                                              the book.

  let quote = "Every face, every shop, bedroom window, public-house, and
dark square is a picture feverishly turned--in search of what?
It is the same with books. What do we seek through millions of pages?";

                                                        Replaces the contains() method
                                                        from listing 2.23 with a match block
    for line in quote.lines() {                         that requires that we handle all
      let contains_substring = re.find(line);           possible cases
      match contains_substring {

        Some(_) => println!("{}", line),                Some(T) is the positive case of an
        None => (),                                     Option, meaning that re.find() was
      }                    None is the negative          successful: it matches all values.
    }                      case of an Option; () can
}                          be thought of as a null
                           placeholder value here.
```

Open a command prompt and move to the root directory of your grep-lite project. Executing cargo run should produce output similar to the following text:

```
$ cargo run
   Compiling grep-lite v0.1.0 (file:///tmp/grep-lite)
    Finished dev [unoptimized + debuginfo] target(s) in 0.48s
     Running `target/debug/grep-lite`
dark square is a picture feverishly turned--in search of what?
```

Admittedly, the code within listing 2.24 hasn't taken significant advantage of its new-found regular expression capabilities. Hopefully, you'll have the confidence to be able to slot those into some of the more complex examples.

2.11.2   *Generating the third-party crate documentation locally*

Documentation for third-party crates is typically available online. Still, it can be useful to know how to generate a local copy in case the internet fails you:

1   Move to the root of the project directory in a terminal: /tmp/grep-lite or %TMP%\grep-lite

2   Execute `cargo doc`. It will inform you of its progress in the console:

```
$ cargo doc
    Checking lazy_static v1.4.0
 Documenting lazy_static v1.4.0
    Checking regex-syntax v0.6.17
 Documenting regex-syntax v0.6.17
    Checking memchr v2.3.3
 Documenting memchr v2.3.3
    Checking thread_local v1.0.1
    Checking aho-corasick v0.7.10
 Documenting thread_local v1.0.1
 Documenting aho-corasick v0.7.10
    Checking regex v1.3.6
 Documenting regex v1.3.6
 Documenting grep-lite v0.1.0 (file:///tmp/grep-lite)
    Finished dev [unoptimized + debuginfo] target(s) in 3.43s
```

Congratulations. You have now created HTML documentation. By opening /tmp/grep-lite/target/doc/grep_lite/index.html in a web browser (also try `cargo doc --open` from the command line), you'll be able to view the documentation for all the crates that yours depend on. It's also possible to inspect the output directory to take a look at what is available to you:

```
$ tree -d -L 1 target/doc/
target/doc/
├── aho_corasick
├── grep_lite
├── implementors
├── memchr
├── regex
├── regex_syntax
├── src
└── thread_local
```

2.11.3   *Managing Rust toolchains with rustup*

rustup is another handy command-line tool, along with cargo. Where cargo manages projects, rustup manages your Rust installation(s). rustup cares about Rust toolchains and enables you to move between versions of the compiler. This means it's possible to compile your projects for multiple platforms and experiment with nightly features of the compiler while keeping the stable version nearby.

rustup also simplifies accessing Rust's documentation. Typing `rustup doc` opens your web browser to a local copy of Rust's standard library.

2.12   *Supporting command-line arguments*

Our program is rapidly increasing its feature count. Yet, there is no way for any options to be specified. To become an actual utility, grep-lite needs to be able to interact with the world.

Sadly, though, Rust has a fairly tight standard library. As with regular expressions, another area with relatively minimalist support is handling command-line arguments. A nicer API is available through a third-party crate called clap (among others).

Now that we've seen how to bring in third-party code, let's take advantage of that to enable users of grep-lite to choose their own pattern. (We'll get to choosing their own input source in the next section.) First, add clap as a dependency in your Cargo.toml:

```
$ cargo add clap@2
    Updating 'https://github.com/rust-lang/crates.io-index' index
      Adding clap v2 to dependencies
```

You can confirm that the crate has been added to your project by inspecting its Cargo.toml file.

Listing 2.25   Adding a dependency to grep-lite/Cargo.toml

```
[package]
name = "grep-lite"
version = "0.1.0"
authors = ["Tim McNamara <author@rustinaction.com>"]

[dependencies]
regex = "1"
clap = "2"
```

Now, adjust src/main.rs.

Listing 2.26   Editing grep-lite/src/main.rs

```
 1 use regex::Regex;
 2 use clap::{App,Arg};            ◄── Brings clap::App and
 3                                      clap::Arg objects into
 4 fn main() {                          local scope
 5   let args = App::new("grep-lite")      ◄──
 6     .version("0.1")                          Incrementally builds a command
 7     .about("searches for patterns")          argument parser, where each
 8     .arg(Arg::with_name("pattern")           argument takes an Arg. In our
 9       .help("The pattern to search for")     case, we only need one.
10       .takes_value(true)
11       .required(true))
12     .get_matches();
13                                                          Extracts the
14   let pattern = args.value_of("pattern").unwrap();   ◄── pattern argument
15   let re = Regex::new(pattern).unwrap();
16
17   let quote = "Every face, every shop, bedroom window, public-house, and
18 dark square is a picture feverishly turned--in search of what?
19 It is the same with books. What do we seek through millions of pages?";
20
21   for line in quote.lines() {
22     match re.find(line) {
```

```
23          Some(_) => println!("{}", line),
24          None => (),
25      }
26   }
27 }
```

With your project updated, executing `cargo run` should set off a few lines in your console:

```
$ cargo run
    Finished dev [unoptimized + debuginfo] target(s) in 2.21 secs
     Running `target/debug/grep-lite`
error: The following required arguments were not provided:
    <pattern>

USAGE:
    grep-lite <pattern>

For more information try --help
```

The error is due to the fact that we haven't passed sufficient arguments through to our resulting executable. To pass arguments through, cargo supports some special syntax. Any arguments appearing after -- are sent through to the resulting executable binary:

```
$ cargo run -- picture
    Finished dev [unoptimized + debuginfo] target(s) in 0.0 secs
     Running `target/debug/grep-lite picture`
dark square is a picture feverishly turned--in search of what?
```

But clap does more than provide parsing. It also generates usage documentation on your behalf. Running `grep-lite --help` provides an expanded view:

```
$ ./target/debug/grep-lite --help
grep-lite 0.1
searches for patterns

USAGE:
    grep-lite <pattern>

FLAGS:
    -h, --help       Prints help information
    -V, --version    Prints version information

ARGS:
    <pattern>    The pattern to search for
```

2.13 *Reading from files*

Searching for text wouldn't be complete without being able to search within files. File I/O can be surprisingly finicky and so has been left until last.

Before adding this functionality to grep-lite, let's take a look at a standalone example in listing 2.27. The code for this listing is in the ch2-read-file.rs file. The general pattern is to open a File object, then wrap that in a BufReader. BufReader takes care of providing *buffered I/O*, which can reduce system calls to the OS if the hard disk is congested.

Listing 2.27 Reading a file manually line by line

```
1 use std::fs::File;
2 use std::io::BufReader;
3 use std::io::prelude::*;
4
5 fn main() {
6   let f = File::open("readme.md").unwrap();
7   let mut reader = BufReader::new(f);
8
9   let mut line = String::new();
10
11  loop {
12    let len = reader.read_line(&mut line)
13                       .unwrap();
14    if len == 0 {
15      break
16    }
17
18    println!("{} ({} bytes long)", line, len);
19
20    line.truncate(0);
21  }
22 }
```

Creates a File object that requires a path argument and error handling if the file does not exist. This program crashes if a readme.md is not present.

Reuses a single String object over the lifetime of the program

Because reading from disk can fail, we need to explicitly handle this. In our case, errors crash the program.

Shrinks the String back to length 0, preventing lines from persisting into the following ones

Manually looping through a file can be cumbersome, despite its usefulness in some cases. For the common case of iterating through lines, Rust provides a helper iterator as the following listing shows. The source code for this listing is in the file ch2/ch2-bufreader-lines.rs.

Listing 2.28 Reading a file line by line via `BufReader::lines()`

```
1 use std::fs::File;
2 use std::io::BufReader;
3 use std::io::prelude::*;
4
5 fn main() {
6   let f = File::open("readme.md").unwrap();
7   let reader = BufReader::new(f);
8
9   for line_ in reader.lines() {
10    let line = line_.unwrap();
11    println!("{} ({} bytes long)", line, line.len());
12  }
13 }
```

A subtle behavior change occurs here. BufReader::lines() removes the trailing newline character from each line.

Unwraps the Result, but at the risk of crashing the program if an error occurs

We're now in a position to add reading from a file into grep-lite's feature list. The following listing creates a complete program that takes a regular expression pattern and an input file as arguments.

Listing 2.29   Reading lines from a file

```
1 use std::fs::File;
2 use std::io::BufReader;
3 use std::io::prelude::*;
4 use regex::Regex;
5 use clap::{App,Arg};
6
7 fn main() {
8   let args = App::new("grep-lite")
9     .version("0.1")
10    .about("searches for patterns")
11    .arg(Arg::with_name("pattern")
12      .help("The pattern to search for")
13      .takes_value(true)
14      .required(true))
15    .arg(Arg::with_name("input")
16      .help("File to search")
17      .takes_value(true)
18      .required(true))
19    .get_matches();
20
21   let pattern = args.value_of("pattern").unwrap();
22   let re = Regex::new(pattern).unwrap();
23
24   let input = args.value_of("input").unwrap();
25   let f = File::open(input).unwrap();
26   let reader = BufReader::new(f);
27
28   for line_ in reader.lines() {
29     let line = line_.unwrap();
30     match re.find(&line) {            ⟵─┐  line is a String, but
31         Some(_) => println!("{}", line),    re.find() takes an &str
32         None => (),                          as an argument.
33     }
34   }
35 }
```

2.14   *Reading from stdin*

A command-line utility wouldn't be complete if it wasn't able to read from stdin. Unfortunately for those readers who skimmed over earlier parts of this chapter, some of the syntax on line 8 might look quite unfamiliar. In short, rather than duplicate code within main(), we'll use a generic function to abstract away the details of whether we are dealing with files or stdin:

Listing 2.30   Searching through a file or stdin

```
1 use std::fs::File;
2 use std::io;
3 use std::io::BufReader;
4 use std::io::prelude::*;
5 use regex::Regex;
```

```
 6 use clap::{App,Arg};
 7
 8 fn process_lines<T: BufRead + Sized>(reader: T, re: Regex) {
 9   for line_ in reader.lines() {
10     let line = line_.unwrap();
11     match re.find(&line) {                    ◁──┐  line is a String, but
12       Some(_) => println!("{}", line),           │  re.find() takes an &str
13       None => (),                                 │  as an argument.
14     }
15   }
16 }
17
18 fn main() {
19   let args = App::new("grep-lite")
20     .version("0.1")
21     .about("searches for patterns")
22     .arg(Arg::with_name("pattern")
23       .help("The pattern to search for")
24       .takes_value(true)
25       .required(true))
26     .arg(Arg::with_name("input")
27       .help("File to search")
28       .takes_value(true)
29       .required(false))
30     .get_matches();
31
32   let pattern = args.value_of("pattern").unwrap();
33   let re = Regex::new(pattern).unwrap();
34
35   let input = args.value_of("input").unwrap_or("-");
36
37   if input == "-" {
38     let stdin = io::stdin();
39     let reader = stdin.lock();
40     process_lines(reader, re);
41   } else {
42     let f = File::open(input).unwrap();
43     let reader = BufReader::new(f);
44     process_lines(reader, re);
45   }
46 }
```

Summary

- Rust has full support for primitive types, such as integers and floating-point numbers.
- Functions are strongly typed and require types to be specified for their parameters and return values.
- Rust features, such as iteration and mathematical operations, rely on traits. The `for` loop is a shorthand for the `std::iter::IntoIterator` trait, for example.
- List-like types are tailored to specific use cases. You will typically reach for `Vec<T>` first.

- All Rust programs have a single entry function: `main()`.
- Every crate has a Cargo.toml file that specifies its metadata.
- The cargo tool is able to compile your code and fetch its dependencies.
- The rustup tool provides access to multiple compiler toolchains and to the language's documentation.

Compound data types 3

Welcome to chapter 3. If we spent the last chapter looking at Rust's atoms, this chapter is focused more on its molecules.

This chapter focuses on two key building blocks for Rust programmers, struct and enum. Both are forms of *compound data types*. Together, struct and enum can compose other types to create something more useful than what those other types would be alone. Consider how a 2D point (x,y) is composed from two numbers, *x* and *y*. We wouldn't want to maintain two variables, x and y, in our program. Instead, we would like to refer to the point as a whole entity. In this chapter, we also discuss how to add methods to types with `impl` blocks. Lastly, we take a deeper look at *traits*, Rust's system for defining interfaces.

Throughout this chapter, you'll work through how to represent files in code. Although conceptually simple—if you're reading this book, it's highly likely you've interacted with a file through code before—there are enough edge cases to make things interesting. Our strategy will be to create a mock version of everything using our own imaginary API. Then, toward the latter part of the chapter, you'll learn how to interact with your actual operating system (OS) and its filesystem(s).

3.1   *Using plain functions to experiment with an API*

To start, let's see how far we can get by making use of the tools we already know. Listing 3.1 lays out a few things that we would expect, such as opening and closing a file. We'll use a rudimentary mock type to model one: a simple alias around `String` that holds a filename and little else.

To make things slightly more interesting than writing lots of boilerplate code, listing 3.1 sprinkles in a few new concepts. These show you how to tame the compiler while you're experimenting with your design. It provides attributes (`#![allow(unused _variables)]`) to relax compiler warnings. The `read` function illustrates how to define a function that never returns. The code actually doesn't do anything, however. That will come shortly. You'll find the source for this listing in the file ch3/ch3-not-quite-file-1.rs.

Listing 3.1   Using type aliases to stub out a type

```
 1 #![allow(unused_variables)]              ⟵┐   Relaxes compiler warnings
 2                                               while working through ideas
 3 type File = String;              ⟵──────┐
 4                                            Creates a type alias. The compiler
 5 fn open(f: &mut File) -> bool {           won't distinguish between String &
 6     true                         ⟵       File, but your source code will.
 7                                        Let's assume for the moment that
 8 fn close(f: &mut File) -> bool {    these two functions always succeed.
 9     true                         ⟵
10 }
11                                 Relaxes a compiler warning
12 #[allow(dead_code)]     ⟵       about an unused function
13 fn read(f: &mut File,
14         save_to: &mut Vec<u8>) -> ! {   ⟵─┐   The ! return type
15     unimplemented!()   ⟵                      indicates to the Rust
16 }                           A macro that crashes   compiler that this
17                             the program if it's     function never returns.
18 fn main() {                 encountered
19     let mut f1 = File::from("f1.txt");   ⟵   With the type declaration at line 3,
20     open(&mut f1);                             File inherits all of String's methods.
21     //read(f1, vec![]);   ⟵─┐
22     close(&mut f1);          There's little point in
23 }                           calling this method.
```

There are *lots* of things that needs to be built on from listing 3.1. For example

- *We haven't created a persistent object that would represent a file.* There's only so much that can be encoded in a string.
- *There's no attempt to implement* read(). If we did, how would we handle the failure case?
- open() *and* close() *return* bool. Perhaps there is a way to provide a more sophisticated result type that might be able to contain an error message if the OS reports one.
- *None of our functions are methods.* From a stylistic point of view, it might be nice to call f.open() rather than open(f).

Let's begin at the top and work our way through this list. Brace yourself for a few scenic detours along the way as we encounter a few side roads that will be profitable to explore.

Special return types in Rust

If you are new to the language, some return types are difficult to interpret. These are also especially difficult to search for because they are made from symbols rather than words.

Known as the *unit type*, () formally is a zero-length tuple. It is used to express that a function returns no value. Functions that appear to have no return type return (), and expressions that are terminated with a semicolon (;) return (). For example, the report() function in the following code block returns the unit type implicitly:

```
use std::fmt::Debug;

fn report<T: Debug>(item: T) {      ◄─── item can be any type
  println!("{:?}", item);               that implements
                                        std::fmt::Debug.
}                                    {:?} directs the println! macro to
                                     use std::fmt::Debug to convert
                                     item to a printable string.
```

And this example returns the unit type explicitly:

```
fn clear(text: &mut String) -> () {    Replaces the string at text
  *text = String::from("");            with an empty string
}
```

The unit type often occurs in error messages. It's common to forget that the last expression of a function shouldn't end with a semicolon.

The exclamation symbol, !, is known as the "Never" type. Never indicates that a function never returns, especially when it is guaranteed to crash. For example, take this code:

```
fn dead_end() -> ! {                  The panic! macro causes the
  panic!("you have reached a dead end");   program to crash. This means
                                           the function is guaranteed
}                                          never to return.
```

(continued)

The following example creates an infinite loop that prevents the function from returning:

```
fn forever() -> ! {
  loop {
    //...
  };
}
```

> Unless it contains a break, the loop never finishes. This prevents the function from returning.

As with the unit type, Never sometimes occurs within error messages. The Rust compiler complains about mismatched types when you forget to add a break in your loop block if you've indicated that the function returns a non-Never type.

3.2   *Modeling files with struct*

We need something to represent that thing we're trying to model. struct allows you to create a composite type made up of other types. Depending on your programming heritage, you may be more familiar with terms such as object or record.

We'll start with requiring that our files have a name and zero or more bytes of data. Listing 3.2 prints the following two lines to the console:

```
File { name: "f1.txt", data: [] }
f1.txt is 0 bytes long
```

To represent data, listing 3.2 uses Vec<u8>, which is a growable list of u8 (single byte) values. The bulk of the main() function demonstrates usage (e.g., field access). The file ch3/ch3-mock-file.rs contains the code for this listing.

Listing 3.2   Defining an instance of struct to represent files

```
 1 #[derive(Debug)]
 2 struct File {
 3   name: String,
 4   data: Vec<u8>,
 5 }
 6
 7 fn main() {
 8   let f1 = File {
 9     name: String::from("f1.txt"),
10     data: Vec::new(),
11   };
12
13   let f1_name = &f1.name;
14   let f1_length = &f1.data.len();
15
16   println!("{:?}", f1);
17   println!("{} is {} bytes long", f1_name, f1_length);
18 }
```

> Allows println! to print File. The std::fmt::Debug trait works in conjunction with {:?} within the macro to enable File as a printable string.

> Using Vec<u8>, provides access to some useful conveniences like dynamic sizing, which makes it possible to simulate writing to a file

> **Here the vec! macro simulates an empty file.**

> String::from generates owned strings from string literals, which are slices.

> Accessing fields uses the . operator. Accessing fields by reference prevents their use after move issues.

Here is a detailed overview of listing 3.2:

- *Lines 1–5 define the `File` struct.* Definitions include fields and their associated types. These also include each field's lifetimes, which happened to be elided here. Explicit lifetimes are required when a field is a reference to another object.
- *Lines 8–11 create our first instance of `File`.* We use a literal syntax here, but typically structs in the wild are created via a convenience method. `String::from()` is one of those convenience methods. It takes a value of another type; in this case, a string slice (`&str`), which returns a `String` instance. `Vec::new()` is the more common case.
- *Lines 13–17 demonstrate accessing our new instance's fields.* We prepend an ampersand to indicate that we want to access this data by reference. In Rust parlance, this means that the variables `f1_name` and `f1_length` are borrowing the data these refer to.

You have probably noticed that our `File` struct doesn't actually store anything to disk at all. That's actually OK for now. If you're interested, figure 3.1 shows its internals. In the figure, its two fields (`name` and `data`) are themselves both created by structs. If you're unfamiliar with the term pointer (`ptr`), consider pointers to be the same thing as references for now. Pointers are variables that refer to some location in memory. The details are explained at length in chapter 6.

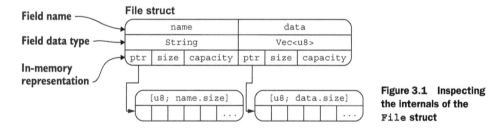

Figure 3.1 **Inspecting the internals of the `File` struct**

We'll leave interacting with the hard disk drive or other persistent storage until later in the chapter. For the meantime, let's recreate listing 3.1 and add the `File` type as promised.

The `newtype` pattern

Sometimes the `type` keyword is all that you need. But what about when you need the compiler to treat your new "type" as a fully-fledged, distinct type rather than just an alias? Enter `newtype`. The `newtype` pattern consists of wrapping a core type within a single field `struct` (or perhaps a `tuple`). The following code shows how to distinguish network hostnames from ordinary strings. You'll find this code in ch3/ch3-newtype-pattern.rs:

```
(continued)
struct Hostname(String);        ⟵ ┐  Hostname is
                                     our new type.         Uses the type system
                                                           to guard against
fn connect(host: Hostname) {    ⟵ ────────────────────     invalid usage
  println!("connected to {}", host.0);  ⟵ ┐
}                                           Accesses the underlying
                                            data with a numeric
fn main() {                                 index
    let ordinary_string = String::from("localhost");
    let host = Hostname ( ordinary_string.clone() );

    connect(ordinary_string);
}
```

Here is the compiler output from rustc:

```
$ rustc ch3-newtype-pattern.rs
error[E0308]: mismatched types
  --> ch3-newtype-pattern.rs:11:13
   |
11 |        connect(ordinary_string);
   |                ^^^^^^^^^^^^^^^ expected struct `Hostname`,
   |                                found struct `String`

error: aborting due to previous error

For more information about this error, try `rustc --explain E0308`.
```

Using the `newtype` pattern can strengthen a program by preventing data from being
silently used in inappropriate contexts. The downside of using the pattern is that each
new type must opt in to all of its intended behavior. This can feel cumbersome.

We can now add a little bit of functionality to the first listing of the chapter. Listing 3.3
(available at ch3/ch3-not-quite-file-2.rs) adds the ability to read a file that has some
data in it. It demonstrates how to use a `struct` to mimic a file and simulate reading its
contents. It then converts opaque data into a `String`. All functions are assumed to
always succeed, but the code is still littered with hard-coded values. Still, the code finally
prints something to the screen. Here is partially obscured output from the program:

```
File { name: "2.txt", data: [114, 117, 115, 116, 33] }
2.txt is 5 bytes long
*****        ⟵ ┐  Revealing this line would
                  spoil all of the fun!
```

Listing 3.3 Using `struct` to mimic a file and simulate reading its contents

```
1 #![allow(unused_variables)]        ⟵ ──────────────┐  Silences
2                                                        warnings
                                   Enables File to work with println!
3 #[derive(Debug)]    ⟵ ┐          and its fmt! sibling macros (used
4 struct File {            at the bottom of the listing)
```

```
 5    name: String,
 6    data: Vec<u8>,
 7  }
 8
 9  fn open(f: &mut File) -> bool {
10    true
11  }
12
13  fn close(f: &mut File) -> bool {
14    true
15  }
16
17  fn read(
18    f: &File,
19    save_to: &mut Vec<u8>,
20  ) -> usize {
21    let mut tmp = f.data.clone();
22    let read_length = tmp.len();
23
24    save_to.reserve(read_length);
25    save_to.append(&mut tmp);
26    read_length
27  }
28
29  fn main() {
30    let mut f2 = File {
31      name: String::from("2.txt"),
32      data: vec![114, 117, 115, 116, 33],
33    };
34
35    let mut buffer: Vec<u8> = vec![];
36
37    open(&mut f2);
38    let f2_length = read(&f2, &mut buffer);
39    close(&mut f2);
40
41    let text = String::from_utf8_lossy(&buffer);
42
43    println!("{:?}", f2);
44    println!("{} is {} bytes long", &f2.name, f2_length);
45    println!("{}", text)
46  }
47
```

These two functions remain inert for now.

Returns the number of bytes read

Makes a copy of the data here because save_to.append() shrinks the input Vec<T>

Ensures that there is sufficient space to fit the incoming data

Allocates sufficient data in the save_to buffer to hold the contents of f

Does the hard work of interacting with the file

Converts Vec<u8> to String. Any bytes that are not valid UTF-8 are replaced with �.

Views the bytes 114, 117, 115, 116, and 33 as an actual word

The code so far has tackled two of the four issues raised at the end of listing 3.1:

- Our File struct is a bona fide type.
- read() is implemented, albeit in a memory-inefficient manner.

These last two points remain:

- open() and close() return bool.
- None of our functions are methods.

3.3   *Adding methods to a struct with impl*

This section explains briefly what methods are and describes how to make use of them in Rust. Methods are functions that are coupled to some object. From a syntactic point of view, these are just functions that don't need to specify one of their arguments. Rather than calling open() and passing a File object in as an argument (read(f, buffer)), methods allow the main object to be implicit in the function call (f.read(buffer)) using the dot operator.[1]

Rust is different than other languages that support methods: there is no class keyword. Types created with struct (and enum, which is described later) feel like classes at times, but as they don't support inheritance, it's probably a good thing that they're named something different.

To define methods, Rust programmers use an impl block, which is physically distinct in source code from the struct and enum blocks that you have already encountered. Figure 3.2 shows the differences.

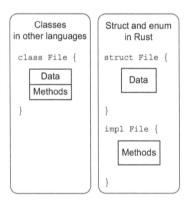

Figure 3.2   **Illustrating syntactic differences between Rust and most object oriented languages. Within Rust, methods are defined separately from fields.**

3.3.1   *Simplifying object creation by implementing new()*

Creating objects with reasonable defaults is done through the new() method. Every struct can be instantiated through a literal syntax. This is handy for getting started, but leads to unnecessary verbosity in most code.

Using new() is a convention within the Rust community. Unlike other languages, new is not a keyword and isn't given some sort of blessed status above other methods. Table 3.1 summarizes the conventions.

---

[1] There are a number of theoretical differences between methods and functions, but a detailed discussion of those computer science topics is available in other books. Briefly, functions are regarded as *pure*, meaning their behavior is determined solely by their arguments. Methods are inherently *impure*, given that one of their arguments is effectively a side effect. These are muddy waters, though. Functions are perfectly capable of acting on side effects themselves. Moreover, methods are implemented with functions. And, to add an exception to an exception, objects sometimes implement *static methods*, which do not include implicit arguments.

Table 3.1 Comparing Rust's literal syntax for creating objects with the use of the `new()` method

Current usage	With File::new()

`File {`
`    name: String::from("f1.txt"),`
`    data: Vec::new(),`
`};`
	`File::new("f1.txt", vec![]);`

`File {`
`  name: String::from("f2.txt"),`
`  data: vec![114, 117, 115, 116, 33],`
`};`
	`File::new("f2.txt", vec![114, 117,`
	`115, 116, 33]);`

To enable these changes, make use of an `impl` block as the next listing shows (see ch3/ch3-defining-files-neatly.rs). The resulting executable should print out the same message as listing 3.3, substituting `f3.txt` for the original's `f1.txt`.

Listing 3.4 Using `impl` blocks to add methods to a struct

```
1  #[derive(Debug)]
2  struct File {
3    name: String,
4    data: Vec<u8>,
5  }
6
7  impl File {
8    fn new(name: &str) -> File {
9      File {
10       name: String::from(name),
11       data: Vec::new(),
12     }
13   }
14 }
15
16 fn main() {
17   let f3 = File::new("f3.txt");
18
19   let f3_name = &f3.name;
20   let f3_length = f3.data.len();
21
22   println!("{:?}", f3);
23   println!("{} is {} bytes long", f3_name, f3_length);
24 }
```

> As File::new() is a completely normal function, we need to tell Rust that it will return a File from this function.

> File::new() does little more than encapsulate the object creation syntax, which is normal.

> Fields are private by default but can be accessed within the module that defines the struct. The module system is discussed later in the chapter.

Merging this new knowledge with the example that we already have, listing 3.5 is the result (see ch3/ch3-defining-files-neatly.rs). It prints the following three lines to the console:

```
File { name: "2.txt", data: [114, 117, 115, 116, 33] }
2.txt is 5 bytes long
*****
```

> **Still hidden!**

Listing 3.5   Using `impl` to improve the ergonomics of `File`

```
1  #![allow(unused_variables)]
2
3  #[derive(Debug)]
4  struct File {
5    name: String,
6    data: Vec<u8>,
7  }
8
9  impl File {
10   fn new(name: &str) -> File {
11     File {
12       name: String::from(name),
13       data: Vec::new(),
14     }
15   }
16
17   fn new_with_data(
18     name: &str,
19     data: &Vec<u8>,
20   ) -> File {
21     let mut f = File::new(name);
22     f.data = data.clone();
23     f
24   }
25
26   fn read(
27     self: &File,
28     save_to: &mut Vec<u8>,
29   ) -> usize {
30     let mut tmp = self.data.clone();
31     let read_length = tmp.len();
32     save_to.reserve(read_length);
33     save_to.append(&mut tmp);
34     read_length
35   }
36 }
37
38 fn open(f: &mut File) -> bool {
39   true
40 }
41
42 fn close(f: &mut File) -> bool {
43   true
44 }
45
46 fn main() {
47   let f3_data: Vec<u8> = vec![
48     114, 117, 115, 116, 33
49   ];
50   let mut f3 = File::new_with_data("2.txt", &f3_data);
51
52   let mut buffer: Vec<u8> = vec![];
53
```

This method sneaked in to deal with cases where we want to simulate that a file has pre-existing data.

Replaces the f argument with self

An explicit type needs to be provided as vec! and can't infer the necessary type through the function boundary.

```
54    open(&mut f3);
55    let f3_length = f3.read(&mut buffer);        ◁─┐  Here is the
56    close(&mut f3);                                 │  change in the
57                                                    │  calling code.
58    let text = String::from_utf8_lossy(&buffer);
59
60    println!("{:?}", f3);
61    println!("{} is {} bytes long", &f3.name, f3_length);
62    println!("{}", text);
63 }
```

3.4   Returning errors

Early on in the chapter, two points were raised discussing dissatisfaction with being unable to properly signify errors:

- *There was no attempt at implementing* read(). If we did, how would we handle the failure case?
- *The methods* open() *and* close() *return* bool. Is there a way to provide a more sophisticated result type to contain an error message if the OS reports one?

The issue arises because dealing with hardware is unreliable. Even ignoring hardware faults, the disk might be full or the OS might intervene and tell you that you don't have permission to delete a particular file. This section discusses different methods for signalling that an error has occurred, beginning with approaches common in other languages and finishing with idiomatic Rust.

3.4.1   Modifying a known global variable

One of the simplest methods for signalling that an error has occurred is by checking the value of a global variable. Although notoriously error-prone, this is a common idiom in systems programming.

C programmers are used to checking the value of errno once system calls return. As an example, the close() system call closes a *file descriptor* (an integer representing a file with numbers assigned by the OS) and can modify errno. The section of the POSIX standard discussing the close() system call includes this snippet:

> "If close() is interrupted by a signal that is to be caught, it shall return -1 with errno set to EINTR and the state of fildes [file descriptor] is unspecified. If an I/O error occurred while reading from or writing to the file system during close(), it may return -1 with errno set to EIO; if this error is returned, the state of fildes is unspecified."

—The Open Group Base Specifications (2018)

Setting errno to either EIO or EINTR means to set it to some magical internal constant. The specific values are arbitrary and defined per OS. With the Rust syntax, checking global variables for error codes would look something like the following listing.

Listing 3.6　Rust-like code that checks error codes from a global variable

```
static mut ERROR: i32 = 0;

// ...

fn main() {
  let mut f = File::new("something.txt");

  read(f, buffer);
  unsafe {
    if ERROR != 0 {
      panic!("An error has occurred while reading the file ")
    }
  }

  close(f);
  unsafe {
    if ERROR != 0 {
      panic!("An error has occurred while closing the file ")
    }
  }
}
```

A global variable, static mut (or mutable static), with a static lifetime that's valid for the life of the program

Accessing and modifying static mut variables requires the use of an unsafe block. This is Rust's way of disclaiming all responsibility.

Checks the ERROR value. Error checking relies on the convention that 0 means no error.

Listing 3.7, presented next, introduces some new syntax. The most significant is probably the unsafe keyword, whose significance we'll discuss later in the book. In the meantime, consider unsafe to be a warning sign rather than an indicator that you're embarking on anything illegal. Unsafe means "the same level of safety offered by C at all times." There are also some other small additions to the Rust language that you know already:

- Mutable global variables are denoted with static mut.
- By convention, global variables use ALL CAPS.
- A const keyword is included for values that never change.

Figure 3.3 provides a visual overview of the flow control error and error handling in listing 3.7.

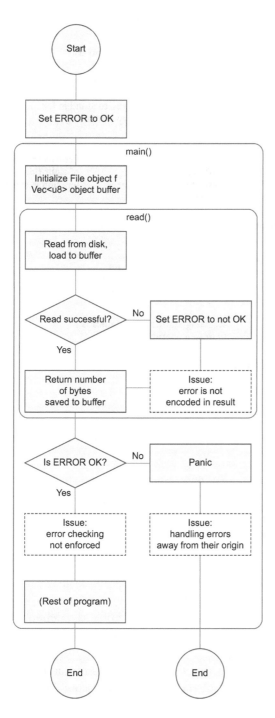

Figure 3.3 A visual overview of listing 3.7, including explanations of problems with using global error codes

Listing 3.7   Using global variables to propagate error information

```
1 use rand::{random};                    ◁──────────────   Brings the rand crate
2                                                           into local scope
3 static mut ERROR: isize = 0;     ◁─────   Initializes ERROR to 0
4
5 struct File;          ◁────────────   Creates a zero-sized type to stand in for
6                                        a struct while we're experimenting
7 #[allow(unused_variables)]
8 fn read(f: &File, save_to: &mut Vec<u8>) -> usize {
9     if random() && random() && random() {     ◁──────   Returns true one out
10        unsafe {                                          of eight times this
11            ERROR = 1;     ◁──────   Sets ERROR to 1, notifying     function is called
12        }                            the rest of the system that
13    }                                an error has occurred
14    0     ◁──────   Always reads 0 bytes
15 }
16
17 #[allow(unused_mut)]     ◁──────   Keeping buffer mutable for
18 fn main() {                        consistency with other code even
19     let mut f = File;              though it isn't touched here
20     let mut buffer = vec![];
21                                    Accessing static mut variables is
22     read(&f, &mut buffer);         an unsafe operation.
23     unsafe {     ◁──────
24         if ERROR != 0 {
25             panic!("An error has occurred!")
26         }
27     }
28 }
```

Here are the commands that you will need to use to experiment with the project at
listing 3.7:

1 git clone --depth=1 https://github.com/rust-in-action/code rust-in-
   action to download the book's source code

2 cd rust-in-action/ch3/globalerror to move into the project directory

3 cargo run to execute the code

If you prefer to do things manually, there are more steps to follow:

1 cargo new --vcs none globalerror to create a new blank project.

2 cd globalerror to move into the project directory.

3 cargo add rand@0.8 to add version 0.8 of the rand crate as a dependency (run
   cargo install cargo-edit if you receive an error message that cargo add command is unavailable).

4 As an optional step, you can verify that the rand crate is now a dependency by
   inspecting Cargo.toml at the root of the project. It will contain the following
   two lines:

```
[dependencies]
rand = "0.8"
```

5 Replace the contents of src/main.rs with the code in listing 3.7 (see ch3/ globalerror/src/main.rs).

6 Now that your source code is in place, execute `cargo run`.

You should see output like this:

```
$ cargo run
  Compiling globalerror v0.1.0 (file:///path/to/globalerror)
   *Finished* dev [unoptimized + debuginfo] target(s) in 0.74 secs
    *Running* `target/debug/globalerror`
```

Most of the time, the program will not do anything. Occasionally, if the book has enough readers with sufficient motivation, it will print a much louder message:

```
$ cargo run
thread 'main' panicked at 'An error has occurred!',
<linearrow />src/main.rs:27:13
note: run with `RUST_BACKTRACE=1` environment variable to display
      a backtrace
```

Experienced programmers will know that using the global variable errno is commonly adjusted by the OS during system calls. This style of programming would typically be discouraged in Rust because it omits both type safety (errors are encoded as plain integers) and can reward sloppy programmers with unstable programs when they forget to check the errno value. However, it's an important style to be aware of because

- Systems programmers may need to interact with OS-defined global values.
- Software that interacts with CPU registers and other low-level hardware needs to get used to inspecting flags to check that operations were completed successfully.

The difference between `const` and `let`

If variables defined with `let` are immutable, then why does Rust include a `const` keyword? The short answer is that data behind `let` *can* change. Rust allows types to have an apparently contradictory property of *interior mutability*.

Some types such as `std:sync::Arc` and `std:rc::Rc` present an immutable façade, yet change their internal state over time. In the case of those two types, these increment a *reference count* as references to those are made and decrement that count when those references expire.

At the level of the compiler, `let` relates more to aliasing than immutability. *Aliasing* in compiler terminology refers to having multiple references to the same location in memory at the same time. Read-only references (borrows) to variables declared with `let` can alias the same data. Read-write references (mutable borrows) are guaranteed to never alias data.

3.4.2   *Making use of the Result return type*

Rust's approach to error handling is to use a type that stands for both the standard case and the error case. This type is known as `Result`. `Result` has two states, `Ok` and `Err`. This two-headed type is versatile and is put to work all through the standard library.

We'll consider *how* a single type can act as two later on. For the moment, let's investigate the mechanics of working with it. Listing 3.8 makes changes from previous iterations:

- Functions that interact with the file system, such as `open()` on line 39, return `Result<File, String>`. This effectively allows two types to be returned. When the function successfully executes, `File` is returned within a wrapper as `Ok(File)`. When the function encounters an error, it returns a `String` within its own wrapper as `Err(String)`. Using a `String` as an error type provides an easy way to report error messages.

- Calling functions that return `Result<File, String>` requires an extra method (`unwrap()`) to actually extract the value. The `unwrap()` call unwraps `Ok(File)` to produce `File`. It will crash the program if it encounters `Err(String)`. More sophisticated error handling is explained in chapter 4.

- `open()` and `close()` now take full ownership of their `File` arguments. While we'll defer a full explanation of the term ownership until chapter 4, it deserves a short explanation here.

  Rust's ownership rules dictate when values are deleted. Passing the `File` argument to `open()` or `close()` without prepending an ampersand, e.g. `&File` or `&mut File`, passes ownership to the function that is being called. This would ordinarily mean that the argument is deleted when the function ends, but these two also return their arguments at the end.

- The `f4` variable now needs to reclaim ownership. Associated with the changes to the `open()` and `close()` functions is a change to the number of times that `let f4` is used. `f4` is now rebound after each call to `open()` and `close()`. Without this, we would run into issues with using data that is no longer valid.

To run the code in listing 3.8, execute these commands from a terminal window:

```
$ git clone --depth=1 https:/ /github.com/rust-in-action/code rust-in-action
$ cd rust-in-action/ch3/fileresult
$ cargo run
```

To do things by hand, here are the recommended steps:

1   Move to a scratch directory, such as `/tmp`; for example, `cd $TMP` (`cd %TMP%` on MS Windows).

2   Execute `cargo new --bin --vcs none fileresult`.

3   Ensure that the crate's Cargo.toml file specifies the 2018 edition and includes the rand crate as a dependency:

```
[package]
name = "fileresult"
version = "0.1.0"
authors = ["Tim McNamara <author@rustinaction.com>"]
edition = "2018"

[dependencies]
rand = "0.8"
```

4 Replace the contents of fileresult/src/main.rs with the code in listing 3.8 (ch3/
   fileresult/src/main.rs).

5 Execute cargo run.

Executing cargo run produces debugging output, but nothing from the executable
itself:

```
$ cargo run
    Compiling fileresult v0.1.0 (file:///path/to/fileresult)
     Finished dev [unoptimized + debuginfo] target(s) in 1.04 secs
      Running `target/debug/fileresult`
```

Listing 3.8   Using `Result` to mark functions liable to filesystem errors

```
 1 use rand::prelude::*;                  ◀─────────────┐   Brings common traits and
 2                                                          types from the rand crate
 3 fn one_in(denominator: u32) -> bool {  ◀────────┐       into this crate's scope
 4    thread_rng().gen_ratio(1, denominator)  ◀──┐ │
 5 }                                             │ │
 6                                               │ │     Helper function
 7 #[derive(Debug)]              thread_rng() creates a    that triggers
 8 struct File {               thread-local random number   sporadic errors
 9    name: String,               generator; gen_ratio(n, m)
10    data: Vec<u8>,            returns a Boolean value with
11 }                              an n/m probability.
12
13 impl File {
14    fn new(name: &str) -> File {
15       File {
16          name: String::from(name),
17       data: Vec::new()
18       }                ◀──┐ Stylistic change to
19    }                      │ shorten the code block
20
21    fn new_with_data(name: &str, data: &Vec<u8>) -> File {
22       let mut f = File::new(name);
23       f.data = data.clone();
24       f
25    }
26
27    fn read(                        First appearance of Result<T, E>,
28       self: &File,                  where T is an integer of type usize
29       save_to: &mut Vec<u8>,         and E is a String. Using String
30    ) -> Result<usize, String> {  ◀── provides arbitrary error messages.
```

```
31      let mut tmp = self.data.clone();
32      let read_length = tmp.len();
33      save_to.reserve(read_length);
34      save_to.append(&mut tmp);
35      Ok(read_length)
36    }
37  }
38
39  fn open(f: File) -> Result<File, String> {
40    if one_in(10_000) {
41      let err_msg = String::from("Permission denied");
42      return Err(err_msg);
43    }
44    Ok(f)
45  }
46
47  fn close(f: File) -> Result<File, String> {
48    if one_in(100_000) {
49      let err_msg = String::from("Interrupted by signal!");
50      return Err(err_msg);
51    }
52    Ok(f)
53  }
54
55  fn main() {
56    let f4_data: Vec<u8> = vec![114, 117, 115, 116, 33];
57    let mut f4 = File::new_with_data("4.txt", &f4_data);
58
59    let mut buffer: Vec<u8> = vec![];
60
61    f4 = open(f4).unwrap();
62    let f4_length = f4.read(&mut buffer).unwrap();
63    f4 = close(f4).unwrap();
67
65    let text = String::from_utf8_lossy(&buffer);
66
67    println!("{:?}", f4);
68    println!("{} is {} bytes long", &f4.name, f4_length);
69    println!("{}", text);
70  }
```

Lines 31–35: In this code, read() never fails, but we still wrap read_length in Ok because we're returning Result.

Lines 39–40: Once in 10,000 executions, returns an error

Line 48: Once in 100,000 executions, returns an error

Lines 61–63: Unwraps T from Ok, leaving T

NOTE Calling .unwrap() on a Result is often considered poor style. When called on an error type, the program crashes without a helpful error message. As the chapter progresses, we'll encounter sophisticated mechanisms to handle errors.

Using Result provides compiler-assisted code correctness: your code won't compile unless you've taken the time to handle the edge cases. This program will fail on error, but at least we have made this explicit.

So, what is a Result? Result is an enum defined in Rust's standard library. It has the same status as any other type but is tied together with the rest of the language through strong community conventions. You may be wondering, "Wait. What is an enum?" I'm glad you asked. That's the topic of our next section.

3.5 *Defining and making use of an enum*

An *enum*, or enumeration, is a type that can represent multiple known variants. Classically, an enum represents several predefined known options like the suits of playing cards or planets in the solar system. The following listing shows one such enum.

> **Listing 3.9 Defining an enum to represent the suits in a deck of cards**

```
enum Suit {
  Clubs,
  Spades,
  Diamonds,
  Hearts,
}
```

If you haven't programmed in a language that makes use of enums, understanding their value takes some effort. As you program with these for a while, though, you're likely to experience a minor epiphany.

Consider creating some code that parses event logs. Each event has a name, perhaps UPDATE or DELETE. Rather than storing those values as strings in your application, which can lead to subtle bugs later on when string comparisons become unwieldy, enums allow you to give the compiler some knowledge of the event codes. Later, you'll be given a warning such as "Hi there, I see that you have considered the UPDATE case, but it looks like you've forgotten the DELETE case. You should fix that."

Listing 3.10 shows the beginnings of an application that parses text and emits structured data. When run, the program produces the following output. You'll find the code for this listing in ch3/ch3-parse-log.rs:

```
(Unknown, "BEGIN Transaction XK342")
(Update, "234:LS/32231 {\"price\": 31.00} -> {\"price\": 40.00}")
(Delete, "342:LO/22111")
```

> **Listing 3.10 Defining an enum and using it to parse an event log**

```
1  #[derive(Debug)]               Prints this enum to the screen
2  enum Event {                    via auto-generated code
3      Update,         Creates three variants of
4      Delete,         Event, including a value
5      Unknown,        for unrecognized events
6  }
7                                                          A function for
8  type Message = String;    A convenient name for String   parsing a line and
9                            for use in this crate's context  converting it into
10 fn parse_log(line: &str) -> (Event, Message) {           semi-structured
11   let parts: Vec<_> = line                               data
12                .splitn(2, ' ')        collect() consumes an iterator from
13                .collect();            line.splitn() and returns Vec<T>.
14   if parts.len() == 1 {
15     return (Event::Unknown, String::from(line))   If line.splitn() doesn't
16   }                                               split log into two parts,
                                                     returns an error
```

Vec<_>
asks Rust
to infer the
elements'
type.

```
17
18   let event = parts[0];                                  | Assigns each part of parts to a
19   let rest = String::from(parts[1]);                     | variable to ease future use
20
21   match event {
22     "UPDATE" | "update" => (Event::Update, rest),        | When we match a known event,
23     "DELETE" | "delete" => (Event::Delete, rest),        | returns structured data
24     _ => (Event::Unknown, String::from(line)),      <──┐
25   }                                                      | If we don't recognize
26 }                                                        | the event type, returns
27                                                          | the whole line
28 fn main() {
29   let log = "BEGIN Transaction XK342
30 UPDATE 234:LS/32231 {\"price\": 31.00} -> {\"price\": 40.00}
31 DELETE 342:LO/22111";
32
33   for line in log.lines() {
34     let parse_result = parse_log(line);
35     println!("{:?}", parse_result);
36   }
37 }
```

Enums have a few tricks up their sleeves:

- These work together with Rust's pattern-matching capabilities to help you build robust, readable code (visible on lines 19–3 of listing 3.10).
- Like structs, enums support methods via impl blocks.
- Rust's enums are more powerful than a set of constants.

It's possible to include data within an enum's variants, granting them a struct-like persona. For example

```
enum Suit {
  Clubs,
  Spades,              | The last element of enums
  Diamonds,            | also ends with a comma to
  Hearts,      <──┘    | ease refactoring.
}

enum Card {
  King(Suit),
  Queen(Suit),         | Face cards
  Jack(Suit),          | have a suit.
  Ace(Suit),
  Pip(Suit, usize),  <──┐ Pip cards have a
}                        | suit and a rank.
```

3.5.1 *Using an enum to manage internal state*

Now that you've seen how to define and use an enum, how is this useful when applied to modelling files? We can expand our File type and allow it to change as it is opened and closed. Listing 3.11 (ch3/ch3-file-states.rs) produces code that prints a short alert to the console:

```
Error checking is working
File { name: "5.txt", data: [], state: Closed }
5.txt is 0 bytes long
```

Listing 3.11 An enum that represents a `File` being open or closed

```
 1 #[derive(Debug,PartialEq)]
 2 enum FileState {
 3   Open,
 4   Closed,
 5 }
 6
 7 #[derive(Debug)]
 8 struct File {
 9   name: String,
10   data: Vec<u8>,
11   state: FileState,
12 }
13
14 impl File {
15   fn new(name: &str) -> File {
16     File {
17       name: String::from(name),
18       data: Vec::new(),
19       state: FileState::Closed,
20     }
21   }
22
23   fn read(
24     self: &File,
25     save_to: &mut Vec<u8>,
26   ) -> Result<usize, String> {
27     if self.state != FileState::Open {
28       return Err(String::from("File must be open for reading"));
29     }
30     let mut tmp = self.data.clone();
31     let read_length = tmp.len();
32     save_to.reserve(read_length);
33     save_to.append(&mut tmp);
34     Ok(read_length)
35   }
36 }
37
38 fn open(mut f: File) -> Result<File, String> {
39   f.state = FileState::Open;
40   Ok(f)
41 }
42
43 fn close(mut f: File) -> Result<File, String> {
44   f.state = FileState::Closed;
45   Ok(f)
46 }
47
48 fn main() {
49   let mut f5 = File::new("5.txt");
```

```
50
51    let mut buffer: Vec<u8> = vec![];
52
53    if f5.read(&mut buffer).is_err() {
54      println!("Error checking is working");
55    }
56
57    f5 = open(f5).unwrap();
58    let f5_length = f5.read(&mut buffer).unwrap();
59    f5 = close(f5).unwrap();
60
61    let text = String::from_utf8_lossy(&buffer);
62
63    println!("{:?}", f5);
64    println!("{} is {} bytes long", &f5.name, f5_length);
65    println!("{}", text);
66 }
```

Enums can be a powerful aide in your quest to produce reliable, robust software. Consider them for your code when you discover yourself introducing "stringly-typed" data, such as message codes.

3.6   *Defining common behavior with traits*

A robust definition of the term *file* needs to be agnostic to storage medium. Files support two main operations: reading and writing streams of bytes. Focusing on those two capabilities allows us to ignore where the reads and writes are actually taking place. These actions can be from a hard disk drive, an in-memory cache, over a network, or via something more exotic.

Irrespective of whether a file is a network connection, a spinning metal platter, or a superposition of an electron, it's possible to define rules that say, "To call yourself a file, you must implement this."

You have already seen traits in action several times. Traits have close relatives in other languages. These are often named interfaces, protocols, type classes, abstract base classes, or, perhaps, contracts.

Every time you've used #[derive(Debug)] in a type definition, you've implemented the Debug trait for that type. Traits permeate the Rust language. Let's see how to create one.

3.6.1   *Creating a Read trait*

Traits enable the compiler (and other humans) to know that multiple types are attempting to perform the same task. Types that use #[derive(Debug)] all print to the console via the println! macro and its relatives. Allowing multiple types to implement a Read trait enables code reuse and allows the Rust compiler to perform its *zero cost abstraction* wizardry.

For the sake of brevity, listing 3.12 (ch3/ch3-skeleton-read-trait.rs) is a bare-bones version of the code that we've already seen. It shows the distinction between the trait keyword, which is used for definitions, and the impl keyword, which attaches a trait to a specific type. When built with rustc and executed, listing 3.12 prints the following line to the console:

```
0 byte(s) read from File
```

Listing 3.12 Defining the bare bones of a Read trait for File

```
1  #![allow(unused_variables)]        ◁──┐  Silences any warnings relating to
2                                         unused variables within functions
3  #[derive(Debug)]
4  struct File;          ◁──┐  Defines a stub File type
5
6  trait Read {     ◁──┐  Provides a specific
7      fn read(         name for the trait
8          self: &Self,                      A trait block includes the type
9          save_to: &mut Vec<u8>,            signatures of functions that
10         ) -> Result<usize, String>;  ◁──  implementors must comply with. The
11 }                                         pseudo-type Self is a placeholder for the
12                                           type that eventually implements Read.
13 impl Read for File {
14     fn read(self: &File, save_to: &mut Vec<u8>) -> Result<usize, String> {
15         Ok(0)   ◁──┐  A simple stub value that
16     }              complies with the type
17 }                  signature required
18
19 fn main() {
20     let f = File{};
21     let mut buffer = vec!();
22     let n_bytes = f.read(&mut buffer).unwrap();
23     println!("{} byte(s) read from {:?}", n_bytes, f);
24 }
```

Defining a trait and implementing it on the same page can feel quite drawn out in small examples such as this. File is spread across three code blocks within listing 3.12. The flip side of this is that many common traits become second nature as your experience grows. Once you've learned what the PartialEq trait does for one type, you'll understand it for every other type.

What does PartialEq do for types? It enables comparisons with the == operator. "Partial" allows for cases where two values that match exactly should not be treated as equal, such as the floating point's NAN value or SQL's NULL.

> **NOTE** If you've spent some time looking through the Rust community's forums and documentation, you might have noticed that they've formed their own idioms of English grammar. When you see a sentence with the following structure, "…T is Debug…", what they're saying is that T implements the Debug trait.

3.6.2 *Implementing std::fmt::Display for your own types*

The println! macro and a number of others live within a family of macros that all use the same underlying machinery. The macros println!, print!, write!, writeln!, and format! all rely on the Display and Debug traits, and these rely on trait implementations provided by programmers to convert from {} to what is printed to the console.

Looking back a few pages to listing 3.11, the `File` type was composed of a few fields and a custom subtype, `FileState`. If you recall, that listing illustrated the use of the Debug trait as repeated in the following listing.

Listing 3.13   Snippets from listing 3.11

```
#[derive(Debug, PartialEq)]
enum FileState {
  Open,
  Closed,
}

#[derive(Debug)]
struct File {
  name: String,
  data: Vec<u8>,
  state: FileState,
}

//...

fn main() {
    let f5 = File::new("f5.txt");

    //...
    println!("{:?}", f5);
    // ...
}
```

Lines skipped from the original →

Debug relies on the colon and question mark syntax.

It's possible to rely on the `Debug` trait auto-implementations as a crutch, but what should you do if you want to provide custom text? `Display` requires that types implement a `fmt` method, which returns `fmt::Result`. The following listing shows this implementation.

Listing 3.14   Using `std::fmt::Display` for `File` and its associated `FileState`

```
impl Display for FileState {
  fn fmt(&self, f:
        &mut fmt::Formatter,
  ) -> fmt::Result {
    match *self {
      FileState::Open => write!(f, "OPEN"),
      FileState::Closed => write!(f, "CLOSED"),
    }
  }
}

impl Display for File {
    fn fmt(&self, f:
          &mut fmt::Formatter,
    ) -> fmt::Result {
      write!(f, "<{} ({})>",
```

To implement std::fmt::Display, a single fmt method must be defined for your type.

```
              self.name, self.state)
    }                                          ◄──────┐  It is common to defer to the inner
}                                                        types' Display implementation via
                                                         the write! macro.
```

The following listing shows how to implement `Display` for a struct that includes fields that also need to implement `Display`. You'll find the code for this listing in ch3/ch3-implementing-display.rs.

Listing 3.15 Working code snippet to implement `Display`

```
 1 #![allow(dead_code)]              ◄─────┐  Silences warnings related to
 2                                             FileState::Open not being used
 3 use std::fmt;                     ◄────┐
 4 use std::fmt::{Display};          ◄───┐
 5                                          Brings the std::fmt crate into local
 6 #[derive(Debug, PartialEq)]             scope, making use of fmt::Result
 7 enum FileState {
 8   Open,                              Brings Display into local scope,
 9   Closed,                            avoiding the need to prefix it as
10 }                                    fmt::Display
11
12 #[derive(Debug)]
13 struct File {
14   name: String,
15   data: Vec<u8>,
16   state: FileState,
17 }
18
19 impl Display for FileState {
20     fn fmt(&self, f: &mut fmt::Formatter) -> fmt::Result {
21       match *self {
22           FileState::Open => write!(f, "OPEN"),         Sneakily, we can make use
23           FileState::Closed => write!(f, "CLOSED"),     of write! to do the grunt
24       }                                                 work for us. Strings
25     }                                                   already implement
26 }                                                       Display, so there's little
27                                                         left for us to do.
28 impl Display for File {
29     fn fmt(&self, f: &mut fmt::Formatter) -> fmt::Result {
30       write!(f, "<{} ({})>",
31           self.name, self.state)    ◄───┐  We can rely on this
32     }                                       FileState Display
33 }                                           implementation.
34
35 impl File {
36   fn new(name: &str) -> File {
37     File {
38         name: String::from(name),
39         data: Vec::new(),
40         state: FileState::Closed,
41     }
42   }
43 }
```

```
44
45 fn main() {
46    let f6 = File::new("f6.txt");
47    //...
48    println!("{:?}", f6);
49    println!("{}", f6);
50 }
```

The Debug implementation prints a familiar message in common with all other implementors of Debug: File { ... }.

Our Display implementation follows its own rules, displaying itself as <f6.txt (CLOSED)>.

We'll see many uses of traits throughout the course of the book. These underlie Rust's generics system and the language's robust type checking. With a little bit of abuse, these also support a form of inheritance that's common in most object oriented languages. For now, though, the thing to remember is that traits represent common behavior that types opt into via the syntax impl Trait for Type.

3.7   *Exposing your types to the world*

Your crates will interact with others that you build over time. You might want to make that process easier for your future self by hiding internal details and documenting what's public. This section describes some of the tooling available within the language and within cargo to make that process easier.

3.7.1   *Protecting private data*

Rust defaults to keeping things private. If you were to create a library with only the code that you have seen so far, importing your crate would provide no extra benefit. To remedy this, use the pub keyword to make things public.

Listing 3.16 provides a few examples of prefixing types and methods with pub. As you'll note, its output is not very exciting:

```
File { name: "f7.txt", data: [], state: Closed }
```

Listing 3.16   Using pub to mark the name and state fields of File public

```
1  #[derive(Debug,PartialEq)]
2  pub enum FileState {
3     Open,
4     Closed,
5  }
6
7  #[derive(Debug)]
8  pub struct File {
9     pub name: String,
10    data: Vec<u8>,
11    pub state: FileState,
12 }
13
14 impl File {
15    pub fn new(name: &str) -> File {
16       File {
17          name: String::from(name),
```

An enum's variants are assumed to be public if the overall type is made public.

File.data remains private if a third party were to import this crate via use.

Even though the File struct is public, its methods must also be explicitly marked as public.

```
18          data: Vec::new(),
19          state: FileState::Closed
20      }
21  }
22 }
23
24 fn main() {
25   let f7 = File::new("f7.txt");
26   //...
27   println!("{:?}", f7);
28 }
```

3.8 *Creating inline documentation for your projects*

When software systems become larger, it becomes more important to document one's progress. This section walks through adding documentation to your code and generating HTML versions of that content.

In listing 3.17, you'll see the familiar code with some added lines beginning with /// or //!. The first form is much more common. It generates documents that refer to the item that immediately follows. The second form refers to the current item as the compiler scans the code. By convention, it is only used to annotate the current module but is available in other places as well. The code for this listing is in the file ch3-file-doced.rs.

Listing 3.17   Adding doc comments to code

```
1 //! Simulating files one step at a time.          ◁──────    //! refers to the current
2                                                              item, the module that's
3 /// Represents a "file",                                     just been entered by the
4 /// which probably lives on a file system.     ◁──────       compiler.
5 #[derive(Debug)]
6 pub struct File {                                            /// annotates whatever
7   name: String,                                             immediately follows it.
8   data: Vec<u8>,
9 }
10
11 impl File {
12   /// New files are assumed to be empty, but a name is required.
13   pub fn new(name: &str) -> File {
14     File {
15       name: String::from(name),
16       data: Vec::new(),
17     }
18   }
19
20   /// Returns the file's length in bytes.
21   pub fn len(&self) -> usize {
22     self.data.len()
23   }
24
25   /// Returns the file's name.
26   pub fn name(&self) -> String {
```

```
27      self.name.clone()
28    }
29  }
30
31  fn main() {
32    let f1 = File::new("f1.txt");
33
34    let f1_name = f1.name();
35    let f1_length = f1.len();
36
37    println!("{:?}", f1);
38    println!("{} is {} bytes long", f1_name, f1_length);
39  }
```

3.8.1 *Using rustdoc to render docs for a single source file*

You may not know it, but you also installed a command-line tool called rustdoc when you installed Rust. rustdoc is like a special-purpose Rust compiler. Instead of producing executable code, it produces HTML versions of your inline documentation.

Here is how to use it. Assuming that you have the code from listing 3.17 saved as ch3-file-doced.rs, follow these steps:

1 Open a terminal.
2 Move to the location of your source file.
3 Execute `rustdoc ch3-file-doced.rs`.

rustdoc creates a directory (doc/) for you. The documentation's entry point is actually within a subdirectory: doc/ch3_file_doced/index.html.

When your programs start to get larger and span multiple files, invoking rustdoc manually can become a bit of a pain. Thankfully, cargo can do the grunt work on your behalf. That's discussed in the next section.

3.8.2 *Using cargo to render docs for a crate and its dependencies*

Your documentation can be rendered as rich HTML output with cargo. cargo works with crates rather than the individual files as we've worked with so far. To get around this, we'll move our project into a crate documentation: To manually create the crate, following these instructions:

1 Open a terminal.
2 Move to a working directory, such as /tmp/, or for Windows, type `cd %TEMP%`.
3 Run `cargo new filebasics`.
   You should end up with a project directory tree that looks like this:

```
filebasics
├──Cargo.toml          This file is what
└──src                 you'll edit in the
     └──main.rs    ◄── following steps.
```

4 Now save the source code from listing 3.17 to filebasics/src/main.rs, overwriting the "Hello World!" boilerplate code that is already in the file.

To skip a few steps, clone the repository. Execute these commands from a terminal:

```
$ git clone https://github.com/rust-in-action/code rust-in-action
$ cd rust-in-action/ch3/filebasics
```

To build an HTML version of the crate's documentation, follow these steps:

1 Move to the project's root directory (filebasics/), which includes the Cargo .toml file.
2 Run cargo doc --open.

Rust will now starts to compile an HTML version of your code's documentation. You should see output similar to the following in the console:

```
Documenting filebasics v0.1.0 (file:///C:/.../Temp/filebasics)
   Finished dev [unoptimized + debuginfo] target(s) in 1.68 secs
     Opening C:\...\Temp\files\target\doc\filebasics\index.html
   Launching cmd /C
```

If you added the --open flag, your web browser will automatically. Figure 3.4 shows the documentation that should now be visible.

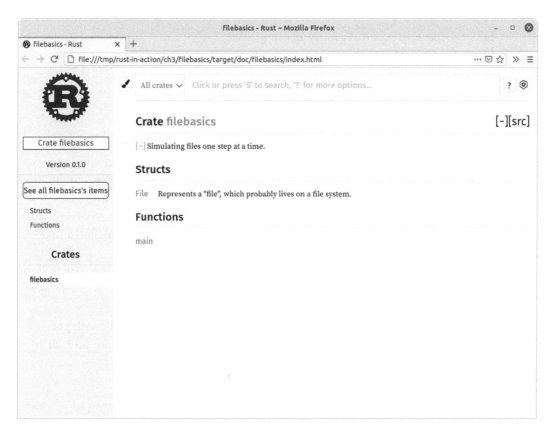

Figure 3.4 Rendered output of cargo doc

TIP   If you have lots of dependencies in your crate, the build process may take a while. A useful flag is `cargo doc --no-deps`. Adding `--no-deps` can significantly restrict the work rustdoc has to do.

rustdoc supports rendering rich text written in Markdown. That allows you to add headings, lists, and links within your documentation. Code snippets that are wrapped in triple backticks (```) are given syntax highlighting.

Listing 3.18   Documenting Rust code with in-line comments

```
 1 //! Simulating files one step at a time.
 2
 3
 4 impl File {
 5   /// Creates a new, empty `File`.
 6   ///
 7   /// # Examples
 8   ///
 9   /// ```
10   /// let f = File::new("f1.txt");
11   /// ```
12   pub fn new(name: &str) -> File {
13     File {
14       name: String::from(name),
15       data: Vec::new(),
16     }
17   }
18 }
```

Summary

- A `struct` is the foundational compound data type. Paired with traits, structs are the closest thing to objects from other domains.
- An `enum` is more powerful than a simple list. Enum's strength lies in its ability to work with the compiler to consider all edge cases.
- Methods are added to types via `impl` blocks.
- You can use global error codes in Rust, but this can be cumbersome and generally is frowned on.
- The `Result` type is the mechanism the Rust community prefers to use to signal the possibility of error.
- Traits enable common behavior through Rust programs.
- Data and methods remain private until they are declared public with `pub`.
- You can use cargo to build the documentation for your crate and all of its dependencies.

Lifetimes, ownership, and borrowing

This chapter covers

- Discovering what the term *lifetime* means in Rust programming
- Working with the borrow checker rather than against it
- Multiple tactics for dealing with issues when these crop up
- Understanding the responsibilities of an owner
- Learning how to borrow values that are owned elsewhere

This chapter explains one of the concepts that trip up most newcomers to Rust—its borrow checker. The *borrow checker* checks that all access to data is legal, which allows Rust to prevent safety issues. Learning how this works will, at the very least, speed up your development time by helping you avoid run-ins with the compiler. More significantly though, learning to work with the borrow checker allows you to build larger software systems with confidence. It underpins the term *fearless concurrency*.

This chapter will explain how this system operates and help you learn how to comply with it when an error is discovered. It uses the somewhat lofty example of simulating a satellite constellation to explain the trade-offs relating to different ways to provide shared access to data. The details of borrow checking are thoroughly explored within the chapter. However, a few points might be useful for readers wanting to quickly get the gist. Borrow checking relies on three interrelated concepts—lifetimes, ownership, and borrowing:

- *Ownership is a stretched metaphor.* There is no relationship to property rights. Within Rust, ownership relates to cleaning values when these are no longer needed. For example, when a function returns, the memory holding its local variables needs to be freed. Owners cannot prevent other parts of the program from accessing their values or report data theft to some overarching Rust authority.

- *A value's lifetime is the period when accessing that value is valid behavior.* A function's local variables live until the function returns, while global variables might live for the life of the program.

- *To borrow a value means to access it.* This terminology is somewhat confusing as there is no obligation to return the value to its owner. Its meaning is used to emphasize that while values can have a single owner, it's possible for many parts of the program to share access to those values.

4.1   *Implementing a mock CubeSat ground station*

Our strategy for this chapter is to use an example that compiles. Then we'll make a minor change that triggers an error that appears to emerge without any adjustment to the program's flow. Working through the fixes to those issues should make the concepts more complete.

The learning example for the chapter is a CubeSat constellation. If you've never encountered that phrase before, here are some definitions:

- *CubeSat*—A miniature artificial satellite, as compared to a conventional satellite, that has increasingly expanded the accessibility of space research.
- *Ground station*—An intermediary between the operators and the satellites themselves. It listens on a radio, checking the status of every satellite in the constellation and transmitting messages to and fro. When introduced in our code, it acts as the gateway between the user and the satellites.
- *Constellation*—The collective noun for satellites in orbit.

Figure 4.1 shows several CubeSats orbiting our ground station.

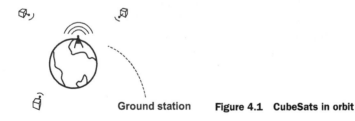

Ground station   **Figure 4.1   CubeSats in orbit**

In figure 4.1, we have three CubeSats. To model this, we'll create a variable for each. This model can happily implement integers for the moment. We don't need to model the ground station explicitly because we're not yet sending messages around the constellations. We'll omit that model for now. These are the variables:

```
let sat_a = 0;
let sat_b = 1;
let sat_c = 2;
```

To check on the status of each of our satellites, we'll use a stub function and an `enum` to represent potential status messages:

For now, all of our CubeSats function perfectly all the time.

```
#[derive(Debug)]
enum StatusMessage {
    Ok,
}

fn check_status(sat_id: u64) -> StatusMessage {
    StatusMessage::Ok
}
```

The `check_status()` function would be extremely complicated in a production system. For our purposes, though, returning the same value every time is perfectly sufficient. Pulling these two snippets into a whole program that "checks" our satellites twice, we end up with something like the following listing. You'll find this code in the file ch4/ch4-check-sats-1.rs.

Listing 4.1 **Checking the status of our integer-based CubeSats**

```
 1 #![allow(unused_variables)]
 2
 3 #[derive(Debug)]
 4 enum StatusMessage {
 5     Ok,
 6 }
 7
 8 fn check_status(sat_id: u64) -> StatusMessage {
 9     StatusMessage::Ok
10 }
11
12 fn main () {
13     let sat_a = 0;          Each satellite variable
14     let sat_b = 1;          is represented by an
15     let sat_c = 2;          integer.
16
17     let a_status = check_status(sat_a);
18     let b_status = check_status(sat_b);
19     let c_status = check_status(sat_c);
20     println!("a: {:?}, b: {:?}, c: {:?}", a_status, b_status, c_status);
21
22     // "waiting" ...
23     let a_status = check_status(sat_a);
```

```
24    let b_status = check_status(sat_b);
25    let c_status = check_status(sat_c);
26    println!("a: {:?}, b: {:?}, c: {:?}", a_status, b_status, c_status);
27  }
```

Running the code in listing 4.1 should be fairly uneventful. The code compiles, albeit begrudgingly. We encounter the following output from our program:

```
a: Ok, b: Ok, c: Ok
a: Ok, b: Ok, c: Ok
```

4.1.1 *Encountering our first lifetime issue*

Let's move closer to idiomatic Rust by introducing *type safety*. Instead of integers, let's create a type to model our satellites. A real implementation of a CubeSat type would probably include lots of information about its position, its RF frequency band, and more. In the following listing, we stick with only recording an identifier.

Listing 4.2 **Modeling a CubeSat as its own type**

```
#[derive(Debug)]
struct CubeSat {
  id: u64,
}
```

Now that we have a `struct` definition, let's inject it into our code. The next listing will not compile (yet). Understanding the details of why it won't is the goal of much of this chapter. The source for this listing is in ch4/ch4-check-sats-2.rs.

Listing 4.3 **Checking the status of our integer-based CubeSats**

```
1  #[derive(Debug)]              Modification 1
2  struct CubeSat {              adds the
3    id: u64,                    definition.
4  }
5
6  #[derive(Debug)]
7  enum StatusMessage {
8    Ok,
9  }
10
11 fn check_status(              Modification 2 uses
12   sat_id: CubeSat             the new type within
13 ) -> StatusMessage {          check_status().
14   StatusMessage::Ok
15 }
16
17 fn main() {
18   let sat_a = CubeSat { id: 0 };    Modification 3
19   let sat_b = CubeSat { id: 1 };    creates three
20   let sat_c = CubeSat { id: 2 };    new instances.
21
```

```
22   let a_status = check_status(sat_a);
23   let b_status = check_status(sat_b);
24   let c_status = check_status(sat_c);
25   println!("a: {:?}, b: {:?}, c: {:?}", a_status, b_status, c_status);
26
27   // "waiting" ...
28   let a_status = check_status(sat_a);
29   let b_status = check_status(sat_b);
30   let c_status = check_status(sat_c);
31   println!("a: {:?}, b: {:?}, c: {:?}", a_status, b_status, c_status);
32 }
```

When you attempt to compile the code for listing 4.3, you will receive a message similar to the following (which has been edited for brevity):

```
error[E0382]: use of moved value: `sat_a`
  --> code/ch4-check-sats-2.rs:26:31
   |
20 |    let a_status = check_status(sat_a);
   |                                 ----- value moved here
...
26 |    let a_status = check_status(sat_a);
   |                                 ^^^^^ value used here after move
   |
   = note: move occurs because `sat_a` has type `CubeSat`,
   = which does not implement the `Copy` trait
```

```
...    ←——| Lines removed
           | for brevity
error: aborting due to 3 previous errors
```

To trained eyes, the compiler's message is helpful. It tells us exactly where the problem is and provides us with a recommendation on how to fix it. To less experienced eyes, it's significantly less useful. We are using a "moved" value and are fully advised to implement the Copy trait on CubeSat. Huh? It turns out that although it is written in English, the term *move* means something very specific within Rust. Nothing physically moves.

Movement within Rust code refers to movement of ownership, rather than the movement of data. *Ownership* is a term used within the Rust community to refer to the compile-time process that checks that every use of a value is valid and that every value is destroyed cleanly.

Every value in Rust is *owned*. In both listings 4.1 and 4.3, sat_a, sat_b, and sat_c own the data that these refer to. When calls to check_status() are made, ownership of the data moves from the variables in the scope of main() to the variable sat_id within the check_status() function. The significant difference is that listing 4.3 places that integer within a CubeSat struct.[1] This type change alters the semantics of how the program behaves.

---

[1] Remember the phrase *zero-cost abstractions*? One of the ways this manifests is by not adding extra data around values within structs.

The next listing provides a stripped-down version of the main() function from listing 4.3. It is centered on sat_a and attempts to show how ownership moves from main() into check_status().

> **Listing 4.4   Extract of listing 4.3, focusing on `main()`**

```
fn main() {
    let sat_a = CubeSat { id: 0 };        ◄──┐ Ownership originates
    // ...                                    here at the creation of
                                             the CubeSat object.

    let a_status = check_status(sat_a);   ◄──┐ Ownership of the object
    // ...                                    moves to check_status() but
                                             is not returned to main().

    // "waiting" ...
    let a_status = check_status(sat_a);   ◄──┐ At line 27, sat_a is no longer
    // ...                                    the owner of the object,
}                                            making access invalid.
```

Lines skipped for brevity

Rebinding is legal when values are not borrowed

If you have experience with programming languages such as JavaScript (from 2015 onward), you may have been surprised to see that the variables for each of the CubeSats were redefined in listing 4.3. In that listing on line 20, a_status is assigned to the result of the first call to check_status(sat_a). On line 26, it is reassigned to the result of the second call. The original value is overwritten.

This is legal Rust code, but one must be aware of ownership issues and lifetime here too. It's possible in this context because there are no live borrows to contend with. Attempting to overwrite a value that's still available from elsewhere in the program causes the compiler to refuse to compile your program.

Figure 4.2 provides a visual walk-through of the interrelated processes of control flow, ownership, and lifetimes. During the call to check_status(sat_a), ownership moves to the check_status() function. When check_status() returns a StatusMessage, it drops the sat_a value. The lifetime of sat_a ends here. Yet, sat_a remains in the local scope of main() after the first call to check_status(). Attempting to access that variable will incur the wrath of the borrow checker.

The distinction between a value's lifetime and its scope—which is what many programmers are trained to rely on—can make things difficult to disentangle. Avoiding and overcoming this type of issue makes up the bulk of this chapter. Figure 4.2 helps to shed some light on this.

4.1.2   *Special behavior of primitive types*

Before carrying on, it might be wise to explain why listing 4.1 compiled at all. Indeed, the only change that we made in listing 4.3 was to wrap our satellite variables in a custom type. As it happens, primitive types in Rust have special behavior. These implement the Copy trait.

Program flow of listing 4.4

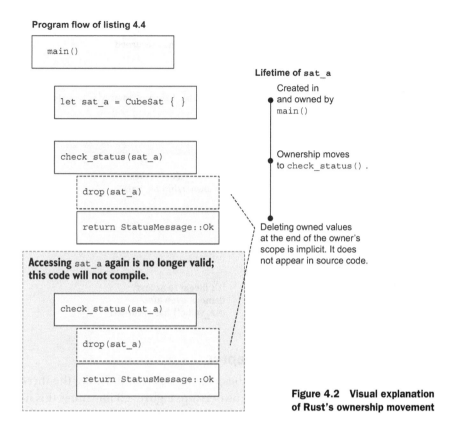

Figure 4.2   Visual explanation of Rust's ownership movement

Types implementing Copy are duplicated at times that would otherwise be illegal. This provides some day-to-day convenience at the expense of adding a trap for newcomers. As you grow out from toy programs using integers, your code suddenly breaks.

Formally, primitive types are said to possess *copy semantics*, whereas all other types have *move semantics*. Unfortunately, for learners of Rust, that special case looks like the default case because beginners typically encounter primitive types first. Listings 4.5 and 4.6 illustrate the difference between these two concepts. The first compiles and runs; the other does not. The only difference is that these listings use different types. The following listing shows not only the primitive types but also the types that implement Copy.

Listing 4.5   The copy semantics of Rust's primitive types

```
1 fn use_value(_val: i32) {
2 }
3
4 fn main() {
5   let a = 123 ;
6   use_value(a);
7
```

use_value() takes ownership of the _val argument. The use_value() function is generic as it's used in the next example.

```
 8    println!("{}", a);
 9
10  }
```

⟵ **It's perfectly legal to access a after use_value() has returned.**

The following listing focuses on those types that do not implement the `Copy` trait. When used as an argument to a function that takes ownership, values cannot be accessed again from the outer scope.

Listing 4.6   The move semantics of types not implementing `Copy`

```
 1  fn use_value(_val: Demo) {
 2  }
 3
 4  struct Demo {
 5    a: i32,
 6  }
 7
 8  fn main() {
 9    let demo = Demo { a: 123 };
10    use_value(demo);
11
12    println!("{}", demo.a);
13  }
```

⟵ **use_value() takes ownership of _val.**

⟵ **It's illegal to access demo.a, even after use_value() has returned.**

4.2   Guide to the figures in this chapter

The figures used in this chapter use a bespoke notation to illustrate the three interrelated concepts of scope, lifetimes, and ownership. Figure 4.3 illustrates this notation.

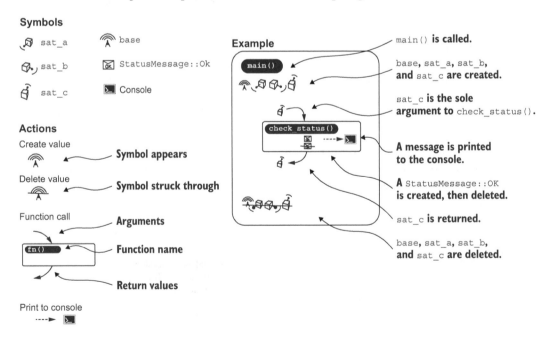

Figure 4.3   How to interpret the figures in this chapter

4.3 *What is an owner? Does it have any responsibilities?*

In the world of Rust, the notion of *ownership* is rather limited. An owner cleans up when its values' lifetimes end.

When values go out of scope or their lifetimes end for some other reason, their destructors are called. A *destructor* is a function that removes traces of the value from the program by deleting references and freeing memory. You won't find a call to any destructors in most Rust code. The compiler injects that code itself as part of the process of tracking every value's lifetime.

To provide a custom destructor for a type, we implement Drop. This typically is needed in cases where we have used unsafe blocks to allocate memory. Drop has one method, drop(&mut self), that you can use to conduct any necessary wind-up activities.

An implication of this system is that values cannot outlive their owner. This kind of situation can make data structures built with references, such as trees and graphs, feel slightly bureaucratic. If the root node of a tree is the owner of the whole tree, it can't be removed without taking ownership into account.

Finally, unlike the Lockean notion of personal property, ownership does not imply control or sovereignty. In fact, the "owners" of values do not have special access to their owned data. Nor do these have the ability to restrict others from trespassing. Owners don't get a say on other sections of code borrowing their values.

4.4 *How ownership moves*

There are two ways to shift ownership from one variable to another within a Rust program. The first is by assignment.[2] The second is by passing data through a function barrier, either as an argument or a return value. Revisiting our original code from listing 4.3, we can see that sat_a starts its life with ownership over a CubeSat object:

```
fn main() {
  let sat_a = CubeSat { id: 0 };
  // ...
```

The CubeSat object is then passed into check_status() as an argument. This moves ownership to the local variable sat_id:

```
fn main() {
  let sat_a = CubeSat { id: 0 };
  // ...
  let a_status = check_status(sat_a);
  // ...
```

Another possibility is that sat_a relinquishes its ownership to another variable within main(). That would look something like this:

---

[2] Within the Rust community, the term *variable binding* is preferred because it is more technically correct.

```
fn main() {
  let sat_a = CubeSat { id: 0 };
  // ...
  let new_sat_a = sat_a;
  // ...
```

Lastly, if there is a change in the check_status() function signature, it too could pass ownership of the CubeSat to a variable within the calling scope. Here is our original function:

```
fn check_status(sat_id: CubeSat) -> StatusMessage {
  StatusMessage::Ok
}
```

And here is an adjusted function that achieves its message notification through a side effect:

```
fn check_status(sat_id: CubeSat) -> CubeSat {

  println!("{:?}: {:?}", sat_id,
                      StatusMessage::Ok);

  sat_id

}
```

Uses the Debug formatting syntax as our types have been annotated with #[derive(Debug)]

Returns a value by omitting the semicolon at the end of the last line

With the adjusted check_status() function used in conjunction with a new main(), it's possible to send ownership of the CubeSat objects back to their original variables. The following listing shows the code. Its source is found in ch4/ch4-check-sats-3.rs.

Listing 4.7   Returning ownership back to the original scope

```
1 #![allow(unused_variables)]
2
3 #[derive(Debug)]
4 struct CubeSat {
5   id: u64,
6 }
7
8 #[derive(Debug)]
9 enum StatusMessage {
10   Ok,
11 }
12
13 fn check_status(sat_id: CubeSat) -> CubeSat {
14   println!("{:?}: {:?}", sat_id, StatusMessage::Ok);
15   sat_id
16 }
17
18 fn main () {
19   let sat_a = CubeSat { id: 0 };
20   let sat_b = CubeSat { id: 1 };
21   let sat_c = CubeSat { id: 2 };
```

```
22
23    let sat_a = check_status(sat_a);
24    let sat_b = check_status(sat_b);
25    let sat_c = check_status(sat_c);
26
27    // "waiting" ...
28
29    let sat_a = check_status(sat_a);
30    let sat_b = check_status(sat_b);
31    let sat_c = check_status(sat_c);
32 }
```

Now that the return value of check_status() is the original sat_a, the new let binding is reset.

The output from the new `main()` function in listing 4.7 now looks like this:

```
CubeSat { id: 0 }: Ok
CubeSat { id: 1 }: Ok
CubeSat { id: 2 }: Ok
CubeSat { id: 0 }: Ok
CubeSat { id: 1 }: Ok
CubeSat { id: 2 }: Ok
```

Figure 4.4 shows a visual overview of the ownership movements within listing 4.7.

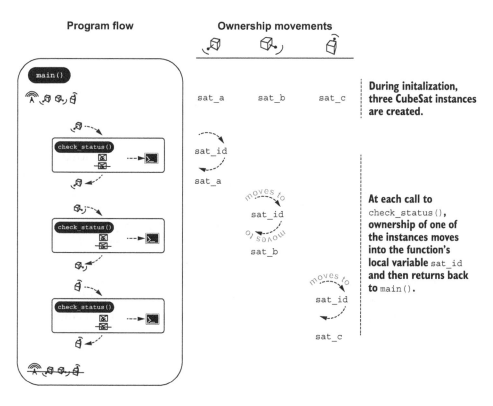

Figure 4.4   The ownership changes within listing 4.7

4.5   *Resolving ownership issues*

Rust's ownership system is excellent. It provides a route to memory safety without needing a garbage collector. There is a "but," however.

The ownership system can trip you up if you don't understand what's happening. This is particularly the case when you bring the programming style from your past experience to a new paradigm. Four general strategies can help with ownership issues:

- Use references where full ownership is not required.
- Duplicate the value.
- Refactor code to reduce the number of long-lived objects.
- Wrap your data in a type designed to assist with movement issues.

To examine each of these strategies, let's extend the capabilities of our satellite network. Let's give the ground station and our satellites the ability to send and receive messages. Figure 4.5 shows what we want to achieve: create a message at Step 1, then transfer it at Step 2. After Step 2, no ownership issues should arise.

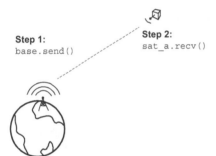

Step 1:
base.send()

Step 2:
sat_a.recv()

Figure 4.5   **Goal: Enable messages to be sent while avoiding ownership issues**

Ignoring the details of implementing the methods, we want to avoid code that looks like the following. Moving ownership of sat_a to a local variable in base.send() ends up hurting us. That value will no longer be accessible for the rest of main():

```
base.send(sat_a, "hello!");      ◁──┐   Moves ownership of sat_a to a
sat_a.recv();                        │   local variable in base.send()
```

To get to a "toy" implementation, we need a few more types to help us out somewhat. In listing 4.8, we add a new field, mailbox, to CubeSat. CubeSat.mailbox is a Mailbox struct that contains a vector of Messages within its messages field. We alias String to Message, giving us the functionality of the String type without needing to implement it ourselves.

Listing 4.8   **Adding a Mailbox type to our system**

```
1 #[derive(Debug)]
2 struct CubeSat {
3   id: u64,
```

```
 4   mailbox: Mailbox,
 5 }
 6
 7 #[derive(Debug)]
 8 enum StatusMessage {
 9   Ok,
10 }
11
12 #[derive(Debug)]
13 struct Mailbox {
14   messages: Vec<Message>,
15 }
16
17 type Message = String;
```

Creating a CubeSat instance has become slightly more complicated. To create one now, we also need to create its associated Mailbox and the mailbox's associated Vec<Message>. The following listing shows this addition.

> **Listing 4.9　Creating a new CubeSat with Mailbox**

```
CubeSat { id: 100, mailbox: Mailbox { messages: vec![] } }
```

Another type to add is one that represents the ground station itself. We will use a bare struct for the moment, as shown in the following listing. That allows us to add methods to it and gives us the option of adding a mailbox as a field later on as well.

> **Listing 4.10　Defining a struct to represent our ground station**

```
struct GroundStation;
```

Creating an instance of GroundStation should be trivial for you now. The following listing shows this implementation.

> **Listing 4.11　Creating a new ground station**

```
GroundStation {};
```

Now that we have our new types in place, let's put these to work. You'll see how in the next section.

4.5.1　*Use references where full ownership is not required*

The most common change you will make to your code is to reduce the level of access you require. Instead of requesting ownership, you can use a "borrow" in your function definitions. For read-only access, use & T. For read-write access, use &mut T.

　　Ownership might be needed in advanced cases, such as when functions want to adjust the lifetime of their arguments. Table 4.1 compares the two different approaches.

Table 4.1   Comparing ownership and mutable references

Using ownership	Using a mutable reference
```fn send(to: CubeSat, msg: Message) { to.mailbox.messages.push(msg); }```	```fn send(to: &mut CubeSat, msg: Message) { to.mailbox.messages.push(msg); }```
Ownership of the `to` variable moves into `send()`. When `send()` returns, `to` is deleted.	Adding the `&mut` prefix to the `CubeSat` type allows the outer scope to retain ownership of data referred to by the `to` variable.

Sending messages will eventually be wrapped up in a method, but with essence functions, implementing that modifies the internal mailbox of the CubeSat. For simplicity's sake, we'll return `()` and hope for the best in case of transmission difficulties caused by solar winds.

The following snippet shows the flow that we want to end up with. The ground station can send a message to sat_a with its send() method, and sat_a then receives the message with its recv() method:

```
base.send(sat_a, "hello!".to_string());

let msg = sat_a.recv();
println!("sat_a received: {:?}", msg); // -> Option("hello!")
```

The next listing shows the implementations of these methods. To achieve that flow, add the implementations to GroundStation and CubeSat types.

Listing 4.12   Adding the `GroundStation.send()` and `CubeSat.recv()` methods

```
 1 impl GroundStation {
 2     fn send(
 3         &self,
 4         to: &mut CubeSat,
 5         msg: Message,
 6     ) {
 7             to.mailbox.messages.push(msg);
 8     }
 9 }
10
11 impl CubeSat {
12     fn recv(&mut self) -> Option<Message> {
13         self.mailbox.messages.pop()
14     }
15 }
```

> **&self** indicates that GroundStation.send() only requires a read-only reference to self. The recipient takes a mutable borrow (&mut) of the CubeSat instance, and msg takes full ownership of its Message instance.

> Ownership of the Message instance transfers from msg to messages.push() as a local variable.

Notice that both GroundStation.send() and CubeSat.recv() require mutable access to a CubeSat instance because both methods modify the underlying CubeSat.messages vector. We move ownership of the message that we're sending into the messages.push(). This provides us with some quality assurance later, notifying us if we access a message after it's already sent. Figure 4.6 illustrates how we can avoid ownership issues.

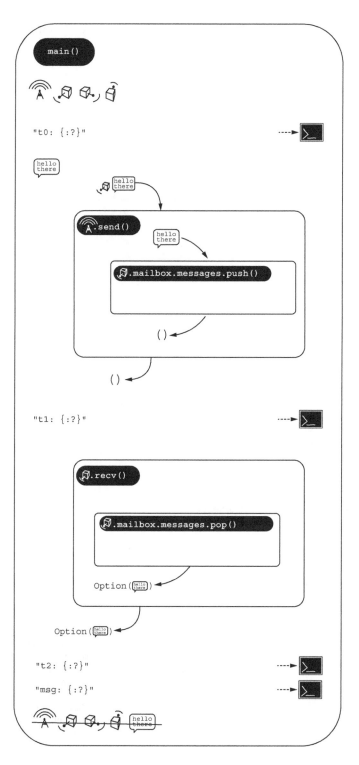

Figure 4.6 Game plan: Use references to avoid ownership issues.

Listing 4.13 (ch4/ch4-sat-mailbox.rs) brings together all of the code snippets in this section thus far and prints the following output. The messages starting with t0 through t2 are added to assist your understanding of how data is flowing through the program:

```
t0: CubeSat { id: 0, mailbox: Mailbox { messages: [] } }
t1: CubeSat { id: 0, mailbox: Mailbox { messages: ["hello there!"] } }
t2: CubeSat { id: 0, mailbox: Mailbox { messages: [] } }
msg: Some("hello there!")
```

Listing 4.13   Avoiding ownership issues with references

```
 1 #[derive(Debug)]
 2 struct CubeSat {
 3   id: u64,
 4   mailbox: Mailbox,
 5 }
 6
 7 #[derive(Debug)]
 8 struct Mailbox {
 9   messages: Vec<Message>,
10 }
11
12 type Message = String;
13
14 struct GroundStation;
15
16 impl GroundStation {
17     fn send(&self, to: &mut CubeSat, msg: Message) {
18         to.mailbox.messages.push(msg);
19     }
20 }
21
22 impl CubeSat {
23     fn recv(&mut self) -> Option<Message> {
24         self.mailbox.messages.pop()
25     }
26 }
27
28 fn main() {
29     let base = GroundStation {};
30     let mut sat_a = CubeSat {
31       id: 0,
32       mailbox: Mailbox {
33         messages: vec![],
34       },
35     };
36
37     println!("t0: {:?}", sat_a);
38
39     base.send(&mut sat_a,
40               Message::from("hello there!"));
```

We don't have a completely ergonomic way to create Message instances yet. Instead, we'll take advantage of the String.from() method that converts &str to String (aka Message).

```
41
42      println!("t1: {:?}", sat_a);
43
44      let msg = sat_a.recv();
45      println!("t2: {:?}", sat_a);
46
47      println!("msg: {:?}", msg);
48  }
```

4.5.2 *Use fewer long-lived values*

If we have a large, long-standing object such as a global variable, it can be somewhat unwieldy to keep this around for every component of your program that needs it. Rather than using an approach involving long-standing objects, consider making objects that are more discrete and ephemeral. Ownership issues can sometimes be resolved by considering the design of the overall program.

In our CubeSat case, we don't need to handle much complexity at all. Each of our four variables—base, sat_a, sat_b, and sat_c—live for the duration of main(). In a production system, there can be hundreds of different components and many thousands of interactions to manage. To increase the manageability of this kind of scenario, let's break things apart. Figure 4.7 presents the game plan for this section.

To implement this kind of strategy, we will create a function that returns CubeSat identifiers. That function is assumed to be a black box that's responsible for communicating with some store of identifiers, such as a database. When we need to communicate with a satellite, we'll create a new object, as the following code snippet shows. In this way, there is no requirement for us to maintain live objects for the whole of the program's duration. It also has the dual benefit that we can afford to transfer ownership of our short-lived variables to other functions:

```
fn fetch_sat_ids() -> Vec<u64> {        ◁───┐  Returns a vector
  vec![1,2,3]                                │  of CubeSat IDs
}
```

We'll also create a method for GroundStation. This method allows us to create a CubeSat instance on demand once:

```
impl GroundStation {
  fn connect(&self, sat_id: u64) -> CubeSat {
    CubeSat { id: sat_id, mailbox: Mailbox { messages: vec![] } } }
  }
}
```

Now we are a bit closer to our intended outcome. Our main function looks like the following code snippet. In effect, we've implemented the first half of figure 4.7.

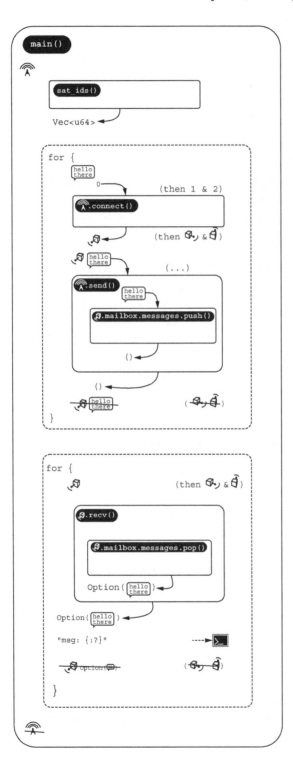

Figure 4.7   Game plan: Short-lived variables to avoid ownership issues

```
fn main() {
  let base = GroundStation();

  let sat_ids = fetch_sat_ids();

  for sat_id in sat_ids {
    let mut sat = base.connect(sat_id);

    base.send(&mut sat, Message::from("hello"));
  }
}
```

But there's a problem. Our CubeSat instances die at the end of the for loop's scope, along with any messages that base sends to them. To carry on with our design decision of short-lived variables, the messages need to live somewhere outside of the CubeSat instances. In a real system, these would live on the RAM of a device in zero gravity. In our not-really-a-simulator, let's put these in a buffer object that lives for the duration of our program.

Our message store will be a Vec<Message> (our Mailbox type defined in one of the first code examples of this chapter). We'll change the Message struct to add a sender and recipient field, as the following code shows. That way our now-proxy CubeSat instances can match their IDs to receive messages:

```
#[derive(Debug)]
struct Mailbox {
  messages: Vec<Message>,
}

#[derive(Debug)]
struct Message {
    to: u64,
    content: String,
}
```

We also need to reimplement sending and receiving messages. Up until now, CubeSat objects have had access to their own mailbox object. The central GroundStation also had the ability to sneak into those mailboxes to send messages. That needs to change now because only one mutable borrow can exist per object.

In the modifications in listing 4.14, the Mailbox instance is given the ability to modify its own message vector. When any of the satellites transmit messages, these take a mutable borrow to the mailbox. These then defer the delivery to the mailbox object. According to this API, although our satellites are able to call Mailbox methods, these are not allowed to touch any internal Mailbox data themselves.

Listing 4.14 Modifications to Mailbox

```
1 impl GroundStation {
2     fn send(
3         &self,
```

```
 4        mailbox: &mut Mailbox,
 5        to: &CubeSat,
 6        msg: Message,
 7    ) {                            ◁——┐  Calls Mailbox.post() to
 8        mailbox.post(to, msg);         │  send messages, yielding
 9    }                                  │  ownership of a Message
10 }
11
12 impl CubeSat {
13    fn recv(
14        &self,                     Calls Mailbox.deliver() to
15        mailbox: &mut Mailbox      receive messages, gaining
16    ) -> Option<Message> {   ◁——┘  ownership of a Message
17        mailbox.deliver(&self)
18    }
19 }                                      Mailbox.post() requires
20                                        mutable access to itself
21 impl Mailbox {                         and ownership over a
22    fn post(&mut self, msg: Message) {  Message.
23        self.messages.push(msg);  ◁——┘
24    }
25
26    fn deliver(
27        &mut self,                 Mailbox.deliver() requires a
28        recipient: &CubeSat        shared reference to a CubeSat
29    ) -> Option<Message> {   ◁——┘  to pull out its id field.
30        for i in 0..self.messages.len() {
31            if self.messages[i].to == recipient.id {
32                let msg = self.messages.remove(i);
33                return Some(msg);  ◁——┐  When we find a message,
34            }                          │  returns early with the
35        }                              │  Message wrapped in Some
36                                       │  per the Option type
37        None   ◁——┐  When no messages are
38    }             │  found, returns None
39 }
```

NOTE   Astute readers of listing 4.14 will notice a strong anti-pattern. On line 32, the `self.messages` collection is modified while it is being iterated over. In this instance, this is legal because of the `return` on the next line. The compiler can prove that another iteration will not occur and allows the mutation to proceed.

With that groundwork in place, we're now able to fully implement the strategy laid out in figure 4.7. Listing 4.15 (ch4/ch4-short-lived-strategy.rs) is the full implementation of the short-lived variables game plan. The output from a compiled version of that listing follows:

```
CubeSat { id: 1 }: Some(Message { to: 1, content: "hello" })
CubeSat { id: 2 }: Some(Message { to: 2, content: "hello" })
CubeSat { id: 3 }: Some(Message { to: 3, content: "hello" })
```

Listing 4.15 Implementing the short-lived variables strategy

```
 1 #![allow(unused_variables)]
 2
 3 #[derive(Debug)]
 4 struct CubeSat {
 5   id: u64,
 6 }
 7
 8 #[derive(Debug)]
 9 struct Mailbox {
10   messages: Vec<Message>,
11 }
12
13 #[derive(Debug)]
14 struct Message {
15     to: u64,
16     content: String,
17 }
18
19 struct GroundStation {}
20
21 impl Mailbox {
22     fn post(&mut self, msg: Message) {
23         self.messages.push(msg);
24     }
25
26     fn deliver(&mut self, recipient: &CubeSat) -> Option<Message> {
27         for i in 0..self.messages.len() {
28             if self.messages[i].to == recipient.id {
29                 let msg = self.messages.remove(i);
30                 return Some(msg);
31             }
32         }
33
34         None
35     }
36 }
37
38 impl GroundStation {
39     fn connect(&self, sat_id: u64) -> CubeSat {
40         CubeSat {
41             id: sat_id,
42         }
43     }
44
45     fn send(&self, mailbox: &mut Mailbox, msg: Message) {
46         mailbox.post(msg);
47     }
48 }
49
50 impl CubeSat {
51     fn recv(&self, mailbox: &mut Mailbox) -> Option<Message> {
52         mailbox.deliver(&self)
53     }
```

```
54 }
55 fn fetch_sat_ids() -> Vec<u64> {
56   vec![1,2,3]
57 }
58
59
60 fn main() {
61   let mut mail = Mailbox { messages: vec![] };
62
63   let base = GroundStation {};
64
65   let sat_ids = fetch_sat_ids();
66
67   for sat_id in sat_ids {
68     let sat = base.connect(sat_id);
69     let msg = Message { to: sat_id, content: String::from("hello") };
70     base.send(&mut mail, msg);
71   }
72
73   let sat_ids = fetch_sat_ids();
74
75   for sat_id in sat_ids {
76     let sat = base.connect(sat_id);
77
78     let msg = sat.recv(&mut mail);
79     println!("{:?}: {:?}", sat, msg);
80   }
81 }
```

4.5.3   *Duplicate the value*

Having a single owner for every object can mean significant up-front planning and/or refactoring of your software. As we saw in the previous section, it can be quite a lot of work to wriggle out of an early design decision.

One alternative to refactoring is to simply copy values. Doing this often is typically frowned upon, however, but it can be useful in a pinch. Primitive types like integers are a good example of that. Primitive types are cheap for a CPU to duplicate—so cheap, in fact, that Rust always copies these if it would otherwise worry about ownership being moved.

Types can opt into two modes of duplication: cloning and copying. Each mode is provided by a trait. Cloning is defined by `std::clone::Clone`, and the copying mode is defined by `std::marker::Copy`. Copy acts implicitly. Whenever ownership would otherwise be moved to an inner scope, the value is duplicated instead. (The bits of object *a* are replicated to create object *b*.) Clone acts explicitly. Types that implement Clone have a `.clone()` method that is permitted to do whatever it needs to do to create a new value. Table 4.2 outlines the major differences between the two modes.

Table 4.2 Distinguishing cloning from copying

Cloning (`std::clone::Clone`)	Copying (`std::marker::Copy`)
■ May be slow and expensive. ■ Never implicit. A call to the `.clone()` method is always required. ■ May differ from original. Crate authors define what cloning means for their types.	■ Always fast and cheap. ■ Always implicit. ■ Always identical. Copies are bit-for-bit duplicates of the original value.

So why do Rust programmers not always use `Copy`? There are three main reasons:

- *The `Copy` trait implies that there will only be negligible performance impact.* This is true for numbers but not true for types that are arbitrarily large, such as `String`.
- *Because `Copy` creates exact copies, it cannot treat references correctly.* Naïvely copying a reference to `T` would (attempt to) create a second owner of `T`. That would cause problems later on because there would be multiple attempts to delete `T` as each reference is deleted.
- *Some types overload the `Clone` trait.* This is done to provide something similar to, yet different from, creating duplicates. For example, `std::rc::Rc<T>` uses `Clone` to create additional references when `.clone()` is called.

NOTE Throughout your time with Rust, you will normally see the `std::clone::Clone` and `std::marker::Copy` traits referred to simply as `Clone` and `Copy`. These are included in every crate's scope via the standard prelude.

IMPLEMENTING COPY

Let's go back to our original example (listing 4.3), which caused the original movement issue. Here it is replicated for convenience, with sat_b and sat_c removed for brevity:

```
#[derive(Debug)]
struct CubeSat {
  id: u64,
}

#[derive(Debug)]
enum StatusMessage {
  Ok,
}

fn check_status(sat_id: CubeSat) -> StatusMessage {
  StatusMessage::Ok
}

fn main() {
  let sat_a = CubeSat { id: 0 };

  let a_status = check_status(sat_a);
  println!("a: {:?}", a_status);
```

```
    let a_status = check_status(sat_a);          The second call to check_status(sat_a)
    println!("a: {:?}", a_status);                is the location of error.
}
```

At this early stage, our program consisted of types that contain types, which themselves implement Copy. That's good because it means implementing it ourselves is fairly straightforward, as the following listing shows.

Listing 4.16   Deriving Copy for types made up of types that implement Copy

```
#[derive(Copy,Clone,Debug)]
struct CubeSat {                        #[derive(Copy,Clone,Debug)]
  id: u64,                              tells the compiler to add an
}                                       implementation of each of
                                        the traits.
#[derive(Copy,Clone,Debug)]
enum StatusMessage {
  Ok,
}
```

The following listing shows how it's possible to implement Copy manually. The impl blocks are impressively terse.

Listing 4.17   Implementing the Copy trait manually

```
impl Copy for CubeSat { }

impl Copy for StatusMessage { }         Implementing Copy
                                        requires an implementation
impl Clone for CubeSat {                of Clone.
  fn clone(&self) -> Self {
    CubeSat { id: self.id }             If desired, we can write out
  }                                     the creation of a new object
}                                       ourselves...

impl Clone for StatusMessage {
  fn clone(&self) -> Self {
    *self                               ...but often we can simply
  }                                     dereference self.
}
```

USING CLONE AND COPY

Now that we know how to implement them, let's put Clone and Copy to work. We've discussed that Copy is implicit. When ownership would otherwise move, such as during assignment and passing through function barriers, data is copied instead.

Clone requires an explicit call to .clone(). That's a useful marker in non-trivial cases, such as in listing 4.18, because it warns the programmer that the process may be expensive. You'll find the source for this listing in ch4/ch4-check-sats-clone-and-copy-traits.rs.

Listing 4.18 Using `Clone` and `Copy`

```
1 #[derive(Debug,Clone,Copy)]      ◄─┐
2 struct CubeSat {                     │   Copy implies
3   id: u64,                           │   Clone, so we
4 }                                    │   can use either
5                                      │   trait later.
6 #[derive(Debug,Clone,Copy)]      ◄─┘
7 enum StatusMessage {
8   Ok,
9 }
10
11 fn check_status(sat_id: CubeSat) -> StatusMessage {
12   StatusMessage::Ok
13 }
14
15 fn main () {
16   let sat_a = CubeSat { id: 0 };
17
18   let a_status = check_status(sat_a.clone());     │ Cloning each object is as
19   println!("a: {:?}", a_status.clone());          │ easy as calling .clone().
20
21   let a_status = check_status(sat_a);             │ Copy works
22   println!("a: {:?}", a_status);                  │ as expected.
23 }
```

4.5.4   *Wrap data within specialty types*

So far in this chapter, we have discussed Rust's ownership system and ways to navigate the constraints it imposes. A final strategy that is quite common is to use *wrapper* types, which allow more flexibility than what is available by default. These, however, incur costs at runtime to ensure that Rust's safety guarantees are maintained. Another way to phrase this is that Rust allows programmers to opt in to garbage collection.[3]

To explain the wrapper type strategy, let's introduce a wrapper type: `std::rc::Rc`. `std:rc::Rc` takes a type parameter T and is typically referred to as Rc<T>. Rc<T> reads as "R. C. of T" and stands for "a reference-counted value of type T." Rc<T> provides *shared ownership* of T. Shared ownership prevents T from being removed from memory until every owner is removed.

As indicated by the name, *reference counting* is used to track valid references. As each reference is created, an internal counter increases by one. When a reference is dropped, the count decreases by one. When the count hits zero, T is also dropped.

Wrapping T involves a calling `Rc::new()`. The following listing, at ch4/ch4-rc-groundstation.rs, shows this approach.

---

[3] Garbage collection (often abbreviated as GC) is a strategy for memory management used by many programming languages, including Python and JavaScript, and all languages built on the JVM (Java, Scala, Kotlin) or the CLR (C#, F#).

Listing 4.19   Wrapping a user-defined type in Rc

```
1 use std::rc::Rc;                          ◄───┐  The use keyword brings
2                                                │  modules from the standard
3 #[derive(Debug)]                               │  library into local scope.
4 struct GroundStation {}
5
6 fn main() {                                          Wrapping involves enclosing
7   let base = Rc::new(GroundStation {});      ◄──┐    the GroundStation instance
8                                                 │    in a call to Rc::new().
9   println!("{:?}", base);      ◄───┐
10 }                                  │  Prints
                                         "GroundStation"
```

Rc<T> implements Clone. Every call to base.clone() increments an internal counter.
Every Drop decrements that counter. When the internal counter reaches zero, the
original instance is freed.

Rc<T> does not allow mutation. To permit that, we need to wrap our wrapper.
Rc<RefCell<T>> is a type that can be used to perform interior mutability, first introduced at the end of of chapter 3 in section 3.4.1. An object that has interior mutability
presents an immutable façade while internal values are being modified.

In the following example, we can modify the variable base despite being marked as
an immutable variable. It's possible to visualize this by looking at the changes to the
internal base.radio_freq:

```
base: RefCell { value: GroundStation { radio_freq: 87.65 } }        value: "<borrowed>"
base_2: GroundStation { radio_freq: 75.31 }                         indicates that base is
base: RefCell { value: GroundStation { radio_freq: 75.31 } }        mutably borrowed
base: RefCell { value: "<borrowed>" }                         ◄──┐  somewhere else and
base_3: GroundStation { radio_freq: 118.52000000000001 }            is no longer generally
                                                                    accessible.
```

The following listing, found at ch4/ch4-rc-refcell-groundstation.rs, uses Rc<RefCell<T>>
to permit mutation within an object marked as immutable. Rc<RefCell<T>> incurs
some additional runtime cost over Rc<T> while allowing shared read/write access to T.

Listing 4.20   Using Rc<RefCell<T>> to mutate an immutable object

```
1 use std::rc::Rc;
2 use std::cell::RefCell;
3
4 #[derive(Debug)]
5 struct GroundStation {
6   radio_freq: f64  // Mhz
7 }
8
9 fn main() {
10   let base: Rc<RefCell<GroundStation>> = Rc::new(RefCell::new(
11     GroundStation {
12       radio_freq: 87.65
13     }
14   ));
```

```
15
16   println!("base: {:?}", base);
17
18   {
19     let mut base_2 = base.borrow_mut();
20     base_2.radio_freq -= 12.34;
21     println!("base_2: {:?}", base_2);
22   }
23
24   println!("base: {:?}", base);
25
26   let mut base_3 = base.borrow_mut();
27   base_3.radio_freq += 43.21;
28
29   println!("base: {:?}", base);
30   println!("base_3: {:?}", base_3);
31 }
```

Introduces a new scope where base can be mutably borrowed

There are two things to note from this example:

- Adding more functionality (e.g., reference-counting semantics rather than move semantics) to types by wrapping these in other types typically reduces their runtime performance.
- If implementing Clone would be prohibitively expensive, Rc<T> can be a handy alternative. This allows two places to "share" ownership.

NOTE Rc<T> is not thread-safe. In multithreaded code, it's much better to replace Rc<T> with Arc<T> and Rc<RefCell<T>> with Arc<Mutex<T>>. *Arc* stands for *atomic reference counter*.

Summary

- A value's owner is responsible for cleaning up after that value when its lifetime ends.
- A value's lifetime is the period when accessing that value is valid behavior. Attempting to access a value after its lifetime has expired leads to code that won't compile.
- To *borrow* a value means to access that value.
- If you find that the borrow checker won't allow your program to compile, several tactics are available to you. This often means that you will need to rethink the design of your program.
- Use shorter-lived values rather than values that stick around for a long time.
- Borrows can be read-only or read-write. Only one read-write borrow can exist at any one time.
- Duplicating a value can be a pragmatic way to break an impasse with the borrow checker. To duplicate a value, implement Clone or Copy.
- It's possible to opt in to reference counting semantics through Rc<T>.
- Rust supports a feature known as interior mutability, which enables types to present themselves as immutable even though their values can change over time.

Part 2

Demystifying systems programming

Part 2 extends your base Rust knowledge by applying Rust to examples from the field of systems programming. Every chapter includes at least one large project that includes a new language feature. You will build command-line utilities, libraries, graphical applications, networked applications, and even your own operating system kernel.

Data in depth

5

This chapter covers

- Learning how the computer represents data
- Building a working CPU emulator
- Creating your own numeric data type
- Understanding floating-point numbers

This chapter is all about understanding how zeroes and ones can become much larger objects like text, images, and sound. We will also touch on how computers do computation.

By the end of the chapter, you will have emulated a fully functional computer with CPU, memory, and user-defined functions. You will break apart floating-point numbers to create a numeric data type of your own that only takes a single byte. The chapter introduces a number of terms, such as *endianness* and *integer overflow*, that may not be familiar to programmers who have never done systems programming.

5.1 *Bit patterns and types*

A small but important lesson is that a single bit pattern can mean different things. The type system of a higher-level language, such as Rust, is just an artificial abstraction over reality. Understanding this becomes important as you begin to unravel some of that abstraction and to gain a deeper understanding of how computers work.

Listing 5.1 (in ch5-int-vs-int.rs) is an example that uses the same bit pattern to represent two different numbers. The type system—not the CPU—is what makes this distinction. The following shows the listing's output:

```
a: 1100001111000011 50115
b: 1100001111000011 -15421
```

Listing 5.1   The data type determines what a sequence of bits represents

```
1 fn main() {
2   let a: u16 = 50115;
3   let b: i16 = -15421;
4
5   println!("a: {:016b} {}", a, a);
6   println!("b: {:016b} {}", b, b);
7 }
```

These two values have
the same bit pattern
but different types.

The different mapping between bit strings and numbers explains part of the distinction between binary files and text files. Text files are just binary files that happen to follow a consistent mapping between bit strings and characters. This mapping is called an *encoding*. Arbitrary files don't describe their meaning to the outside world, which makes these opaque.

We can take this process one step further. What happens if we ask Rust to treat a bit pattern produced by one type as another? The following listing provides an answer. The source code for this listing is in ch5/ch5-f32-as-u32.rs.

Listing 5.2   Interpreting a float's bit string as an integer

```
1 fn main() {
2   let a: f32 = 42.42;
3   let frankentype: u32 = unsafe {
4     std::mem::transmute(a)
5   };
6
7   println!("{}", frankentype);
8   println!("{:032b}", frankentype);
9
10  let b: f32 = unsafe {
11    std::mem::transmute(frankentype)
12  };
13  println!("{}", b);
14  assert_eq!(a, b);
15 }
```

No semicolon here. We want the
result of this expression to feed
into the outer scope.

Views the bits of a 42.42_f32
value as a decimal integer

{:032b} means to format as a binary
via the std::fmt::Binary trait with 32
zeroes padded on the left.

Confirms that the
operation is symmetrical

When compiled and run, the code from listing 5.2 produces the following output:

```
1110027796
01000010001010011010111000010100
42.42
```

Some further remarks about some of the unfamiliar Rust that listing 5.2 introduces includes the following:

- *Line 8 demonstrates a new directive to the* `println!()` *macro:* `{:032b}`. The `032` reads as "left-pad with 32 zeros" and the right-hand b invokes the `std::fmt::Binary` trait. This contrasts with the default syntax (`{}`), which invokes the `std::fmt::Display` trait, or the question mark syntax (`{:?}`), which invokes `std::fmt::Debug`.

  Unfortunately for us, `f32` doesn't implement `std::fmt::Binary`. Luckily, Rust's integer types do. There are two integer types guaranteed to take up the same number of bits as `f32`—`i32` and `u32`. The decision about which to choose is somewhat arbitrary.

- *Lines 3–5 perform the conversion discussed in the previous bulleted point.* The `std::mem::transmute()` function asks Rust to naïvely interpret an `f32` as an `u32` without affecting any of the underlying bits. The inverse conversion is repeated later on lines 10–12.

Mixing data types in a program is inherently chaotic, so we need to wrap these operation within `unsafe` blocks. `unsafe` tells the Rust compiler, "Stand back, I'll take care of things from here. I've got this." It's a signal to the compiler that you have more context than it does to verify the correctness of the program.

Using the `unsafe` keyword does not imply that code is *inherently* dangerous. For example, it does not allow you to bypass Rust's borrow checker. It indicates that the compiler is not able to guarantee that the program's memory is safe by itself. Using `unsafe` means that the programmer is fully responsible for maintaining the program's integrity.

> **WARNING** Some functionality allowed within `unsafe` blocks is more difficult to verify than others. For example, the `std::mem::transmute()` function is one of the least safe in the language. It shreds all type safety. Investigate alternatives before using it in your own code.

Needlessly using `unsafe` blocks is heavily frowned upon within the Rust community. It can expose your software to critical security vulnerabilities. Its primary purpose is to allow Rust to interact with external code, such as libraries written in other languages and OS interfaces. This book uses `unsafe` more frequently than many projects because its code examples are teaching tools, not industrial software. `unsafe` allows you to peek at and poke at individual bytes, which is essential knowledge for people seeking to understand how computers work.

5.2 *Life of an integer*

During earlier chapters, we spent some time discussing what it means for an integer to be an `i32`, an `u8`, or an `usize`. Integers are like small, delicate fish. They do what they do remarkably well, but take them outside of their natural range and they die a quick, painful death.

Integers live within a fixed range. When represented inside the computer, these occupy a fixed number of bits per type. Unlike floating-point numbers, integers cannot sacrifice their precision to extend their bounds. Once those bits have been filled with 1s, the only way forward is back to all 0s.

A 16-bit integer can represent numbers between 0 and 65,535, inclusive. What happens when you want to count to 65,536? Let's find out.

The technical term for the class of problem that we are investigating is *integer overflow*. One of the most innocuous ways of overflowing an integer is by incrementing forever. The following listing (ch5/ch5-to-oblivion.rs) is a trivial example of this.

Listing 5.3   Exploring the effect of incrementing an integer past its range

```
 1 fn main() {
 2    let mut i: u16 = 0;
 3    print!("{}..", i);
 4
 5    loop {
 6        i += 1000;
 7        print!("{}..", i);
 8        if i % 10000 == 0 {
 9            print!{"\n"}
10        }
11    }
12 }
```

When we try to run listing 5.3, things don't end well for our program. Let's look at the output:

```
$ rustc ch5-to-oblivion.rs && ./ch5-to-oblivion
0..1000..2000..3000..4000..5000..6000..7000..8000..9000..10000..
11000..12000..13000..14000..15000..16000..17000..18000..19000..20000..
21000..22000..23000..24000..25000..26000..27000..28000..29000..30000..
31000..32000..33000..34000..35000..36000..37000..38000..39000..40000..
41000..42000..43000..44000..45000..46000..47000..48000..49000..50000..
51000..52000..53000..54000..55000..56000..57000..58000..59000..60000..
thread 'main' panicked at 'attempt to add with overflow',
                    ch5-to-oblivion.rs:5:7
note: run with `RUST_BACKTRACE=1` environment variable
      to display a backtrace
61000..62000..63000..64000..65000..
```

A panicked program is a dead program. Panic means that the programmer has asked the program to do something that's impossible. It doesn't know what to do to proceed and shuts itself down.

To understand why this is such a critical class of bugs, let's take a look at what's going on under the hood. Listing 5.4 (ch5/ch5-bit-patterns.rs) prints six numbers with their bit patterns laid out in literal form. When compiled, the listing prints the following short line:

```
0, 1, 2, ..., 65533, 65534, 65535
```

Try compiling the code with optimizations enabled via `rustc -O ch5-to-oblivion.rs` and running the resulting executable. The behavior is quite different. The problem we're interested in is what happens when there's no more bits left. 65,536 cannot be represented by `u16`.

Listing 5.4 **How `u16` bit patterns translate to a fixed number of integers**

```
fn main() {
  let zero: u16 = 0b0000_0000_0000_0000;
  let one:  u16 = 0b0000_0000_0000_0001;
  let two:  u16 = 0b0000_0000_0000_0010;
  // ...
  let sixtyfivethousand_533: u16 = 0b1111_1111_1111_1101;
  let sixtyfivethousand_534: u16 = 0b1111_1111_1111_1110;
  let sixtyfivethousand_535: u16 = 0b1111_1111_1111_1111;

  print!("{}, {}, {}, ..., ", zero, one, two);
  println!("{}, {}, {}", sixty5_533, sixty5_534, sixty5_535);
}
```

There is another (easy) way to kill a program using a similar technique. In listing 5.5, we ask Rust to fit 400 into an `u8`, which can only count up to 255 values. Look in ch5/ch5-impossible-addition.rs for the source code for this listing.

Listing 5.5 **Impossible addition**

```
#[allow(arithmetic_overflow)]          ◁─┐  Required declaration. The
                                          │  Rust compiler can detect this
fn main() {                               │  obvious overflow situation.
  let (a, b) = (200, 200);
  let c: u8 = a + b;                   ◁─┐  Without the type declaration, Rust
  println!("200 + 200 = {}", c);         │  won't assume that you're trying to
}                                         │  create an impossible situation.
```

The code compiles, but one of two things happen:

- The program panics:

```
thread 'main' panicked at 'attempt to add with overflow',
    5-impossible-add.rs:3:15
note: Run with `RUST_BACKTRACE=1` for a backtrace
```

This behavior can be invoked via executing `rustc` with its default options: `rustc ch5-impossible-add.rs && ch5-impossible-add`.

- The program gives you the wrong answer:

```
200 + 200 = 144
```

This behavior can be invoked by executing `rustc` with the `-O` flag: `rustc -O ch5-impossible-add.rs && ch5-impossible-add`.

There are two small lessons here:

- It's important to understand the limitations of your types.
- Despite Rust's strengths, programs written in Rust can still break.

Developing strategies for preventing integer overflow is one of the ways that system programmers are distinguished from others. Programmers who only have experience with dynamic languages are extremely unlikely to encounter an integer overflow. Dynamic languages typically check to see that the results of integer expressions will fit. When these can't, the variable that's receiving the result is promoted to a wider integer type.

When developing performance critical code, you get to choose which parameters to adjust. If you use fixed-sized types, you gain speed, but you need to accept some risk. To mitigate the risk, you can check to see that overflow won't occur at runtime. Imposing those checks will slow you down, however. Another, much more common option, is to sacrifice space by using a large integer type, such as i64. To go higher still, you'll need to move to arbitrarily sized integers, which come with their own costs.

5.2.1   *Understanding endianness*

CPU vendors argue about how the individual bytes that make up integers should be laid out. Some CPUs order multibyte sequences left to right and others are right to left. This characteristic is known as a CPU's *endianness*. The is one of the reasons why copying an executable file from one computer to another might not work.

Let's consider a 32-bit integer that represents a number made up of four bytes: AA, BB, CC, and DD. Listing 5.6 (ch5/ch5-endianness.rs), with the help of our friend sys::mem::transmute(), demonstrates that byte order matters. When compiled and executed, the code from listing 5.6 prints one of two things, depending on the endianness of your machine. Most computers that people run for day-to-day work print the following:[1]

```
-573785174 vs. -1430532899
```

But more exotic hardware swaps the two numbers around like this:

```
-1430532899 vs.  -573785174
```

Listing 5.6   Inspecting endianness

```
use std::mem::transmute;

fn main() {
    let big_endian: [u8; 4]    = [0xAA, 0xBB, 0xCC, 0xDD];
    let little_endian: [u8; 4] = [0xDD, 0xCC, 0xBB, 0xAA];
```

---

[1] In 2021, the x86-64/AMD64 CPU architecture is dominant.

```
    let a: i32 = unsafe { transmute(big_endian)    };
    let b: i32 = unsafe { transmute(little_endian) };

    println!("{} vs {}", a, b);
}
```

> std::mem::transmute()
> **instructs the compiler to**
> **interpret its argument as**
> **the type on the left (i32).**

The terminology comes from the *significance* of the bytes in the sequence. To take you back to when you learned addition, we can factor the number 123 into three parts:

100 × 1	100
10 × 2	20
1 × 3	3

Summing all of these parts gets us back to our original number. The first part, 100, is labeled as the most significant. When written out in the conventional way, 123 as 123, we are writing in *big endian* format. Were we to invert that ordering by writing 123 as 321, we would be writing in *little endian* format.

Binary numbers work in a similar way. Each number part is a power of 2 (2^0, 2^1, 2^2,..., $2n$), rather than a power of 10 (10^0, 10^1, 10^2,..., $10n$).

Before the late-1990s, endianness was a big issue, especially in the server market. Glossing over the fact that a number of processors can support bidirectional endianness, Sun Microsystems, Cray, Motorola, and SGI went one way. ARM decided to hedge its bet and developed a *bi-endian* architecture. Intel went the other way. The other way won. Integers are almost certainly stored in *little endian* format.

In addition to multibyte sequences, there is a related problem within a byte. Should an u8 that represents 3 look like 0000_0011, or should it look like 1100_0000? The computer's preference for layout of individual bits is known as its *bit numbering* or *bit endianness*. It's unlikely, however, that this internal ordering will affect your day-to-day programming. To investigate further, look for your platform's documentation to find out on which end its *most significant* bit lies.

> **NOTE** The abbreviation MSB can be deceptive. Different authors use the same abbreviation to refer to two concepts: most significant *bit* and most significant *byte*. To avoid confusion, this text uses the term *bit numbering* to refer to the most significant bit and *endianness* to refer to most significant byte.

5.3 *Representing decimal numbers*

One of the claims made at the start of this chapter was that understanding more about bit patterns enables you to compress your data. Let's put that into practice. In this section, you will learn how to pull bits out of a floating-point number and inject those into a single byte format of your own creation.

Here is some context for the problem at hand. Machine learning practitioners often need to store and distribute large models. A model for our purposes here is just a large array of numbers. The numbers within those models often fall within the ranges `0..=1` or `-1..=1` (using Rust's range syntax), depending on the application. Given that we don't need the whole range that `f32` or `f64` supports, why use all of these bytes? Let's see how far we can get with 1. Because there is a known limited range, it's possible to create a decimal number format that can model that range compactly.

To start, we're going to need to learn about how decimal numbers are represented inside today's computers. This means learning about the internals of floating-point numbers.

5.4   Floating-point numbers

Each floating-point number is laid out in memory as scientific notation. If you're unfamiliar with scientific notation, here is a quick primer.

Scientists describe the mass of Jupiter as 1.898×10^{27} kg and the mass of an ant as 3.801×10^{-4} kg. The key insight is that the same number of characters are used to describe vastly different scales. Computer scientists have taken advantage of that insight to create a fixed-width format that encodes a wide range of numbers. Each position within a number in scientific notation is given a role:

- A *sign*, which is implied in our two examples, would be present for negative numbers (negative infinity to 0).
- The *mantissa*, also known as the *significand*, can be thought of as being the value in question (1.898 and 3.801, for example).
- The *radix*, also known as the *base*, is the value that is raised to the power of the exponent (10 in both of our examples).
- The *exponent* describes the scale of the values (27 and –4).

This crosses over to floating point quite neatly. A floating-point value is a container with three fields:

- A sign bit
- An exponent
- A mantissa

Where is the radix? The standard defines it as 2 for all floating-point types. This definition allows the radix to be omitted from the bit pattern itself.

5.4.1   Looking inside an f32

Figure 5.1 presents the memory layout of the `f32` type in Rust. The layout is called *binary32* within the IEEE 754-2019 and IEEE 754-2008 standards and *single* by their predecessor, IEE 754-1985.

The value 42.42 is encoded as `f32` with the bit pattern `01000010001010011010111000010100`. That bit pattern is more compactly represented as `0x4229AE14`. Table 5.1 shows the values of each of the three fields and what these represent..

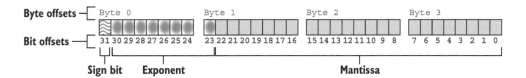

Figure 5.1 **An overview of the three components encoded within the bits of a floating-point number for the f32 type in Rust**

Table 5.1 **The components of 42.42 represented by the bit pattern 0x4229AE14 as a f32 type**

Component name	Component in binary	Component as base-10 (u32)	Decoded value
Sign bit (s)	0	0	1
Exponent (t)	10000100	132	5
Mantissa/significand (m)	01010011010111000010100	2,731,540	1.325625
Base/radix			2
Exponent bias			127

NOTE See listing 5.9 for an explanation provided of how the bit pattern 01010011010111000010100 represents 1.325625.

The following equation decodes the fields of a floating-point number into a single number. Variables from the standard (Radix, Bias) appear in title case. Variables from the bit pattern (`sign_bit`, `mantissa`, `exponent`) occur as lowercase and monospace.

$$n = -1^{\texttt{sign\_bit}} \times \texttt{mantissa} \times \text{Radix}^{(\texttt{exponent}-\text{Bias})}$$
$$n = -1^{\texttt{sign\_bit}} \times \texttt{mantissa} \times \text{Radix}^{(\texttt{exponent} - 127)}$$
$$n = -1^{\texttt{sign\_bit}} \times \texttt{mantissa} \times \text{Radix}^{(132 - 127)}$$
$$n = -1^{\texttt{sign\_bit}} \times \texttt{mantissa} \times 2^{(132 - 127)}$$
$$n = -1^{\texttt{sign\_bit}} \times 1.325625 \times 2^{(132 - 127)}$$
$$n = -1^{0} \times 1.325625 \times 2^{5}$$
$$n = 1 \times 1.325625 \times 32$$
$$n = 42.42$$

One quirk of floating-point numbers is that their sign bits allow for both 0 and –0. That is, floating-point numbers that have different bit patterns compare as equal (0 and –0) and have identical bit patterns (NAN values) that compare as unequal.

5.4.2   *Isolating the sign bit*

To isolate the sign bit, shift the other bits out of the way. For f32, this involves a right shift of 31 places (>> 31). The following listing is a short snippet of code that performs the right shift.

Listing 5.7   Isolating and decoding the sign bit from an f32

```
1 let n: f32 = 42.42;
2 let n_bits: u32 = n.to_bits();
3 let sign_bit = n_bits >> 31;
```

To provide you with a deeper intuition about what is happening, these steps are detailed graphically here:

1. Start with a f32 value:

   ```
   1 let n: f32 = 42.42;
   ```

2. Interpret the bits of the f32 as a u32 to allow for bit manipulation:

   ```
   2 let n_bits: u32 = n.to_bits();
   ```

   The issue that needs to be resolved is the sign bit's position. Treated naïvely, it represents 4,294,967,296 (2^{32}) or 0, rather than 1 (2^0) or 0.

3. Shift the bits within n 31 places to the right:

   ```
   3 let sign_bit = n_bits >> 31;
   ```

   The sign bit has now been moved to the least significant position.

5.4.3   *Isolating the exponent*

To isolate the exponent, two bit manipulations are required. First, perform a right shift to overwrite the mantissa's bits (>> 23). Then use an AND mask (& 0xff) to exclude the sign bit.

The exponent's bits also need to go through a decoding step. To decode the exponent, interpret its 8 bits a signed integer, then subtract 127 from the result. (As shown in table 5.1, 127 is known as the *bias*.) The following listing shows the code that describes the steps given in the last two paragraphs.

Listing 5.8   Isolating and decoding the exponent from an f32

```
1 let n: f32 = 42.42;
2 let n_bits: u32 = n.to_bits();
3 let exponent_ = n_bits >> 23;
4 let exponent_ = exponent_ & 0xff;
5 let exponent = (exponent_ as i32) - 127;
```

And to further explain the process, these steps are repeated graphically as follows:

1 Start with an f32 number:

```
1 let n: f32 = 42.42;
```

2 Interpret the bits of that f32 as u32 to allow for bit manipulation:

```
2 let n_bits: u32 = n.to_bits();
```

Problem: exponent bits are not aligned to the right.

3 Shift the exponent's 8 bits to the right, overwriting the mantissa:

```
3 let exponent_ = n_bits >> 23;
```

Problem: The sign bit remains at bit 8.

4 Filter the sign bit away with an AND mask. Only the 8 rightmost bits can pass through the mask:

```
4 let exponent_ = exponent_ & 0xff;
```

The sign bit has now been removed.

5 Interpret the remaining bits as a signed integer and subtract the bias as defined by the standard:

```
5 let exponent = (exponent_ as i32) - 127;
```

5.4.4   *Isolate the mantissa*

To isolate the mantissa's 23 bits, you can use an AND mask to remove the sign bit and the exponent (`& 0x7fffff`). However, it's actually not necessary to do so because the following decoding steps can simply ignore bits as irrelevant. Unfortunately, the mantissa's decoding step is significantly more complex than the exponent's.

To decode the mantissa's bits, multiply each bit by its weight and sum the result. The first bit's weight is 0.5, and each subsequent bit's weight is half of the current weight; for example, 0.5 (2^{-1}), 0.25 (2^{-2}),..., 0.00000011920928955078125 (2^{-23}). An implicit 24th bit that represents 1.0 (2^{-0}) is always considered to be on, except when special cases are triggered. Special cases are triggered by the state of the exponent:

- *When the exponent's bits are all 0s, then the treatment of mantissa's bits changes to represent subnormal numbers (also known as "denormal numbers").* In practical terms, this change increases the number of decimal numbers near zero that can be represented. Formally, a subnormal number is one between 0 and the smallest number that the normal behavior would otherwise be able to represent.

- *When the exponent's bits are all 1s, then the decimal number is infinity (∞), negative infinity ($-\infty$), or Not a Number (NAN).* NAN values indicate special cases where the numeric result is mathematically undefined (such as $0 \div 0$) or that are otherwise invalid.

  Operations involving NAN values are often counterintuitive. For example, testing whether two values are equal is always `false`, even when the two bit patterns are exactly the same. An interesting curiosity is that f32 has approximately 4.2 million (~2^{22}) bit patterns that represent NAN.

The following listing provides the code that implements nonspecial cases.

Listing 5.9   **Isolating and decoding the mantissa from an f32**

```
1 let n: f32 = 42.42;
2 let n_bits: u32 = n.to_bits();
3 let mut mantissa: f32 = 1.0;
4
5 for i in 0..23 {
6     let mask = 1 << i;
7     let one_at_bit_i = n_bits & mask;
8     if one_at_bit_i != 0 {
9         let i_ = i as f32;
10        let weight = 2_f32.powf( i_ - 23.0 );
11        mantissa += weight;
12    }
13 }
```

Repeating that process slowly:

1 Start with an f32 value:

```
1 let n: f32 = 42.42;
```

2 Cast f32 as u32 to allow for bit manipulation:

```
2 let n_bits: u32 = n.to_bits();
```

3 Create a mutable f32 value initialized to 1.0 (2^{-0}). This represents the weight of the implicit 24th bit:

```
3 let mut mantissa: f32 = 1.0;
```

4 Iterate through the fractional bits of the mantissa, adding those bit's defined values to the mantissa variable:

```
 5 for i in 0..23 {
 6     let mask = 1 << i;
 7     let one_at_bit_i = n_bits & mask;
 8     if one_at_bit_i != 0 {
 9         let i_ = i as f32;
10         let weight = 2_f32.powf( i_ - 23.0 );
11         mantissa += weight;
12     }
13 }
```

a Iterate from 0 to 23 with a temporary variable i assigned to the iteration number:

```
5 for i in 0..23 {
```

b Create a bit mask with the iteration number as the bit allowed to pass through and assign the result to mask. For example, when i equals 5, the bit mask is 0b00000000_00000000_00000000_00100000:

```
6 let mask = 1 << i;
```

c Use mask as a filter against the bits from the original number stored as n_bits. When the original number's bit at position i is non-zero, one_at_bit_i will be assigned to a non-zero value:

```
7 let one_at_bit_i = n_bits & mask;
```

d If one_at_bit_i is non-zero, then proceed:

```
8 if one_at_bit_i != 0 {
```

e Calculate the weight of the bit at position i, which is $2i^{-23}$:

```
 9 let i_ = i as f32;
10 let weight = 2_f32.powf( i_ - 23.0 );
```

f Add the weight to mantissa in place:

```
11 mantissa += weight;
```

Parsing Rust's floating-point literals is harder than it looks

Rust's numbers have methods. To return the nearest integer to 1.2, Rust uses the method `1.2_f32.ceil()` rather than the function call `ceil(1.2)`. While often convenient, this can cause some issues when the compiler parses your source code.

For example, unary minus has lower precedence than method calls, which means unexpected mathematical errors can occur. It is often helpful to use parentheses to make your intent clear to the compiler. To calculate -1^0, wrap 1.0 in parentheses

```
(-1.0_f32).powf(0.0)
```

rather than

```
-1.0_f32.powf(0.0)
```

which is interpreted as $-(1^0)$. Because both -1^0 and $-(1^0)$ are mathematically valid, Rust will not complain when parentheses are omitted.

5.4.5 *Dissecting a floating-point number*

As mentioned at the start of section 5.4, floating-point numbers are a container format with three fields. Sections 5.4.1–5.4.3 have given us the tools that we need to extract each of these fields. Let's put those to work.

Listing 5.10 does a round trip. It extracts the fields from the number 42.42 encoded as an `f32` into individual parts, then assembles these again to create another number. To convert the bits within a floating-point number to a number, there are three tasks:

1 Extract the bits of those values from the container (`to_parts()` on lines 1–26)
2 Decode each value from its raw bit pattern to its actual value (`decode()` on lines 28–47)
3 Perform the arithmetic to convert from scientific notation to an ordinary number (`from_parts()` on lines 49–55)

When we run listing 5.10, it provides two views of the internals of the number 42.42 encoded as an `f32`:

```
42.42 -> 42.42
field    | as bits | as real number
sign     |       0 | 1
exponent | 10000100 | 32
mantissa | 01010011010111000010100 | 1.325625
```

In listing 5.10, `deconstruct_f32()` extracts each field of a floating-point value with bit manipulation techniques. `decode_f32_parts()` demonstrates how to convert those fields to the relevant number. The `f32_from_parts()` method combines these to create a single decimal number. The source for this file is located in ch5/ch5-visualizing-f32.rs.

Listing 5.10 Deconstructing a floating-point value

```
 1 const BIAS: i32 = 127;              Similar constants are accessible
 2 const RADIX: f32 = 2.0;             via the std::f32 module.
 3
 4 fn main() {                    ◄──── main() lives happily at
 5   let n: f32 = 42.42;                the beginning of a file.
 6
 7   let (sign, exp, frac) = to_parts(n);
 8   let (sign_, exp_, mant) = decode(sign, exp, frac);
 9   let n_ = from_parts(sign_, exp_, mant);
10
11   println!("{} -> {}", n, n_);
12   println!("field    | as bits | as real number");
13   println!("sign     |     {:01b} | {}", sign, sign_);
14   println!("exponent | {:08b} | {}", exp, exp_);
15   println!("mantissa | {:023b} | {}", frac, mant);
16 }
17
18 fn to_parts(n: f32) -> (u32, u32, u32) {        Strips 31 unwanted bits
19   let bits = n.to_bits();                       away by shifting these
20                                                 nowhere, leaving only
21   let sign     = (bits >> 31) & 1;      ◄────   the sign bit
22   let exponent = (bits >> 23) & 0xff;   ◄────   Filters out the top bit with a
23   let fraction =  bits & 0x7fffff ;     ◄────   logical AND mask, then strips
24                                                 23 unwanted bits away
25   (sign, exponent, fraction)     ◄────
26 }                                               Retains only the 23 least
27                     The mantissa part           significant bits via an AND mask
28 fn decode(         is called a fraction
29   sign: u32,       here as it becomes
30   exponent: u32,   the mantissa once
31   fraction: u32    it's decoded.              Converts the sign bit to 1.0 or
32 ) -> (f32, f32, f32) {                        −1.0 (−lsign). Parentheses are
33   let signed_1 = (-1.0_f32).powf(sign as f32); ◄── required around −1.0_f32 to
34                                                clarify operator precedence as
35   let exponent = (exponent as i32) - BIAS;     method calls rank higher than
36   let exponent = RADIX.powf(exponent as f32);  a unary minus.
37
38   for i in 0..23 {                          exponent must become an
39     let mask = 1 << i;                      i32 in case subtracting the
40     let one_at_bit_i = fraction & mask;     BIAS results in a negative
41     if one_at_bit_i != 0 {                  number; then it needs to be
42       let i_ = i as f32;                    cast as a f32 so that it can
43       let weight = 2_f32.powf( i_ - 23.0 ); be used for exponentiation.
44       mantissa += weight;
45     }
46   }
47
48   (signed_1, exponent, mantissa)
49 }
50                              Cheats a bit by using f32 values
51 fn from_parts(       ◄────  in intermediate steps. Hopefully,
52   sign: f32,                it is a forgivable offense.
53   exponent: f32,
```

Decodes the mantissa using the logic described in section 5.4.4

```
54    mantissa: f32,
55 ) -> f32 {
56      sign *  exponent * mantissa
57 }
```

Understanding how to unpack bits from bytes means that you'll be in a much stronger position when you're faced with interpreting untyped bytes flying in from the network throughout your career.

5.5   *Fixed-point number formats*

In addition to representing decimal numbers with floating-point formats, fixed point is also available. These can be useful for representing fractions and are an option for performing calculations on CPUs without a floating point unit (FPU), such as micro-controllers. Unlike floating-point numbers, the decimal place does not move to dynamically accommodate different ranges. In our case, we'll be using a fixed-point number format to compactly represent values between $-1..=1$. Although it loses accuracy, it saves significant space.[2]

The *Q format* is a fixed-point number format that uses a single byte.[3] It was created by Texas Instruments for embedded computing devices. The specific version of the Q format that we will implement is called *Q7*. This indicates that there are 7 bits available for the represented number plus 1 sign bit. We'll disguise the decimal nature of the type by hiding the 7 bits within an i8. That means that the Rust compiler will be able to assist us in keeping track of the value's sign. We will also be able to derive traits such as `PartialEq` and `Eq`, which provide comparison operators for our type, for free.

The following listing, an extract from listing 5.14, provides the type's definition. You'll find the source in ch5/ch5-q/src/lib.rs.

> **Listing 5.11   Definition of the Q7 format**

```
1 #[derive(Debug,Clone,Copy,PartialEq,Eq)]
2 pub struct Q7(i8);      ◁──┐ Q7 is a tuple struct.
```

A struct created from unnamed fields (for example, `Q7(i8)`), is known as a *tuple struct*. It offers a concise notation when the fields are not intended to be accessed directly. While not shown in listing 5.11, tuple structs can include multiple fields by adding further types separated by commas. As a reminder, the `#[derive(...)]` block asks Rust to implement several traits on our behalf:

---

[2] This practice is known as *quantizing the model* in the machine learning community.

[3] *Q*, often written as ℚ (this style is called *blackboard bold*), is the mathematical symbol for the so-called rational numbers. Rational numbers are numbers that can be represented as a fraction of two integers, such as 1/3.

- Debug—Used by the println!() macro (and others); allows Q7 to be converted to a string by the {:?} syntax.
- Clone—Enables Q7 to be duplicated with a .clone() method. This can be derived because i8 implements the Clone trait.
- Copy—Enables cheap and implicit duplications where ownership errors might otherwise occur. Formally, this changes Q7 from a type that uses *move semantics* to one that uses *copy semantics.*
- PartialEq—Enables Q7 values to be compared with the equality operator (==).
- Eq—Indicates to Rust that all possible Q7 values can be compared against any other possible Q7 value.

Q7 is intended as a compact storage and data transfer type only. Its most important role is to convert to and from floating-point types. The following listing, an extract from listing 5.14, shows the conversion to f64. The source for this listing is in ch5/ch5-q/src/lib.rs.

Listing 5.12 Converting from f64 to Q7

```
4  impl From<f64> for Q7 {
5      fn from (n: f64) -> Self {
6          // assert!(n >= -1.0);
7          // assert!(n <= 1.0);
8          if n >= 1.0 {
9              Q7(127)                      ◁──┐  Coerces any out-of-
10         } else if n <= -1.0 {   ◁─────────┘  bounds input to fit
11             Q7(-128)
12         } else {
13             Q7((n * 128.0) as i8)
14         }
15     }
16 }
17
18 impl From<Q7> for f64 {                       Equivalent to the
19     fn from(n: Q7) -> f64 {                    iteration approach
20         (n.0 as f64) * 2_f64.powf(-7.0)  ◁──┘  taken in listing 5.9.
21     }
22 }
```

The two impl From<T> for U blocks in listing 5.12 explain to Rust how to convert from type T to type U. In the listing

- Lines 4 and 18 introduce the impl From<T> for U blocks. The std::convert::From trait is included in local scope as From, which is part of the standard prelude. It requires type U to implement from() that takes a T value as its sole argument.

- Lines 6–7 present an option for handling unexpected input data: crashes. It is not used here, but is available to you in your own projects.
- Lines 13–16 truncate out-of-bounds input. For our purposes, we know that out-of-bounds input will not occur and so accept the risk of losing information.

TIP   Conversions using the From trait should be mathematically equivalent. For type conversions that can fail, consider implementing the std::convert ::TryFrom trait instead.

We can also quickly implement converting from f32 to Q7 using the From<f64> implementation that we've just seen. The following listing, an extract from listing 5.14, shows this conversion. Its source is in ch5/ch5-q/src/lib.rs.

Listing 5.13   Converting from f32 to Q7 via f64

```
22 impl From<f32> for Q7 {
23     fn from (n: f32) -> Self {
24         Q7::from(n as f64)          ◁──  By design, it's safe to convert from f32 to f64.
25     }                                     A number that can be represented in 32 bits,
26 }                                         it can also be represented in 64 bits.
27
28 impl From<Q7> for f32 {
29     fn from(n: Q7) -> f32 {             Generally, converting an f64 into a f32 risks a
30         f64::from(n) as f32        ◁──  loss of precision. In this application, that risk
31     }                                   doesn't apply as we only have numbers
32 }                                       between −1 and 1 to convert from.
```

Now, we've covered both floating-point types. But how do we know that the code that we've written actually does what we intend? And how do we test what we've written? As it happens, Rust has excellent support for unit testing via cargo.

The Q7 code that you've seen is available as a complete listing. But first, to test the code, enter the root directory of the crate and run cargo test. The following shows the output from listing 5.14 (the complete listing):

```
$ cargo test
   Compiling ch5-q v0.1.0 (file:///path/to/ch5/ch5-q)
    Finished dev [unoptimized + debuginfo] target(s) in 2.86 s
     Running target\debug\deps\ch5_q-013c963f84b21f92

running 3 tests
test tests::f32_to_q7 ... ok
test tests::out_of_bounds ... ok
test tests::q7_to_f32 ... ok
```

```
test result: ok. 3 passed; 0 failed; 0 ignored; 0 measured; 0 filtered out

    Doc-tests ch5-q

running 0 tests

test result: ok. 0 passed; 0 failed; 0 ignored; 0 measured; 0 filtered out
```

The following listing implements the Q7 format and its conversion to and from f32 and f64 types. You'll find the source for this listing in ch5/ch5-q/src/lib.rs.

Listing 5.14 Full code implementation of the Q7 format

```
1  #[derive(Debug,Clone,Copy,PartialEq,Eq)]
2  pub struct Q7(i8);
3
4  impl From<f64> for Q7 {
5      fn from (n: f64) -> Self {
6          if n >= 1.0 {
7              Q7(127)
8          } else if n <= -1.0 {
9              Q7(-128)
10         } else {
11             Q7((n * 128.0) as i8)
12         }
13     }
14 }
15
16 impl From<Q7> for f64 {
17     fn from(n: Q7) -> f64 {
18         (n.0 as f64) * 2f64.powf(-7.0)
19     }
20 }
21
22 impl From<f32> for Q7 {
23     fn from (n: f32) -> Self {
24         Q7::from(n as f64)
25     }
26 }
27
28 impl From<Q7> for f32 {
29     fn from(n: Q7) -> f32 {
30         f64::from(n) as f32
31     }
32 }
33
```

```
34  #[cfg(test)]
35  mod tests {                    ⟵⎤   Defines a submodule within this file
36      use super::*;              ⟵⎤   Brings the parent module within the submodule's local
37      #[test]                        │  scope. Items that are marked as pub are accessible here.
38      fn out_of_bounds() {
39          assert_eq!(Q7::from(10.), Q7::from(1.));
40          assert_eq!(Q7::from(-10.), Q7::from(-1.));
41      }
42
43      #[test]
44      fn f32_to_q7() {
45          let n1: f32 = 0.7;
46          let q1 = Q7::from(n1);
47
48          let n2 = -0.4;
49*          let q2 = Q7::from(n2);
50
51          let n3 = 123.0;
52          let q3 = Q7::from(n3);
53
54          assert_eq!(q1, Q7(89));
55          assert_eq!(q2, Q7(-51));
56          assert_eq!(q3, Q7(127));
57      }
58
59      #[test]
60      fn q7_to_f32() {
61          let q1 = Q7::from(0.7);
62          let n1 = f32::from(q1);
63          assert_eq!(n1, 0.6953125);
64
65          let q2 = Q7::from(n1);
66          let n2 = f32::from(q2);
67          assert_eq!(n1, n2);
68      }
69  }
```

A brief look at Rust's module system

Rust includes a powerful and ergonomic module system. To keep the examples simple, however, this book does not make heavy use of its system. But here are some basic guidelines:

- Modules are combined into crates.
- Modules can be defined by a project's directory structure. Subdirectories under src/ become a module when that directory contains a mod.rs file.
- Modules can also be defined within a file with the mod keyword.
- Modules can be nested arbitrarily.
- All members of a module including its submodules are *private* by default. Private items can be accessed within the module and any of the module's descendants.

- Prefix things that you want to make public with the `pub` keyword. The `pub` keyword has some specialized cases:
  - **a** `pub(crate)` exposes an item to other modules within the crate.
  - **b** `pub(super)` exposes an item to the parent module.
  - **c** `pub(in path)` exposes an item to a module within *path*.
  - **d** `pub(self)` explicitly keeps the item private.
- Bring items from other modules into local scope with the `use` keyword.

5.6 Generating random probabilities from random bytes

Here is an interesting exercise to test the knowledge that you have developed over the preceding pages. Imagine that you have a source of random bytes (`u8`), and you want to convert one of those into a floating-point (`f32`) value between 0 and 1. Naively interpreting the incoming bytes as `f32`/`f64` via `mem::transmute` results in massive variations in scale. The following listing demonstrates the division operation that generates an `f32` value that lies between 0 and 1 from an arbitrary input byte.

Listing 5.15 Generating `f32` values in interval [0,1] from a `u8` with division

```
fn mock_rand(n: u8) -> f32 {
    (n as f32) / 255.0          255 is the maximum value
}                               that u8 can represent.
```

As division is a slow operation, perhaps there is something faster than simply dividing by the largest value that a byte can represent. Perhaps it's possible to assume a constant exponent value, then shift the incoming bits into the mantissa, such that these would form a range between 0 and 1. Listing 5.16 with bit manipulation is the best result that I could achieve.

With an exponent of –1 represented as `0b01111110` (126 in base 10), the source byte achieves a range of 0.5 to 0.998. That can be normalized to 0.0 to 0.996 with subtraction and multiplication. But is there a better way to do this?

Listing 5.16 Generating `f32` values in interval [0,1] from a `u8`

```
 1 fn mock_rand(n: u8) -> f32 {
 2
 3     let base: u32 = 0b0_01111110_00000000000000000000000;
 4
 5     let large_n = (n as u32) << 15;        Aligns the input byte n to 32 bits,
 6                                            then increases its value by shifting
 7     let f32_bits = base | large_n;         its bits 15 places to the left
 8
 9     let m = f32::from_bits(f32_bits);      Takes a bitwise OR, merging
10                                            the base with the input byte
11     2.0 * ( m - 0.5 )
12 }              Normalizes the           Interprets f32_bits (which
                  output range             is type u32) as an f32
```

As a complete program, you can incorporate `mock_rand()` from listing 5.16 into a test program fairly easily. Listing 5.17 (ch5/ch5-u8-to-mock-rand.rs) generates an `f32` value that lies between 0 and 1 from an arbitrary input byte without division. Here's its output:

```
max of input range: 11111111 -> 0.99609375
mid of input range: 01111111 -> 0.49609375
min of input range: 00000000 -> 0
```

Listing 5.17   Generating an `f32` value without division

```
 1 fn mock_rand(n: u8) -> f32 {
 2     let base: u32 = 0b0_01111110_00000000000000000000000;
 3     let large_n =  (n as u32) << 15;
 4     let f32_bits = base | large_n;
 5     let m = f32::from_bits(f32_bits);
 6     2.0 * ( m - 0.5 )
 7 }
 8
 9 fn main() {
10     println!("max of input range: {:08b} -> {:?}", 0xff, mock_rand(0xff));
11     println!("mid of input range: {:08b} -> {:?}", 0x7f, mock_rand(0x7f));
12     println!("min of input range: {:08b} -> {:?}", 0x00, mock_rand(0x00));
13 }
```

5.7 *Implementing a CPU to establish that functions are also data*

One of the fairly mundane, yet utterly intriguing details about computing is that instructions are also just numbers. Operations and the data that is being operated on share the same encoding. This means that, as a general computing device, your computer can emulate other computers' *instruction sets* by emulating those in software. While we cannot pull apart a CPU to see how it works, we can construct one with code.

After working through this section, you will learn how a computer operates at a fundamental level. This section shows how functions operate and what the term *pointer* means. We won't have an assembly language; we'll actually be programming directly in hex. This section also introduces you to another term you may have heard of in passing: *the stack.*

We'll implement a subset of a system called CHIP-8, which was available to consumers in the 1970s. CHIP-8 was supported by a number of manufacturers, but it was fairly primitive even by the standards of that time. (It was created to write games rather than for commercial or scientific applications.)

One device that used the CHIP-8 CPU was the COSMAC VIP. It had a single-color display with a resolution of 64x32 (0.0002 megapixels), 2 KB RAM, 1.76 MHz CPU, and sold for $275 USD. Oh, and you needed to assemble the computer yourself. It also contained games programmed by the world's first female game developer, Joyce Weisbecker.

5.7.1   *CPU RIA/1: The Adder*

We'll build our understanding by starting with a minimal core. Let's first construct an emulator that only supports a single instruction: addition. To understand what's happening within listing 5.22 later in this section, there are three main things to learn:

- Becoming familiar with new terminology
- How to interpret opcodes
- Understanding the main loop

TERMS RELATED TO CPU EMULATION

Dealing with CPUs and emulation involves learning some terms. Take a moment to look at and understand the following:

- *An operation (often shortened to "op") refers to procedures that are supported natively by the system.* You might also encounter equivalent phrases such as *implemented in hardware* or *intrinsic operation* as you explore further.
- *Registers are containers for data that the CPU accesses directly.* For most operations, operands must be moved to registers for an operation to function. For the CHIP-8, each register is a u8 value.
- *An opcode is a number that maps to an operation.* On the CHIP-8 platform, opcodes include both the operation and the operands' registers.

DEFINING THE CPU

The first operation that we want to support is addition. The operation takes two registers (x and y) as operands and adds the value stored in y to x. To implement this, we'll use the minimal amount of code possible, as the following listing shows. Our initial CPU contains only two registers and the space for a single opcode.

> **Listing 5.18   Definition of the CPU used in listing 5.22**

```
struct CPU {                      All CHIP-8 opcodes
                                  are u16 values.
    current_operation: u16,  ◁──┘
    registers: [u8; 2],  ◁──┐
                            │  These two registers are
}                           │  sufficient for addition.
```

So far, the CPU is inert. To perform addition, we'll need to take the following steps, but there is no ability to store data in memory as yet:

1. Initialize a CPU.
2. Load u8 values into registers.
3. Load the addition opcode into current_operation.
4. Perform the operation.

LOADING VALUES INTO REGISTERS

The process for booting up the CPU consists of writing to the fields of the CPU struct. The following listing, an extract from listing 5.22, shows the CPU initialization process.

Listing 5.19   Initializing the CPU

```
32  fn main() {
33    let mut cpu = CPU {                     Initializes with a
34      current_operation: 0,            ◁——┐ no-op (do nothing)
35      registers: [0; 2],
36    };
37
38    cpu.current_operation = 0x8014;
39    cpu.registers[0] = 5;                   Registers can only
40    cpu.registers[1] = 10;                  hold u8 values.
```

Line 38 from listing 5.19 is difficult to interpret without context. The constant 0x8014 is the opcode that the CPU will interpret. To decode it, split it into four parts:

- 8 signifies that the operation involves two registers.
- 0 maps to cpu.registers[0].
- 1 maps to cpu.registers[1].
- 4 indicates addition.

UNDERSTANDING THE EMULATOR'S MAIN LOOP

Now that we've loaded the data, the CPU is almost able to do some work. The run() method performs the bulk of our emulator's work. Using the following steps, it emulates CPU cycles:

1 Reads the opcode (eventually, from memory)
2 Decodes instruction
3 Matches decoded instruction to known opcodes
4 Dispatches execution of the operation to a specific function

The following listing, an extract from listing 5.22, shows the first functionality being added to the emulator.

Listing 5.20   Reading the opcode

```
 6  impl CPU {
 7    fn read_opcode(&self) -> u16 {          read_opcode() becomes more
 8      self.current_operation                complex when we introduce
 9    }                                       reading from memory.
10
11    fn run(&mut self) {                     Avoids running this
12      // loop {                       ◁——┐  code in a loop for now
13        let opcode = self.read_opcode();
14
15        let c = ((opcode & 0xF000) >> 12) as u8;   The opcode decoding
16        let x = ((opcode & 0x0F00) >>  8) as u8;   process is explained fully
17        let y = ((opcode & 0x00F0) >>  4) as u8;   in the next section.
18        let d = ((opcode & 0x000F) >>  0) as u8;
19
20        match (c, x, y, d) {                       Dispatches execution to the
21            (0x8, _, _, 0x4) => self.add_xy(x, y),  ◁—  hardware circuit responsible
                                                        for performing it
```

```
22               _   =>  todo!("opcode {:04x}", opcode),
23        }
24    // }
25  }
26
27  fn add_xy(&mut self, x: u8, y: u8) {
28      self.registers[x as usize] += self.registers[y as usize];
29  }
30 }
```

Line 22 annotation: **A full emulator contains several dozen operations.**

Line 24 annotation: **Avoids running this code in a loop for now**

HOW TO INTERPRET CHIP-8 OPCODES

It is important for our CPU to be able to interpret its opcode (0x8014). This section provides a thorough explanation of the process used in the CHIP-8 and its naming conventions.

CHIP-8 opcodes are u16 values made up of 4 nibbles. A *nibble* is half of a byte. That is, a nibble is a 4-bit value. Because there isn't a 4-bit type in Rust, splitting the u16 values into those parts is fiddly. To make matters more complicated, CHIP-8 nibbles are often recombined to form either 8-bit or 12-bit values depending on context.

To simplify talking about the parts of each opcode, let's introduce some standard terminology. Each opcode is made up of two bytes: the *high byte* and the *low byte*. And each byte is made up of two nibbles, the *high nibble* and the *low nibble*, respectively. Figure 5.2 illustrates each term.

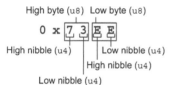

Figure labels: High byte (u8)   Low byte (u8)
0 x 7 3 E E
High nibble (u4)   Low nibble (u4)   High nibble (u4)   Low nibble (u4)

Figure 5.2   Terms used to refer to parts of CHIP-8 opcodes

Documentation manuals for the CHIP-8 introduce several variables, including *kk*, *nnn*, *x*, and *y*. Table 5.2 explains their role, location, and width.

Table 5.2   Variables used within CHIP-8 opcode descriptions

Variable	Bit length	Location	Description
n^*	4	low byte, low nibble	Number of bytes
x	4	high byte, low nibble	CPU register
y	4	low byte, high nibble	CPU register
$c^†$	4	high byte, high nibble	Opcode group
$d^{†*†}$	4	low byte, low nibble	Opcode subgroup
$kk^†$	8	low byte, both nibbles	Integer

Table 5.2   Variables used within CHIP-8 opcode descriptions *(continued)*

Variable	Bit length	Location	Description
nnn[†]	12	high byte, low nibble and low byte, both nibbles	Memory address

[*] *n* and *d* occupy the same location but are used in mutually exclusive contexts.

[†] The variable names *c* and *d* are used within this book but not in other CHIP-8 documentation.

[‡] Used in CPU RIA/3 (listing 5.29).

There are three main forms of opcodes, as illustrated in figure 5.3. The decoding process involves matching on the high nibble of the first byte and then applying one of three strategies.

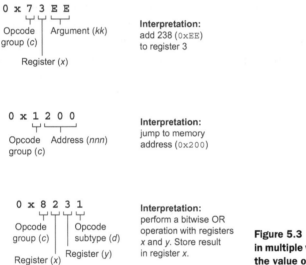

Figure 5.3   CHIP-8 opcodes are decoded in multiple ways. Which to use depends on the value of the leftmost nibble.

To extract nibbles from bytes, we'll need to use the right shift (>>) and logical AND (&) bitwise operations. These operations were introduced in section 5.4, especially in sections 5.4.1–5.4.3. The following listing demonstrates applying these bitwise operations to the current problem.

Listing 5.21   Extracting variables from an opcode

```
fn main() {
    let opcode: u16 = 0x71E4;

    let c = (opcode & 0xF000) >> 12;
    let x = (opcode & 0x0F00) >>  8;
    let y = (opcode & 0x00F0) >>  4;
    let d = (opcode & 0x000F) >>  0;
```

Select single nibbles with the AND operator (&) to filter bits that should be retained, then shift to move the bits to the lowest significant place. Hexadecimal notation is convenient for these operations as each hexadecimal digit represents 4 bits. A 0xF value selects all bits from a nibble.

```
assert_eq!(c, 0x7);
assert_eq!(x, 0x1);
assert_eq!(y, 0xE);
assert_eq!(d, 0x4);
```

> **The four nibbles from opcode are available as individual variables after processing.**

```
let nnn = opcode & 0x0FFF;
let kk  = opcode & 0x00FF;

assert_eq!(nnn, 0x1E4);
assert_eq!(kk,  0xE4);
}
```

> **Select multiple nibbles by increasing the width of the filter. For our purposes, shifting bits rightward is unnecessary.**

We're now able to decode the instructions. The next step is actually executing these.

5.7.2 *Full code listing for CPU RIA/1: The Adder*

The following listing is the full code for our proto-emulator, the Adder. You'll find its source in ch5/ch5-cpu1/src/main.rs.

Listing 5.22 Implementing the beginnings of CHIP-8 emulator

```
 1 struct CPU {
 2   current_operation: u16,
 3   registers: [u8; 2],
 4 }
 5
 6 impl CPU {
 7   fn read_opcode(&self) -> u16 {
 8     self.current_operation
 9   }
10
11   fn run(&mut self) {
12     // loop {
13       let opcode = self.read_opcode();
14
15       let c = ((opcode & 0xF000) >> 12) as u8;
16       let x = ((opcode & 0x0F00) >>  8) as u8;
17       let y = ((opcode & 0x00F0) >>  4) as u8;
18       let d = ((opcode & 0x000F) >>  0) as u8;
19
20       match (c, x, y, d) {
21         (0x8, _, _, 0x4) => self.add_xy(x, y),
22         _ => todo!("opcode {:04x}", opcode),
23       }
24     // }
25   }
26
27   fn add_xy(&mut self, x: u8, y: u8) {
28     self.registers[x as usize] += self.registers[y as usize];
29   }
30 }
31
32 fn main() {
33   let mut cpu = CPU {
```

```
34      current_operation: 0,
35      registers: [0; 2],
36    };
37
38    cpu.current_operation = 0x8014;
39    cpu.registers[0] = 5;
40    cpu.registers[1] = 10;
41
42    cpu.run();
43
44    assert_eq!(cpu.registers[0], 15);
45
46    println!("5 + 10 = {}", cpu.registers[0]);
47 }
```

The Adder doesn't do much. When executed, it prints the following line:

```
5 + 10 = 15
```

5.7.3   *CPU RIA/2: The Multiplier*

CPU RIA/1 can execute a single instruction: addition. CPU RIA/2, the Multiplier, can execute several instructions in sequence. The Multiplier includes RAM, a working main loop, and a variable that indicates which instruction to execute next that we'll call position_in_memory. Listing 5.26 makes the following substantive changes to listing 5.22:

- Adds 4 KB of memory (line 8).
- Includes a fully-fledged main loop and stopping condition (lines 14–31).

  At each step in the loop, memory at position_in_memory is accessed and decoded into an opcode. position_in_memory is then incremented to the next memory address, and the opcode is executed. The CPU continues to run forever until the stopping condition (an opcode of 0x0000) is encountered.
- Removes the current_instruction field of the CPU struct, which is replaced by a section of the main loop that decodes bytes from memory (lines 15–17).
- Writes the opcodes into memory (lines 51–53).

EXPANDING THE CPU TO SUPPORT MEMORY

We need to implement some modifications to make our CPU more useful. To start, the computer needs memory.

Listing 5.23, an extract from listing 5.26, provides CPU RIA/2's definition. CPU RIA/2 contains general-purpose registers for calculations (registers) and one special-purpose register (position_in_memory). For convenience, we'll also include the system's memory within the CPU struct itself as the memory field.

Listing 5.23   Defining a CPU struct

```
1 struct CPU {
2   registers: [u8; 16],
```

```
3    position_in_memory: usize,
4    memory: [u8; 0x1000],
5 }
```

> **Using usize rather that u16 diverges from the original spec, but we'll use usize as Rust allows these to be used for indexing.**

Some features of the CPU are quite novel:

- *Having 16 registers means that a single hexadecimal number (0 to F) can address those.* That allows all opcodes to be compactly represented as u16 values.
- *The CHIP-8 only has 4096 bytes of RAM (0x1000 in hexadecimal).* This allows CHIP-8's equivalent of a usize type to only be 12 bits wide: $2^{12} = 4,096$. Those 12 bits become the *nnn* variable discussed earlier.

Rust in Action deviates from standard practice in two ways:

- *What we call the "position in memory" is normally referred to as the "program counter."* As a beginner, it can be difficult to remember what the program counter's role is. So instead, this book uses a name that reflects its usage.
- *Within the CHIP-8 specification, the first 512 bytes (0x100) are reserved for the system, while other bytes are available for programs.* This implementation relaxes that restriction.

READING OPCODES FROM MEMORY

With the addition of memory within the CPU, the read_opcode() method requires updating. The following listing, an extract from listing 5.26, does that for us. It reads an opcode from memory by combining two u8 values into a single u16 value.

Listing 5.24   Reading an opcode from memory

```
 8 fn read_opcode(&self) -> u16 {
 9    let p = self.position_in_memory;
10    let op_byte1 = self.memory[p] as u16;
11    let op_byte2 = self.memory[p + 1] as u16;
12
13    op_byte1 << 8 | op_byte2
14 }
```

> **To create a u16 opcode, we combine two values from memory with the logical OR operation. These need to be cast as u16 to start with; otherwise, the left shift sets all of the bits to 0.**

HANDLING INTEGER OVERFLOW

Within the CHIP-8, we use the last register as a *carry flag*. When set, this flag indicates that an operation has overflowed the u8 register size. The following listing, an extract from listing 5.26, shows how to handle this overflow.

Listing 5.25   Handling overflow in CHIP-8 operations

```
34 fn add_xy(&mut self, x: u8, y: u8) {
35    let arg1 = self.registers[x as usize];
36    let arg2 = self.registers[y as usize];
37
38    let (val, overflow) = arg1.overflowing_add(arg2);
39    self.registers[x as usize] = val;
40
```

> **The overflowing_add() method for u8 returns (u8, bool). The bool is true when overflow is detected.**

```
41   if overflow {
42     self.registers[0xF] = 1;
43   } else {
44     self.registers[0xF] = 0;
45   }
46 }
```

FULL CODE LISTING FOR CPU RIA/2: THE MULTIPLIER

The following listing shows the complete code for our second working emulator, the Multiplier. You'll find the source for this listing in ch5/ch5-cpu2/src/main.rs.

Listing 5.26   Enabling the emulator to process multiple instructions

```
 1 struct CPU {
 2   registers: [u8; 16],
 3   position_in_memory: usize,
 4   memory: [u8; 0x1000],
 5 }
 6
 7 impl CPU {
 8   fn read_opcode(&self) -> u16 {
 9     let p = self.position_in_memory;
10     let op_byte1 = self.memory[p] as u16;
11     let op_byte2 = self.memory[p + 1] as u16;
12
13     op_byte1 << 8 | op_byte2
14   }
15
16   fn run(&mut self) {
17     loop {
18       let opcode = self.read_opcode();
19       self.position_in_memory += 2;
20
21       let c = ((opcode & 0xF000) >> 12) as u8;
22       let x = ((opcode & 0x0F00) >>  8) as u8;
23       let y = ((opcode & 0x00F0) >>  4) as u8;
24       let d = ((opcode & 0x000F) >>  0) as u8;
25
26       match (c, x, y, d) {
27           (0, 0, 0, 0)      => { return; },
28           (0x8, _, _, 0x4) => self.add_xy(x, y),
29           _                 => todo!("opcode {:04x}", opcode),
30       }
31     }
32   }
33
34   fn add_xy(&mut self, x: u8, y: u8) {
35     let arg1 = self.registers[x as usize];
36     let arg2 = self.registers[y as usize];
37
38     let (val, overflow) = arg1.overflowing_add(arg2);
39     self.registers[x as usize] = val;
40
41     if overflow {
```

Annotations (in right margin):

— **Continues execution beyond processing a single instruction** (points to line 17, `loop {`)

— **Increments position_in_memory to point to the next instruction** (points to line 19)

— **Short-circuits the function to terminate execution when the opcode 0x0000 is encountered** (points to line 27)

```
42          self.registers[0xF] = 1;
43      } else {
44          self.registers[0xF] = 0;
45      }
46  }
47 }
48
49 fn main() {
50   let mut cpu = CPU {
51     registers: [0; 16],
52     memory: [0; 4096],
53     position_in_memory: 0,
54   };
55
56   cpu.registers[0] = 5;
57   cpu.registers[1] = 10;
58   cpu.registers[2] = 10;          Initializes a few
59   cpu.registers[3] = 10;          registers with values
60
                                    Loads opcode 0x8014, which
61   let mem = &mut cpu.memory;      adds register 1 to register 0
62   mem[0] = 0x80; mem[1] = 0x14;
63   mem[2] = 0x80; mem[3] = 0x24;       Loads opcode 0x8024, which
64   mem[4] = 0x80; mem[5] = 0x34;       adds register 2 to register 0
65
66   cpu.run();                      Loads opcode 0x8034. which
67                                   adds register 3 to register 0
68   assert_eq!(cpu.registers[0], 35);
69
70   println!("5 + 10 + 10 + 10 = {}", cpu.registers[0]);
71 }
```

When executed, CPU RIA/2 prints its impressive mathematical calculations:

```
5 + 10 + 10 + 10 = 35
```

5.7.4   CPU RIA/3: The Caller

We have nearly built all of the emulator machinery. This section adds the ability for you to call functions. There is no programming language support, however, so any programs still need to be written in binary. In addition to implementing functions, this section validates an assertion made at the start—functions are also data.

EXPANDING THE CPU TO INCLUDE SUPPORT FOR A STACK

To build functions, we need to implement some additional opcodes. These are as follows:

- The CALL opcode (0x2nnn, where nnn is a memory address) sets position_ in_memory to nnn, the address of the function.
- The RETURN opcode (0x00EE) sets position_in_memory to the memory address of the previous CALL opcode.

To enable these to opcodes to work together, the CPU needs to have some specialized memory available for storing addresses. This is known as *the stack*. Each CALL opcode adds an address to the stack by incrementing the stack pointer and writing *nnn* to that position in the stack. Each RETURN opcode removes the top address by decrementing the stack pointer. The following listing, an extract from listing 5.29, provides the details to emulate the CPU.

Listing 5.27   Including a stack and stack pointer

```
1 struct CPU {
2    registers: [u8; 16],
3    position_in_memory: usize,
4    memory: [u8; 4096],
5    stack: [u16; 16],
6    stack_pointer: usize,
7 }
```

The stack's maximum height is 16. After 16 nested function calls, the program encounters a stack overflow.

Giving the stack_pointer type usize makes it easier to index values within the stack.

DEFINING A FUNCTION AND LOADING IT INTO MEMORY

Within computer science, a function is just a sequence of bytes that can be executed by a CPU.[4] CPUs start at the first opcode, then make their way to the end. The next few code snippets demonstrate how it is possible to move from a sequence of bytes, then convert that into executable code within CPU RIA/3.

1   Define the function. Our function performs two addition operations and then returns—modest, yet informative. It is three opcodes long. The function's internals look like this in a notation that resembles assembly language:

```
add_twice:
    0x8014
    0x8014
    0x00EE
```

2   Convert opcodes into Rust data types. Translating these three opcodes into Rust's array syntax involves wrapping them in square brackets and using a comma for each number. The function has now become a [u16;3]:

```
let add_twice: [u16;3] = [
    0x8014,
    0x8014,
    0x00EE,
];
```

We want to be able to deal with one byte in the next step, so we'll decompose the [u16;3] array further into a [u8;6] array:

```
let add_twice: [u8;6] = [
    0x80, 0x14,
    0x80, 0x14,
    0x00, 0xEE,
];
```

---

[4] The sequence of bytes must also be tagged as executable. The tagging process is explained in section 6.1.4.

3   Load the function into RAM. Assuming that we wish to load that function into memory address 0x100, here are two options. First, if we have our function available as a slice, we can copy it across to `memory` with the `copy_from_slice()` method:

```
fn main() {
  let mut memory: [u8; 4096] = [0; 4096];
  let mem = &mut memory;

  let add_twice = [
    0x80, 0x14,
    0x80, 0x14,
    0x00, 0xEE,
  ];

  mem[0x100..0x106].copy_from_slice(&add_twice);

  println!("{:?}", &mem[0x100..0x106]);          ◄───┤ Prints [128, 20,
}                                                      128, 20, 0, 238]
```

An alternative approach that achieves the same effect within `memory` without requiring a temporary array is to overwrite bytes directly:

```
fn main() {
  let mut memory: [u8; 4096] = [0; 4096];
  let mem = &mut memory;

  mem[0x100] = 0x80; mem[0x101] = 0x14;
  mem[0x102] = 0x80; mem[0x103] = 0x14;
  mem[0x104] = 0x00; mem[0x105] = 0xEE;
                                                        Prints [128, 20,
  println!("{:?}", &mem[0x100..0x106]);          ◄───┤ 128, 20, 0, 238]
}
```

The approach taken in the last snippet is exactly what is used within the `main()` function of lines 96–98 of listing 5.29. Now that we know how to load a function into memory, it's time to learn how to instruct a CPU to actually call it.

IMPLEMENTING THE **CALL** AND **RETURN** OPCODES

Calling a function is a three-step process:

1   Store the current memory location on the stack.
2   Increment the stack pointer.
3   Set the current memory location to the intended memory address.

Returning from a function involves reversing the calling process:

1   Decrement the stack pointer.
2   Retrieve the calling memory address from the stack.
3   Set the current memory location to the intended memory address.

The following listing, an extract from listing 5.29, focuses on the `call()` and `ret()` methods.

Listing 5.28   Adding the `call()` and `ret()` methods

```
41 fn call(&mut self, addr: u16) {
42     let sp = self.stack_pointer;
43     let stack = &mut self.stack;
44
45     if sp > stack.len() {
46         panic!("Stack overflow!")
47     }
48
49     stack[sp] = self.position_in_memory as u16;
50     self.stack_pointer += 1;
51     self.position_in_memory = addr as usize;
52 }
53
54 fn ret(&mut self) {
55     if self.stack_pointer == 0 {
56         panic!("Stack underflow");
57     }
58
59     self.stack_pointer -= 1;
60     let call_addr = self.stack[self.stack_pointer];
61     self.position_in_memory = call_addr as usize;
62 }
```

Modifies self.position_in_memory to affect jumping to that address → (lines 49–51)

Adds the current position_in_memory to the stack. This memory address is two bytes higher than the calling location as it is incremented within the body of the run() method. (line 49)

Increments self.stack_pointer to prevent self.position_in_memory from being overwritten until it needs to be accessed again in a subsequent return (line 50)

Jumps to the position in memory where an earlier call was made (lines 60–61)

FULL CODE LISTING FOR CPU RIA/3: THE CALLER

Now that we have all of the pieces ready, let's assemble those into a working program. Listing 5.29 is able to compute a (hard-coded) mathematical expression. Here's its output:

```
5 + (10 * 2) + (10 * 2) = 45
```

This calculation is made without the source code that you may be used to. You will need to make do with interpreting hexadecimal numbers. To help, figure 5.4 illustrates what happens within the CPU during cpu.run(). The arrows reflect the state of the cpu.position_in_memory variable as it makes its way through the program.

Listing 5.29 shows our completed emulator for CPU RIA/3, the Caller. You'll find the source code for this listing in ch5/ch5-cpu3/src/main.rs.

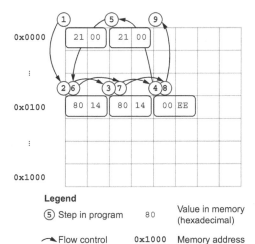

Legend

⑤ Step in program

↰ Flow control

▭ Opcode

`80`   Value in memory (hexadecimal)

`0x1000`   Memory address

   Address space (not to scale)

Figure 5.4   **Illustrating the control flow of the function implemented within CPU RIA/3 in listing 5.29**

Listing 5.29   Emulating a CPU that incorporates user-defined functions

```
1 struct CPU {
2   registers: [u8; 16],
3   position_in_memory: usize,
4   memory: [u8; 4096],
5   stack: [u16; 16],
6   stack_pointer: usize,
7 }
8
9 impl CPU {
10   fn read_opcode(&self) -> u16 {
11     let p = self.position_in_memory;
12     let op_byte1 = self.memory[p] as u16;
13     let op_byte2 = self.memory[p + 1] as u16;
14
15     op_byte1 << 8 | op_byte2
16   }
17
18   fn run(&mut self) {
19     loop {
20       let opcode = self.read_opcode();
21       self.position_in_memory += 2;
22
23       let c = ((opcode & 0xF000) >> 12) as u8;
24       let x = ((opcode & 0x0F00) >>  8) as u8;
25       let y = ((opcode & 0x00F0) >>  4) as u8;
26       let d = ((opcode & 0x000F) >>  0) as u8;
27
28       let nnn = opcode & 0x0FFF;
29       // let kk  = (opcode & 0x00FF) as u8;
30
31       match (c, x, y, d) {
```

```
32                ( 0,    0,   0,    0) => { return; },
33                ( 0,    0, 0xE, 0xE) => self.ret(),
34                (0x2,   _,   _,    _) => self.call(nnn),
35                (0x8,   _,   _,  0x4) => self.add_xy(x, y),
36                 _                   => todo!("opcode {:04x}", opcode),
37            }
38        }
39    }
40
41    fn call(&mut self, addr: u16) {
42      let sp = self.stack_pointer;
43      let stack = &mut self.stack;
44
45      if sp > stack.len() {
46        panic!("Stack overflow!")
47      }
48
49      stack[sp] = self.position_in_memory as u16;
50      self.stack_pointer += 1;
51      self.position_in_memory = addr as usize;
52    }
53
54    fn ret(&mut self) {
55      if self.stack_pointer == 0 {
56        panic!("Stack underflow");
57      }
58
59      self.stack_pointer -= 1;
60      let addr = self.stack[self.stack_pointer];
61      self.position_in_memory = addr as usize;
62    }
63
64    fn add_xy(&mut self, x: u8, y: u8) {
65      let arg1 = self.registers[x as usize];
66      let arg2 = self.registers[y as usize];
67
68      let (val, overflow_detected) = arg1.overflowing_add(arg2);
69      self.registers[x as usize] = val;
70
71      if overflow_detected {
72        self.registers[0xF] = 1;
73      } else {
74        self.registers[0xF] = 0;
75      }
76    }
77 }
78
79 fn main() {
80   let mut cpu = CPU {
81     registers: [0; 16],
82     memory: [0; 4096],
83     position_in_memory: 0,
84     stack: [0; 16],
85     stack_pointer: 0,
86   };
```

```
87
88    cpu.registers[0] = 5;
89    cpu.registers[1] = 10;
90
91    let mem = &mut cpu.memory;
92    mem[0x000] = 0x21; mem[0x001] = 0x00;
93    mem[0x002] = 0x21; mem[0x003] = 0x00;
94    mem[0x004] = 0x00; mem[0x005] = 0x00;
95
96    mem[0x100] = 0x80; mem[0x101] = 0x14;
97    mem[0x102] = 0x80; mem[0x103] = 0x14;
98    mem[0x104] = 0x00; mem[0x105] = 0xEE;
99
100   cpu.run();
101
102   assert_eq!(cpu.registers[0], 45);
103   println!("5 + (10 * 2) + (10 * 2) = {}", cpu.registers[0]);
104 }
```

Sets opcode to 0x00EE: RETURN

Sets opcode to 0x2100: CALL the function at 0x100

Sets opcode to 0x2100: CALL the function at 0x100

Sets opcode to 0x0000: HALT (not strictly necessary as cpu.memory is initialized with null bytes)

Sets opcode to 0x8014: ADD register 1's value to register 0

Sets opcode to 0x8014: ADD register 1's value to register 0

As you delve into systems' documentation, you will find that real-life functions are more complicated than simply jumping to a predefined memory location. Operating systems and CPU architectures differ in calling conventions and in their capabilities. Sometimes operands will need to be added to the stack; sometimes they'll need to be inserted into defined registers. Still, while the specific mechanics can differ, the process is roughly similar to what you have just encountered. Congratulations on making it this far.

5.7.5   *CPU 4: Adding the rest*

With a few extra opcodes, it's possible to implement multiplication and many more functions within your inchoate CPU. Check the source code that comes along with the book, specifically the ch5/ch5-cpu4 directory at https://github.com/rust-in-action/code for a fuller implementation of the CHIP-8 specification.

The last step in learning about CPUs and data is to understand how control flow works. Within CHIP-8, control flow works by comparing values in registers, then modifying position_in_memory, depending on the outcome. There are no while or for loops within a CPU. Creating these in programming languages is the art of the compiler writer.

Summary

- The same bit pattern can represent multiple values, depending on its data type.
- Integer types within Rust's standard library have a fixed width. Attempting to increment past an integer's maximum value is an error called an integer overflow. Decrementing past its lowest value is called integer underflow.
- Compiling programs with optimization enabled (for example, via cargo build --release) can expose your programs to integer overflow and underflow as run-time checks are disabled.

- Endianness refers to the layout of bytes in multibyte types. Each CPU manufacturer decides the endianness of its chips. A program compiled for a little-endian CPU malfunctions if one attempts to run it on a system with a big-endian CPU.

- Decimal numbers are primarily represented by floating-point number types. The standard that Rust follows for its f32 and f64 types is IEEE 754. These types are also known as single precision and double precision floating point.

- Within f32 and f64 types, identical bit patterns can compare as unequal (e.g., f32::NAN != f32::NAN), and differing bit patterns can compare as equal (e.g., -0 == 0). Accordingly, f32 and f64 only satisfy a partial equivalence relation. Programmers should be mindful of this when comparing floating-point values for equality.

- Bitwise operations are useful for manipulating the internals of data structures. However, doing so can often be highly unsafe.

- Fixed-point number formats are also available. These represent numbers by encoding a value as the nominator and using an implicit denominator.

- Implement std::convert::From when you want to support type conversions. But in cases where the conversion may fail, the std::convert::TryFrom trait is the preferred option.

- A CPU opcode is a number that represents an instruction rather than data. Memory addresses are also just numbers. Function calls are just sequences of numbers.

Memory

6

This chapter covers

- What pointers are and why some are smart
- What the terms stack and heap mean
- How a program views its memory

This chapter provides you with some of the tacit knowledge held by systems programmers about how a computer's memory operates. It aims to be the most accessible guide to pointers and memory management available. You will learn how applications interact with an operating system (OS). Programmers who understand these dynamics can use that knowledge to maximize their programs' performance, while minimizing their memory footprint.

Memory is a shared resource, and the OS is an arbiter. To make its life easier, the OS lies to your program about how much memory is available and where it's located. Revealing the truth behind those lies requires us to work through some prior knowledge. This is the work of the first two sections of the chapter.

Each of the four sections in this chapter builds on the previous one. None of these sections assume that you've encountered the topic before. There is a fairly large body of theory to cover, but all of it is explained by examples.

In this chapter, you'll create your first graphical application. The chapter introduces little new Rust syntax, as the material is quite dense. You'll learn how to construct pointers, how to interact with an OS via its native API, and how to interact with other programs through Rust's foreign function interface.

6.1   *Pointers*

Pointers are how computers refer to data that isn't immediately accessible. This topic tends to have an aura of mystique to it. That's not necessary. If you've ever read a book's table of contents, then you've used a pointer. Pointers are just numbers that refer to somewhere else.

If you've never encountered systems programming before, there is a lot of terminology to grapple with that describes unfamiliar concepts. Thankfully, though, what's sitting underneath the abstraction is not too difficult to understand. The first thing to grasp is the notation used in this chapter's figures. Figure 6.1 introduces three concepts:

- The arrow refers to some location in memory that is determined at runtime rather than at compile time.
- Each box represents a block of memory, and each block refers to a `usize` width. Other figures use a byte or perhaps even a bit as the chunk of memory these refer to.
- The rounded box underneath the Value label represents three contiguous blocks of memory.

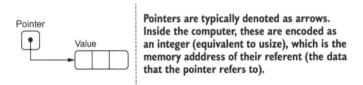

Figure 6.1   Depicting notation used in this chapter's figures for illustrating a pointer. In Rust, pointers are most frequently encountered as `&T` and `&mut T`, where `T` is the type of the value.

For newcomers, pointers are scary and, at the same time, awe-inspiring. Their proper use requires that you know exactly how your program is laid out in memory. Imagine reading a table of contents that says chapter 4 starts on page 97, but it actually starts on page 107. That would be frustrating, but at least you could cope with the mistake.

A computer doesn't experience frustration. It also lacks any intuition that it has pointed to the wrong place. It just keeps working, correctly or incorrectly, as if it had been given the correct location. The fear of pointers is that you will introduce some impossible-to-debug error.

We can think of data stored within the program's memory as being scattered around somewhere within physical RAM. To make use of that RAM, there needs to be some sort of retrieval system in place. An *address space* is that retrieval system.

Pointers are encoded as memory addresses, which are represented as integers of type usize. An address points to somewhere within the address space. For the moment, think of the address space as all of your RAM laid out end to end in a single line.

Why are memory addresses encoded as usize? Surely there's no 64-bit computer with 2^{64} bytes of RAM. The range of the address space is a façade provided by the OS and the CPU. Programs only know an orderly series of bytes, irrespective of the amount of RAM that is actually available in the system. We discuss how this works later in the virtual memory section of this chapter.

NOTE Another interesting example is the Option<T> type. Rust uses null pointer optimization to ensure that an Option<T> occupies 0 bytes in the compiled binary. The None variant is represented by a *null pointer* (a pointer to invalid memory), allowing the Some(T) variant to have no additional indirection.

What are the differences between references, pointers, and memory addresses?

References, pointers, and memory addresses are confusingly similar:

- *A memory address, often shortened to address, is a number that happens to refer to a single byte in memory.* Memory addresses are abstractions provided by assembly languages.
- *A pointer, sometimes expanded to raw pointer, is a memory address that points to a value of some type.* Pointers are abstractions provided by higher-level languages.
- *A reference is a pointer, or in the case of dynamically sized types, a pointer and an integer with extra guarantees.* References are abstractions provided by Rust.

Compilers are able to determine spans of valid bytes for many types. For example, when a compiler creates a pointer to an i32, it can verify that there are 4 bytes that encode an integer. This is more useful than simply having a memory address, which may or may not point to any valid data type. Unfortunately, the programmer bears the responsibility for ensuring the validity for types with no known size at compile time.

Rust's references offer substantial benefits over pointers:

- *References always refer to valid data.* Rust's references can only be used when it's legal to access their referent. I'm sure you're familiar with this core tenet of Rust by now!
- *References are correctly aligned to multiples of usize.* For technical reasons, CPUs become quite temperamental when asked to fetch unaligned memory.

(continued)

> They operate much more slowly. To mitigate this problem, Rust's types actually include padding bytes so that creating references to these does not slow down your program.
>
> - *References are able to provide these guarantees for dynamically sized types.* For types with no fixed width in memory, Rust ensures that a length is kept alongside the internal pointer. That way Rust can ensure that the program never overruns the type's space in memory.

NOTE The distinguishing characteristic between memory addresses and the two higher abstractions is that the latter two have information about the type of their referent.

6.2   *Exploring Rust's reference and pointer types*

This section teaches you how to work with several of Rust's pointer types. *Rust in Action* tries to stick to the following guidelines when discussing these types:

- *References*—Signal that the Rust compiler will provide its safety guarantees.
- *Pointers*—Refer to something more primitive. This also includes the implication that we are responsible for maintaining safety. (There is an implied connotation of being unsafe.)
- *Raw pointers*—Used for types where it's important to make their unsafe nature explicit.

Throughout this section, we'll expand on a common code fragment introduced by listing 6.1. Its source code is available in ch6/ch6-pointer-intro.rs. In the listing, two global variables, B and C, are pointed to by references. Those references hold the addresses of B and C, respectively. A view of what's happening follows the code in figures 6.2 and 6.3.

Listing 6.1   Mimicking pointers with references

```
static B: [u8; 10] = [99, 97, 114, 114, 121, 116, 111, 119, 101, 108];
static C: [u8; 11] = [116, 104, 97, 110, 107, 115, 102, 105, 115, 104, 0];

fn main() {
    let a = 42;
    let b = &B;
    let c = &C;

    println!("a: {}, b: {:p}, c: {:p}", a, b, c);
}
```

For simplicity, uses the same reference type for this example. Later examples distinguish smart pointers from raw pointers and require different types.

The {:p} syntax asks Rust to format the variable as a pointer and prints the memory address that the value points to.

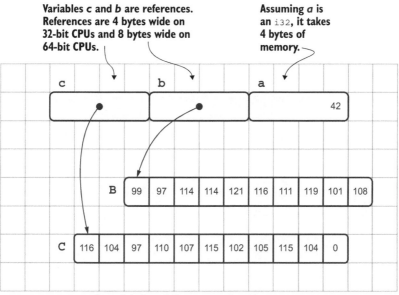

A partial view of the program's address space

Figure 6.2   An abstract view of how two pointers operate alongside a standard integer. The important lesson here is that the programmer might not know the location of the referent data beforehand.

Listing 6.1 has three variables within its `main()` function. a is rather trivial; it's just an integer. The other two are more interesting. b and c are references. These refer to two opaque arrays of data, B and C. For the moment, consider Rust references as equivalent to pointers. The output from one execution on a 64-bit machine is as follows:

```
a: 42, b: 0x556fd40eb480, c: 0x556fd40eb48a
```
If you run the code, the exact memory addresses will be different on your machine.

Figure 6.3 provides a view of the same example in an imaginary address space of 49 bytes. It has a pointer width of two bytes (16 bits). You'll notice that the variables b and c look different in memory, despite being the same type as in listing 6.1. That's due to that because the listing is lying to you. The gritty details and a code example that more closely represents the diagram in figure 6.3 are coming shortly.

As evidenced in figure 6.2, there's one problem with portraying pointers as arrows to disconnected arrays. These tend to de-emphasize that the address space is contiguous and shared between all variables.

For a more thorough examination of what happens under the hood, listing 6.2 produces much more output. It uses more sophisticated types instead of references to

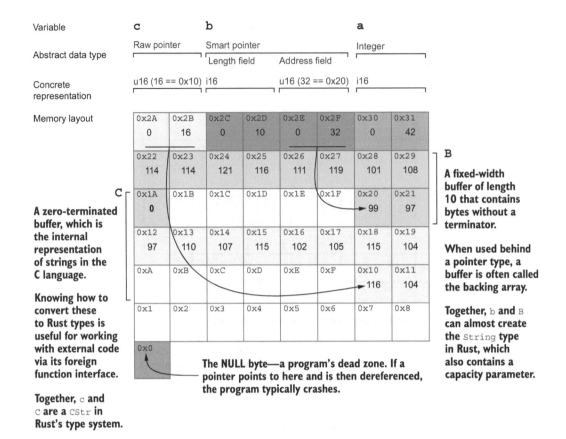

Figure 6.3 An illustrative address space of the program provided in listing 6.1. It provides an illustration of the relationship between addresses (typically written in hexadecimal) and integers (typically written in decimal). White cells represent unused memory.

demonstrate how these differ internally and to correlate more accurately what is presented in figure 6.3. The following shows the output from listing 6.2:

```
a  (an unsigned integer):
   location: 0x7ffe8f7ddfd0
   size:     8 bytes
   value:    42

b (a reference to B):
   location:  0x7ffe8f7ddfd8
   size:      8 bytes
   points to: 0x55876090c830

c (a "box" for C):
   location:  0x7ffe8f7ddfe0
   size:      16 bytes
   points to: 0x558762130a40
```

```
B (an array of 10 bytes):
  location: 0x55876090c830
  size:     10 bytes
  value:    [99, 97, 114, 114, 121, 116, 111, 119, 101, 108]

C (an array of 11 bytes):
  location: 0x55876090c83a
  size:     11 bytes
  value:    [116, 104, 97, 110, 107, 115, 102, 105, 115, 104, 0
```

Listing 6.2 Comparing references and `Box<T>` to several types

&[u8; 10] reads as "a reference to an array of 10 bytes." The array is located in static memory, and the reference itself (a pointer of width usize bytes) is placed on the stack.

```
 1 use std::mem::size_of;
 2
 3 static B: [u8; 10] = [99, 97, 114, 114, 121, 116, 111, 119, 101, 108];
 4 static C: [u8; 11] = [116, 104, 97, 110, 107, 115, 102, 105, 115, 104, 0];
 5
 6 fn main() {
 7     let a: usize      = 42;
 8
 9     let b: &[u8; 10] = &B;
10
11     let c: Box<[u8]> = Box::new(C);
12
13     println!("a (an unsigned integer):");
14     println!("  location: {:p}", &a);
15     println!("  size:     {:?} bytes", size_of::<usize>());
16     println!("  value:    {:?}", a);
17     println!();
18
19     println!("b (a reference to B):");
20     println!("  location: {:p}", &b);
21     println!("  size:     {:?} bytes", size_of::<&[u8; 10]>());
22     println!("  points to: {:p}", b);
23     println!();
24
25     println!("c (a \"box\" for C):");
26     println!("  location: {:p}", &c);
27     println!("  size:     {:?} bytes", size_of::<Box<[u8]>>());
28     println!("  points to: {:p}", c);
29     println!();
30
31     println!("B (an array of 10 bytes):");
32     println!("  location: {:p}",  &B);
33     println!("  size:     {:?} bytes", size_of::<[u8; 10]>());
34     println!("  value:    {:?}", B);
35     println!();
36
37     println!("C (an array of 11 bytes):");
38     println!("  location: {:p}",  &C);
39     println!("  size:     {:?} bytes", size_of::<[u8; 11]>());
40     println!("  value:    {:?}", C);
41 }
```

usize is the memory address size for the CPU the code is compiled for. That CPU is called the compile target. (annotation for line 7)

The Box<[u8]> type is a boxed byte slice. When we place values inside a box, ownership of the value moves to the owner of the box. (annotation for line 11)

For readers who are interested in decoding the text within B and C, listing 6.3 is a short program that (almost) creates a memory address layout that resembles figure 6.3 more closely. It contains a number of new Rust features and some relatively arcane syntax, both of which haven't been introduced yet. These will be explained shortly.

Listing 6.3   Printing from strings provided by external sources

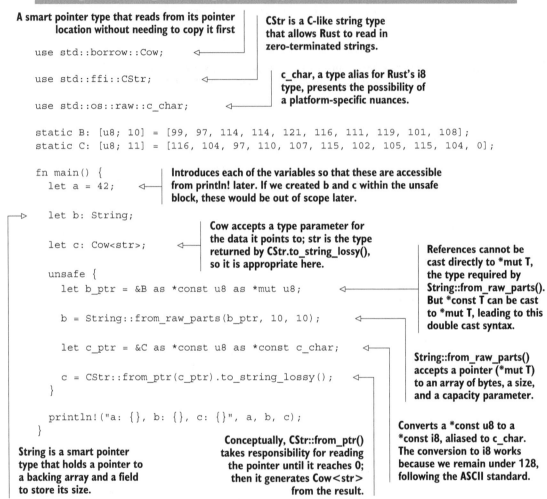

A smart pointer type that reads from its pointer location without needing to copy it first

CStr is a C-like string type that allows Rust to read in zero-terminated strings.

```rust
use std::borrow::Cow;

use std::ffi::CStr;

use std::os::raw::c_char;

static B: [u8; 10] = [99, 97, 114, 114, 121, 116, 111, 119, 101, 108];
static C: [u8; 11] = [116, 104, 97, 110, 107, 115, 102, 105, 115, 104, 0];

fn main() {
    let a = 42;

    let b: String;

    let c: Cow<str>;

    unsafe {
        let b_ptr = &B as *const u8 as *mut u8;

        b = String::from_raw_parts(b_ptr, 10, 10);

        let c_ptr = &C as *const u8 as *const c_char;

        c = CStr::from_ptr(c_ptr).to_string_lossy();
    }

    println!("a: {}, b: {}, c: {}", a, b, c);
}
```

c_char, a type alias for Rust's i8 type, presents the possibility of a platform-specific nuances.

Introduces each of the variables so that these are accessible from println! later. If we created b and c within the unsafe block, these would be out of scope later.

Cow accepts a type parameter for the data it points to; str is the type returned by CStr.to_string_lossy(), so it is appropriate here.

References cannot be cast directly to *mut T, the type required by String::from_raw_parts(). But *const T can be cast to *mut T, leading to this double cast syntax.

String::from_raw_parts() accepts a pointer (*mut T) to an array of bytes, a size, and a capacity parameter.

Converts a *const u8 to a *const i8, aliased to c_char. The conversion to i8 works because we remain under 128, following the ASCII standard.

String is a smart pointer type that holds a pointer to a backing array and a field to store its size.

Conceptually, CStr::from_ptr() takes responsibility for reading the pointer until it reaches 0; then it generates Cow<str> from the result.

In listing 6.3, Cow stands for *copy on write*. This smart pointer type is handy when an external source provides a buffer. Avoiding copies increases runtime performance. std::ffi is the foreign function interface module from Rust's standard library. use std::os::raw::c_char; is not strictly needed, but it does make the code's intent clear. C does not define the width of its char type in its standard, although it's one byte wide in practice. Retrieving the type alias c_char from the std::os:raw module allows for differences.

To thoroughly understand the code in listing 6.3, there is quite a bit of ground to cover. We first need to work through what raw pointers are and then discuss a number of feature-rich alternatives that have been built around them.

6.2.1 *Raw pointers in Rust*

A *raw pointer* is a memory address without Rust's standard guarantees. These are inherently unsafe. For example, unlike references (`&T`), raw pointers can be `null`.

If you'll forgive the syntax, raw pointers are denoted as `*const T` and `*mut T` for immutable and mutable raw pointers, respectively. Even though each is a single type, these contain three tokens: `*`, `const` or `mut`. Their type, T, a raw pointer to a `String`, looks like `*const String`. A raw pointer to an `i32` looks like `*mut i32`. But before we put pointers into practice, here are two other things that are useful to know:

- *The difference between a `*mut T` and a `*const T` is minimal.* These can be freely cast between one another and tend to be used interchangeably, acting as in-source documentation.
- *Rust references (`&mut T` and `&T`) compile down to raw pointers.* That means that it's possible to access the performance of raw pointers without needing to venture into `unsafe` blocks.

The next listing provides a small example that coerces a reference to a value (`&T`), creating a raw pointer from an `i64` value. It then prints the value and its address in memory via the `{:p}` syntax.

Listing 6.4   Creating a raw pointer (`*const T`)

```
fn main() {
    let a: i64 = 42;
    let a_ptr = &a as *const i64;        ◁──┐ Casts a reference to the
                                              variable a (&a) to a constant
                                              raw pointer i64 (*const i64)
    println!("a: {} ({:p})", a, a_ptr);  ◁──┐
}                                              Prints the value of the variable
                                               a (42) and its address in
                                               memory (0x7ff…)
```

The terms *pointer* and *memory address* are sometimes used interchangeably. These are integers that represent a location in virtual memory. From the compiler's point of view, though, there is one important difference. Rust's pointer types `*const T` and `*mut T` always point to the starting byte of T, and these also know the width of type T in bytes. A memory address might refer to anywhere in memory.

An `i64` is 8-bytes wide (64 bits ÷ 8 bits per byte). Therefore, if an `i64` is stored at address `0x7fffd`, then each of the bytes between `0x7ffd..0x8004` must be fetched from RAM to recreate the integer's value. The process of fetching data from RAM from a pointer is known as *dereferencing a pointer*. The following listing identifies a value's address by casting a reference to it as a raw pointer via `std::mem::transmute`.

Listing 6.5   Identifying a value's address

```
fn main() {
    let a: i64 = 42;
    let a_ptr = &a as *const i64;
    let a_addr: usize = unsafe {
      std::mem::transmute(a_ptr)
    };

    println!("a: {} ({:p}...0x{:x})", a, a_ptr, a_addr + 7);

}
```

> Interprets *const i64 as usize.
> Using transmute() is highly unsafe
> but is used here to postpone
> introducing more syntax.

Under the hood, references (`&T` and `&mut T`) are implemented as raw pointers. These come with extra guarantees and should always be preferred.

> **WARNING**   Accessing the value of a raw pointer is always unsafe. Handle with care.

Using raw pointers in Rust code is like working with pyrotechnics. Usually the results are fantastic, sometimes they're painful, and occasionally they're tragic. Raw pointers are often handled in Rust code by the OS or a third-party library.

To demonstrate their volatility, let's work through a quick example with Rust's raw pointers. Creating a pointer of arbitrary types from any integer is perfectly legal. Dereferencing that pointer must occur within an `unsafe` block, as the following snippet shows. An `unsafe` block implies that the programmer takes full responsibility for any consequences:

```
fn main() {
    let ptr = 42 as *const Vec<String>;

    unsafe {
        let new_addr = ptr.offset(4);
        println!("{:p} -> {:p}", ptr, new_addr);
    }
}
```

> You can create pointers safely from
> any integral value. An i32 is not a
> Vec<String>, but Rust is quite
> comfortable ignoring that here.

To reiterate, raw pointers are not safe. These have a number of properties that mean that their use is strongly discouraged within day-to-day Rust code:

- *Raw pointers do not own their values.* The Rust compiler does not check that the referent data is still valid when these are accessed.
- *Multiple raw pointers to the same data are allowed.* Every raw pointer can have write, read-write access to data. This means that there is no time when Rust can guarantee that shared data is valid.

Notwithstanding those warnings, there are a small number of valid reasons to make use of raw pointers:

- *It's unavoidable.* Perhaps some OS call or third-party code requires a raw pointer. Raw pointers are common within C code that provides an external interface.
- *Shared access to something is essential and runtime performance is paramount.* Perhaps multiple components within your application require equal access to some expensive-to-compute variable. If you're willing to take on the risk of one of those components poisoning every other component with some silly mistake, then raw pointers are an option of last resort.

6.2.2 Rust's pointer ecosystem

Given that raw pointers are unsafe, what is the safer alternative? The alternative is to use smart pointers. In the Rust community, a *smart pointer* is a pointer type that has some kind of superpower, over and above the ability to deference a memory address. You will probably encounter the term *wrapper type* as well. Rust's smart pointer types tend to wrap raw pointers and bestow them with added semantics.

A narrower definition of smart pointer is common in the C communities. There authors (generally) imply that the term smart pointer means the C equivalents of Rust's `core::ptr::Unique`, `core::ptr::Shared`, and `std::rc::Weak` types. We will introduce these types shortly.

> **NOTE** The term *fat pointer* refers to memory layout. Thin pointers, such as raw pointers, are a single `usize` wide. Fat pointers are usually two `usize` wide, and occasionally more.

Rust has an extensive set of pointer (and pointer-like) types in its standard library. Each has its own role, strengths, and weaknesses. Given their unique properties, rather than writing these out as a list, let's model these as characters in a card-based role-playing game, as shown in figure 6.4.

Each of the pointer types introduced here are used extensively throughout the book. As such, we'll give these fuller treatment when that's needed. For now, the two novel attributes that appear within the Powers section of some of these cards are interior mutability and shared ownership. These two terms warrant some discussion.

With interior mutability, you may want to provide an argument to a method that takes immutable values, yet you need to retain mutability. If you're willing to pay the runtime performance cost, it's possible to fake immutability. If the method requires an owned value, wrap the argument in `Cell<T>`. References can also be wrapped in `RefCell<T>`. It is common when using the reference counted types `Rc<T>` and `Arc<T>`, which only accept immutable arguments, to also wrap those in `Cell<T>` or `RefCell<T>`. The resulting type might look like `Rc<RefCell<T>>`. This means that you pay the runtime cost twice but with significantly more flexibility.

With shared ownership, some objects, such as a network connection or, perhaps, access to some OS service, are difficult to mould into the pattern of having a single place with read-write access at any given time. Code might be simplified if two parts of

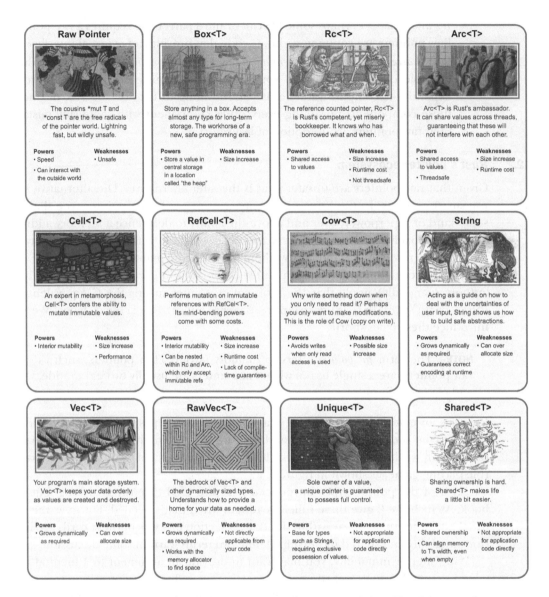

Figure 6.4　A fictitious role-playing card game describing the characteristics of Rust's smart pointer types

the program can share access to that single resource. Rust allows you to do this, but again, at the expense of a runtime cost.

6.2.3　*Smart pointer building blocks*

You might find yourself in a situation where you want to build your own smart pointer type with its own semantics. Perhaps a new research paper has been released, and you want to incorporate its results into your own work. Perhaps you're conducting the research. Regardless, it might be useful to know that Rust's pointer types are extensible—these are designed with extension in mind.

All of the programmer-facing pointer types like Box<T> are built from more primitive types that live deeper within Rust, often in its core or alloc modules. Additionally, the C++ smart pointer types have Rust counterparts. Here are some useful starting points for you when building your own smart pointer types:

- core::ptr::Unique is the basis for types such as String, Box<T>, and the pointer field Vec<T>.
- core::ptr::Shared is the basis for Rc<T> and Arc<T>, and it can handle situations where shared access is desired.

In addition, the following tools can also be handy in certain situations:

- *Deeply interlinked data structures can benefit from* std::rc::Weak *and* std::arc::Weak *for single and multi-threaded programs, respectively.* These allow access to data within an Rc/Arc without incrementing its reference count. This can prevent never-ending cycles of pointers.
- *The* alloc::raw_vec::RawVec *type underlies* Vec<T> *and* VecDeq<T>. An expandable, double-ended queue that hasn't appeared in the book so far, it understands how to allocate and deallocate memory in a smart way for any given type.
- *The* std::cell::UnsafeCell *type sits behind both* Cell<T> *and* RefCell<T>. If you would like to provide interior mutability to your types, its implementation is worth investigating.

A full treatment of building new safe pointers touches on some of Rust's internals. These building blocks have their own building blocks. Unfortunately, explaining every detail will diverge too far from our goals for this chapter.

> **NOTE** Inquisitive readers should investigate the source code of the standard library's pointer types. For example, the std::cell::RefCell type is documented at https://doc.rust-lang.org/std/cell/struct.RefCell.html. Clicking the [src] button on that web page directs you to the type's definition.

6.3   *Providing programs with memory for their data*

This section attempts to demystify the terms *the stack* and *the heap*. These terms often appear in contexts that presuppose you already know what they mean. That isn't the case here. We'll cover the details of what they are, why they exist, and how to make use of that knowledge to make your programs leaner and faster.

Some people hate wading through the details, though. For those readers, here is the salient difference between the stack and the heap:

- The stack is fast.
- The heap is slow.

That difference leads to the following axiom: "When in doubt, prefer the stack." To place data onto the stack, the compiler must know the type's size at compile time.

Translated to Rust, that means, "When in doubt, use types that implement `Sized`." Now that you've got the gist of those terms, it's time to learn when to take the slow path and how to avoid it when you want to take a faster one.

6.3.1   *The stack*

The stack is often described by analogy. Think of a stack of dinner plates waiting in the cupboard of a commercial kitchen. Cooks are taking plates off the stack to serve food, and dishwashers are placing new plates on the top.

The unit (the plate) of a computing stack is the stack frame, also known as the *allocation record*. You are probably used to thinking of this as a group of variables and other data. Like many descriptions in computing, the stack and the heap are analogies that only partially fit. Even though the stack is often compared by analogy to a stack of dinner plates waiting in the cupboard, unfortunately, that mental picture is inaccurate. Here are some differences:

- The stack actually contains two levels of objects: stack frames and data.
- The stack grants programmers access to multiple elements stored within it, rather than the top item only.
- The stack can include elements of arbitrary size, where the implication of the dinner plate analogy is that all elements must be of the same size.

So why is the stack called the stack? Because of the usage pattern. Entries on the stack are made in a Last In, First Out (LIFO) manner.

The entries in the stack are called *stack frames*. Stack frames are created as function calls are made. As a program progresses, a cursor within the CPU updates to reflect the current address of the current stack frame. The cursor is known as the *stack pointer*.

As functions are called within functions, the stack pointer decreases in value as the stack grows. When a function returns, the stack pointer increases.

Stack frames contain a function's state during the call. When a function is called within a function, the older function's values are effectively frozen in time. Stack frames are also known as *activation frames*, and less commonly *allocation records.*[1]

Unlike dinner plates, every stack frame is a different size. The stack frame contains space for its function's arguments, a pointer to the original call site, and local variables (except the data which is allocated on the heap).

NOTE If you are unfamiliar with what the term *call site* means, see the CPU emulation section in chapter 5.

To understand what is happening more fully, let's consider a thought experiment. Imagine a diligent, yet absurdly single-minded cook in a commercial kitchen. The cook takes each table's docket and places those in a queue. The cook has a fairly bad memory, so each current order is written down a notebook. As new orders come in,

---

[1] To be precise, the activation frame is called a stack frame when allocated on the stack.

the cook updates the notebook to refer to the new order. When orders are complete, the notebook page is changed to the next item in the queue. Unfortunately, for customers in this restaurant, the book operates in a LIFO manner. Hopefully, you will not be one of the early orders during tomorrow's lunch rush.

In this analogy, the notebook plays the role of the stack pointer. The stack itself is comprised of variable-length dockets, representing stack frames. Like stack frames, restaurant dockets contain some metadata. For example, the table number can act as the return address.

The stack's primary role is to make space for local variables. Why is the stack fast? All of a function's variables are side by side in memory. That speeds up access.

Improving the ergonomics of functions that can only accept `String` or `&str`

As a library author, it can simplify downstream application code if your functions can accept both `&str` and `String` types. Unfortunately, these two types have different representations in memory. One (`&str`) is allocated on the stack, the other (`String`) allocates memory on the heap. That means that types cannot be trivially cast between one another. It's possible, however, to work around this with Rust's generics.

Consider the example of validating a password. For the purposes of the example, a strong password is one that's at least 6 characters long. The following shows how to validate the password by checking its length:

```
fn is_strong(password: String) -> bool {
    password.len() > 5
}
```

`is_strong` can only accept `String`. That means that the following code won't work:

```
let pw = "justok";
let is_strong = is_strong(pw);
```

But generic code can help. In cases where read-only access is required, use functions with the type signature `fn x<T: AsRef<str>> (a: T)` rather than `fn x (a: String)`. The fairly unwieldy type signature reads "as function x takes an argument `password` of type T, where T implements `AsRef<str>`." Implementors of `AsRef<str>` behave as a reference to `str` even when these are not.

Here is the code snippet again for the previous listing, accepting any type T that implements `AsRef<str>`. It now has the new signature in place:

```
fn is_strong<T: AsRef<str>>(password: T) -> bool {
    password.as_ref().len() > 5
}
```
← **Provides a String or a &str as password**

When read-write access to the argument is required, normally you can make use of `AsRef<T>`'s sibling trait `AsMut<T>`. Unfortunately for this example, `&'static str` cannot become mutable and so another strategy can be deployed: implicit conversion.

(continued)

It's possible to ask Rust to accept only those types that can be converted to String. The following example performs that conversion within the function and applies any required business logic to that newly created String. This can circumvent the issue of &str being an immutable value.

```
fn is_strong<T: Into<String>>(password: T) -> bool {
    password.into().len() > 5
}
```

This implicit conversion strategy does have significant risks, though. If a string-ified version of the password variable needs to be created multiple times in the pipeline, it would be much more efficient to require an explicit conversion within the calling application. That way the String would be created once and reused.

6.3.2   *The heap*

This section introduces the heap. The heap is an area of program memory for types that do not have known sizes at compile time.

What does it mean to have no known size at compile time? In Rust, there are two meanings. Some types grow and shrink over time as required. Obvious cases are String and Vec<T>. Other types are unable to tell the Rust compiler how much memory to allocate even though these don't change size at runtime. These are known as dynamically sized types. Slices ([T]) are the commonly cited example. Slices have no compile-time length. Internally, these are a pointer to some part of an array. But slices actually represent some number of elements within that array.

Another example is a *trait object*, which we've not described in this book so far. Trait objects allow Rust programmers to mimic some features of dynamic languages by allowing multiple types to be wedged into the same container.

WHAT IS THE HEAP?

You will gain a fuller understanding of *what* the heap is once you work through the next section on virtual memory. For now, let's concentrate on what it is *not*. Once those points are clarified, we'll then work our way back toward some form of truth.

The word "heap" implies disorganization. A closer analogy would be warehouse space in some medium-sized business. As deliveries arrive (as variables are created), the warehouse makes space available. As the business carries out its work, those materials are used, and the warehouse space can now be made available for new deliveries. At times, there are gaps and perhaps a bit of clutter. But overall, there is a good sense of order.

Another mistake is that the heap has no relationship to the data structure that is also known as a heap. That data structure is often used to create priority queues. It's an incredibly clever tool in its own right, but right now it's a complete distraction. The heap is not a data structure. It's an area of memory.

Now that those two distinctions are made, let's inch toward an explanation. The critical difference from a usage point of view is that variables on the heap must be accessed via a pointer, whereas this is not required with variables accessed on the stack.

Although it's a trivial example, let's consider two variables, a and b. These both represent the integers 40 and 60, respectively. In one of those cases though, the integer happens to live on the heap, as in this example:

```
let a: i32 = 40;
let b: Box<i32> = Box::new(60);
```

Now, let's demonstrate that critical difference. The following code won't compile:

```
let result = a + b;
```

The boxed value assigned to b is only accessible via a pointer. To access that value, we need to dereference it. The dereference operator is a unary *, which prefixes the variable name:

```
let result = a + *b;
```

This syntax can be difficult to follow at first because the symbol is also used for multiplication. It does, however, become more natural over time. The following listing shows a complete example where creating variables on the heap implies constructing that variable via a pointer type such as Box<T>.

Listing 6.6 Creating variables on the heap

```
fn main() {
    let a: i32 = 40;                              ◁──┐  40 lives on the stack.
    let b: Box<i32> = Box::new(60);            ◁──┐  60 lives on the heap.

    println!("{} + {} = {}", a, b, a + *b);    ◁──┐  To access 60, we need
}                                                     to dereference it.
```

To get a feel for what the heap is and what is happening within memory as a program runs, let's consider a tiny example. In this example, all we will do is to create some numbers on the heap and then add their values together. When run, the program in listing 6.7 produces some fairly trivial output: two 3s. Still, it's really the internals of the program's memory that are important here, not its results.

The code for the next listing is in the file ch6/ch6-heap-via-box/src/main.rs. A pictorial view of the program's memory as it runs (figure 6.5) follows the code. Let's first look at the program's output:

```
3 3
```

Listing 6.7 Allocating and deallocating memory on the heap via Box<T>

```
 1 use std::mem::drop;          ◁────┐   Brings manual drop()
 2                                   │   into local scope
 3 fn main() {
 4     let a = Box::new(1);
 5     let b = Box::new(1);              Allocates values
 6     let c = Box::new(1);              on the heap
 7
 8     let result1 = *a + *b + *c;   ◁────────   The unary *, the dereference operator,
 9                                               returns the value within the box, and
10     drop(a);                 ◁────────        result1 holds the value 3.
11     let d = Box::new(1);
12     let result2 = *b + *c + *d;           Invokes drop(), freeing
13                                           memory for other uses
14     println!("{} {}", result1, result2);
15 }
```

Listing 6.7 places four values on the heap and removes one. It contains some new or, at least, less familiar syntax that might be worthwhile to cover and/or recap:

- *Box::new(T) allocates T on the heap. Box* is a term that can be deceptive if you don't share its intuition.

  Something that has been *boxed* lives on the heap, with a pointer to it on the stack. This is demonstrated in the first column of figure 6.5, where the number 0x100 at address 0xfff points to the value 1 at address 0x100. However, no actual box of bytes encloses a value, nor is the value hidden or concealed in some way.

- *std::mem::drop brings the function drop() into local scope.* drop() deletes objects before their scope ends.

  Types that implement Drop have a drop() method, but explicitly calling it is illegal within user code. std::mem::drop is an escape hatch from that rule.

- *Asterisks next to variables (*a, *b, *c, and *d) are unary operators.* This is the *dereference operator*. Dereferencing a Box::(T) returns T. In our case, the variables a, b, c, and d are references that refer to integers.

In figure 6.5, each column illustrates what happens inside memory at 6 lines of code. The stack appears as the boxes along the top, and the heap appears along the bottom. The figure omits several details, but it should help you gain an intuition about the relationship between the stack and the heap.

> **NOTE** If you have experience with a debugger and want to explore what is happening, be sure to compile your code with no optimizations. Compile your code with cargo build (or cargo run) rather than cargo build --release. Using the --release flag actually ends up optimizing all the allocations and arithmetic. If you are invoking rustc manually, use the command rustc --codegen opt-level=0.

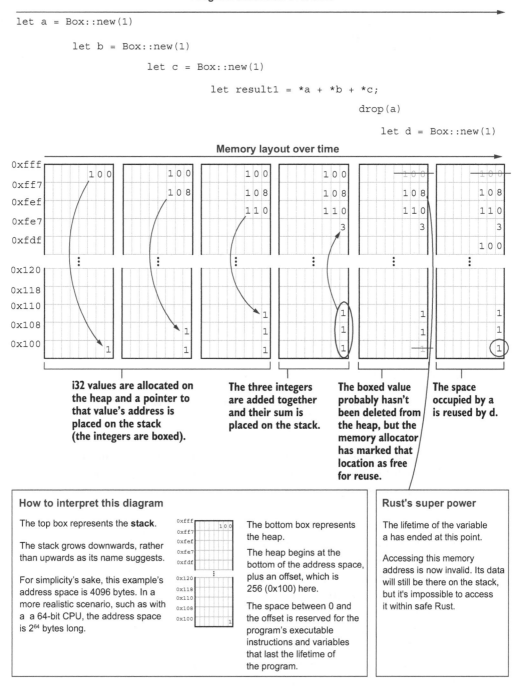

Figure 6.5 A view into a program's memory layout during the execution of listing 6.7

6.3.3 *What is dynamic memory allocation?*

At any given time, a running program has a fixed number of bytes with which to get its work done. When the program would like more memory, it needs to ask for more from the OS. This is known as *dynamic memory allocation* and is shown in figure 6.6. Dynamic memory allocation is a three-step process:

1 Request memory from the OS via a system call. In the UNIX family of operating systems, this system call is `alloc()`. In MS Windows, the call is `HeapAlloc()`.

2 Make use of the allocated memory in the program.

3 Release memory that isn't needed back to the OS via `free()` for UNIX systems and `HeapFree()` for Windows.

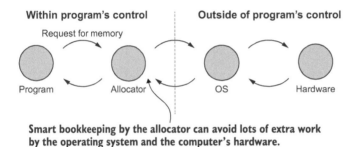

Smart bookkeeping by the allocator can avoid lots of extra work by the operating system and the computer's hardware.

Figure 6.6 Conceptual view of dynamic memory allocation. Requests for memory originate and terminate at the program level but involve several other components. At each stage, the components may short-circuit the process and return quickly.

As it turns out, there is an intermediary between the program and the OS: the *allocator,* a specialist subprogram that is embedded in your program behind the scenes. It will often perform optimizations that avoid lots of work within the OS and CPU.

Let's examine the performance impact of dynamic memory allocation and strategies to reduce that impact. Before starting, let's recap why there's a performance difference between the stack and the heap. Remember that the stack and the heap are conceptual abstractions only. These do not exist as physical partitions of your computer's memory. What accounts for their different performance characteristics?

Accessing data on the stack is fast because a function's local variables, which are allocated on the stack, reside next to each other in RAM. This is sometimes referred to as a *contiguous layout.*

A contiguous layout is cache-friendly. Alternatively, variables allocated on the heap are unlikely to reside next to each other. Moreover, accessing data on the heap involves dereferencing the pointer. That implies a page table lookup and a trip to main memory. Table 6.1 summarizes these differences.

Table 6.1 A simplistic, yet practical table for comparing the stack and the heap

Stack	Heap
Simple	Complex
Safe	Dangerous*
Fast	Slow
Rigid	Flexible

* Not in safe Rust!

There is a trade-off for the stack's increased speed. Data structures on the stack must stay the same size during the lifetime of the program. Data structures allocated on the heap are more flexible. Because these are accessed via a pointer, that pointer can be changed.

To quantify this impact, we need to learn how to measure the cost. To get a large number of measurements, we need a program that creates and destroys many values. Let's create a toy program. Figure 6.7 shows show a background element to a video game.

Figure 6.7   Screenshots from the result of running listing 6.9

After running listing 6.9, you should see a window appear on your screen filled with a dark grey background. White snow-like dots will start to float from the bottom and fade as they approach the top. If you check the console output, streams of numbers will appear. Their significance will be explained once we discuss the code. Listing 6.9 contains three major sections:

- A memory allocator (the ReportingAllocator struct) records the time that dynamic memory allocations take.
- Definitions of the structs World and Particle and how these behave over time.
- The main() function deals with window creation and initialization.

The following listing shows the dependencies for our toy program (listing 6.9). The source for the following listing is in ch6/ch6-particles/Cargo.toml. The source for listing 6.9 is in ch6/ch6-particles/main.rs.

Listing 6.8   Build dependencies for listing 6.9

```
[package]
name = "ch6-particles"
version = "0.1.0"
authors = ["TS McNamara <author@rustinaction.com>"]
edition = "2018"

[dependencies]
piston_window = "0.117"

piston2d-graphics = "0.39"

rand = "0.8"
```

Provides a wrapper around the core functionality of the piston game engine, letting us easily draw things onscreen; largely irrespective of the host environment

Provides vector mathematics, which is important to simulate movement

Provides random number generators and associated functionality

Listing 6.9   A graphical application to create and destroy objects on the heap

rand provides random number generators and related functionality.

graphics::math::Vec2d provides mathematical operations and conversion functionality for 2D vectors.

```
 1 use graphics::math::{Vec2d, add, mul_scalar};
 2
 3 use piston_window::*;
 4
 5 use rand::prelude::*;
 6
 7 use std::alloc::{GlobalAlloc, System, Layout};
 8
 9 use std::time::Instant;
10
11
12 #[global_allocator]
13 static ALLOCATOR: ReportingAllocator = ReportingAllocator;
14
15 struct ReportingAllocator;
16
17 unsafe impl GlobalAlloc for ReportingAllocator {
18   unsafe fn alloc(&self, layout: Layout) -> *mut u8 {
19     let start = Instant::now();
20     let ptr = System.alloc(layout);
21     let end = Instant::now();
22     let time_taken = end - start;
23     let bytes_requested = layout.size();
24
25     eprintln!("{}\t{}", bytes_requested, time_taken.as_nanos());
26     ptr
27   }
28
29   unsafe fn dealloc(&self, ptr: *mut u8, layout: Layout) {
```

piston_window provides the tools to create a GUI program and draws shapes to it.

std::alloc provides facilities for controlling memory allocation.

std::time provides access to the system's clock.

#[global_allocator] marks the following value (ALLOCATOR) as satisfying the GlobalAlloc trait.

Prints the time taken for each allocation to STDOUT as the program runs. This provides a fairly accurate indication of the time taken for dynamic memory allocation.

Defers the actual memory allocation to the system's default memory allocator

```
30      System.dealloc(ptr, layout);
31    }
32 }
33
34 struct World {
35    current_turn: u64,
36    particles: Vec<Box<Particle>>,
37    height: f64,
38    width: f64,
39    rng: ThreadRng,
40 }
41
42 struct Particle {
43    height: f64,
44    width: f64,
45    position: Vec2d<f64>,
46    velocity: Vec2d<f64>,
47    acceleration: Vec2d<f64>,
48    color: [f32; 4],
49 }
50
51 impl Particle {
52    fn new(world : &World) -> Particle {
53      let mut rng = thread_rng();
54      let x = rng.gen_range(0.0..=world.width);
55      let y = world.height;
56      let x_velocity = 0.0;
57      let y_velocity = rng.gen_range(-2.0..0.0);
58      let x_acceleration = 0.0;
59      let y_acceleration = rng.gen_range(0.0..0.15);
60
61      Particle {
62        height: 4.0,
63        width: 4.0,
64        position: [x, y].into(),
65        velocity: [x_velocity, y_velocity].into(),
66        acceleration: [x_acceleration,
67                       y_acceleration].into(),
68        color: [1.0, 1.0, 1.0, 0.99],
69      }
70    }
71
72    fn update(&mut self) {
73      self.velocity = add(self.velocity,
74                          self.acceleration);
75      self.position = add(self.position,
76                          self.velocity);
77      self.acceleration = mul_scalar(
78        self.acceleration,
79        0.7
80      );
81      self.color[3] *= 0.995;
82    }
83 }
84
```

Contains the data that is useful for the lifetime of the program (lines 34–40)

Defines an object in 2D space (lines 42–49)

Starts at a random position along the bottom of the window (lines 54–55)

Rises vertically over time (line 57)

Increases the speed of the rise over time (line 59)

into() converts the arrays of type [f64; 2] into Vec2d. (lines 64–67)

Inserts a fully saturated white that has a tiny amount of transparency (line 68)

Moves the particle to its next position (lines 73–76)

Slows down the particle's rate of increase as it travels across the screen (lines 77–80)

Makes the particle more transparent over time (line 81)

```
85 impl World {
86   fn new(width: f64, height: f64) -> World {
87     World {
88       current_turn: 0,
89       particles: Vec::<Box<Particle>>::new(),
90       height: height,
91       width: width,
92       rng: thread_rng(),
93     }
94   }
95
96   fn add_shapes(&mut self, n: i32) {
97     for _ in 0..n.abs() {
98       let particle = Particle::new(&self);
99       let boxed_particle = Box::new(particle);
100      self.particles.push(boxed_particle);
101    }
102  }
103
104  fn remove_shapes(&mut self, n: i32) {
105    for _ in 0..n.abs() {
106      let mut to_delete = None;
107
108      let particle_iter = self.particles
109        .iter()
110        .enumerate();
111
112      for (i, particle) in particle_iter {
113        if particle.color[3] < 0.02 {
114          to_delete = Some(i);
115        }
116        break;
117      }
118
119      if let Some(i) = to_delete {
120        self.particles.remove(i);
121      } else {
122        self.particles.remove(0);
123      };
124    }
125  }
126
127  fn update(&mut self) {
128    let n = self.rng.gen_range(-3..=3);
129
130    if n > 0 {
131      self.add_shapes(n);
132    } else {
133      self.remove_shapes(n);
134    }
135
136    self.particles.shrink_to_fit();
137    for shape in &mut self.particles {
138      shape.update();
139    }
```

Uses Box<Particle> rather than Particle to incur an extra memory allocation when every particle is created

Creates a Particle as a local variable on the stack

Takes ownership of particle, moving its data to the heap, and creates a reference to that data on the stack

Pushes the reference into self.shapes

particle_iter is split into its own variable to more easily fit on the page.

For n iterations, removes the first particle that's invisible. If there are no invisible particles, then removes the oldest.

Returns a random integer between –3 and 3, inclusive

```
140      self.current_turn += 1;
141    }
142 }
143
144 fn main() {
145   let (width, height) = (1280.0, 960.0);
146   let mut window: PistonWindow = WindowSettings::new(
147     "particles", [width, height]
148   )
149   .exit_on_esc(true)
150   .build()
151   .expect("Could not create a window.");
152
153   let mut world = World::new(width, height);
154   world.add_shapes(1000);
155
156   while let Some(event) = window.next() {
157     world.update();
158
159     window.draw_2d(&event, |ctx, renderer, _device| {
160       clear([0.15, 0.17, 0.17, 0.9], renderer);
161
162       for s in &mut world.particles {
163         let size = [s.position[0], s.position[1], s.width, s.height];
164         rectangle(s.color, size, ctx.transform, renderer);
165       }
166     });
167   }
168 }
```

Listing 6.9 is a fairly long code example, but hopefully, it does not contain any code that's too alien compared to what you've already seen. Toward the end, the code example introduces Rust's closure syntax. If you look at the call to window.draw_2d(), it has a second argument with vertical bars surrounding two variable names (|ctx, renderer, _device| { ... }). Those vertical bars provide space for the closure's arguments, and the curly braces are its body.

A *closure* is a function that is defined in line and can access variables from its surrounding scope. These are often called *anonymous* or *lambda* functions.

Closures are a common feature within idiomatic Rust code, but this book tends to avoid those where possible to keep examples approachable to programmers from an imperative or object-oriented background. Closures are explained fully in chapter 11. In the interim, it's sufficient to say that these are a convenient shorthand for defining functions. Let's next focus on generating some evidence that allocating variables on the heap (many millions of times) can have a performance impact on your code.

6.3.4   *Analyzing the impact of dynamic memory allocation*

If you run listing 6.9 from a terminal window, you'll soon see two columns of numbers filling it up. These columns represent the number of bytes allocated, and the duration in nanoseconds taken to fulfil the request. That output can be sent to a file for further analysis, as shown in the following listing, which redirects stderr from ch6-particles to a file.

Listing 6.10 Creating a report of memory allocations

```
$ cd ch6-particles

$ cargo run -q 2> alloc.tsv          ◁─┐   Runs ch6-particles
                                         │   in quiet mode

$ head alloc.tsv   ◁─┐   Views the first 10
4       219          │   lines of output
5       83
48      87
9       78
9       93
19      69
15      960
16      40
14      70
16      53
```

One interesting aspect from this short extract is that memory allocation speed is not well-correlated with allocation size. When every heap allocation is plotted, this becomes even clearer as figure 6.8 shows.

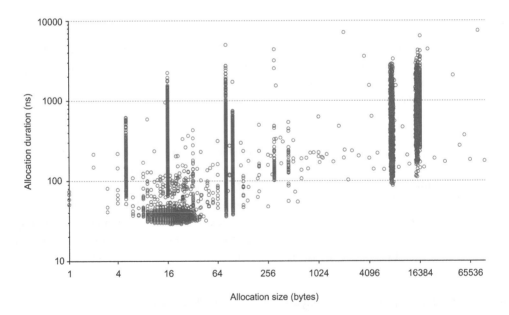

Figure 6.8 Plotting heap allocation times against allocation size shows that there is no clear relationship between the two. The time taken to allocate memory is essentially unpredictable, even when requesting the same amount of memory multiple times.

To generate your own version of figure 6.8, the following listing shows a gnuplot script that can be tweaked as desired. You'll find this source in the file ch6/alloc.plot.

Listing 6.11   Script used to generate figure 6.8 with gnuplot

```
set key off
set rmargin 5
set grid ytics noxtics nocbtics back
set border 3 back lw 2 lc rgbcolor "#222222"

set xlabel "Allocation size (bytes)"
set logscale x 2
set xtics nomirror out
set xrange [0 to 100000]

set ylabel "Allocation duration (ns)"
set logscale y
set yrange [10 to 10000]
set ytics nomirror out

plot "alloc.tsv" with points \
    pointtype 6 \
    pointsize 1.25 \
    linecolor rgbcolor "#22dd3131"
```

Although larger memory allocations do tend to take longer than shorter ones, it's not guaranteed. The range of durations for allocating memory of the same number is over an order of magnitude. It might take 100 nanoseconds; it might take 1,000.

Does it matter? Probably not. But it might. If you have a 3 GHz CPU, then your processor is capable of performing 3 billion operations per second. If there is a 100 nanosecond delay between each of those operations, your computer can only perform 30 million operations in the same time frame. Perhaps those hundreds of microseconds really do count for your application. Some general strategies for minimizing heap allocations include

- *Using arrays of uninitialized objects.* Instead of creating objects from scratch as required, create a bulk lot of those with zeroed values. When the time comes to activate one of those objects, set its values to non-zero. This can be a very dangerous strategy because you're circumventing Rust's lifetime checks.
- *Using an allocator that is tuned for your application's access memory profile.* Memory allocators are often sensitive to the sizes where these perform best.
- *Investigate* arena::Arena *and* arena::TypedArena. These allow objects to be created on the fly, but alloc() and free() are only called when the arena is created and destroyed.

6.4   *Virtual memory*

This section explains what the term virtual memory means and why it exists. You will be able to use this knowledge to speed up your programs by building software that goes with the grain. CPUs can compute faster when they're able to access memory quickly. Understanding some of the dynamics of the computer architecture can help to provide CPUs with memory efficiently.

6.4.1   *Background*

I have spent far too much of my life playing computer games. As enjoyable and challenging as I've found these, I've often wondered about whether I would have been better off spending my teenage years doing something more productive. Still, it's left me with plenty of memories. But some of those memories still leave a bitter taste.

Occasionally, someone would enter the game and obliterate everyone with near perfect aim and seemingly impossibly high health ratings. Other players would decry, "Cheater!" but were more or less helpless in defeat. While waiting in in-game purgatory, I would sit wondering, "How is that possible? How are those tweaks to the game actually made?"

By working through this section's examples, you would have built the core of a tool that's capable of inspecting and modifying values of a running program.

Terms related to virtual memory

Terminology within this area is particularly arcane. It is often tied to decisions made many decades ago when the earliest computers were being designed. Here is a quick reference to some of the most important terms:

- *Page*—A fixed-size block of words of real memory. Typically 4 KB in size for 64-bit operating systems.
- *Word*—Any type that is size of a pointer. This corresponds to the width of the CPU's registers. In Rust, `usize` and `isize` are word-length types.
- *Page fault*—An error raised by the CPU when a valid memory address is requested that is not currently in physical RAM. This signals to the OS that at least one page must be swapped back into memory.
- *Swapping*—Migrating a page of memory stored temporarily on disk from main memory upon request.
- *Virtual memory*—The program's view of its memory. All data accessible to a program is provided in its address space by the OS.
- *Real memory*—The operating system's view of the physical memory available on the system. In many technical texts, real memory is defined independently from physical memory, which becomes much more of an electrical engineering term.
- *Page table*—The data structure maintained by the OS to manage translating from virtual to real memory.

- *Segment*—A block within virtual memory. Virtual memory is divided into blocks to minimize the space required to translate between virtual and physical addresses.
- *Segmentation fault*—An error raised by the CPU when an illegal memory address is requested.
- *MMU*—A component of the CPU that manages memory address translation. Maintains a cache of recently translated addresses (called the TLB), which stands for the translation lookaside buffer, although that terminology has fallen from fashion.

One term that has not been defined in any technical sense so far in this book is *process*. If you've encountered it before and have been wondering why it has been omitted, it will be introduced properly when we talk about concurrency. For now, consider the terms *process* and its peer *operating system process* to refer to a running program.

6.4.2 *Step 1: Having a process scan its own memory*

Intuitively, a program's memory is a series of bytes that starts at location 0 and ends at location *n*. If a program reports 100 KB of RAM usage, it would seem that *n* would be somewhere near 100,000. Let's test that intuition.

We'll create a small command-line program that looks through memory, starting at location 0 and ending at 10,000. As it's a small program, it shouldn't occupy more than 10,000 bytes. But when executed, the program will not perform as intended. Sadly, it will crash. You'll learn why the crash occurs as you follow through this section.

Listing 6.12 shows the command-line program. You can find its source in ch6/ch6-memscan-1/src/main.rs. The listing scans through a running program's memory byte by byte, starting at 0. It introduces the syntax for creating raw pointers and dereferencing (reading) those.

Listing 6.12 Attempting to scan a running program's memory byte by byte

```
 1 fn main() {
 2     let mut n_nonzero = 0;
 3
 4     for i in 0..10000 {
 5         let ptr = i as *const u8;
 6         let byte_at_addr = unsafe { *ptr };
 7
 8         if byte_at_addr != 0 {
 9             n_nonzero += 1;
10         }
11     }
12
13     println!("non-zero bytes in memory: {}", n_nonzero);
14 }
```

Converts i to a *const T, a raw pointer of type u8 to inspect raw memory addresses. We treat every address as a unit, ignoring the fact that most values span multiple bytes.

Dereferences the pointer, it reads the value at address i. Another way of saying this is "read the value being pointed to."

Listing 6.12 crashes because it is attempting to dereference a NULL pointer. When i equals 0, ptr can't really be dereferenced. Incidentally, this is why all raw pointer dereferences must occur within an unsafe block.

How about we attempt to start from a non-zero memory address? Given that the program is executable code, there should be at least several thousand bytes of non-zero data to iterate through. The following listing scans the process's memory starting from 1 to avoid dereferencing a NULL pointer.

Listing 6.13   Scanning a process's memory

```
 1 fn main() {
 2     let mut n_nonzero = 0;          Starts at 1 rather
 3                                     than 0 to avoid a NULL
 4     for i in 1..10000 {             pointer exception
 5         let ptr = i as *const u8;
 6         let byte_at_addr = unsafe { *ptr };
 7
 8         if byte_at_addr != 0 {
 9             n_nonzero += 1;
10         }
11     }
12
13     println!("non-zero bytes in memory: {}", n_nonzero);
14 }
```

This unfortunately does not completely solve the issue. Listing 6.13 still crashes upon execution, and the number of non-zero bytes is never printed to the console. This is due to what's known as a *segmentation fault.*

Segmentation faults are generated when the CPU and OS detect that your program is attempting to access memory regions that they aren't entitled to. Memory regions are divided into segments. That explains the name.

Let's try a different approach. Rather than attempting to scan through bytes, let's look for the addresses of things that we know exist. We've spent lots of time learning about pointers, so let's put that to use. Listing 6.14 creates several values, examining their addresses.

Every run of listing 6.14 may generate unique values. Here is the output of one run:

```
GLOBAL:    0x7ff6d6ec9310
local_str: 0x7ff6d6ec9314
local_int: 0x23d492f91c
boxed_int: 0x18361b78320
boxed_str: 0x18361b78070
fn_int:    0x23d492f8ec
```

As you can see, values appear to be scattered across a wide range. So despite your program (hopefully) only needing a few kilobytes of RAM, a few variables live in giant locations. These are *virtual addresses.*

As explained in the heap versus stack section, the stack starts at the top of the address space and the heap starts near the bottom. In this run, the highest value is `0x7ff6d6ec9314`. That's approximately $2^{64} \div 2$. That number is due to the OS reserving half of the address space for itself.

The following listing returns the address of several variables within a program to examine its address space. The source for this listing in ch6/ch6-memscan-3/src/main.rs.

> **Listing 6.14   Printing the address of variables within a program**

```
static GLOBAL: i32 = 1000;              ◁──────  Creates a global static, which is a
                                                 global variable in Rust programs
fn noop() -> *const i32 {
    let noop_local = 12345;             ◁──────  Creates a global static, which is a
    &noop_local as *const i32           ◁──────  global variable in Rust programs
}
                                                 Creates a local variable within noop() so that
                                                 something outside of main() has a memory address
fn main() {
    let local_str = "a";
    let local_int = 123;                         Creates various values of
    let boxed_str = Box::new('b');               several types including
    let boxed_int = Box::new(789);               values on the heap
    let fn_int = noop();

    println!("GLOBAL:    {:p}", &GLOBAL as *const i32);
    println!("local_str: {:p}", local_str as *const str);
    println!("local_int: {:p}", &local_int as *const i32);
    println!("boxed_int: {:p}", Box::into_raw(boxed_int));
    println!("boxed_str: {:p}", Box::into_raw(boxed_str));
    println!("fn_int:    {:p}", fn_int);}
```

By now, you should be pretty good at accessing addresses of stored values. There are actually two small lessons that you may have also picked up on:

- *Some memory addresses are illegal.* The OS will shut your program down if it attempts to access memory that is out of bounds.
- *Memory addresses are not arbitrary.* Although values seem to be spread quite far apart within the address space, values are clustered together within pockets.

Before pressing on with the cheat program, let's step back and look at the system that's operating behind the scenes to translate these virtual addresses to real memory.

6.4.3   *Translating virtual addresses to physical addresses*

Accessing data in a program requires virtual addresses—the only addresses that the program itself has access to. These get translated into physical addresses. This process involves a dance between the program, the OS, the CPU, the RAM hardware, and occasionally hard drives and other devices. The CPU is responsible for performing this translation, but the OS stores the instructions.

CPUs contain a *memory management unit* (MMU) that is designed for this one job. For every running program, every virtual address is mapped to a physical address. Those instructions are stored at a predefined address in memory as well. That means, in the worst case, every attempt at accessing memory addresses incurs two memory lookups. But it's possible to avoid the worst case.

The CPU maintains a cache of recently translated addresses. It has its own (fast) memory to speed up accessing memory. For historic reasons, this cache is known as the *translation lookaside buffer*, often abbreviated as TLB. Programmers optimizing for performance need to keep data structures lean and avoid deeply nested structures. Reaching the capacity of the TLB (typically around 100 pages for x86 processors) can be costly.

Looking into how the translation system operates reveals more, often quite complex, details. Virtual addresses are grouped into blocks called *pages*, which are typically 4 KB in size. This practice avoids the need to store a translation mapping for every single variable in every program. Having a uniform size for each page also assists in avoiding a phenomenon known as *memory fragmentation*, where pockets of empty, yet unusable, space appear within available RAM.

> **NOTE**   This is a general guide only. The details of how the OS and CPU cooperate to manage memory differs significantly in some environments. In particular, constrained environments such as microcontrollers can use real addressing. For those interested in learning more, the research field is known as *computer architecture.*

The OS and CPU can play some interesting tricks when data lives within pages of virtual memory. For example

- *Having a virtual address space allows the OS to overallocate.* Programs that ask for more memory than the machine can physically provide are able to be accommodated.
- *Inactive memory pages can be swapped to disk in a byte-for-byte manner until it's requested by the active program.* Swapping is often used during periods of high contention for memory but can be used more generally, depending on an operating system's whims.
- *Other size optimizations such as compression can be performed.* A program sees its memory intact. Behind the scenes, the OS compresses the program's wasteful data usage.
- *Programs are able to share data quickly.* If your program requests a large block of zeroes, say, for a newly created array, the OS might point you towards a page filled with zeroes that is currently being used by three other programs. None of the programs are aware that the others are looking at the same physical memory, and the zeroes have different positions within their virtual address space.

- *Paging can speed up the loading of shared libraries.* As a special case of the previous point, if a shared library is already loaded by another program, the OS can avoid loading it into memory twice by pointing the new program to the old data.

- *Paging adds security between programs.* As you discovered earlier in this section, some parts of the address space are illegal to access. The OS has other attributes that it can add. If an attempt is made to write to a read-only page, the OS terminates the program.

Making effective use of the virtual memory system in day-to-day programs requires thinking about how data is represented in RAM. Here are some guidelines:

- *Keep hot working portions of your program within 4 KB of size.* This maintains fast lookups.

- *If 4 KB is unreasonable for your application, then the next target to keep under is 4 KB * 100.* That rough guide should mean that the CPU can maintain its translation cache (the TLB) in good order to support your program.

- *Avoid deeply nested data structures with pointer spaghetti.* If a pointer points to another page, then performance suffers.

- *Test the ordering of your nested loops.* CPUs read small blocks of bytes, known as a *cache line*, from the RAM hardware. When processing an array, you can take advantage of this by investigating whether you are doing column-wise or row-wise operations.

One thing to note: virtualization makes this situation worse. If you're running an app inside a virtual machine, the hypervisor must also translate addresses for its guest operating systems. This is why many CPUs ship with virtualization support, which can reduce this extra overhead. Running containers within virtual machines adds another layer of indirection and, therefore, latency. For bare-metal performance, run apps on bare metal.

How does an executable file turn into a program's virtual address space?

The layout of executable files (aka binaries) has many similarities to the address space diagram that we saw earlier in the heap versus stack section of the chapter.

While the exact process is dependent on the OS and file format, the following figure shows a representative example. Each of the segments of the address space that we have discussed are described by binary files. When the executable is started, the OS loads the right bytes into the right places. Once the virtual address space is created, the CPU can be told to jump to the start of the .text segment, and the program begins executing.

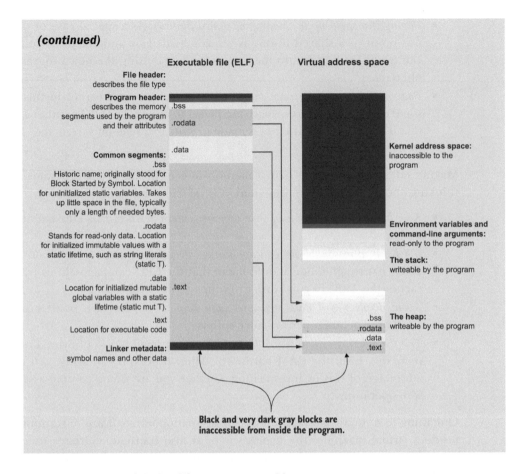

(continued)

Black and very dark gray blocks are inaccessible from inside the program.

6.4.4   *Step 2: Working with the OS to scan an address space*

Our task is to scan our program's memory while it's running. As we've discovered, the OS maintains the instructions for mapping between a virtual address and a physical address. Can we ask the OS to tell us what is happening?

Operating systems provide an interface for programs to be able to make requests; this is known as a *system call*. Within Windows, the KERNEL.DLL provides the necessary functionality to inspect and manipulate the memory of a running process.

NOTE   Why Windows? Well, many Rust programmers use MS Windows as a platform. Also, its functions are well named and don't require as much prior knowledge as the POSIX API.

When you run listing 6.16, you should see lots of output with many sections. This may be similar to the following:

```
MEMORY_BASIC_INFORMATION {
    BaseAddress: 0x00007ffbe8d9b000,
```

This struct is defined within the Windows API.

```
        AllocationBase: 0x0000000000000000,
        AllocationProtect: 0,
        RegionSize: 17568124928,
        State: 65536,
        Protect: 1,
        Type: 0
}
MEMORY_BASIC_INFORMATION {
        BaseAddress: 0x00007fffffe0000,
        AllocationBase: 0x00007fffffe0000,
        AllocationProtect: 2,
        RegionSize: 65536,
        State: 8192,
        Protect: 1,
        Type: 131072
```

> These fields are the integer representations of enums defined in the Windows API. It's possible to decode these to the enum variant names, but this isn't available without adding extra code to the listing.

The following listing shows the dependencies for listing 6.16. You can find its source in ch6/ch6-meminfo-win/Cargo.toml.

Listing 6.15 Dependencies for listing 6.16

```
[package]
name = "meminfo"
version = "0.1.0"
authors = ["Tim McNamara <author@rustinaction.com>"]
edition = "2018"

[dependencies]
winapi = "0.2" #
kernel32-sys = "0.2" #
```

Defines some useful type aliases

Provides interaction with KERNEL.DLL from the Windows API

The following listing shows how to inspect memory via the Windows API. The source code for this listing is in ch6/ch6-meminfo-win/src/main.rs.

Listing 6.16 Inspecting a program's memory

```
use kernel32;
use winapi;

use winapi::{
    DWORD,
    HANDLE,
    LPVOID,
    PVOID,
    SIZE_T,
    LPSYSTEM_INFO,
    SYSTEM_INFO,
    MEMORY_BASIC_INFORMATION as MEMINFO,
};
```

In Rust, this would be a u32.

Pointer types for various internal APIs without an associated type. In Rust, std::os::raw::c_void defines void pointers; a HANDLE is a pointer to some opaque resource within Windows.

In Windows, data type names are often prefixed with a shorthand for their type. P stands for pointer; LP stands for long pointer (e.g., 64 bit).

u64 is the usize on this machine.

A pointer to a SYSTEM_INFO struct

Some structs defined by Windows internally

```
fn main() {
    let this_pid: DWORD;
    let this_proc: HANDLE;
    let min_addr: LPVOID;
    let max_addr: LPVOID;
    let mut base_addr: PVOID;
    let mut proc_info: SYSTEM_INFO;
    let mut mem_info: MEMORY_BASIC_INFORMATION;

    const MEMINFO_SIZE: usize = std::mem::size_of::<MEMINFO>();

    unsafe {
        base_addr = std::mem::zeroed();
        proc_info = std::mem::zeroed();
        mem_info = std::mem::zeroed();
    }

    unsafe {
        this_pid = kernel32::GetCurrentProcessId();
        this_proc = kernel32::GetCurrentProcess();
        kernel32::GetSystemInfo(
          &mut proc_info as LPSYSTEM_INFO
        );
    };

    min_addr = proc_info.lpMinimumApplicationAddress;
    max_addr = proc_info.lpMaximumApplicationAddress;

    println!("{:?} @ {:p}", this_pid, this_proc);
    println!("{:?}", proc_info);
    println!("min: {:p}, max: {:p}", min_addr, max_addr);

    loop {
        let rc: SIZE_T = unsafe {
            kernel32::VirtualQueryEx(
                                    this_proc, base_addr,
                                    &mut mem_info, MEMINFO_SIZE as SIZE_T)
        };

        if rc == 0 {
            break
        }

        println!("{:#?}", mem_info);
        base_addr = ((base_addr as u64) + mem_info.RegionSize) as PVOID;
    }
}
```

Initializes these variables from within unsafe blocks. To make these accessible in the outer scope, these need to be defined here.

This block guarantees that all memory is initialized.

Rather than use a return value, this function makes use of a C idiom to provide its result to the caller. We provide a pointer to some predefined struct, then read that struct's new values once the function returns to see the results.

This block of code is where system calls are made.

Renaming these variables for convenience

This loop does the work of scanning through the address space.

Provides information about a specific segment of the running program's memory address space, starting at base_addr

Finally, we have been able to explore an address space without the OS killing our program. Now the question remains: How do we inspect individual variables and modify those?

6.4.5   *Step 3: Reading from and writing to process memory*

Operating systems provide tools to read and write memory, even in other programs. This is essential for Just-In-Time compilers (JITs), debuggers, and programs to help people "cheat" at games. On Windows, the general process looks something like this in Rust-like pseudocode:

```
let pid = some_process_id;
OpenProcess(pid);

loop address space {
    *call* VirtualQueryEx() to access the next memory segment

    *scan* the segment by calling ReadProcessMemory(),
    looking for a selected pattern

    *call* WriteProcessMemory() with the desired value
}
```

Linux provides an even simpler API via `process_vm_readv()` and `process_vm_writev()`. These are analogous to `ReadProcessMemory()` and `WriteProcessMemory()` in Windows.

Memory management is a complicated area with many levels of abstraction to uncover. This chapter has tried to focus on those elements that are most salient to your work as a programmer. Now, when you read your next blog post on some low-level coding technique, you should be able to follow along with the terminology.

Summary

- Pointers, references, and memory addresses are identical from the CPU's perspective, but these are significantly different at the programming language level.
- Strings and many other data structures are implemented with a backing array pointed to by a pointer.
- The term *smart pointer* refers to data structures that behave like pointers but have additional capabilities. These almost always incur a space overhead. Additionally, data can include integer length and capacity fields or things that are more sophisticated, such as locks.
- Rust has a rich collection of smart pointer types. Types with more features typically incur greater runtime costs.
- The standard library's smart pointer types are built from building blocks that you can also use to define your own smart pointers if required.
- The heap and the stack are abstractions provided by operating systems and programming languages. These do not exist at the level of the CPU.
- Operating systems often provide mechanisms such as memory allocations to inspect a program's behavior.

Files and storage

This chapter covers

- Learning how data is represented on physical storage devices
- Writing data structures to your preferred file format
- Building a tool to read from a file and inspect its contents
- Creating a working key-value store that's immune from corruption

Storing data permanently on digital media is trickier than it looks. This chapter takes you though some of the details. To transfer information held by ephemeral electrical charges in RAM to (semi)permanent storage media and then be able to retrieve it again later takes several layers of software indirection.

The chapter introduces some new concepts such as how to structure projects into library crates for Rust developers. This task is needed because one of the projects is ambitious. By the end of the chapter, you'll have built a working key-value store that's guaranteed to be durable to hardware failure at any stage. During the chapter, we'll work through a small number of side quests. For example, we implement parity bit checking and explore what it means to hash a value. To start with, however, let's see if we can create patterns from the raw byte sequence within files.

7.1 What is a file format?

File formats are standards for working with data as an single, ordered sequence of bytes. Storage media like hard disk drives work faster when reading or writing large blocks of data in serial. This contrasts with in-memory data structures, where data layout has less of an impact.

File formats live in a large design space with trade-offs in performance, human-readability, and portability. Some formats are highly portable and self-describing. Others restrict themselves to being accessible within a single environment and are unable to be read by third-party tools, yet they are high performance.

Table 7.1 illustrates some of the design space for file formats. Each row reveals the file format's internal patterns, which are generated from the same source text. By color-coding each byte within the file, it's possible to see structural differences between each representation.

Table 7.1 The internals of four digital versions of William Shakespeare's *Much Ado About Nothing* produced by Project Gutenberg.

The plain text version of the play contains printable characters only. These are indicated by dark grey for letters and punctuation, and white for whitespace.
Visually, the image appears to be noisy. It lacks internal structure. That's due to the variation in length of the natural language that the file represents. A file with regular, repeating structures, such as a file format designed to hold arrays of floating-point numbers, tends to look quite different.

The EPUB format is actually a compressed ZIP archive with a bespoke file extension. There are many bytes within the file that fall out of the range of the printable category as indicated by the mid-grey pixels.

MOBI includes four bands of NULL bytes (0x00), represented as black pixels. These bands probably represent the result of an engineering trade-off. In some sense, these empty bytes are wasted space. They're probably added as padding so that the file's sections are easy to parse later on.
The other notable feature of this file is its size. It's larger than the other versions of the play. This might imply that the file is harboring more data than just the text. Candidates include display elements like fonts, or encryption keys that enforce anti-copying restrictions within the file.

Table 7.1 The internals of four digital versions of William Shakespeare's *Much Ado About Nothing* **produced by Project Gutenberg.** *(continued)*

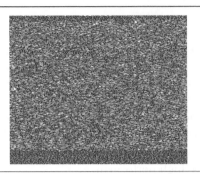	The HTML file contains a high proportion of whitespace characters. These are indicated by white pixels. Markup languages like HTML tend to add whitespace to aid readability.

7.2   *Creating your own file formats for data storage*

When working with data that needs to be stored over a long time, the proper thing to do is to use a battle-tested database. Despite this, many systems use plain text files for data storage. Configuration files, for example, are commonly designed to be both human-readable and machine-readable. The Rust ecosystem has excellent support for converting data to many on-disk formats.

7.2.1   *Writing data to disk with serde and the bincode format*

The serde crate *serializes* and *deserializes* Rust values to and from many formats. Each format has its own strengths: many are human-readable, while others prefer to be compact so that they can be speedily sent across the network.

Using serde takes surprisingly little ceremony. As an example, let's use statistics about the Nigerian city of Calabar and store those in multiple output formats. To start, let's assume that our code contains a City struct. The serde crate provides the Serialize and Deserialize traits, and most code implements these with this derived annotation:

```
#[derive(Serialize)]
struct City {
    name: String,
    population: usize,
    latitude: f64,
    longitude: f64,
}
```

Provides the tooling to enable external formats to interact with Rust code

Populating that struct with data about Calabar is straightforward. This code snippet shows the implementation:

```
let calabar = City {
    name: String::from("Calabar"),
    population: 470_000,
    latitude: 4.95,
    longitude: 8.33,
};
```

Now to convert that `calabar` variable to JSON-encoded `String`. Performing the conversion is one line of code:

```
let as_json = to_json(&calabar).unwrap();
```

serde understands many more formats than JSON. The code in listing 7.2 (shown later in this section) also provides similar examples for two lesser-known formats: CBOR and bincode. CBOR and bincode are more compact than JSON but at the expense of being machine-readable only.

The following shows the output, formatted for the page, that's produced by listing 7.2. It provides a view of the bytes of the `calabar` variable in several encodings:

```
$ cargo run
   Compiling ch7-serde-eg v0.1.0 (/rust-in-action/code/ch7/ch7-serde-eg)
    Finished dev [unoptimized + debuginfo] target(s) in 0.27s
     Running `target/debug/ch7-serde-eg`
json:
{"name":"Calabar","population":470000,"latitude":4.95,"longitude":8.33}

cbor:
[164, 100, 110, 97, 109, 101, 103, 67, 97, 108, 97, 98, 97, 114, 106,
112, 111, 112, 117, 108, 97, 116, 105, 111, 110, 26, 0, 7, 43, 240, 104,
108, 97, 116, 105, 116, 117, 100, 101, 251, 64, 19, 204, 204, 204, 204,
204, 205, 105, 108, 111, 110, 103, 105, 116, 117, 100, 101, 251, 64, 32,
168, 245, 194, 143, 92, 41]

bincode:
[7, 0, 0, 0, 0, 0, 0, 0, 67, 97, 108, 97, 98, 97, 114, 240, 43, 7, 0, 0,
0, 0, 0, 205, 204, 204, 204, 204, 204, 19, 64, 41, 92, 143, 194, 245, 168,
32, 64]

json (as UTF-8):
{"name":"Calabar","population":470000,"latitude":4.95,"longitude":8.33}

cbor (as UTF-8):
�dnamegCalabarjpopulation+��@�����ilongitude�@ ��\)

bincode (as UTF-8):
Calabar�+�����@)\���� @
```

To download the project, enter these commands in the console:

```
$ git clone https://github.com/rust-in-action/code rust-in-action
$ cd rust-in-action/ch7/ch7-serde-eg
```

To create the project manually, create a directory structure that resembles the following snippet and populate its contents with the code in listings 7.1 and 7.2 from the ch7/ch7-serde-eg directory:

```
ch7-serde-eg
├── src
```

```
|
|___ main.rs          ⟵___|    See listing 7.2.
|___ Cargo.toml       ⟵____    See listing 7.1.
```

Listing 7.1   Declaring dependencies and setting metadata for listing 7.2

```
[package]
name = "ch7-serde-eg"
version = "0.1.0"
authors = ["Tim McNamara <author@rustinaction.com>"]
edition = "2018"

[dependencies]
bincode = "1"
serde = "1"
serde_cbor = "0.8"
serde_derive = "1"
serde_json = "1"
```

Listing 7.2   Serialize a Rust struct to multiple formats

```
 1 use bincode::serialize as to_bincode;        These functions are
 2 use serde_cbor::to_vec as to_cbor;           renamed to shorten
 3 use serde_json::to_string as to_json;        lines where used.
 4 use serde_derive::{Serialize};
 5
 6 #[derive(Serialize)]              ⟵____  Instructs the serde_derive
 7 struct City {                             crate to write the necessary
 8     name: String,                         code to carry out the
 9     population: usize,                    conversion from an in-memory
10     latitude: f64,                        City to on-disk City
11     longitude: f64,
12 }
13
14 fn main() {
15     let calabar = City {
16         name: String::from("Calabar"),
17         population: 470_000,
18         latitude: 4.95,
19         longitude: 8.33,
20     };
21
22     let as_json    =    to_json(&calabar).unwrap();      Serializes
23     let as_cbor    =    to_cbor(&calabar).unwrap();      into different
24     let as_bincode = to_bincode(&calabar).unwrap();      formats
25
26     println!("json:\n{}\n", &as_json);
27     println!("cbor:\n{:?}\n", &as_cbor);
28     println!("bincode:\n{:?}\n", &as_bincode);
29     println!("json (as UTF-8):\n{}\n",
30         String::from_utf8_lossy(as_json.as_bytes())
31     );
32     println!("cbor (as UTF-8):\n{:?}\n",
33         String::from_utf8_lossy(&as_cbor)
```

```
34      );
35      println!("bincode (as UTF-8):\n{:?}\n",
36          String::from_utf8_lossy(&as_bincode)
37      );
38 }
```

7.3 *Implementing a hexdump clone*

A handy utility for inspecting a file's contents is hexdump, which takes a stream of bytes, often from a file, and then outputs those bytes in pairs of hexadecimal numbers. Table 7.2 provides an example. As you know from previous chapters, two hexadecimal numbers can represent all digits from 0 to 255, which is the number of bit patterns representable within a single byte. We'll call our clone fview (short for file view).

Table 7.2 fview in operation

fview input	`fn main() {`
	`println!("Hello, world!");`
	`}`

fview output	`[0x00000000] 0a 66 6e 20 6d 61 69 6e 28 29 20 7b 0a 20 20 20`
	`[0x00000010] 20 70 72 69 6e 74 6c 6e 21 28 22 48 65 6c 6c 6f`
	`[0x00000020] 2c 20 77 6f 72 6c 64 21 22 29 3b 0a 7d`

Unless you're familiar with hexadecimal notation, the output from fview can be fairly opaque. If you're experienced at looking at similar output, you may notice that there are no bytes above 0x7e (127). There are also few bytes less than 0x21 (33), with the exception of 0x0a (10). 0x0a represents the newline character (\n). These byte patterns are markers for a plain text input source.

Listing 7.4 provides the source code that builds the complete fview. But because a few new features of Rust need to be introduced, we'll take a few steps to get to the full program.

We'll start with listing 7.3, which uses a string literal as input and produces the output in table 7.2. It demonstrates the use of multiline string literals, importing the std::io traits via std::io::prelude. This enables &[u8] types to be read as files via the std::io::Read trait. The source for this listing is in ch7/ch7-fview-str/src/main.rs.

Listing 7.3 A hexdump clone with hard-coded input that mocks file I/O

```
1 use std::io::prelude::*;
2
3 const BYTES_PER_LINE: usize = 16;
4 const INPUT: &'static [u8] = br#"
5 fn main() {
6     println!("Hello, world!");
7 }"#;
8
9 fn main() -> std::io::Result<()> {
```

prelude imports heavily used traits such as Read and Write in I/O operations. It's possible to include the traits manually, but they're so common that the standard library provides this convenience line to help keep your code compact.

Multiline string literals don't need double quotes escaped when built with raw string literals (the r prefix and the # delimiters). The additional b prefix indicates that this should be treated as bytes (&[u8]) not as UTF-8 text (&str).

```
10        let mut buffer: Vec<u8> = vec!();              ◄─────┐   Makes space for the
11        INPUT.read_to_end(&mut buffer)?;              ◄──┐   │   program's input with
12                                                          │   │   an internal buffer
13        let mut position_in_input = 0;                    │
14        for line in buffer.chunks(BYTES_PER_LINE) {       │       Reads our input and
15            print!("[0x{:08x}] ", position_in_input);  ◄──┤       inserts it into our
16            for byte in line {                            │       internal buffer
17                print!("{:02x} ", byte);
18            }                                                     Writes the current
19            println!();                               ◄───────   position with up to 8
20            position_in_input += BYTES_PER_LINE;                 left-padded zeros
21        }
22                                                          ┌── Shortcut for printing
23        Ok(())                                            │   a newline to stdout
24  }
```

Now that we have seen the intended operation of fview, let's extend its capabilities to
read real files. The following listing provides a basic hexdump clone that demonstrates
how to open a file in Rust and iterate through its contents. You'll find this source in
ch7/ch7-fview/src/main.rs.

Listing 7.4 Opening a file in Rust and iterating through its contents

```
1 use std::fs::File;
2 use std::io::prelude::*;
3 use std::env;                              ┐   Changing this constant
4                                            │   changes the program's
5 const BYTES_PER_LINE: usize = 16;    ◄─────┘   output.
6
7 fn main() {
8   let arg1 = env::args().nth(1);
9
10   let fname = arg1.expect("usage: fview FILENAME");
11
12   let mut f = File::open(&fname).expect("Unable to open file.");
13   let mut pos = 0;
14   let mut buffer = [0; BYTES_PER_LINE];
15
16     while let Ok(_) = f.read_exact(&mut buffer) {
17         print!("[0x{:08x}] ", pos);
18         for byte in &buffer {
19             match *byte {
20                 0x00 => print!(".  "),
21                 0xff => print!("## "),
22                 _ => print!("{:02x} ", byte),
23             }
24         }
25
26         println!("");
27         pos += BYTES_PER_LINE;
28     }
29 }
```

Listing 7.4 introduces some new Rust. Let's look at some of those constructs now:

- `while let Ok(_) { … }`— With this control-flow structure, the program continues to loop until `f.read_exact()` returns `Err`, which occurs when it has run out of bytes to read.
- `f.read_exact()`—This method from the `Read` trait transfers data from the source (in our case, `f`) to the buffer provided as an argument. It stops when that buffer is full.

`f.read_exact()` provides greater control to you as a programmer for managing memory than the `chunks()` option used in listing 7.3, but it comes with some quirks. If the buffer is longer than the number of available bytes to read, the file returns an error, and the state of the buffer is undefined. Listing 7.4 also includes some stylistic additions:

- *To handle command-line arguments without using third-party libraries, we make use of* `std::env::args()`. It returns an iterator over the arguments provided to the program. Iterators have an `nth()` method, which extracts the element at the *n*th position.
- *Every iterator's* `nth()` *method returns an* `Option`. When *n* is larger than the length of the iterator, `None` is returned. To handle these `Option` values, we use calls to `expect()`.
- *The* `expect()` *method is considered a friendlier version of* `unwrap()`. `expect()` takes an error message as an argument, whereas `unwrap()` simply panics abruptly.

Using `std::env::args()` directly means that input is not validated. That's a problem in our simple example, but is something to consider for larger programs.

7.4 *File operations in Rust*

So far in this chapter, we have invested a lot of time considering how data is translated into sequences of bytes. Let's spend some time considering another level of abstraction—the file. Previous chapters have covered basic operations like opening and reading from a file. This section contains some other helpful techniques, which provide more granular control.

7.4.1 *Opening a file in Rust and controlling its file mode*

Files are an abstraction that's maintained by the operating system (OS). It presents a façade of names and hierarchy above a nest of raw bytes.

Files also provide a layer of security. These have attached permissions that the OS enforces. This (in principle, at least) is what prevents a web server running under its own user account from reading files owned by others.

`std::fs::File` is the primary type for interacting with the filesystem. There are two methods available for creating a file: `open()` and `create()`. Use `open()` when you know the file already exists. Table 7.3 explains more of their differences.

Table 7.3 Creating File values in Rust and the effects on the underlying filesystem

Method	Return value when the file already exists	Effect on the underlying file	Return value when no file exists
File::open	Ok(File)*	Opened as is in read-only mode.	Err
File::create	Ok(File)*	All existing bytes are truncated, and the file is opened at the beginning of the new file.	Ok(File)*

* Assuming the user account has sufficient permission.

When you require more control, std::fs::OpenOptions is available. It provides the necessary knobs to turn for any intended application. Listing 7.16 provides a good example of a case where an append mode is requested. The application requires a writeable file that is also readable, and if it doesn't already exist, it's created. The following shows an excerpt from listing 7.16 that demonstrates the use of std::fs:Open-Options to create a writeable file. The file is not truncated when it's opened.

Listing 7.5 Using std::fs:OpenOptions to create a writeable file

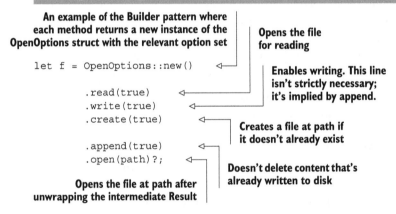

7.4.2 Interacting with the filesystem in a type-safe manner with std::fs::Path

Rust provides type-safe variants of str and String in its standard library: std::path::Path and std::path::PathBuf. You can use these variants to unambiguously work with path separators in a cross-platform way. Path can address files, directories, and related abstractions, such as symbolic links. Path and PathBuf values often start their lives as plain string types, which can be converted with the from() static method:

```
let hello = PathBuf::from("/tmp/hello.txt")
```

From there, interacting with these variants reveals methods that are specific to paths:

```
hello.extension()        ⟵——— Returns Some("txt")
```

The full API is straightforward for anyone who has used code to manipulate paths before, so it won't be fleshed out here. Still, it may be worth discussing why it's included within the language because many languages omit this.

> **NOTE** As an implementation detail, `std::fs::Path` and `std::fs::PathBuf` are implemented on top of `std::ffi::OsStr` and `std::ffi::OsString`, respectively. This means that `Path` and `PathBuf` are *not* guaranteed to be UTF-8 compliant.

Why use `Path` rather than manipulating strings directly? Here are some good reasons for using `Path`:

- *Clear intent*—`Path` provides useful methods like `set_extension()` that describe the intended outcome. This can assist programmers who later read the code. Manipulating strings doesn't provide that level of self-documentation.
- *Portability*—Some operating systems treat filesystem paths as case-insensitive. Others don't. Using one operating system's conventions can result in issues later, when users expect their host system's conventions to be followed. Additionally, path separators are specific to operating systems and, thus, can differ. This means that using raw strings can lead to portability issues. Comparisons require exact matches.
- *Easier debugging*—If you're attempting to extract /tmp from the path /tmp/hello.txt, doing it manually can introduce subtle bugs that may only appear at runtime. Further, miscounting the correct number of index values after splitting the string on / introduces a bug that can't be caught at compile time.

To illustrate the subtle errors, consider the case of separators. Slashes are common in today's operating systems, but those conventions took some time to become established:

- \ is commonly used on MS Windows.
- / is the convention for UNIX-like operating systems.
- : was the path separator for the classic Mac OS.
- > is used in the Stratus VOS operating system.

Table 7.4 compares the two strings: `std::String` and `std::path::Path`.

Table 7.4 Using `std::String` and `std::path::Path` to extract a file's parent directory

```
fn main() {
    let hello = String::from("/tmp/
hello.txt");
    let tmp_dir = hello.split("/").nth(0);
    println!("{:?}", tmp_dir);
}
```
Splits hello at its backslashes, then takes the 0th element of the resulting Vec<String>

Mistake! Prints Some("").

```
use std::path::PathBuf;

fn main() {
    let mut hello = PathBuf::from("/tmp/
hello.txt");
    hello.pop();
    println!("{:?}", hello.display());
}
```
Truncates hello in place

Success! Prints "/tmp".

Table 7.4   Using `std::String` **and** `std::path::Path` **to extract a file's parent directory** *(continued)*

The plain `String` code lets you use familiar methods, but it can introduce subtle bugs that are difficult to detect at compile time. In this instance, we've used the wrong index number to access the parent directory (`/tmp`).	Using `path::Path` doesn't make your code immune to subtle errors, but it can certainly help to minimize their likelihood. `Path` provides dedicated methods for common operations such as setting a file's extension.

7.5   *Implementing a key-value store with a log-structured, append-only storage architecture*

It's time to tackle something larger. Let's begin to lift the lid on database technology. Along the way, we'll learn the internal architecture of a family of database systems using a *log-structured, append-only* model.

Log-structured, append-only database systems are significant as case studies because these are designed to be extremely resilient while offering optimal read performance. Despite storing data on fickle media like flash storage or a spinning hard disk drive, databases using this model are able to guarantee that data will never be lost and that backed up data files will never be corrupted.

7.5.1   *The key-value model*

The key-value store implemented in this chapter, actionkv, stores and retrieves sequences of bytes (`[u8]`) of arbitrary length. Each sequence has two parts: the first is a key and the second is a value. Because the `&str` type is represented as `[u8]` internally, table 7.5 shows the plain text notation rather than the binary equivalent.

Table 7.5   Illustrating keys and values by matching countries with their capital cities

Key	Value
`"Cook Islands"`	`"Avarua"`
`"Fiji"`	`"Suva"`
`"Kiribati"`	`"South Tarawa"`
`"Niue"`	`"Alofi"`

The key-value model enables simple queries such as "What is the capital city of Fiji?" But it doesn't support asking broader queries such as "What is the list of capital cities for all Pacific Island states?"

7.5.2   *Introducing actionkv v1: An in-memory key-value store with a command-line interface*

The first version of our key-value store, actionkv, exposes us to the API that we'll use throughout the rest of the chapter and also introduces the main library code. The library code will not change as the subsequent two systems are built on top of it. Before we get to that code, though, there are some prerequisites that need to be covered.

Unlike other projects in this book, this one uses the library template to start with (cargo new --lib actionkv). It has the following structure:

```
actionkv
├── src
│   ├── akv_mem.rs
│   └── lib.rs
└── Cargo.toml
```

Using a library crate allows programmers to build reusable abstractions within their projects. For our purposes, we'll use the same lib.rs file for multiple executables. To avoid future ambiguity, we need to describe the executable binaries the actionkv project produces.

To do so, provide a bin section within two square bracket pairs ([[bin]]) to the project's Cargo.toml file. See lines 14–16 of the following listing. Two square brackets indicate that the section can be repeated. The source for this listing is in ch7/ch7-actionkv/Cargo.toml.

Listing 7.6   Defining dependencies and other metadata

```
 1 [package]
 2 name = "actionkv"
 3 version = "1.0.0"
 4 authors = ["Tim McNamara <author@rustinaction.com>"]
 5 edition = "2018"
 6
 7 [dependencies]
 8 byteorder = "1.2"
 9 crc = "1.7"
10
11 [lib]
12 name = "libactionkv"
13 path = "src/lib.rs"
14
15 [[bin]]
16 name = "akv_mem"
17 path = "src/akv_mem.rs"
```

Extends Rust types with extra traits to write those to disk, then reads those back into a program in a repeatable, easy-to-use way

Provides the checksum functionality that we want to include

This section of Cargo.toml lets you define a name for the library you're building. Note that a crate can only have one library.

A [[bin]] section, of which there can be many, defines an executable file that's built from this crate. The double square bracket syntax is required because it unambiguously describes bin as having one or more elements.

Our actionkv project will end up with several files. Figure 7.1 illustrates the relationships and how these work together to build the akv_mem executable, referred to within the [[bin]] section of the project's Cargo.toml file.

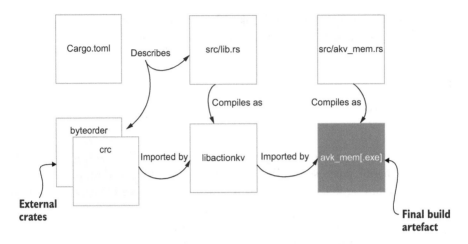

Figure 7.1 An outline of how the different files and their dependencies work together in the actionkv project. The project's Cargo.toml coordinates lots of activity that ultimately results in an executable.

7.6   *Actionkv v1: The front-end code*

The public API of actionkv is comprised of four operations: get, delete, insert, and update. Table 7.6 describes these operations.

Table 7.6 Operations supported by actionkv v1

Command	Description
get <key>	Retrieves the value at key from the store
insert <key> <value>	Adds a key-value pair to the store
delete <key>	Removes a key-value pair from the store
update <key> <value>	Replaces an old value with a new one

> **Naming is difficult**
>
> To access stored key-value pairs, should the API provide a get, retrieve, or, perhaps, fetch? Should setting values be insert, store, or set? actionkv attempts to stay neutral by deferring these decisions to the API provided by std::collections:: HashMap.

The following listing, an excerpt from listing 7.8, shows the naming considerations mentioned in the preceding sidebar. For our project, we use Rust's matching facilities to efficiently work with the command-line arguments and to dispatch to the correct internal function.

Listing 7.7 Demonstrating the public API

```
32 match action {
33   "get" => match store.get(key).unwrap() {
34     None => eprintln!("{:?} not found", key),
35     Some(value) => println!("{:?}", value),
36   },
37
38   "delete" => store.delete(key).unwrap(),
39
40   "insert" => {
41     let value = maybe_value.expect(&USAGE).as_ref();
42     store.insert(key, value).unwrap()
43   }
44
45   "update" => {
46     let value = maybe_value.expect(&USAGE).as_ref();
47     store.update(key, value).unwrap()
48   }
49
50   _ => eprintln!("{}", &USAGE),
51 }
```

The action command-line argument has the type &str.

println! needs to use the Debug syntax ({:?}) because [u8] contains arbitrary bytes and doesn't implement Display.

A future update that can be added for compatibility with Rust's HashMap, where insert returns the old value if it exists.

In full, listing 7.8 presents the code for actionkv v1. Notice that the heavy lifting of interacting with the filesystem is delegated to an instance of `ActionKV` called `store`. How `ActionKV` operates is explained in section 7.7. The source for this listing is in ch7/ch7-actionkv1/src/akv_mem.rs.

Listing 7.8 In-memory key-value store command-line application

```
1 use libactionkv::ActionKV;
2
3 #[cfg(target_os = "windows")]
4 const USAGE: &str = "
5 Usage:
6     akv_mem.exe FILE get KEY
7     akv_mem.exe FILE delete KEY
8     akv_mem.exe FILE insert KEY VALUE
9     akv_mem.exe FILE update KEY VALUE
10 ";
11
12 #[cfg(not(target_os = "windows"))]
13 const USAGE: &str = "
14 Usage:
15     akv_mem FILE get KEY
16     akv_mem FILE delete KEY
17     akv_mem FILE insert KEY VALUE
18     akv_mem FILE update KEY VALUE
19 ";
20
21 fn main() {
22   let args: Vec<String> = std::env::args().collect();
23   let fname = args.get(1).expect(&USAGE);
```

Although src/lib.rs exists within our project, it's treated the same as any other crate within the src/bin.rs file.

The cfg attribute allows Windows users to see the correct file extension in their help documentation. This attribute is explained in the next section.

```
24    let action = args.get(2).expect(&USAGE).as_ref();
25    let key = args.get(3).expect(&USAGE).as_ref();
26    let maybe_value = args.get(4);
27
28    let path = std::path::Path::new(&fname);
29    let mut store = ActionKV::open(path).expect("unable to open file");
30    store.load().expect("unable to load data");
31
32    match action {
33      "get" => match store.get(key).unwrap() {
34        None => eprintln!("{:?} not found", key),
35        Some(value) => println!("{:?}", value),
36      },
37
38      "delete" => store.delete(key).unwrap(),
39
40      "insert" => {
41        let value = maybe_value.expect(&USAGE).as_ref();
42        store.insert(key, value).unwrap()
43      }
44
45      "update" => {
46        let value = maybe_value.expect(&USAGE).as_ref();
47        store.update(key, value).unwrap()
48      }
49
50      _ => eprintln!("{}", &USAGE),
51    }
52 }
```

7.6.1 *Tailoring what is compiled with conditional compilation*

Rust provides excellent facilities for altering what is compiled depending on the *compiler target architecture*. Generally, this is the target's OS but can be facilities provided by its CPU. Changing what is compiled depending on some compile-time condition is known as *conditional compilation*.

To add conditional compilation to your project, annotate your source code with cfg attributes. cfg works in conjunction with the target parameter provided to rustc during compilation.

Listing 7.8 provides a usage string common as quick documentation for command-line utilities for multiple operating systems. It's replicated in the following listing, which uses conditional compilation to provide two definitions of const USAGE in the code. When the project is built for Windows, the usage string contains a .exe file extension. The resulting binary files include only the data that is relevant for their target.

Listing 7.9 Demonstrating the use of conditional compilation

```
3 #[cfg(target_os = "windows")]
4 const USAGE: &str = "
5 Usage:
6     akv_mem.exe FILE get KEY
```

```
 7     akv_mem.exe FILE delete KEY
 8     akv_mem.exe FILE insert KEY VALUE
 9     akv_mem.exe FILE update KEY VALUE
10  ";
11
12  #[cfg(not(target_os = "windows"))]
13  const USAGE: &str = "
14  Usage:
15      akv_mem FILE get KEY
16      akv_mem FILE delete KEY
17      akv_mem FILE insert KEY VALUE
18      akv_mem FILE update KEY VALUE
19  ";
```

There is no negation operator for these matches. That is, `#[cfg(target_os != "windows")]` does not work. Instead, there is a function-like syntax for specifying matches. Use `#[cfg(not(...))]` for negation. `#[cfg(all(...))]` and `#[cfg(any(...))]` are also available to match elements of a list. Lastly, it's possible to tweak `cfg` attributes when invoking cargo or rustc via the `--cfg ATTRIBUTE` command-line argument.

The list of conditions that can trigger compilation changes is extensive. Table 7.7 outlines several of these.

Table 7.7 Options available to match against with `cfg` attributes

Attribute	Valid options	Notes
target_arch	aarch64, arm, mips, powerpc, powerpc64, x86, x86_64	Not an exclusive list.
target_os	android, bitrig, dragonfly, freebsd, haiku, ios, linux, macos, netbsd, redox, openbsd, windows	Not an exclusive list.
target_family	unix, windows	
target_env	"", gnu, msvc, musl	This is often an empty string ("").
target_endian	big, little	
target_pointer_width	32, 64	The size (in bits) of the target architecture's pointer. Used for `isize`, `usize`, `* const`, and `* mut` types.
target_has_atomic	8, 16, 32, 64, ptr	Integer sizes that have support for atomic operations. During atomic operations, the CPU takes responsibility for preventing race conditions with shared data at the expense of performance. The word *atomic* is used in the sense of indivisible.

Table 7.7   Options available to match against with `cfg` attributes *(continued)*

Attribute	Valid options	Notes
`target_vendor`	`apple, pc, unknown`	
`test`		No available options; just uses a simple Boolean check.
`debug_assertions`		No available options; just uses a simple Boolean check. This attribute is present for non-optimized builds and supports the `debug_assert!` macro.

7.7   Understanding the core of actionkv: The libactionkv crate

The command-line application built in section 7.6 dispatches its work to `libactionkv::ActionKV`. The responsibilities of the `ActionKV` struct are to manage interactions with the filesystem and to encode and decode data from the on-disk format. Figure 7.2 depicts the relationships.

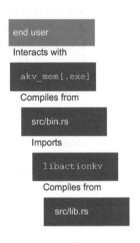

Figure 7.2   Relationship between `libactionkv` and other components of the actionkv project

7.7.1   Initializing the ActionKV struct

Listing 7.10, an excerpt from listing 7.8, shows the initialization process of `libactionkv::ActionKV`. To create an instance of `libactionkv::ActionKV`, we need to do the following:

1 Point to the file where the data is stored
2 Load an in-memory index from the data within the file

Listing 7.10   Initializing `libactionkv::ActionKV`

```
30 let mut store = ActionKV::open(path)          Opens the file at path
31               .expect("unable to open file");
32
33 store.load().expect("unable to load data");   Creates an in-memory index by
                                                  loading the data from path
```

Both steps return `Result`, which is why the calls to `.expect()` are also present. Let's now look inside the code of `ActionKV::open()` and `ActionKV::load()`. `open()` opens the file from disk, and `load()` loads the offsets of any pre-existing data into an in-memory index. The code uses two type aliases, `ByteStr` and `ByteString`:

```
type ByteStr = [u8];
```

We'll use the `ByteStr` type alias for data that tends to be used as a string but happens to be in a binary (raw bytes) form. Its text-based peer is the built-in `str`. Unlike `str`, `ByteStr` is not guaranteed to contain valid UTF-8 text.

Both `str` and `[u8]` (or its alias `ByteStr`) are seen in the wild as `&str` and `&[u8]` (or `&ByteStr`). These are both called *slices*.

```
type ByteString = Vec<u8>;
```

The alias `ByteString` will be the workhorse when we want to use a type that behaves like a `String`. It's also one that can contain arbitrary binary data. The following listing, an excerpt from listing 7.16, demonstrates the use of `ActionKV::open()`.

Listing 7.11 Using `ActionKV::open()`

```
12 type ByteString = Vec<u8>;          ◁──┐   This code processes lots of Vec<u8> data.
13                                          Because that's used in the same way as String
14 type ByteStr = [u8];                     tends to be used, ByteString is a useful alias.
15
16 #[derive(Debug, Serialize, Deserialize)]  ◁──
17 pub struct KeyValuePair {                       Instructs the compiler to generate
18     pub key: ByteString,                         serialized code to enable writing
19     pub value: ByteString,                       KeyValuePair data to disk. Serialize
20 }                                                and Deserialize are explained in
21                                                  section 7.2.1.
22 #[derive(Debug)]
23 pub struct ActionKV {
24     f: File,
25     pub index: HashMap<ByteString, u64>,   ◁──   Maintains a mapping
26 }                                                between keys and
27                                                  file locations
28 impl ActionKV {
29     pub fn open(path: &Path) -> io::Result<Self> {
30         let f = OpenOptions::new()
31                     .read(true)
32                     .write(true)
33                     .create(true)
34                     .append(true)
35                     .open(path)?;
36         let index = HashMap::new();
37         Ok(ActionKV { f, index })
38     }
                                              ActionKV::load() populates the
                                              index of the ActionKV struct,
79 pub fn load(&mut self) -> io::Result<()> {  ◁──┘  mapping keys to file positions.
80
81   let mut f = BufReader::new(&mut self.f);          File::seek() returns the
82                                                      number of bytes from the
83   loop {                                             start of the file. This becomes
84     let position = f.seek(SeekFrom::Current(0))?;  ◁──┘  the value of the index.
85
86     let maybe_kv = ActionKV::process_record(&mut f);   ◁──
87                                               ActionKV::process_record() reads a record
88     let kv = match maybe_kv {                 in the file at its current position.
```

ByteStr is to &str what ByteString is to Vec<u8>.

```
 89        Ok(kv) => kv,
 90        Err(err) => {
 91          match err.kind() {
 92            io::ErrorKind::UnexpectedEof => {
 93              break;
 94            }
 95            _ => return Err(err),
 96          }
 97        }
 98      };
 99
100      self.index.insert(kv.key, position);
101    }
102
103    Ok(())
104  }
```

Unexpected is relative. The application might not have expected to encounter the end of the file, but we expect files to be finite, so we'll deal with that eventuality.

What is EOF?

File operations in Rust might return an error of type `std::io::ErrorKind::UnexpectedEof`, but what is `Eof`? The end of file (EOF) is a convention that operating systems provide to applications. There is no special marker or delimiter at the end of a file within the file itself.

EOF is a zero byte (`0u8`). When reading from a file, the OS tells the application how many bytes were successfully read from storage. If no bytes were successfully read from disk, yet no error condition was detected, then the OS and, therefore, the application assume that EOF has been reached.

This works because the OS has the responsibility for interacting with physical devices. When a file is read by an application, the application notifies the OS that it would like to access the disk.

7.7.2 *Processing an individual record*

actionkv uses a published standard for its on-disk representation. It is an implementation of the Bitcask storage backend that was developed for the original implementation of the Riak database. Bitcask belongs to a family of file formats known in the literature as *Log-Structured Hash Tables*.

What is Riak?

Riak, a NoSQL database, was developed during the height of the NoSQL movement and competed against similar systems such as MongoDB, Apache CouchDB, and Tokyo Tyrant. It distinguished itself with its emphasis on resilience to failure.

Although it was slower than its peers, it guaranteed that it never lost data. That guarantee was enabled in part because of its smart choice of a data format.

Bitcask lays every record in a prescribed manner. Figure 7.3 illustrates a single record in the Bitcask file format.

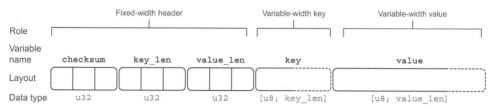

Specifying an array's type with a variable is not legal Rust but is added here to demonstrate the relationship between the header and the body of each record.

Figure 7.3 A single record in the Bitcask file format. To parse a record, read the header information, then use that information to read the body. Lastly, verify the body's contents with the checksum provided in the header.

Every key-value pair is prefixed by 12 bytes. Those bytes describe its length (key_len + val_len) and its content (checksum).

The process_record() function does the processing for this within ActionKV. It begins by reading 12 bytes that represent three integers: a checksum, the length of the key, and the length of the value. Those values are then used to read the rest of the data from disk and verify what's intended. The following listing, an extract from listing 7.16, shows the code for this process.

Listing 7.12 Focusing on the `ActionKV::process_record()` method

```
43 fn process_record<R: Read>(              f may be any type that implements Read, such as
44   f: &mut R                            ◁── a type that reads files, but can also be &[u8].
45 ) -> io::Result<KeyValuePair> {
46    let saved_checksum =
47       f.read_u32::<LittleEndian>()?;        The byteorder crate allows
48    let key_len =                            on-disk integers to be read
49       f.read_u32::<LittleEndian>()?;        in a deterministic manner
50    let val_len =                            as discussed in the
51       f.read_u32::<LittleEndian>()?;        following section.
52    let data_len = key_len + val_len;
53
54    let mut data = ByteString::with_capacity(data_len as usize);
55
56    {
57      f.by_ref()                         ◁──   f.by_ref() is required because take(n)
58        .take(data_len as u64)                 creates a new Read value. Using a
59        .read_to_end(&mut data)?;              reference within this short-lived
60    }                                          block sidesteps ownership issues.
```

```
61        debug_assert_eq!(data.len(), data_len as usize);        ◄─┐  debug_assert! tests
62                                                                   │  are disabled in
63        let checksum = crc32::checksum_ieee(&data);                │  optimized builds,
64        if checksum != saved_checksum {                            │  enabling debug
65          panic!(                                                  │  builds to have more
66            "data corruption encountered ({:08x} != {:08x})",      │  runtime checks.
67            checksum, saved_checksum
68          );
69        }
70
71        let value = data.split_off(key_len as usize);          ◄─┐  The split_off(n)
72        let key = data;                                           │  method splits a
73                                                                   │  Vec<T> in two
74        Ok( KeyValuePair { key, value } )                         │  at n.
75  }
```

A checksum (a number) verifies that the bytes read from disk are the
same as what was intended. This process is discussed in section 7.7.4.

7.7.3   *Writing multi-byte binary data to disk in a guaranteed byte order*

One challenge that our code faces is that it needs to be able to store multi-byte data to
disk in a deterministic way. This sounds easy, but computing platforms differ as to how
numbers are read. Some read the 4 bytes of an i32 from left to right; others read from
right to left. That could potentially be a problem if the program is designed to be written by one computer and loaded by another.

The Rust ecosystem provides some support here. The byteorder crate can extend
types that implement the standard library's std::io::Read and std::io::Write traits.
std::io::Read and std::io::Write are commonly associated with std::io::File
but are also implemented by other types such as [u8] and TcpStream. The extensions can guarantee how multi-byte sequences are interpreted, either as little endian
or big endian.

To follow what's going on with our key-value store, it will help to have an understanding of how byteorder works. Listing 7.14 is a toy application that demonstrates
the core functionality. Lines 11–23 show how to write to a file and lines 28–35 show
how to read from one. The two key lines are

```
use byteorder::{LittleEndian};
use byteorder::{ReadBytesExt, WriteBytesExt};
```

byteorder::LittleEndian and its peers BigEndian and NativeEndian (not used in
listing 7.14) are types that declare how multi-byte data is written to and read from
disk. byteorder::ReadBytesExt and byteorder::WriteBytesExt are traits. In some
sense, these are invisible within the code.

These extend methods to primitive types such as f32 and i16 without further ceremony. Bringing those into scope with a use statement immediately adds powers to the
types that are implemented within the source of byteorder (in practice, that means
primitive types). Rust, as a statically-typed language, makes this transformation at

compile time. From the running program's point of view, integers always have the ability to write themselves to disk in a predefined order.

When executed, listing 7.14 produces a visualization of the byte patterns that are created by writing `1_u32`, `2_i8`, and `3.0_f32` in little-endian order. Here's the output:

```
[1, 0, 0, 0]
[1, 0, 0, 0, 2]
[1, 0, 0, 0, 2, 0, 0, 0, 0, 0, 0, 8, 64]
```

The following listing shows the metadata for the project in listing 7.14. You'll find the source code for the following listing in ch7/ch7-write123/Cargo.toml. The source code for listing 7.14 is in ch7/ch7-write123/src/main.rs.

Listing 7.13   Metadata for listing 7.14

```
[package]
name = "write123"
version = "0.1.0"
authors = ["Tim McNamara <author@rustinaction.com>"]
edition = "2018"

[dependencies]
byteorder = "1.2"
```

Listing 7.14   Writing integers to disk

As files support the ability to seek(), moving backward and forward to different positions, something is necessary to enable a Vec<T> to mock being a file. io::Cursor plays that role, enabling an in-memory Vec<T> to be file-like.

Used as a type argument for a program's various read_*() and write_*() methods

```
 1 use std::io::Cursor;
 2 use byteorder::{LittleEndian};
 3 use byteorder::{ReadBytesExt, WriteBytesExt};
 4
 5 fn write_numbers_to_file() -> (u32, i8, f64) {
 6   let mut w = vec![];
 7
 8   let one: u32   = 1;
 9   let two: i8    = 2;
10   let three: f64 = 3.0;
11
12   w.write_u32::<LittleEndian>(one).unwrap();
13   println!("{:?}", &w);
14
15   w.write_i8(two).unwrap();
16   println!("{:?}", &w);
17
18   w.write_f64::<LittleEndian>(three).unwrap();
19   println!("{:?}", &w);
20
21   (one, two, three)
```

Traits that provide read_*() and write_*()

The variable w stands for writer.

Single byte types i8 and u8 don't take an endianness parameter.

Writes values to disk. These methods return io::Result, which we swallow here as these won't fail unless something is seriously wrong with the computer that's running the program.

```
22 }
23
24 fn read_numbers_from_file() -> (u32, i8, f64) {
25   let mut r = Cursor::new(vec![1, 0, 0, 0, 2, 0, 0, 0, 0, 0, 0, 8, 64]);
26   let one_ = r.read_u32::<LittleEndian>().unwrap();
27   let two_ = r.read_i8().unwrap();
28   let three_ = r.read_f64::<LittleEndian>().unwrap();
29
30   (one_, two_, three_)
31 }
32
33 fn main() {
34   let (one, two, three) = write_numbers_to_file();
35   let (one_, two_, three_) = read_numbers_from_file();
36
37   assert_eq!(one, one_);
38   assert_eq!(two, two_);
39   assert_eq!(three, three_);
40 }
```

7.7.4 *Validating I/O errors with checksums*

actionkv v1 has no method of validating that what it has read from disk is what was written to disk. What if something is interrupted during the original write? We may not be able to recover the original data if this is the case, but if we could recognize the issue, then we would be in a position to alert the user.

A well-worn path to overcome this problem is to use a technique called a *checksum*. Here's how it works:

- *Saving to disk*—Before data is written to disk, a checking function (there are many options as to which function) is applied to those bytes. The result of the checking function (the checksum) is written alongside the original data.

  No checksum is calculated for the bytes of the checksum. If something breaks while writing the checksum's own bytes to disk, this will be noticed later as an error.

- *Reading from disk*—Read the data and the saved checksum, applying the checking function to the data. Then compare the results of the two checking functions. If the two results do not match, an error has occurred, and the data should be considered corrupted.

Which checking function should you use? Like many things in computer science, it depends. An ideal checksum function would

- Return the same result for the same input
- Always return a different result for different inputs
- Be fast
- Be easy to implement

Table 7.8 compares the different checksum approaches. To summarize

- The parity bit is easy and fast, but it is somewhat prone to error.
- CRC32 (cyclic redundancy check returning 32 bits) is much more complex, but its results are more trustworthy.
- Cryptographic hash functions are more complex still. Although being significantly slower, they provide high levels of assurance.

Table 7.8   A simplistic evaluation of different checksum functions

Checksum technique	Size of result	Simplicity	Speed	Reliability
Parity bit	1 bit	★★★★★	★★★★★	★★☆☆☆
CRC32	32 bits	★★★☆☆	★★★★☆	★★★☆☆
Cryptographic hash function	128–512 bits (or more)	★☆☆☆☆	★★☆☆☆	★★★★★

Functions that you might see in the wild depend on your application domain. More traditional areas might see the use of simpler systems, such as a parity bit or CRC32.

IMPLEMENTING PARITY BIT CHECKING

This section describes one of the simpler checksum schemes: *parity checking*. Parity checks count the number of 1s within a bitstream. These store a bit that indicates whether the count was even or odd.

Parity bits are traditionally used for error detection within noisy communication systems, such as transmitting data over analog systems such as radio waves. For example, the ASCII encoding of text has a particular property that makes it quite convenient for this scheme. Its 128 characters only require 7 bits of storage ($128 = 2^7$). That leaves 1 spare bit in every byte.

Systems can also include parity bits in larger streams of bytes. Listing 7.15 presents an (overly chatty) implementation. The `parity_bit()` function in lines 1–10 takes an arbitrary stream of bytes and returns a u8, indicating whether the count of the input's bits was even or odd. When executed, listing 7.15 produces the following output:

```
input: [97, 98, 99]
97 (0b01100001) has 3 one bits
98 (0b01100010) has 3 one bits
99 (0b01100011) has 4 one bits
output: 00000001
```

input: [97, 98, 99] represents
b"abc" as seen by the internals
of the Rust compiler.

```
input: [97, 98, 99, 100]
97 (0b01100001) has 3 one bits
98 (0b01100010) has 3 one bits
99 (0b01100011) has 4 one bits
100 (0b01100100) has 3 one bits
result: 00000000
```

input: [97, 98, 99,
100] represents
b"abcd".

NOTE   The code for the following listing is in ch7/ch7-paritybit/src/main.rs.

Listing 7.15   Implementing parity bit checking

All of Rust's integer types come equipped with
count_ones() and count_zeros() methods.

Takes a byte slice as the bytes
argument and returns a single
byte as output. This function could
have easily returned a bool value,
but returning u8 allows the result
to bit shift into some future
desired position.

```
 1 fn parity_bit(bytes: &[u8]) -> u8 {
 2   let mut n_ones: u32 = 0;
 3
 4   for byte in bytes {
 5     let ones = byte.count_ones();
 6     n_ones += ones;
 7     println!("{} (0b{:08b}) has {} one bits", byte, byte, ones);
 8   }
 9   (n_ones % 2 == 0) as u8
10 }
11
12 fn main() {
13   let abc = b"abc";
14   println!("input: {:?}", abc);
15   println!("output: {:08x}", parity_bit(abc));
16   println!();
17   let abcd = b"abcd";
18   println!("input: {:?}", abcd);
19   println!("result: {:08x}", parity_bit(abcd))
20 }
```

There are plenty of methods to optimize this
function. One fairly simple approach is to hard
code a const [u8; 256] array of 0s and 1s,
corresponding to the intended result, then
index that array with each byte.

7.7.5   *Inserting a new key-value pair into an existing database*

As discussed in section 7.6, there are four operations that our code needs to support: insert, get, update, and delete. Because we're using an append-only design, this means that the last two operations can be implemented as variants of insert.

You may have noticed that during load(), the inner loop continues until the end of the file. This allows more recent updates to overwrite stale data, including deletions. Inserting a new record is almost the inverse of process_record(), described in section 7.7.2. For example

```
164 pub fn insert(
165   &mut self,
166   key: &ByteStr,
167   value: &ByteStr
168 ) -> io::Result<()> {
169   let position = self.insert_but_ignore_index(key, value)?;
170
171   self.index.insert(key.to_vec(), position);
172   Ok(())
173 }
174
175 pub fn insert_but_ignore_index(
176   &mut self,
177   key: &ByteStr,
178   value: &ByteStr
179 ) -> io::Result<u64> {
180   let mut f = BufWriter::new(&mut self.f);
181
```

key.to_vec() converts the
&ByteStr to a ByteString.

The std::io::BufWriter type batches
multiple short write() calls into
fewer actual disk operations,
resulting in a single one. This
increases throughput while keeping
the application code neater.

```
182    let key_len = key.len();
183    let val_len = value.len();
184    let mut tmp = ByteString::with_capacity(key_len + val_len);
185
186    for byte in key {
187        tmp.push(*byte);
188    }
189
190    for byte in value {
191        tmp.push(*byte);
192    }
193
194    let checksum = crc32::checksum_ieee(&tmp);
195
196    let next_byte = SeekFrom::End(0);
197    let current_position = f.seek(SeekFrom::Current(0))?;
198    f.seek(next_byte)?;
199    f.write_u32::<LittleEndian>(checksum)?;
200    f.write_u32::<LittleEndian>(key_len as u32)?;
201    f.write_u32::<LittleEndian>(val_len as u32)?;
202    f.write_all(&mut tmp)?;
203
204    Ok(current_position)
205 }
```

Lines 186–192: **Iterating through one collection to populate another is slightly awkward, but gets the job done.**

7.7.6   *The full code listing for actionkv*

libactionkv performs the heavy lifting in our key-value stores. You have already explored much of the actionkv project throughout section 7.7. The following listing, which you'll find in the file ch7/ch7-actionkv1/src/lib.rs, presents the project code in full.

Listing 7.16   The actionkv project (full code)

```
 1 use std::collections::HashMap;
 2 use std::fs::{File, OpenOptions};
 3 use std::io;
 4 use std::io::prelude::*;
 5 use std::io::{BufReader, BufWriter, SeekFrom};
 6 use std::path::Path;
 7
 8 use byteorder::{LittleEndian, ReadBytesExt, WriteBytesExt};
 9 use crc::crc32;
10 use serde_derive::{Deserialize, Serialize};
11
12 type ByteString = Vec<u8>;
13 type ByteStr = [u8];
14
15 #[derive(Debug, Serialize, Deserialize)]
16 pub struct KeyValuePair {
17   pub key: ByteString,
18   pub value: ByteString,
19 }
20
```

```
21 #[derive(Debug)]
22 pub struct ActionKV {
23   f: File,
24   pub index: HashMap<ByteString, u64>,
25 }
26
27 impl ActionKV {
28   pub fn open(
29     path: &Path
30   ) -> io::Result<Self> {
31     let f = OpenOptions::new()
32       .read(true)
33       .write(true)
34       .create(true)
35       .append(true)
36       .open(path)?;
37     let index = HashMap::new();
38     Ok(ActionKV { f, index })
39   }
40
41   fn process_record<R: Read>(
42     f: &mut R
43   ) -> io::Result<KeyValuePair> {
44     let saved_checksum =
45       f.read_u32::<LittleEndian>()?;
46     let key_len =
47       f.read_u32::<LittleEndian>()?;
48     let val_len =
49       f.read_u32::<LittleEndian>()?;
50     let data_len = key_len + val_len;
51
52     let mut data = ByteString::with_capacity(data_len as usize);
53
54     {
55       f.by_ref()
56         .take(data_len as u64)
57         .read_to_end(&mut data)?;
58     }
59     debug_assert_eq!(data.len(), data_len as usize);
60
61     let checksum = crc32::checksum_ieee(&data);
62     if checksum != saved_checksum {
63       panic!(
64         "data corruption encountered ({:08x} != {:08x})",
65         checksum, saved_checksum
66       );
67     }
68
69     let value = data.split_off(key_len as usize);
70     let key = data;
71
72     Ok(KeyValuePair { key, value })
73   }
74
75   pub fn seek_to_end(&mut self) -> io::Result<u64> {
```

Line 41 annotation: **process_record() assumes that f is already at the right place in the file.**

Line 55 annotation: **f.by_ref() is required because .take(n) creates a new Read instance. Using a reference within this block allows us to sidestep ownership issues.**

```
76      self.f.seek(SeekFrom::End(0))
77    }
78
79    pub fn load(&mut self) -> io::Result<()> {
80      let mut f = BufReader::new(&mut self.f);
81
82      loop {
83        let current_position = f.seek(SeekFrom::Current(0))?;
84
85        let maybe_kv = ActionKV::process_record(&mut f);
86        let kv = match maybe_kv {
87          Ok(kv) => kv,
88          Err(err) => {
89            match err.kind() {
90              io::ErrorKind::UnexpectedEof => {
91                break;
92              }
93              _ => return Err(err),
94            }
95          }
96        };
97
98        self.index.insert(kv.key, current_position);
99      }
100
101     Ok(())
102   }
103
104   pub fn get(
105     &mut self,
106     key: &ByteStr
107   ) -> io::Result<Option<ByteString>> {
108     let position = match self.index.get(key) {
109       None => return Ok(None),
110       Some(position) => *position,
111     };
112
113     let kv = self.get_at(position)?;
114
115     Ok(Some(kv.value))
116   }
117
118   pub fn get_at(
119     &mut self,
120     position: u64
121   ) -> io::Result<KeyValuePair> {
122     let mut f = BufReader::new(&mut self.f);
123     f.seek(SeekFrom::Start(position))?;
124     let kv = ActionKV::process_record(&mut f)?;
125
126     Ok(kv)
127   }
128
129   pub fn find(
130     &mut self,
```

⟵ **"Unexpected" is relative. The application may not have expected it, but we expect files to be finite.**

⟵ **Wraps Option within Result to allow for the possibility of an I/O error as well as tolerating missing values**

```
131       target: &ByteStr
132     ) -> io::Result<Option<(u64, ByteString)>> {
133       let mut f = BufReader::new(&mut self.f);
134
135       let mut found: Option<(u64, ByteString)> = None;
136
137       loop {
138         let position = f.seek(SeekFrom::Current(0))?;
139
140         let maybe_kv = ActionKV::process_record(&mut f);
141         let kv = match maybe_kv {
142           Ok(kv) => kv,
143           Err(err) => {
144             match err.kind() {
145               io::ErrorKind::UnexpectedEof => {
146                 break;
147               }
148               _ => return Err(err),
149             }
150           }
151         };
152
153         if kv.key == target {
154           found = Some((position, kv.value));
155         }
156
157         // important to keep looping until the end of the file,
158         // in case the key has been overwritten
159       }
160
161       Ok(found)
162     }
163
164     pub fn insert(
165       &mut self,
166       key: &ByteStr,
167       value: &ByteStr
168     ) -> io::Result<()> {
169       let position = self.insert_but_ignore_index(key, value)?;
170
171       self.index.insert(key.to_vec(), position);
172       Ok(())
173     }
174
175     pub fn insert_but_ignore_index(
176       &mut self,
177       key: &ByteStr,
178       value: &ByteStr
179     ) -> io::Result<u64> {
180       let mut f = BufWriter::new(&mut self.f);
181
182       let key_len = key.len();
183       let val_len = value.len();
184       let mut tmp = ByteString::with_capacity(key_len + val_len);
185
```

> **"Unexpected" is relative. The application may not have expected it, but we expect files to be finite.** (line 145)

```
186      for byte in key {
187        tmp.push(*byte);
188      }
189
190      for byte in value {
191        tmp.push(*byte);
192      }
193
194      let checksum = crc32::checksum_ieee(&tmp);
195
196      let next_byte = SeekFrom::End(0);
197      let current_position = f.seek(SeekFrom::Current(0))?;
198      f.seek(next_byte)?;
199      f.write_u32::<LittleEndian>(checksum)?;
200      f.write_u32::<LittleEndian>(key_len as u32)?;
201      f.write_u32::<LittleEndian>(val_len as u32)?;
202      f.write_all(&tmp)?;
203
204      Ok(current_position)
205    }
206
207    #[inline]
208    pub fn update(
209      &mut self,
210      key: &ByteStr,
211      value: &ByteStr,
212    ) -> io::Result<()> {
213      self.insert(key, value)
214    }
215
216    #[inline]
217    pub fn delete(
218      &mut self,
219      key: &ByteStr,
220    ) -> io::Result<()> {
221      self.insert(key, b"")
222    }
223  }
```

If you've made it this far, you should congratulate yourself. You've implemented a key-value store that will happily store and retrieve whatever you have to throw at it.

7.7.7 *Working with keys and values with HashMap and BTreeMap*

Working with key-value pairs happens in almost every programming language. For the tremendous benefit of learners everywhere, this task and the data structures that support it have many names:

- You might encounter someone with a computer science background who prefers to use the term *hash table*.
- Perl and Ruby call these *hashes*.
- Lua does the opposite and uses the term *table*.

- Many communities name the structure after a metaphor such as a *dictionary* or a *map*.
- Other communities prefer naming based on the role that the structure plays.
- PHP describes these as *associative arrays*.
- JavaScript's objects tend to be implemented as a key-value pair collection and so the generic term *object* suffices.
- Static languages tend to name these according to how they are implemented.
- C++ and Java distinguish between a *hash map* and a *tree map*.

Rust uses the terms `HashMap` and `BTreeMap` to define two implementations of the same abstract data type. Rust is closest to C++ and Java in this regard. In this book, the terms *collection of key-value pairs* and *associative array* refer to the abstract data type. *Hash table* refers to associative arrays implemented with a hash table, and a `HashMap` refers to Rust's implementation of hash tables.

What is a hash? What is hashing?

If you've ever been confused by the term *hash*, it may help to understand that this relates to an implementation decision made to enable non-integer keys to map to values. Hopefully, the following definitions will clarify the term:

- A `HashMap` *is implemented with a hash function*. Computer scientists will understand that this implies a certain behavior pattern in common cases. A hash map has a constant time lookup in general, formally denoted as $O(1)$ in big O notation. (Although a hash map's performance can suffer when its underlying hash function encounters some pathological cases as we'll see shortly.)
- A hash function *maps between values of variable-length to fixed-length*. In practice, the return value of a hash function is an integer. That fixed-width value can then be used to build an efficient lookup table. This internal lookup table is known as a *hash table*.

The following example shows a basic hash function for `&str` that simply interprets the first character of a string as an unsigned integer. It, therefore, uses the first character of the string as an hash value:

```
fn basic_hash(key: &str) -> u32 {
    let first = key.chars()

                    .next()

                    .unwrap_or('\0');

    u32::from(first)
}
```

The .chars() iterator converts the string into a series of char values, each 4 bytes long.

Returns an Option that's either Some(char) or None for empty strings

Interprets the memory of first as an u32, even though its type is char

If an empty string, provides NULL as the default. unwrap_or() behaves as unwrap() but provides a value rather than panicking when it encounters None.

basic_hash can take any string as input—an infinite set of possible inputs—and return a fixed-width result for all of those in a deterministic manner. That's great! But, although basic_hash is fast, it has some significant faults.

If multiple inputs start with the same character (for example, *Tonga* and *Tuvalu*), these result in the same output. This happens in every instance when an infinite input space is mapped into a finite space, but it's particularly bad here. Natural language text is not uniformly distributed.

Hash tables, including Rust's HashMap, deal with this phenomenon, which is called a *hash collision*. These provide a backup location for keys with the same hash value. That secondary storage is typically a Vec<T> that we'll call the *collision store*. When collisions occur, the collision store is scanned from front to back when it is accessed. That linear scan takes longer and longer to run as the store's size increases. Attackers can make use of this characteristic to overload the computer that is performing the hash function.

In general terms, faster hash functions do less work to avoid being attacked. These will also perform best when their inputs are within a defined range.

Fully understanding the internals of how hash tables are implemented is too much detail for this sidebar. But it's a fascinating topic for programmers who want to extract optimum performance and memory usage from their programs.

7.7.8   *Creating a HashMap and populating it with values*

The next listing provides a collection of key-value pairs encoded as JSON. It uses some Polynesian island nations and their capital cities to show the use of an associative array.

Listing 7.17   Demonstrating the use of an associative array in JSON notation

```json
{
  "Cook Islands": "Avarua",
  "Fiji": "Suva",
  "Kiribati": "South Tarawa",
  "Niue": "Alofi",
  "Tonga": "Nuku'alofa",
  "Tuvalu": "Funafuti"
}
```

Rust does not provide a literal syntax for HashMap within the standard library. To insert items and get them out again, follow the example provided in listing 7.18, whose source is available in ch7/ch7-pacific-basic/src/main.rs. When executed, listing 7.18 produces the following line in the console:

```
Capital of Tonga is: Nuku'alofa
```

Listing 7.18   An example of the basic operations of HashMap

```
1 use std::collections::HashMap;
2
3 fn main() {
```

```
 4    let mut capitals = HashMap::new();
 5
 6    capitals.insert("Cook Islands", "Avarua");
 7    capitals.insert("Fiji", "Suva");
 8    capitals.insert("Kiribati", "South Tarawa");
 9    capitals.insert("Niue", "Alofi");
10    capitals.insert("Tonga", "Nuku'alofa");
11    capitals.insert("Tuvalu", "Funafuti");
12
13    let tongan_capital = capitals["Tonga"];
14
15    println!("Capital of Tonga is: {}", tongan_capital);
16 }
```

Type declarations of keys and values are not required here as these are inferred by the Rust compiler.

HashMap implements Index, which allows for values to be retrieved via the square bracket indexing style.

Writing everything out as method calls can feel needlessly verbose at times. With some support from the wider Rust ecosystem, it's possible to inject JSON string literals into Rust code. It's best that the conversion is done at compile time, meaning no loss of runtime performance. The output of listing 7.19 is also a single line:

```
Capital of Tonga is: "Nuku'alofa"
```

Uses double quotes because the json! macro returns a wrapper around String, its default representation

The next listing uses a serde-json crate to include JSON literals within your Rust source code. Its source code is in the ch7/ch7-pacific-json/src/main.rs file.

Listing 7.19 Including JSON literals with serde-json

```
 1 #[macro_use]
 2 extern crate serde_json;
 3
 4 fn main() {
 5   let capitals = json!({
 6     "Cook Islands": "Avarua",
 7     "Fiji": "Suva",
 8     "Kiribati": "South Tarawa",
 9     "Niue": "Alofi",
10     "Tonga": "Nuku'alofa",
11     "Tuvalu": "Funafuti"
12   });
13
14   println!("Capital of Tonga is: {}", capitals["Tonga"])
15 }
```

Incorporates the serde_json crate and makes use of its macros, bringing the json! macro into scope

json! takes a JSON literal and some Rust expressions to implement String values. It converts these into a Rust value of type serde_json::Value, an enum that can represent every type within the JSON specification.

7.7.9   *Retrieving values from HashMap and BTreeMap*

The main advantage that a key-value store provides is the ability to access its values. There are two ways to achieve this. To demonstrate, let's assume that we have initialized capitals from listing 7.19. The approach (already demonstrated) is to access values via square brackets:

```
capitals["Tonga"]
```

Returns "Nuku'alofa"

This approach returns a read-only reference to the value, which is deceptive when dealing with examples containing string literals because their status as references is somewhat disguised. In the syntax used by Rust's documentation, this is described as &V, where & denotes a read-only reference and V is the type of the value. If the key is not present, the program will panic.

> **NOTE** Index notation is supported by all types that implement the Index trait. Accessing capitals["Tonga"] is syntactic sugar for capitals.index("Tonga").

It's also possible to use the .get() method on HashMap. This returns an Option<&V>, providing the opportunity to recover from cases where values are missing. For example

```
capitals.get("Tonga")        ◄─────────  Returns Some("Nuku'alofa")
```

Other important operations supported by HashMap include

- Deleting key-value pairs with the .remove() method
- Iterating over keys, values, and key-value pairs with the .keys(), .values(), and .iter() methods, respectively, as well as their read-write variants, .keys_mut(), .values_mut(), and .iter_mut()

There is no method for iterating through a subset of the data. For that, we need to use BTreeMap.

7.7.10 How to decide between HashMap and BTreeMap

If you're wondering about which backing data structure to choose, here is a simple guideline: use HashMap unless you have a good reason to use BTreeMap. BTreeMap is faster when there is a natural ordering between the keys, and your application makes use of that arrangement. Table 7.9 highlights the differences.

Let's demonstrate these two use cases with a small example from Europe. The Dutch East India Company, known as VOC after the initials of its Dutch name, Vereenigde Oostindische Compagnie, was an extremely powerful economic and political force at its peak. For two centuries, VOC was a dominant trader between Asia and Europe. It had its own navy and currency, and established its own colonies (called trading posts). It was also the first company to issue bonds. In the beginning, investors from six business chambers (kamers) provided capital for the business.

Let's use these investments as key-value pairs. When listing 7.20 is compiled, it produces an executable that generates the following output:

```
$ cargo run -q
Rotterdam invested 173000
Hoorn invested 266868
Delft invested 469400
Enkhuizen invested 540000
Middelburg invested 1300405
Amsterdam invested 3697915
smaller chambers: Rotterdam Hoorn Delft
```

Listing 7.20 Demonstrating range queries and ordered iteration of `BTreeMap`

```
1 use std::collections::BTreeMap;
2
3 fn main() {
4   let mut voc = BTreeMap::new();
5
6   voc.insert(3_697_915, "Amsterdam");
7   voc.insert(1_300_405, "Middelburg");
8   voc.insert(  540_000, "Enkhuizen");
9   voc.insert(  469_400, "Delft");
10  voc.insert(  266_868, "Hoorn");
11  voc.insert(  173_000, "Rotterdam");
12
13  for (guilders, kamer) in &voc {
14    println!("{} invested {}", kamer, guilders);
15  }
16
17  print!("smaller chambers: ");
18  for (_guilders, kamer) in voc.range(0..500_000) {
19    print!("{} ", kamer);
20  }
21  println!("");
22 }
```

Prints in sorted order

BTreeMap lets you select a portion of the keys that are iterated through with the range syntax.

Table 7.9 Deciding on which implementation to use to map keys to values

`std::collections::HashMap` with a default hash function (known as SipHash in the literature)	Cryptographically secure and resistant to denial of service attacks but slower than alternative hash functions
`std::collections::BTreeMap`	Useful for keys with an inherent ordering, where cache coherence can provide a boost in speed

7.7.11 Adding a database index to actionkv v2.0

Databases and filesystems are much larger pieces of software than single files. There is a large design space involved with storage and retrieval systems, which is why new ones are always being developed. Common to all of those systems, however, is a component that is the real smarts behind the database.

Built in section 7.5.2, actionkv v1 contains a major issue that prevents it from having a decent startup time. Every time it's run, it needs to rebuild its index of where keys are stored. Let's add the ability for actionkv to store its own data that indexes *within* the same file that's used to store its application data. It will be easier than it sounds. No changes to libactionkv are necessary. And the front-end code only requires minor additions. The project folder now has a new structure with an extra file (shown in the following listing).

Listing 7.21   The updated project structure for actionkv v2.0

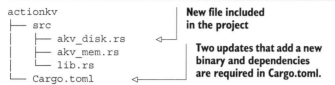

```
actionkv
├── src
│   ├── akv_disk.rs      ◁
│   ├── akv_mem.rs
│   └── lib.rs
└── Cargo.toml           ◁
```

**New file included
in the project**

**Two updates that add a new
binary and dependencies
are required in Cargo.toml.**

The project's Cargo.toml adds some new dependencies along with a second `[[bin]]` entry, as the last three lines of the following listing show. The source for this listing is in ch7/ch7-actionkv2/Cargo.toml.

Listing 7.22   Updating the Cargo.toml file for actionkv v2.0

```toml
[package]
name = "actionkv"
version = "2.0.0"
authors = ["Tim McNamara <author@rustinaction.com>"]
edition = "2018"

[dependencies]
bincode = "1"
byteorder = "1"
crc = "1"
serde = "1"
serde_derive = "1"

[lib]
name = "libactionkv"
path = "src/lib.rs"

[[bin]]
name = "akv_mem"
path = "src/akv_mem.rs"

[[bin]]
name = "akv_disk"
path = "src/akv_disk.rs"
```

**New dependencies to
assist with writing
the index to disk**

**New executable
definition**

When a key is accessed with the get operation, to find its location on disk, we first need to load the index from disk and convert it to its in-memory form. The following listing is an excerpt from listing 7.24. The on-disk implementation of actionkv includes a hidden `INDEX_KEY` value that allows it to quickly access other records in the file.

Listing 7.23   Highlighting the main change from listing 7.8

```
48 match action {
49     "get" => {
50         let index_as_bytes = a.get(&INDEX_KEY)   ◁
51                                 .unwrap()
52                                 .unwrap();
```

**INDEX_KEY is an internal hidden name
of the index within the database.**

**Two unwrap() calls are required
because a.index is a HashMap
that returns Option, and values
themselves are stored within an
Option to facilitate possible
future deletes.**

```
53
54    let index_decoded = bincode::deserialize(&index_as_bytes);
55
56    let index: HashMap<ByteString, u64> = index_decoded.unwrap();
57
58    match index.get(key) {
59      None => eprintln!("{:?} not found", key),
60      Some(&i) => {
61        let kv = a.get_at(i).unwrap();
62        println!("{:?}", kv.value)
63      }
64    }
65  }
```

Retrieving a value now involves fetching the index first, then identifying the correct location on disk.

The following listing shows a key-value store that persists its index data between runs. The source for this listing is in ch7/ch7-actionkv2/src/akv_disk.rs.

Listing 7.24 Persisting index data between runs

```
1 use libactionkv::ActionKV;
2 use std::collections::HashMap;
3
4 #[cfg(target_os = "windows")]
5 const USAGE: &str = "
6 Usage:
7     akv_disk.exe FILE get KEY
8     akv_disk.exe FILE delete KEY
9     akv_disk.exe FILE insert KEY VALUE
10    akv_disk.exe FILE update KEY VALUE
11 ";
12
13 #[cfg(not(target_os = "windows"))]
14 const USAGE: &str = "
15 Usage:
16    akv_disk FILE get KEY
17    akv_disk FILE delete KEY
18    akv_disk FILE insert KEY VALUE
19    akv_disk FILE update KEY VALUE
20 ";
21
22 type ByteStr = [u8];
23 type ByteString = Vec<u8>;
24
25 fn store_index_on_disk(a: &mut ActionKV, index_key: &ByteStr) {
26   a.index.remove(index_key);
27   let index_as_bytes = bincode::serialize(&a.index).unwrap();
28   a.index = std::collections::HashMap::new();
29   a.insert(index_key, &index_as_bytes).unwrap();
30 }
31
32 fn main() {
33   const INDEX_KEY: &ByteStr = b"+index";
34
35   let args: Vec<String> = std::env::args().collect();
```

```
36    let fname = args.get(1).expect(&USAGE);
37    let action = args.get(2).expect(&USAGE).as_ref();
38    let key = args.get(3).expect(&USAGE).as_ref();
39    let maybe_value = args.get(4);
40
41    let path = std::path::Path::new(&fname);
42    let mut a = ActionKV::open(path).expect("unable to open file");
43
44    a.load().expect("unable to load data");
45
46    match action {
47      "get" => {
48        let index_as_bytes = a.get(&INDEX_KEY)
49                                        .unwrap()
50                                        .unwrap();
51
52        let index_decoded = bincode::deserialize(&index_as_bytes);
53
54        let index: HashMap<ByteString, u64> = index_decoded.unwrap();
55
56        match index.get(key) {
57          None => eprintln!("{:?} not found", key),
58          Some(&i) => {
59            let kv = a.get_at(i).unwrap();
60            println!("{:?}", kv.value)           ◁——┐  To print values, we need to
61          }                                           use Debug as an [u8] value
62        }                                             contains arbitrary bytes.
63      }
64
65      "delete" => a.delete(key).unwrap(),
66
67      "insert" => {
68        let value = maybe_value.expect(&USAGE).as_ref();
69        a.insert(key, value).unwrap();
70        store_index_on_disk(&mut a, INDEX_KEY);      ◁——┐
71      }
72                                                          The index must
73      "update" => {                                       also be updated
74        let value = maybe_value.expect(&USAGE).as_ref();  whenever the
75        a.update(key, value).unwrap();                    data changes.
76        store_index_on_disk(&mut a, INDEX_KEY);      ◁——┘
77      }
78      _ => eprintln!("{}", &USAGE),
79    }
80 }
```

Summary

- Converting between in-memory data structures and raw byte streams to be stored in files or sent over the network is known as *serialization* and *deserialization*. In Rust, serde is the most popular choice for these two tasks.
- Interacting with the filesystem almost always implies handling std::io::Result. Result is used for errors that are not part of normal control flow.

- Filesystem paths have their own types: `std::path::Path` and `std::path::PathBuf`. While it adds to the learning burden, implementing these allows you to avoid common mistakes that can occur by treating paths directly as strings.

- To mitigate the risk of data corruption during transit and storage, use checksums and parity bits.

- Using a library crate makes it easier to manage complex software projects. Libraries can be shared between projects, and you can make these more modular.

- There are two primary data structures for handling key-value pairs within the Rust standard library: `HashMap` and `BTreeMap`. Use `HashMap` unless you know that you want to make use of the features offered by `BTreeMap`.

- The `cfg` attribute and `cfg!` macro allow you to compile platform-specific code.

- To print to standard error (stderr), use the `eprintln!` macro. Its API is identical to the `println!` macro that is used to print to standard output (stdout).

- The `Option` type is used to indicate when values may be missing, such as asking for an item from an empty list.

Networking

This chapter covers

- Implementing a networking stack
- Handling multiple error types within local scope
- When to use trait objects
- Implementing state machines in Rust

This chapter describes how to make HTTP requests multiple times, stripping away a layer of abstraction each time. We start by using a user-friendly library, then boil that away until we're left with manipulating raw TCP packets. When we're finished, you'll be able to distinguish an IP address from a MAC address. And you'll learn why we went straight from IPv4 to IPv6.

You'll also learn lots of Rust in this chapter, most of it related to advanced error handling techniques that become essential for incorporating upstream crates. Several pages are devoted to error handling. This includes a thorough introduction to trait objects.

Networking is a difficult subject to cover in a single chapter. Each layer is a fractal of complexity. Networking experts will hopefully overlook my lack of depth in treating such a diverse topic.

Figure 8.1 provides an overview of the topics that the chapter covers. Some of the projects that we cover include implementing DNS resolution and generating standards-compliant MAC addresses, including multiple examples of generating HTTP requests. A bit of a role-playing game is added for light relief.

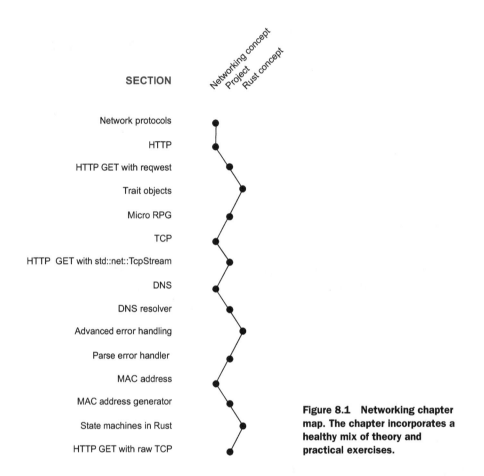

Figure 8.1   Networking chapter map. The chapter incorporates a healthy mix of theory and practical exercises.

8.1 *All of networking in seven paragraphs*

Rather than trying to learn the whole networking stack, let's focus on something that's of practical use. Most readers of this book will have encountered web programming. Most web programming involves interacting with some sort of framework. Let's look there.

HTTP is the protocol that web frameworks understand. Learning more about HTTP enables us to extract the most performance out of our web frameworks. It can also help us to more easily diagnose any problems that occur. Figure 8.2 shows networking protocols for content delivery over the internet.

Networking is comprised of layers. If you're new to the field, don't be intimidated by a flood of acronyms. The most important thing to remember is that lower levels are

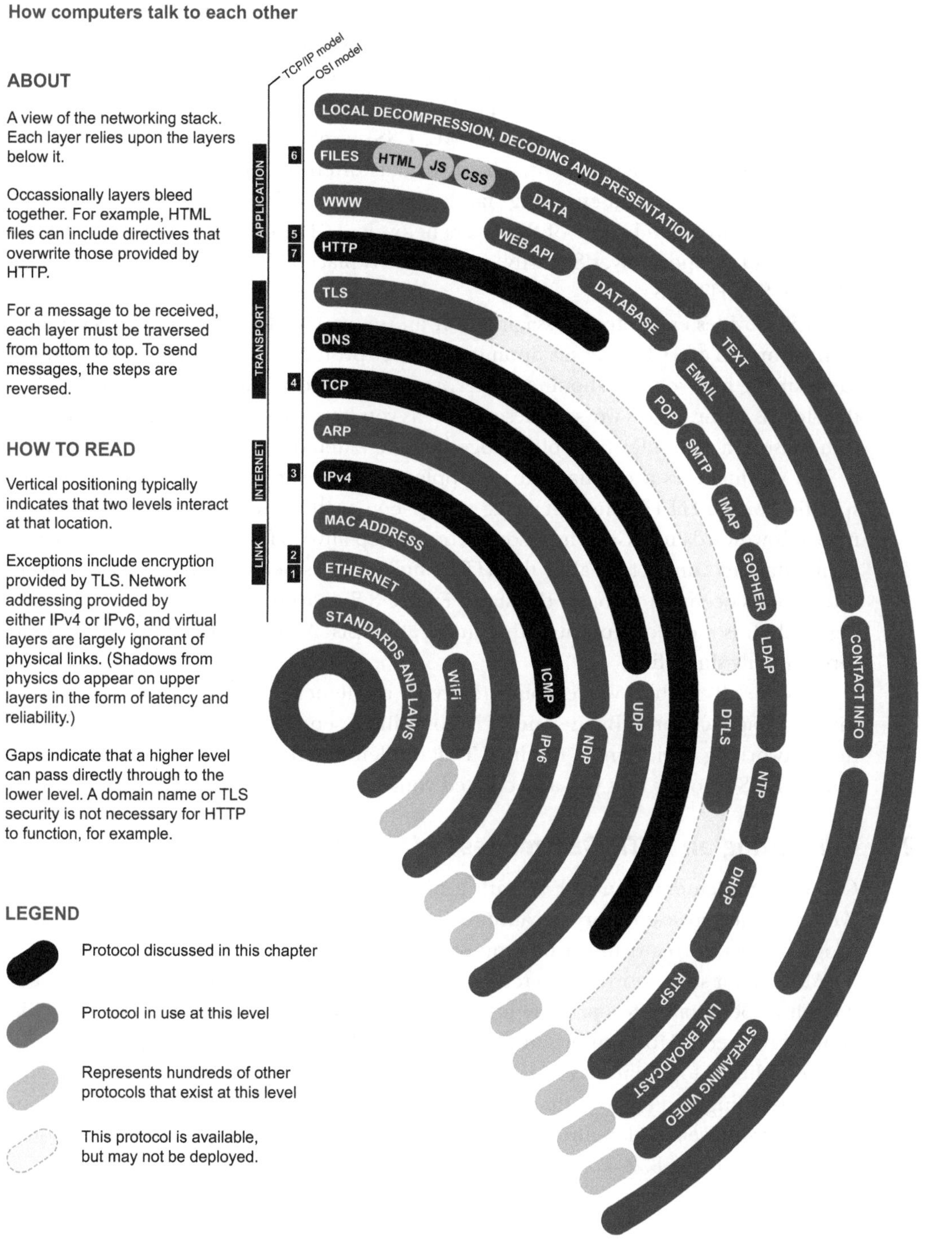

How computers talk to each other

TCP/IP model
OSI model

ABOUT

A view of the networking stack. Each layer relies upon the layers below it.

Occassionally layers bleed together. For example, HTML files can include directives that overwrite those provided by HTTP.

For a message to be received, each layer must be traversed from bottom to top. To send messages, the steps are reversed.

HOW TO READ

Vertical positioning typically indicates that two levels interact at that location.

Exceptions include encryption provided by TLS. Network addressing provided by either IPv4 or IPv6, and virtual layers are largely ignorant of physical links. (Shadows from physics do appear on upper layers in the form of latency and reliability.)

Gaps indicate that a higher level can pass directly through to the lower level. A domain name or TLS security is not necessary for HTTP to function, for example.

LEGEND

Protocol discussed in this chapter

Protocol in use at this level

Represents hundreds of other protocols that exist at this level

This protocol is available, but may not be deployed.

APPLICATION — TRANSPORT — INTERNET — LINK

6 FILES — HTML — JS — CSS
WWW
5 / 7 HTTP
TLS
DNS
4 TCP
ARP
3 IPv4
MAC ADDRESS
2 / 1 ETHERNET
STANDARDS AND LAWS

LOCAL DECOMPRESSION, DECODING AND PRESENTATION
DATA
WEB API
DATABASE
TEXT
EMAIL
POP — SMTP — IMAP — GOPHER — LDAP
CONTACT INFO

WiFi
ICMP
IPv6
NDP
UDP
DTLS
NTP
DHCP
RTSP
LIVE BROADCAST
STREAMING VIDEO

Figure 8.2   Several layers of networking protocols involved with delivering content over the internet. The figure compares some common models, including the seven-layer OSI model and the four-layer TCP/IP model.

unaware of what's happening above them, and higher levels are agnostic to what's happening below them. Lower levels receive a stream of bytes and pass it on. Higher levels don't care how messages are sent; they just want them sent.

Let's consider one example: HTTP. HTTP is known as an *application-level protocol.* Its job is to transport content like HTML, CSS, JavaScript, WebAssembly modules, images, video, and other formats. These formats often include other embedded formats via compression and encoding standards. HTTP itself often redundantly includes information provided by one of the layers below it, TCP. Between HTTP and TCP sits TLS. TLS (Transport Layer Security), which has replaced SSL (Secure Sockets Layer), adds the S to HTTPS.

TLS provides encrypted messaging over an unencrypted connection. TLS is implemented on top of TCP. TCP sits upon many other protocols. These go all the way down to specifying how voltages should be interpreted as 0s and 1s. And yet, as complicated as this story is so far, it gets worse. These layers, as you have probably seen in your dealings with those as a computer user, bleed together like watercolor paint.

HTML includes a mechanism to supplement or overwrite directives omitted or specified within HTTP: the `<meta>` tag's `http-equiv` attribute. HTTP can make adjustments downwards to TCP. The "Connection: keep-alive" HTTP header instructs TCP to maintain its connection after this HTTP message has been received. These sorts of interactions occur all through the stack. Figure 8.2 provides one view of the networking stack. It is more complicated than most attempts. And even that complicated picture is highly simplified.

Despite all of that, we're going to try to implement as many layers as possible within a single chapter. By the end of it, you will be sending HTTP requests with a virtual networking device and a minimal TCP implementation that you created yourself, using a DNS resolver that you also created yourself.

8.2   *Generating an HTTP GET request with reqwest*

Our first implementation will be with a high-level library that is focused on HTTP. We'll use the reqwest library because its focus is primarily on making it easy for Rust programmers to create an HTTP request.

Although it's the shortest, the reqwest implementation is the most feature-complete. As well as being able to correctly interpret HTTP headers, it also handles cases like content redirects. Most importantly, it understands how to handle TLS properly.

In addition to expanded networking capabilities, reqwest also validates the content's encoding and ensures that it is sent to your application as a valid `String`. None of our lower-level implementations do any of that. The following shows the project structure for listing 8.2:

```
ch8-simple/
├── src
│   └── main.rs
└── Cargo.toml
```

The following listing shows the metadata for listing 8.2. The source code for this listing is in ch8/ch8-simple/Cargo.toml.

Listing 8.1 Crate metadata for listing 8.2

```
[package]
name = "ch8-simple"
version = "0.1.0"
authors = ["Tim McNamara <author@rustinaction.com>"]
edition = "2018"

[dependencies]
reqwest = "0.9"
```

The following listing illustrates how to make an HTTP request with the reqwest library. You'll find the source in ch8/ch8-simple/src/main.rs.

Listing 8.2 Making an HTTP request with `reqwest`

```
 1 use std::error::Error;
 2
 3 use reqwest;
 4
 5 fn main() -> Result<(), Box<dyn Error>> {       ◁─┐  Box<dyn Error>
 6    let url = "http://www.rustinaction.com/";        represents a trait
 7    let mut response = reqwest::get(url)?;           object, which we'll
 8                                                     cover in section 8.3.
 9    let content = response.text()?;
10    print!("{}", content);
11
12    Ok(())
13 }
```

If you've ever done any web programming, listing 8.2 should be straightforward. reqwest::get() issues an HTTP GET request to the URL represented by url. The response variable holds a struct representing the server's response. The response .text() method returns a Result that provides access to the HTTP body after validating that the contents are a legal String.

One question, though: What on earth is the error side of the Result return type Box<dyn std::error::Error>? This is an example of a trait object that enables Rust to support polymorphism at runtime. *Trait objects* are proxies for concrete types. The syntax Box<dyn std::error::Error> means a Box (a pointer) to any type that implements std::error:Error's.

Using a library that knows about HTTP allows our programs to omit many details. For example

- *Knowing when to close the connection.* HTTP has rules for telling each of the parties when the connection ends. This isn't available to us when manually making requests. Instead, we keep the connection open for as long as possible and hope that the server will close.

- *Converting the byte stream to content.* Rules for translating the message body from `[u8]` to `String` (or perhaps an image, video, or some other content) are handled as part of the protocol. This can be tedious to handle manually as HTTP allows content to be compressed into several methods and encoded into several plain text formats.
- *Inserting or omitting port numbers.* HTTP defaults to port 80. A library that is tailored for HTTP, such as reqwest, allows you to omit port numbers. When we're building requests by hand with generic TCP crates, however, we need to be explicit.
- *Resolving the IP addresses.* The TCP protocol doesn't actually know about domain names like www.rustinaction.com, for example. The library resolves the IP address for www.rustinaction.com on our behalf.

8.3　Trait objects

This section describes trait objects in detail. You will also develop the world's next best-selling fantasy role-playing game—the rpg project. If you would like to focus on networking, feel free to skip ahead to section 8.4.

There is a reasonable amount of jargon in the next several paragraphs. Brace yourself. You'll do fine. Let's start by introducing trait objects by what they achieve and what they do, rather than focusing on what they are.

8.3.1　What do trait objects enable?

While trait objects have several uses, they are immediately helpful by allowing you to create containers of multiple types. Although players of our role-playing game can choose different races, and each race is defined in its own `struct`, you'll want to treat those as a single type. A `Vec<T>` won't work here because we can't easily have types `T`, `U`, and `V` wedged into `Vec<T>` without introducing some type of wrapper object.

8.3.2　What is a trait object?

Trait objects add a form of *polymorphism*—the ability to share an interface between types—to Rust via *dynamic dispatch*. Trait objects are similar to generic objects. Generics offer polymorphism via *static dispatch*. Choosing between generics and type objects typically involves a trade off between disk space and time:

- Generics use more disk space with faster runtimes.
- Trait objects use less disk space but incur a small runtime overhead caused by pointer indirection.

Trait objects are *dynamically-sized types*, which means that these are always seen in the wild behind a pointer. Trait objects appear in three forms: `&dyn Trait`, `&mut dyn Trait`, and `Box<dyn Trait>`.[1] The primary difference between the three forms is that `Box<dyn Trait>` is an owned trait object, whereas the other two are borrowed.

---

[1] In old Rust code, you may see `&Trait`, and `Box<Trait>`. While legal syntax, these are officially deprecated. Adding dyn keyword is strongly encouraged.

8.3.3 Creating a tiny role-playing game: The rpg project

Listing 8.4 is the start of our game. Characters in the game can be one of three races: humans, elves, and dwarves. These are represented by the Human, Elf, and Dwarf structs, respectively.

Characters interact with things. Things are represented by the Thing type.[2] Thing is an enum that currently represents swords and trinkets. There's only one form of interaction right now: enchantment. Enchanting a thing involves calling the enchant() method:

```
character.enchant(&mut thing)
```

When enchantment is successful, thing glows brightly. When a mistake occurs, thing is transformed into a trinket. Within listing 8.4, we create a party of characters with the following syntax:

```
58 let d = Dwarf {};
59 let e = Elf {};
60 let h = Human {};
61
62 let party: Vec<&dyn Enchanter> = vec![&d, &h, &e];
```

> Although d, e, and h are different types, using the type hint &dyn Enchanter tells the compiler to treat each value as a trait object. These now all have the same type.

Casting the spell involves choosing a spellcaster. We make use of the rand crate for that:

```
58 let spellcaster = party.choose(&mut rand::thread_rng()).unwrap();
59 spellcaster.enchant(&mut it)
```

The choose() method originates from the rand::seq::SliceRandom trait that is brought into scope in listing 8.4. One of the party is chosen at random. The party then attempts to enchant the object it. Compiling and running listing 8.4 results in a variation of this:

```
$ cargo run
 . . .
   Compiling rpg v0.1.0 (/rust-in-action/code/ch8/ch8-rpg)
    Finished dev [unoptimized + debuginfo] target(s) in 2.13s
     Running `target/debug/rpg`
Human mutters incoherently. The Sword glows brightly.

$ target/debug/rpg
Elf mutters incoherently. The Sword fizzes, then turns into a worthless
    trinket.
```

> Re-executes the command without recompiling

The following listing shows the metadata for our fantasy role-playing game. The source code for the rpg project is in ch8/ch8-rpg/Cargo.toml.

---

[2] Naming is hard.

Listing 8.3   Crate metadata for the rpg project

```
[package]
name = "rpg"
version = "0.1.0"
authors = ["Tim McNamara <author@rustinaction.com>"]
edition = "2018"

[dependencies]
rand = "0.7"
```

Listing 8.4 provides an example of using a trait object to enable a container to hold several types. You'll find its source in ch8/ch8-rpg/src/main.rs.

Listing 8.4   Using the trait object &dyn Enchanter

```
 1 use rand;
 2 use rand::seq::SliceRandom;
 3 use rand::Rng;
 4
 5 #[derive(Debug)]
 6 struct Dwarf {}
 7
 8 #[derive(Debug)]
 9 struct Elf {}
10
11 #[derive(Debug)]
12 struct Human {}
13
14 #[derive(Debug)]
15 enum Thing {
16   Sword,
17   Trinket,
18 }
19
20 trait Enchanter: std::fmt::Debug {
21   fn competency(&self) -> f64;
22
23   fn enchant(&self, thing: &mut Thing) {
24     let probability_of_success = self.competency();
25     let spell_is_successful = rand::thread_rng()
26       .gen_bool(probability_of_success);           ◄──┐
27
28     print!("{:?} mutters incoherently. ", self);
29     if spell_is_successful {
30       println!("The {:?} glows brightly.", thing);
31     } else {
32       println!("The {:?} fizzes, \
33               then turns into a worthless trinket.", thing);
34       *thing = Thing::Trinket {};
35     }
36   }
37 }
38
```

gen_bool() generates a Boolean value, where true occurs in proportion to its argument. For example, a value of 0.5 returns true 50% of the time.

```
39 impl Enchanter for Dwarf {
40    fn competency(&self) -> f64 {
41        0.5
42    }
43 }
44 impl Enchanter for Elf {
45    fn competency(&self) -> f64 {
46        0.95
47    }
48 }
49 impl Enchanter for Human {
50    fn competency(&self) -> f64 {
51        0.8
52    }
53 }
54
55 fn main() {
56    let mut it = Thing::Sword;
57
58    let d = Dwarf {};
59    let e = Elf {};
60    let h = Human {};
61
62    let party: Vec<&dyn Enchanter> = vec![&d, &h, &e];
63    let spellcaster = party.choose(&mut rand::thread_rng()).unwrap();
64
65    spellcaster.enchant(&mut it);
66 }
```

◁— **Dwarves are poor spellcasters, and their spells regularly fail.**

◁— **Spells cast by elves rarely fail.**

◁— **Humans are proficient at enchanting things. Mistakes are uncommon.**

We can hold members of different types within the same Vec as all these implement the Enchanter trait. ◁—

Trait objects are a powerful construct in the language. In a sense, they provide a way to navigate Rust's rigid type system. As you learn about this feature in more detail, you will encounter some jargon. For example, trait objects are a form of *type erasure*. The compiler does not have access to the original type during the call to enchant().

Trait vs. type

One of the frustrating things about Rust's syntax for beginners is that trait objects and type parameters look similar. But types and traits are used in different places. For example, consider these two lines:

```
use rand::Rng;
use rand::rngs::ThreadRng;
```

Although these both have something to do with random number generators, they're quite different. rand::Rng is a trait; rand::rngs::ThreadRng is a struct. Trait objects make this distinction harder.

When used as a function argument and in similar places, the form &dyn Rng is a reference to something that implements the Rng trait, whereas &ThreadRng is a reference to a value of ThreadRng. With time, the distinction between traits and types becomes easier to grasp. Here's some common use cases for trait objects:

(continued)

- Creating collections of heterogeneous objects.
- Returning a value. Trait objects enable functions to return multiple concrete types.
- Supporting dynamic dispatch, whereby the function that is called is determined at runtime rather than at compile time.

Before the Rust 2018 edition, the situation was even more confusing. The dyn keyword did not exist. This meant that context was needed to decide between &Rng and &ThreadRng.

Trait objects are not objects in the sense that an object-oriented programmer would understand. They're perhaps closer to a mixin class. Trait objects don't exist on their own; they are agents of some other type.

An alternative analogy would be a singleton object that is delegated with some authority by another concrete type. In listing 8.4, the &Enchanter is delegated to act on behalf of three concrete types.

8.4 TCP

Dropping down from HTTP, we encounter TCP (Transmission Control Protocol). Rust's standard library provides us with cross-platform tools for making TCP requests. Let's use those. The file structure for listing 8.6, which creates an HTTP GET request, is provided here:

```
ch8-stdlib
├── src
│   └── main.rs
└── Cargo.toml
```

The following listing shows the metadata for listing 8.6. You'll find the source for this listing in ch8/ch8-stdlib/Cargo.toml.

Listing 8.5   Project metadata for listing 8.6

```
[package]
name = "ch8-stdlib"
version = "0.1.0"
authors = ["Tim McNamara <author@rustinaction.com>"]
edition = "2018"


[dependencies]
```

The next listing shows how to use the Rust standard library to construct an HTTP GET request with std::net::TcpStream. The source for this listing is in ch8/ch8-stdlib/src/main.rs.

Listing 8.6   Constructing an HTTP GET request

```
 1 use std::io::prelude::*;                           Explicitly specifying the
 2 use std::net::TcpStream;                            port (80) is required.
 3                                                     TcpStream does not know
 4 fn main() -> std::io::Result<()> {                  that this will become a
 5   let host = "www.rustinaction.com:80";        ◁──┘ HTTP request.
 6
 7   let mut conn =
 8     TcpStream::connect(host)?;
 9                                                  In many networking
10   conn.write_all(b"GET / HTTP/1.0")?;            protocols, \r\n signifies
11   conn.write_all(b"\r\n")?;                  ◁── a new line.
12
13   conn.write_all(b"Host: www.rustinaction.com")?;
14   conn.write_all(b"\r\n\r\n")?;             ◁──┐ Two blank new
15                                                 │ lines signify end
16   std::io::copy(                std::io::copy()  │ of request
17     &mut conn,                  streams bytes
18     &mut std::io::stdout()      from a Reader
19   )?;                           to a Writer.
20
21   Ok(())
22 }
```

Some remarks about listing 8.6:

- On line 10, we specify HTTP 1.0. Using this version of HTTP ensures that the connection is closed when the server sends its response. HTTP 1.0, however, does not support "keep alive" requests. Specifying HTTP 1.1 actually confuses this code as the server will refuse to close the connection until it has received another request, and the client will never send one.

- On line 13, we include the hostname. This may feel redundant given that we used that exact hostname when we connected on lines 7–8. However, one should remembers that the connection is established over IP, which does not have host names. When `TcpStream::connect()` connects to the server, it only uses an IP address. Adding the Host HTTP header allows us to inject that information back into the context.

8.4.1   *What is a port number?*

Port numbers are purely virtual. They are simply `u16` values. Port numbers allow a single IP address to host multiple services.

8.4.2   *Converting a hostname to an IP address*

So far, we've provided the hostname www.rustinaction.com to Rust. But to send messages over the internet, the IP (internet protocol) address is required. TCP knows nothing about domain names. To convert a domain name to an IP address, we rely on the Domain Name System (DNS) and its process called *domain name resolution*.

We're able to resolve names by asking a server, which can recursively ask other servers. DNS requests can be made over TCP, including encryption with TLS, but are also sent over UDP (User Datagram Protocol). We'll use DNS here because it's more useful for learning purposes.

To explain how the translation from a domain name to an IP address works, we'll create a small application that does the translation. We'll call the application *resolve*. You'll find its source code in listing 8.9. The application makes use of public DNS services, but you can easily add your own with the -s argument.

Public DNS providers

At the time of writing, several companies provide DNS servers for public use. Any of the IP addresses listed here should offer roughly equivalent service:

- 1.1.1.1 and 1.0.0.1 by Cloudflare
- 8.8.8.8 and 8.8.4.4. by Google
- 9.9.9.9 by Quad9 (founded by IBM)
- 64.6.64.6 and 64.6.65.6 by VeriSign

Our resolve application only understands a small portion of DNS protocol, but that portion is sufficient for our purposes. The project makes use of an external crate, trust-dns, to perform the hard work. The trust-dns crate implements RFC 1035, which defines DNS and several later RFCs quite faithfully using terminology derived from it. Table 8.1 outlines some of the terms that are useful to understand.

Table 8.1   Terms that are used in RFC 1035, the trust_dns crate, and listing 8.9, and how these interlink

Term	Definition	Representation in code

Domain name	A domain name is almost what you probably think of when you use the term *domain name* in your everyday language.
	
	The technical definition includes some special cases such as the *root* domain, which is encoded as a single dot, and domain names that need to be case-insensitive.
		Defined in `trust_dns::domain::Name`
		`pub struct Name {`
		`    is_fqdn: bool,`
		`    labels: Vec<Label>,`
		`}`
		
		fqdn stands for fully-qualified domain name.

Table 8.1 Terms that are used in RFC 1035, the trust_dns crate, and listing 8.9, and how these interlink *(continued)*

Term	Definition	Representation in code

Message	A message is a container for both requests to DNS servers (called *queries*) and responses back to clients (called *answers*).
	
	Messages must contain a header, but other fields are not required. A `Message` struct represents this and includes several `Vec<T>` fields. These do not need to be wrapped in `Option` to represent missing values as their length can be 0.
		Defined in `trust_dns::domain::Name`
		
		``rust
		struct Message {
		    header: Header,
		    queries: Vec<Query>,
		    answers: Vec<Record>,
		    name_servers: Vec<Record>,
		    additionals: Vec<Record>,
		    sig0: Vec<Record>,
		    edns: Option<Edns>,
		}
		``
		
		edns indicates whether the message includes extended DNS.
		
		sig0, a cryptographically signed record, verifies the message's integrity. It is defined in RFC 2535.

Message type	A message type identifies the message as a query or as an answer. Queries can also be updates, which are functionality that our code ignores.	Defined in `trust_dns::op::MessageType`
		
		``rust
		pub enum MessageType {
		    Query,
		    Response,
		}
		``

Message ID	A number that is used for senders to link queries and answers.	`u16`

Resource record type	The resource record type refers to the DNS codes that you've probably encountered if you've ever configured a domain name.
	
	Of note is how trust_dns handles invalid codes. The `RecordType` enum contains an `Unknown(u16)` variant that can be used for codes that it doesn't understand.
		Defined in `trust_dns::rr::record_type::RecordType`
		
		``rust
		pub enum RecordType {
		    A,
		    AAAA,
		    ANAME,
		    ANY,
		    // ...
		    Unknown(u16),
		    ZERO,
		}
		``

Query	A `Query` struct holds the domain name and the record type that we're seeking the DNS details for. These traits also describe the DNS class and allow queries to distinguish between messages sent over the internet from other transport protocols.	Defined in `trust_dns::op::Query`
		
		``rust
		pub struct Query {
		    name: Name,
		    query_type: RecordType,
		    query_class: DNSClass,
		}
		``

Table 8.1 Terms that are used in RFC 1035, the trust_dns crate, and listing 8.9, and how these interlink *(continued)*

Term	Definition	Representation in code

Opcode	An `OpCode` enum is, in some sense, a subtype of `Message-Type`. This is an extensibility mechanism that allows future functionality. For example, RFC 1035 defines the `Query` and `Status` opcodes but others were defined later. The `Notify` and `Update` opcodes are defined by RFC 1996 and RFC 2136, respectively.	Defined in `trust_dns::op::OpCode`
		`pub enum OpCode {`
		    `Query,`
		    `Status,`
		    `Notify,`
		    `Update,`
		`}`

An unfortunate consequence of the protocol, which I suppose is a consequence of reality, is that there are many options, types, and subtypes involved. Listing 8.7, an excerpt from listing 8.9, shows the process of constructing a message that asks, "Dear DNS server, what is the IPv4 address for domain_name?" The listing constructs the DNS message, whereas the trust-dns crate requests an IPv4 address for domain_name.

Listing 8.7   Constructing a DNS message in Rust

```
                     A Message is a container for
                        queries (or answers).          Generates a random
                                                       u16 number
35 let mut msg = Message::new();
36 msg
37    .set_id(rand::random::<u16>())               Multiple queries can be
38    .set_message_type(MessageType::Query)        included in the same
39    .add_query(                                   message.
40       Query::query(domain_name, RecordType::A)         The equivalent
41    )                                                    type for IPv6
42    .set_op_code(OpCode::Query)       Requests that the  addresses is
43    .set_recursion_desired(true);     DNS server asks    AAAA.
                                        other DNS servers
                                        if it doesn't know
                                        the answer
```

We're now in a position where we can meaningfully inspect the code. It has the following structure:

- Parses command-line arguments
- Builds a DNS message using trust_dns types
- Converts the structured data into a stream of bytes
- Sends those bytes across the wire

After that, we need to accept the response from the server, decode the incoming bytes, and print the result. Error handling remains relatively ugly, with many calls to unwrap() and expect(). We'll address that problem shortly in section 8.5. The end process is a command-line application that's quite simple.

Running our resolve application involves little ceremony. Given a domain name, it provides an IP address:

```
$ resolve www.rustinaction.com 35.185.44.232
```

Listings 8.8 and 8.9 are the project's source code. While you are experimenting with the project, you may want to use some features of cargo run to speed up your process:

```
$ cargo run -q -- www.rustinaction.com    ◁─┐  Sends arguments to the right of -- to the
35.185.44.232                                  executable it compiles. The -q option
                                               mutes any intermediate output.
```

To compile the resolve application from the official source code repository, execute these commands in the console:

```
$ git clone https://github.com/rust-in-action/code rust-in-action
Cloning into 'rust-in-action'...

$ cd rust-in-action/ch8/ch8-resolve

$ cargo run -q -- www.rustinaction.com    ◁─┐
35.185.44.232
```
It may take a while to download the project's dependencies and compile the code. The -q flag mutes intermediate output. Adding two dashes (--) sends further arguments to the compiled executable.

To compile and build from scratch, follow these instructions to establish the project structure:

1 At the command-line, enter these commands:

```
$ cargo new resolve
    Created binary (application) `resolve` package

$ cargo install cargo-edit
...

$ cd resolve

$ cargo add rand@0.6
    Updating 'https://github.com/rust-lang/crates.io-index' index
      Adding rand v0.6 to dependencies

$ cargo add clap@2
    Updating 'https://github.com/rust-lang/crates.io-index' index
      Adding rand v2 to dependencies

$ cargo add trust-dns@0.16 --no-default-features
    Updating 'https://github.com/rust-lang/crates.io-index' index
      Adding trust-dns v0.16 to dependencies
```

2 Once the structure has been established, you check that your Cargo.toml matches listing 8.8, available in ch8/ch8-resolve/Cargo.toml.

3 Replace the contents of src/main.rs with listing 8.9. It is available from ch8/ch8-resolve/src/main.rs.

The following snippet provides a view of how the files of the project and the listings are interlinked:

```
ch8-resolve
├── Cargo.toml        ⊲─┘   See listing 8.8
└── src
     └── main.rs      ⊲─┘   See listing 8.9
```

Listing 8.8   Crate metadata for the resolve app

```
[package]
name = "resolve"
version = "0.1.0"
authors = ["Tim McNamara <author@rustinaction.com>"]
edition = "2018"

[dependencies]
rand = "0.6"
clap = "2.33"
trust-dns = { version = "0.16", default-features = false }
```

Listing 8.9   A command-line utility to resolve IP addresses from hostnames

```
 1 use std::net::{SocketAddr, UdpSocket};
 2 use std::time::Duration;
 3
 4 use clap::{App, Arg};
 5 use rand;
 6 use trust_dns::op::{Message, MessageType, OpCode, Query};
 7 use trust_dns::rr::domain::Name;
 8 use trust_dns::rr::record_type::RecordType;
 9 use trust_dns::serialize::binary::*;
10
11 fn main() {
12   let app = App::new("resolve")
13     .about("A simple to use DNS resolver")
14     .arg(Arg::with_name("dns-server").short("s").default_value("1.1.1.1"))
15     .arg(Arg::with_name("domain-name").required(true))
16     .get_matches();
17
18   let domain_name_raw = app
19     .value_of("domain-name").unwrap();
20   let domain_name =
21     Name::from_ascii(&domain_name_raw).unwrap();
22
23   let dns_server_raw = app
24     .value_of("dns-server").unwrap();
25   let dns_server: SocketAddr =
26     format!("{}:53", dns_server_raw)
27     .parse()
28     .expect("invalid address");
29
```

Converts the command-line argument to a typed domain name

Converts the command-line argument to a typed DNS server

```
30      let mut request_as_bytes: Vec<u8> =
31        Vec::with_capacity(512);
32      let mut response_as_bytes: Vec<u8> =
33        vec![0; 512];
34
35      let mut msg = Message::new();
36      msg
37        .set_id(rand::random::<u16>())
38        .set_message_type(MessageType::Query)
39        .add_query(Query::query(domain_name, RecordType::A))
40        .set_op_code(OpCode::Query)
41        .set_recursion_desired(true);
42
43      let mut encoder =
44        BinEncoder::new(&mut request_as_bytes);
45      msg.emit(&mut encoder).unwrap();
46
47      let localhost = UdpSocket::bind("0.0.0.0:0")
48        .expect("cannot bind to local socket");
49      let timeout = Duration::from_secs(3);
50      localhost.set_read_timeout(Some(timeout)).unwrap();
51      localhost.set_nonblocking(false).unwrap();
52
53      let _amt = localhost
54        .send_to(&request_as_bytes, dns_server)
55        .expect("socket misconfigured");
56
57      let (_amt, _remote) = localhost
58        .recv_from(&mut response_as_bytes)
59        .expect("timeout reached");
60
61      let dns_message = Message::from_vec(&response_as_bytes)
62        .expect("unable to parse response");
63
64      for answer in dns_message.answers() {
65        if answer.record_type() == RecordType::A {
66          let resource = answer.rdata();
67          let ip = resource
68            .to_ip_addr()
69            .expect("invalid IP address received");
70          println!("{}", ip.to_string());
71        }
72      }
73  }
```

An explanation of why two forms of initializing are used is provided after the listing.

Message represents a DNS message, which is a container for queries and other information such as answers.

Specifies that this is a DNS query, not a DNS answer. Both have the same representation over the wire, but not in Rust's type system.

Converts the Message type into raw bytes with BinEncoder

0.0.0.0:0 means listen to all addresses on a random port. The OS selects the actual port.

Listing 8.9 includes some business logic that deserves explaining. Lines 30–33, repeated here, use two forms of initializing a Vec<u8>. Why?

```
30      let mut request_as_bytes: Vec<u8> =
31        Vec::with_capacity(512);
32      let mut response_as_bytes: Vec<u8> =
33        vec![0; 512];
```

Each form creates a subtly different outcome:

- `Vec::with_capacity(512)` creates a `Vec<T>` with length 0 and capacity 512.
- `vec![0; 512]` creates a `Vec<T>` with length 512 and capacity 512.

The underlying array looks the same, but the difference in length is significant. Within the call to `recv_from()` at line 58, the trust-dns crate includes a check that `response_as_bytes` has sufficient space. That check uses the length field, which results in a crash. Knowing how to wriggle around with initialization can be handy for satisfying an APIs' expectations.

> ### How DNS supports connections within UDP
>
> UDP does not have a notion of long-lived connections. Unlike TCP, all messages are short-lived and one-way. Put another way, UDP does not support two-way (*duplex*) communications. But DNS requires a response to be sent from the DNS server back to the client.
>
> To enable two-way communications within UDP, both parties must act as clients and servers, depending on context. That context is defined by the protocol built on top of UDP. Within DNS, the client becomes a DNS server to receive the server's reply. The following table provides a flow chart of the process.
>
> | Stage | DNS client role | DNS server role |
> | --- | --- | --- |
> | Request sent from DNS client | UDP client | UDP server |
> | Reply sent from DNS server | UDP server | UDP client |

It's time to recap. Our overall task in this section was to make HTTP requests. HTTP is built on TCP. Because we only had a domain name (www.rustinaction.com) when we made the request, we needed to use DNS. DNS is primarily delivered over UDP, so we needed to take a diversion and learn about UDP.

Now it's almost time to return to TCP. Before we're able to do that, though, we need to learn how to combine error types that emerge from multiple dependencies.

8.5 *Ergonomic error handling for libraries*

Rust's error handling is safe and sophisticated. However, it offers a few challenges. When a function incorporates `Result` types from two upstream crates, the `?` operator no longer works because it only understands a single type. This proves to be important when we refactor our domain resolution code to work alongside our TCP code. This section discusses some of those challenges as well as strategies for managing them.

8.5.1   *Issue: Unable to return multiple error types*

Returning a Result<T, E> works great when there is a single error type E. But things become more complicated when we want to work with multiple error types.

> **TIP** For single files, compile the code with rustc <filename> rather than using cargo build. For example, if a file is named io-error.rs, then the shell command is rustc io-error.rs && ./io-error[.exe].

To start, let's look at a small example that covers the easy case of a single error type. We'll try to open a file that does not exist. When run, listing 8.10 prints a short message in Rust syntax:

```
$ rustc ch8/misc/io-error.rs && ./io-error
Error: Os { code: 2, kind: NotFound, message: "No such file or directory" }
```

We won't win any awards for user experience here, but we get a chance to learn a new language feature. The following listing provides the code that produces a single error type. You'll find its source in ch8/misc/io-error.rs.

> **Listing 8.10   A Rust program that always produces an I/O error**

```
1 use std::fs::File;
2
3 fn main() -> Result<(), std::io::Error> {
4     let _f = File::open("invisible.txt")?;
5
6     Ok(())
7 }
```

Now, let's introduce another error type into main(). The next listing produces a compiler error, but we'll work through some options to get the code to compile. The code for this listing is in ch8/misc/multierror.rs.

> **Listing 8.11   A function that attempts to return multiple Result types**

```
 1 use std::fs::File;
 2 use std::net::Ipv6Addr;
 3
 4 fn main() -> Result<(), std::io::Error> {
 5   let _f = File::open("invisible.txt")?;
 6
 7   let _localhost = "::1"
 8     .parse::<Ipv6Addr>()?;
 9
10   Ok(())
11 }
```

File::open() returns Result<(), std::io::Error>.

"".parse::<Ipv6Addr>() returns Result<Ipv6Addr, std::net::AddrParseError>.

To compile listing 8.11, enter the ch8/misc directory and use rustc. This produces quite a stern, yet helpful, error message:

```
$ rustc multierror.rs
error[E0277]: `?` couldn't convert the error to `std::io::Error`
 --> multierror.rs:8:25
  |
4 | fn main() -> Result<(), std::io::Error> {
  |                         ------------------------- expected `std::io::Error`
  |                                                   because of this
...
8 |         .parse::<Ipv6Addr>()?;
  |                              ^ the trait `From<AddrParseError>`
  |                                is not implemented for `std::io::Error`
  |
  = note: the question mark operation (`?`) implicitly performs a
          conversion on the error value using the `From` trait
  = help: the following implementations were found:
            <std::io::Error as From<ErrorKind>>
            <std::io::Error as From<IntoInnerError<W>>>
            <std::io::Error as From<NulError>>
  = note: required by `from`

error: aborting due to previous error

For more information about this error, try `rustc --explain E0277`.
```

The error message can be difficult to interpret if you don't know what the question mark operator (?) is doing. Why are there multiple messages about std::convert::From? Well, the ? operator is syntactic sugar for the try! macro. try! performs two functions:

- When it detects Ok(value), the expression evaluates to value.
- When Err(err) occurs, try!/? returns early after attempting to convert err to the error type defined in the calling function.

In Rust-like pseudocode, the try! macro could be defined as

```
macro try {
  match expression {
    Result::Ok(val) => val,
    Result::Err(err) => {
      let converted = convert::From::from(err);
      return Result::Err(converted);
    }
  });
}
```

Uses val when an expression matches Result::Ok(val)

Converts err to the outer function's error type when it matches Result::Err(err) and then returns early

Returns from the calling function, not the try! macro itself

Looking at listing 8.11 again, we can see the try! macro in action as ?:

```
4 fn main() -> Result<(), std::io::Error> {
5   let _f = File::open("invisible.txt")?;
6
7   let _localhost = "::1"
8       .parse::<Ipv6Addr>()?;
```

File::open() returns std::io::Error, so no conversion is necessary.

"".parse() presents ? with a std::net::AddrParseError. We don't define how to convert std::net::AddrParseError to std::io::Error, so the program fails to compile.

```
 9
10   Ok(())
11 }
```

In addition to saving you from needing to use explicit pattern matching to extract the value or return an error, the ? operator also attempts to convert its argument into an error type if required. Because the signature of main is main() ? Result<(), std::io ::Error>, Rust attempts to convert the std::net::AddrParseError produced by parse::<Ipv6Addr>() into a std::io::Error. Don't worry, though; we can fix this! Earlier, in section 8.3, we introduced trait objects. Now we'll be able to put those to good use.

Using Box<dyn Error> as the error variant in the main() function allows us to progress. The dyn keyword is short for *dynamic*, implying that there is a runtime cost for this flexibility. Running listing 8.12 produces this output:

```
$ rustc ch8/misc/traiterror.rs && ./traiterror
Error: Os { code: 2, kind: NotFound, message: "No such file or directory" }
```

I suppose it's a limited form of progress, but progress nonetheless. We've circled back to the error we started with. But we've passed through the compiler error, which is what we wanted.

Going forward, let's look at listing 8.12. It implements a trait object in a return value to simplify error handling when errors originate from multiple upstream crates. You can find the source for this listing in ch8/misc/traiterror.rs.

Listing 8.12   Using a trait object in a return value

```
 1 use std::fs::File;
 2 use std::error::Error;
 3 use std::net::Ipv6Addr;                    A trait object, Box<dyn
 4                                            Error>, represents any type
 5 fn main() -> Result<(), Box<dyn Error>> {   that implements Error.
 6
 7   let _f = File::open("invisible.txt")?;    Error type is
 8                                             std::io::Error
 9   let _localhost = "::1"
10     .parse::<Ipv6Addr>()?        Error type is
11                                  std::net::AddrParseError
12   Ok(())
13 }
```

Wrapping trait objects in Box is necessary because their size (in bytes on the stack) is unknown at compile time. In the case of listing 8.12, the trait object might originate from either File::open() or "::1".parse(). What actually happens depends on the circumstances encountered at runtime. A Box has a known size on the stack. Its raison d'être is to point to things that don't, such as trait objects.

8.5.2 *Wrapping downstream errors by defining our own error type*

The problem that we are attempting to solve is that each of our dependencies defines its own error type. Multiple error types in one function prevent returning Result. The first strategy we looked at was to use trait objects, but trait objects have a potentially significant downside.

Using trait objects is also known as *type erasure*. Rust is no longer aware that an error has originated upstream. Using Box<dyn Error> as the error variant of a Result means that the upstream error types are, in a sense, lost. The original errors are now converted to exactly the same type.

It is possible to retain the upstream errors, but this requires more work on our behalf. We need to bundle upstream errors in our own type. When the upstream errors are needed later (say, for reporting errors to the user), it's possible to extract these with pattern matching. Here is the process:

1 Define an enum that includes the upstream errors as variants.
2 Annotate the enum with #[derive(Debug)].
3 Implement Display.
4 Implement Error, which almost comes for free because we have implemented Debug and Display.
5 Use map_err() in your code to convert the upstream error to your omnibus error type.

NOTE You haven't previously encountered the map_err() function. We'll explain what it does when we get there later in this section.

It's possible to stop with the previous steps, but there's an optional extra step that improves the ergonomics. We need to implement std::convert::From to remove the need to call map_err(). To begin, let's start back with listing 8.11, where we know that the code fails:

```
use std::fs::File;
use std::net::Ipv6Addr;

fn main() -> Result<(), std::io::Error> {
  let _f = File::open("invisible.txt")?;

  let _localhost = "::1"
    .parse::<Ipv6Addr>()?;

  Ok(())
}
```

This code fails because "".parse::<Ipv6Addr>() does not return a std::io::Error. What we want to end up with is code that looks a little more like the following listing.

> **Listing 8.13 Hypothetical example of the kind of code we want to write**

```
 1 use std::fs::File;
 2 use std::io::Error;                          Brings upstream errors
 3 use std::net::AddrParseError;                into local scope
 4 use std::net::Ipv6Addr;
 5
 6 enum UpstreamError{
 7   IO(std::io::Error),
 8   Parsing(AddrParseError),
 9 }
10
11 fn main() -> Result<(), UpstreamError> {
12   let _f = File::open("invisible.txt")?
13     .maybe_convert_to(UpstreamError);
14
15   let _localhost = "::1"
16     .parse::<Ipv6Addr>()?
17     .maybe_convert_to(UpstreamError);
18
19   Ok(())
20 }
```

DEFINE AN ENUM THAT INCLUDES THE UPSTREAM ERRORS AS VARIANTS

The first thing to do is to return a type that can hold the upstream error types. In Rust, an enum works well. Listing 8.13 does not compile, but does do this step. We'll tidy up the imports slightly, though:

```
use std::io;
use std::net;

enum UpstreamError{
  IO(io::Error),
  Parsing(net::AddrParseError),
}
```

ANNOTATE THE ENUM WITH #[DERIVE(DEBUG)]

The next change is easy. It's a single-line change—the best kind of change. To annotate the enum, we'll add #[derive(Debug)], as the following shows:

```
use std::io;
use std::net;

#[derive(Debug)]
enum UpstreamError{
  IO(io::Error),
  Parsing(net::AddrParseError),
}
```

IMPLEMENT STD::FMT::DISPLAY

We'll cheat slightly and implement Display by simply using Debug. We know that this is available to us because errors must define Debug. Here's the updated code:

```
use std::fmt;
use std::io;
use std::net;

#[derive(Debug)]
enum UpstreamError{
  IO(io::Error),
  Parsing(net::AddrParseError),
}

impl fmt::Display for UpstreamError {
  fn fmt(&self, f: &mut fmt::Formatter<'_>) -> fmt::Result {
    write!(f, "{:?}", self)        ◄─────┐  Implements Display in terms
  }                                         of Debug via the "{:?}" syntax
}
```

IMPLEMENT STD::ERROR::ERROR

Here's another easy change. To end up with the kind of code that we'd like to write, let's make the following change:

```
use std::error;        ◄─────┐  Brings the
use std::fmt;                   std::error::Error trait
use std::io;                    into local scope
use std::net;

#[derive(Debug)]
enum UpstreamError{
  IO(io::Error),
  Parsing(net::AddrParseError),
}

impl fmt::Display for UpstreamError {
  fn fmt(&self, f: &mut fmt::Formatter<'_>) -> fmt::Result {
    write!(f, "{:?}", self)
  }                                          Defers to default method
}                                            implementations. The compiler
                                             will fill in the blanks.
impl error::Error for UpstreamError { }  ◄───┘
```

The impl block is—well, we can rely on default implementations provided by the compiler—especially terse. Because there are default implementations of every method defined by std::error::Error, we can ask the compiler to do all of the work for us.

USE MAP_ERR()

The next fix is to add map_err() to our code to convert the upstream error to the omnibus error type. Back at listing 8.13, we wanted to have a main() that looks like this:

```
fn main() -> Result<(), UpstreamError> {
  let _f = File::open("invisible.txt")?
    .maybe_convert_to(UpstreamError);

  let _localhost = "::1"
    .parse::<Ipv6Addr>()?
```

```
  .maybe_convert_to(UpstreamError);

  Ok(())
}
```

I can't offer you that. I can, however, give you this:

```
fn main() -> Result<(), UpstreamError> {
  let _f = File::open("invisible.txt")
    .map_err(UpstreamError::IO)?;

  let _localhost = "::1"
    .parse::<Ipv6Addr>()
    .map_err(UpstreamError::Parsing)?;

  Ok(())
}
```

This new code works! Here's how. The `map_err()` function maps an error to a function. (Variants of our `UpstreamError` enum can be used as functions here.) Note that the `?` operator needs to be at the end. Otherwise, the function can return before the code has a chance to convert the error.

Listing 8.14 provides the new code. When run, it produces this message to the console:

```
$ rustc ch8/misc/wraperror.rs && ./wraperror
Error: IO(Os { code: 2, kind: NotFound, message: "No such file or directory" })
```

To retain type safety, we can use the new code in the following listing. You'll find its source in ch8/misc/wraperror.rs.

Listing 8.14 Wrapping upstream errors in our own type

```
 1 use std::io;
 2 use std::fmt;
 3 use std::net;
 4 use std::fs::File;
 5 use std::net::Ipv6Addr;
 6
 7 #[derive(Debug)]
 8 enum UpstreamError{
 9   IO(io::Error),
10   Parsing(net::AddrParseError),
11 }
12
13 impl fmt::Display for UpstreamError {
14   fn fmt(&self, f: &mut fmt::Formatter<'_>) -> fmt::Result {
15     write!(f, "{:?}", self)
16   }
17 }
18
19 impl error::Error for UpstreamError { }
```

```
20
21 fn main() -> Result<(), UpstreamError> {
22   let _f = File::open("invisible.txt")
23     .map_err(UpstreamError::IO)?;
24
25   let _localhost = "::1"
26     .parse::<Ipv6Addr>()
27     .map_err(UpstreamError::Parsing)?;
28
29   Ok(())
30 }
```

It's also possible to remove the calls to map_err(). But to enable that, we need to implement From.

IMPLEMENT STD::CONVERT::FROM TO REMOVE THE NEED TO CALL MAP_ERR()

The std::convert::From trait has a single required method, from(). We need two impl blocks to enable our two upstream error types to be convertible. The following snippet shows how:

```
impl From<io::Error> for UpstreamError {
  fn from(error: io::Error) -> Self {
    UpstreamError::IO(error)
  }
}

impl From<net::AddrParseError> for UpstreamError {
  fn from(error: net::AddrParseError) -> Self {
    UpstreamError::Parsing(error)
  }
}
```

Now the main() function returns to a simple form of itself:

```
fn main() -> Result<(), UpstreamError> {
  let _f = File::open("invisible.txt")?;
  let _localhost = "::1".parse::<Ipv6Addr>()?;

  Ok(())
}
```

The full code listing is provided in listing 8.15. Implementing From places the burden of extra syntax on the library writer. It results in a much easier experience when using your crate, simplifying its use by downstream programmers. You'll find the source for this listing in ch8/misc/wraperror2.rs.

Listing 8.15   Implementing std::convert::From **for our wrapper error type**

```
1 use std::io;
2 use std::fmt;
3 use std::net;
```

```
 4 use std::fs::File;
 5 use std::net::Ipv6Addr;
 6
 7 #[derive(Debug)]
 8 enum UpstreamError{
 9   IO(io::Error),
10   Parsing(net::AddrParseError),
11 }
12
13 impl fmt::Display for UpstreamError {
14   fn fmt(&self, f: &mut fmt::Formatter<'_>) -> fmt::Result {
15     write!(f, "{:?}", self)                                     1((CO20-1))
16   }
17 }
18
19 impl error::Error for UpstreamError { }
20
21 impl From<io::Error> for UpstreamError {
22   fn from(error: io::Error) -> Self {
23     UpstreamError::IO(error)
24   }
25 }
26
27 impl From<net::AddrParseError> for UpstreamError {
28   fn from(error: net::AddrParseError) -> Self {
29     UpstreamError::Parsing(error)
30   }
31 }
32
33 fn main() -> Result<(), UpstreamError> {
34   let _f = File::open("invisible.txt")?;
35   let _localhost = "::1".parse::<Ipv6Addr>()?;
36
37   Ok(())
38 }
```

8.5.3 Cheating with unwrap() and expect()

The final approach for dealing with multiple error types is to use unwrap() and expect(). Now that we have the tools to handle multiple error types in a function, we can continue our journey.

> **NOTE** This is a reasonable approach when writing a main() function, but it isn't recommended for library authors. Your users don't want their programs to crash because of things outside of their control.

8.6 MAC addresses

Several pages ago in listing 8.9, you implemented a DNS resolver. That enabled conversions from a host name such as www.rustinaction.com to an IP address. Now we have an IP address to connect to.

The internet protocol enables devices to contact each other via their IP addresses. But that's not all. Every hardware device also includes a unique identifier that's independent of the network it's connected to. Why a second number? The answer is partially technical and partially historical.

Ethernet networking and the internet started life independently. Ethernet's focus was on local area networks (LANs). The internet was developed to enable communication between networks, and Ethernet is the addressing system understood by devices that share a physical link (or a radio link in the case of WiFi, Bluetooth, and other wireless technologies).

Perhaps a better way to express this is that MAC (short for *media access control*) addresses are used by devices that share electrons (figure 8.3). But there are a few differences:

- *IP addresses are hierarchical, but MAC addresses are not.* Addresses appearing close together numerically are not close together physically, or organizationally.
- *MAC addresses are 48 bits (6 bytes) wide.* IP addresses are 32 bits (4 bytes) wide for IPv4 and 128 bits (16 bytes) for IPv6.

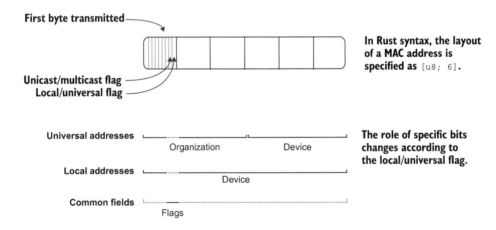

Figure 8.3   In-memory layout for MAC addresses

There are two forms of MAC addresses:

- *Universally administered (or universal) addresses are set when devices are manufactured.* Manufacturers use a prefix assigned by the IEEE Registration Authority and a scheme of their choosing for the remaining bits.
- *Locally administered (or local) addresses allow devices to create their own MAC addresses without registration.* When setting a device's MAC address yourself in software, you should make sure that your address is set to the local form.

MAC addresses have two modes: *unicast* and *multicast*. The transmission behavior for these forms is identical. The distinction is made when a device makes a decision about whether to accept a frame. A *frame* is a term used by the Ethernet protocol for a byte slice at this level. Analogies to frame include a packet, wrapper, and envelope. Figure 8.4 shows this distinction.

Unicast vs. multicast MAC addresses

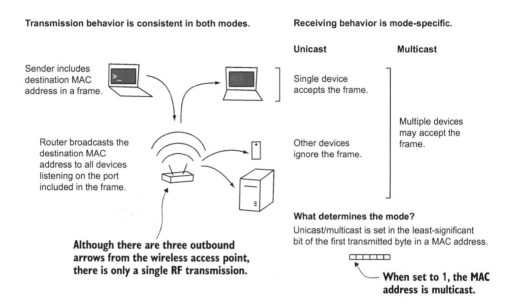

Figure 8.4 The differences between multicast and unicast MAC addresses

Unicast addresses are intended to transport information between two points that are in direct contact (say, between a laptop and a router). Wireless access points complicate matters somewhat but don't change the fundamentals. A multicast address can be accepted by multiple recipients, whereas unicast has a single recipient. The term *unicast* is somewhat misleading, though. Sending an Ethernet packet involves more than two devices. Using a unicast address alters what devices do when they receive packets but not which data is transmitted over the wire (or through the radio waves).

8.6.1 Generating MAC addresses

When we begin talking about raw TCP in section 8.8, we'll create a virtual hardware device in listing 8.22. To convince anything to talk to us, we need to learn how to assign our virtual device a MAC address. The macgen project in listing 8.17 generates the MAC addresses for us. The following listing shows the metadata for that project. You can find its source in ch8/ch8-mac/Cargo.toml.

Listing 8.16   Crate metadata for the macgen project

```
[package]
name = "ch8-macgen"
version = "0.1.0"
authors = ["Tim McNamara <author@rustinaction.com>"]
edition = "2018"

[dependencies]
rand = "0.7"
```

The following listing shows the macgen project, our MAC address generator. The source code for this project is in the ch8/ch8-mac/src/main.rs file.

Listing 8.17   Creating macgen, a MAC address generator

```
 1 extern crate rand;
 2
 3 use rand::RngCore;
 4 use std::fmt;
 5 use std::fmt::Display;
 6
 7 #[derive(Debug)]
 8 struct MacAddress([u8; 6]);        ◁── Uses the newtype pattern to
 9                                         wrap a bare array without
10 impl Display for MacAddress {         any extra overhead
11    fn fmt(&self, f: &mut fmt::Formatter<'_>) -> fmt::Result {
12      let octet = &self.0;
13      write!(
14        f,
15        "{:02x}:{:02x}:{:02x}:{:02x}:{:02x}:{:02x}",   Converts each byte
16        octet[0], octet[1], octet[2],                  to hexadecimal
17        octet[3], octet[4], octet[5]                   notation
18      )
19    }
20 }
21
22 impl MacAddress {
23    fn new() -> MacAddress {
24      let mut octets: [u8; 6] = [0; 6];              Sets the MAC
25      rand::thread_rng().fill_bytes(&mut octets);    address to local
26      octets[0] |= 0b_0000_0011;            ◁──      and unicast
27      MacAddress { 0: octets }
28    }
29
30    fn is_local(&self) -> bool {
31      (self.0[0] & 0b_0000_0010) == 0b_0000_0010
32    }
33
34    fn is_unicast(&self) -> bool {
35      (self.0[0] & 0b_0000_0001) == 0b_0000_0001
```

```
36    }
37  }
38
39  fn main() {
40    let mac = MacAddress::new();
41    assert!(mac.is_local());
42    assert!(mac.is_unicast());
43    println!("mac: {}", mac);
44  }
```

The code from listing 8.17 should feel legible. Line 25 contains some relatively obscure syntax, though. `octets[0] |= 0b_0000_0011` coerces the two flag bits described at figure 8.3 to a state of 1. That designates every MAC address we generate as locally assigned and unicast.

8.7   *Implementing state machines with Rust's enums*

Another prerequisite for handling network messages is being able to define a state machine. Our code needs to adapt to changes in connectivity.

Listing 8.22 contains a state machine, implemented with a `loop`, a `match`, and a Rust enum. Because of Rust's expression-based nature, control flow operators also return values. Every time around the loop, the state is mutated in place. The following listing shows the pseudocode for how a repeated `match` on a enum works together.

Listing 8.18   Pseudocode for a state machine implementation

```
enum HttpState {
    Connect,
    Request,
    Response,
}

loop {
    state = match state {
        HttpState::Connect if !socket.is_active() => {
            socket.connect();
            HttpState::Request
        }

        HttpState::Request if socket.may_send() => {
            socket.send(data);
            HttpState::Response
        }

        HttpState::Response if socket.can_recv() => {
            received = socket.recv();
            HttpState::Response
        }

        HttpState::Response if !socket.may_recv() => {
            break;
        }
```

```
        _ => state,
    }
}
```

More advanced methods to implement finite state machines do exist. This is the simplest, however. We'll make use of it in listing 8.22. Making use of an enum embeds the state machine's transitions into the type system itself.

But we're still at a level that is far too high! To dig deeper, we're going to need to get some assistance from the OS.

8.8   Raw TCP

Integrating with the raw TCP packets typically requires root/superuser access. The OS starts to get quite grumpy when an unauthorized user asks to make raw network requests. We can get around this (on Linux) by creating a proxy device that non-super users are allowed to communicate with directly.

> **Don't have Linux?**
> If you're running another OS, there are many virtualization options available. Here are a few:
>
> - The Multipass project (https://multipass.run/) provides fast Ubuntu virtual machines on macOS and Windows hosts.
> - WSL, the Windows Subsystem for Linux (https://docs.microsoft.com/en-us/windows/wsl/about), is another option to look into.
> - Oracle VirtualBox (https://www.virtualbox.org/) is an open source project with excellent support for many host operating systems.

8.9   Creating a virtual networking device

To proceed with this section, you will need to create virtual networking hardware. Using virtual hardware provides more control to freely assign IP and MAC addresses. It also avoids changing your hardware settings, which could affect its ability to connect to the network. To create a TAP device called tap-rust, execute the following command in your Linux console:

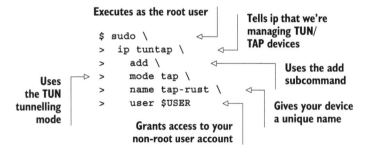

When successful, `ip` prints no output. To confirm that our tap-rust device was added, we can use the `ip tuntap list` subcommand as in the following snippet. When executed, you should see the tap-rust device in the list of devices in the output:

```
$ ip tuntap list
tap-rust: tap persist user
```

Now that we have created a networking device, we also need to allocate an IP address for it and tell our system to forward packets to it. The following shows the commands to enable this functionality:

```
                  Establishes a network device
                  called tap-rust and activates it
                                                                    Assigns the IP address
                                                                    192.168.42.100 to
$ sudo ip link set tap-rust up      <──┘                            the device
$ sudo ip addr add 192.168.42.100/24 dev tap-rust   <──┘

$ sudo iptables \
>    -t nat\                        Enables internet packets to reach the source IP
>    -A POSTROUTING \               address mask (-s 192.168.42.100/24) by appending
>    -s 192.168.42.0/24 \           a rule (-A POSTROUTING) that dynamically maps IP
>    -j MASQUERADE                  addresses to a device (-j MASQUERADE)

                                          Instructs the kernel to enable
$ sudo sysctl net.ipv4.ip_forward=1   <──┘ IPv4 packet forwarding
```

The following shows how to remove the device (once you have completed this chapter) by using `del` rather than `add`:

```
$ sudo ip tuntap del mode tap name tap-rust
```

8.10 *"Raw" HTTP*

We should now have all the knowledge we need to take on the challenge of using HTTP at the TCP level. The mget project (mget is short for *manually get*) spans listings 8.20–8.23. It is a large project, but you'll find it immensely satisfying to understand and build. Each file provides a different role:

- *main.rs (listing 8.20)*—Handles command-line parsing and weaves together the functionality provided by its peer files. This is where we combine the error types using the process outlined in section 8.5.2.
- *ethernet.rs (listing 8.21)*—Generates a MAC address using the logic from listing 8.17 and converts between MAC address types (defined by the smoltcp crate) and our own.
- *http.rs (listing 8.22)*—Carries out the work of interacting with the server to make the HTTP request.
- *dns.rs (listing 8.23)*—Performs DNS resolution, which converts a domain name to an IP address.

NOTE   The source code for these listings (and every code listing in the book) is available from https://github.com/rust-in-action/code or https://www.manning.com/books/rust-in-action.

It's important to acknowledge that listing 8.22 was derived from the HTTP client example within the smoltcp crate itself. whitequark (https://whitequark.org/) has built an absolutely fantastic networking library. Here's the file structure for the mget project:

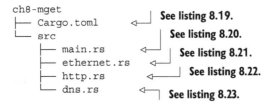

```
ch8-mget
├── Cargo.toml          ◁── │  See listing 8.19.
└── src                         See listing 8.20.
    ├── main.rs         ◁── │    See listing 8.21.
    ├── ethernet.rs     ◁──┘  See listing 8.22.
    ├── http.rs         ◁──│
    └── dns.rs          ◁──┐  See listing 8.23.
```

To download and run the mget project from source control, execute these commands at the command line:

```
$ git clone https://github.com/rust-in-action/code rust-in-action
Cloning into 'rust-in-action'...

$ cd rust-in-action/ch8/ch8-mget
```

Here are the project setup instructions for those readers who enjoy doing things step by step (with the output omitted).

  1   Enter these commands at the command-line:

```
$ cargo new mget

$ cd mget

$ cargo install cargo-edit

$ cargo add clap@2

$ cargo add url@02

$ cargo add rand@0.7

$ cargo add trust-dns@0.16 --no-default-features

$ cargo add smoltcp@0.6 --features='proto-igmp proto-ipv4 verbose log'
```

  2   Check that your project's Cargo.toml matches listing 8.19.
  3   Within the src directory, listing 8.20 becomes main.rs, listing 8.21 becomes ethernet.rs, listing 8.22 becomes http.rs, and listing 8.23 becomes dns.rs.

The following listing shows the metadata for mget. You'll find its source code in the ch8/ch8-mget/Cargo.toml file.

Listing 8.19   Crate metadata for mget

```
[package]
name = "mget"
version = "0.1.0"
authors = ["Tim McNamara <author@rustinaction.com>"]
edition = "2018"

[dependencies]
clap = "2"                          Provides command-line argument parsing
rand = "0.7"                        Selects a random port number
smoltcp = {                         Provides a TCP implementation
  version = "0.6",
  features = ["proto-igmp", "proto-ipv4", "verbose", "log"]
}
trust-dns = {                       Enables connecting to a DNS server
  version = "0.16",
  default-features = false
}
url = "2"          Parses and validates URLs
```

The following listing shows the command-line parsing for our project. You'll find this source in ch8/ch8-mget/src/main.rs.

Listing 8.20   mget command-line parsing and overall coordination

```
 1 use clap::{App, Arg};
 2 use smoltcp::phy::TapInterface;
 3 use url::Url;
 4
 5 mod dns;
 6 mod ethernet;
 7 mod http;
 8
 9 fn main() {
10   let app = App::new("mget")
11     .about("GET a webpage, manually")
12     .arg(Arg::with_name("url").required(true))          Requires a URL to download data from
13     .arg(Arg::with_name("tap-device").required(true))    Requires a TAP networking device to connect with
14     .arg(
15       Arg::with_name("dns-server")                       Makes it possible for the user to select which DNS server to use
16         .default_value("1.1.1.1"),
17     )
18     .get_matches();          Parses the command-line arguments
19
20   let url_text = app.value_of("url").unwrap();
21   let dns_server_text =
22     app.value_of("dns-server").unwrap();
23   let tap_text = app.value_of("tap-device").unwrap();
24
```

```
25    let url = Url::parse(url_text)                          ⊲┐
26      .expect("error: unable to parse <url> as a URL");      │
27                                                              │
28    if url.scheme() != "http" {                             ⊲┤
29      eprintln!("error: only HTTP protocol supported");      │
30      return;                                                │
31    }                                                        │
32                                                             │
33    let tap = TapInterface::new(&tap_text)                  ⊲┤  Validates the
34      .expect(                                               │  command-line
35        "error: unable to use <tap-device> as a \            │  arguments
36        network interface",                                  │
37      );                                                     │
38                                                             │
39    let domain_name =                                        │
40      url.host_str()                                        ⊲┤
41        .expect("domain name required");                     │
42                                                             │
43    let _dns_server: std::net::Ipv4Addr =                    │
44      dns_server_text                                        │
45        .parse()                                            ⊲┘
46        .expect(
47          "error: unable to parse <dns-server> as an \
48          IPv4 address",
49        );
                                                                   Converts the URL's domain
50                                                                  name into an IP address
51    let addr =                                                    that we can connect to
52      dns::resolve(dns_server_text, domain_name)          ⊲┘
53        .unwrap()
54        .unwrap();                                             Generates a
55                                                               random unicode
56    let mac = ethernet::MacAddress::new().into();         ⊲    MAC address
57
58    http::get(tap, mac, addr, url).unwrap();              ⊲┐  Makes the HTTP
59                                                            │  GET request
60  }
```

The following listing generates our MAC address and converts between MAC address types defined by the smoltcp crate and our own. The code for this listing is in ch8/ch8-mget/src/ethernet.rs.

Listing 8.21 Ethernet type conversion and MAC address generation

```
1 use rand;
2 use std::fmt;
3 use std::fmt::Display;
4
5 use rand::RngCore;
6 use smoltcp::wire;
7
8 #[derive(Debug)]
9 pub struct MacAddress([u8; 6]);
10
```

```
11 impl Display for MacAddress {
12    fn fmt(&self, f: &mut fmt::Formatter<'_>) -> fmt::Result {
13       let octet = self.0;
14       write!(
15          f,
16          "{:02x}:{:02x}:{:02x}:{:02x}:{:02x}:{:02x}",
17          octet[0], octet[1], octet[2],
18          octet[3], octet[4], octet[5]
19       )
20    }
21 }
22
23 impl MacAddress {
24    pub fn new() -> MacAddress {
25       let mut octets: [u8; 6] = [0; 6];
26       rand::thread_rng().fill_bytes(&mut octets);          ◄──┘  Generates a random number
27       octets[0] |= 0b_0000_0010;          ◄──┐  Ensures that the local address bit is set to 1
28       octets[0] &= 0b_1111_1110;          ◄──┘
29       MacAddress { 0: octets }
30    }                                           Ensures the unicast bit is set to 0
31 }
32
33 impl Into<wire::EthernetAddress> for MacAddress {
34    fn into(self) -> wire::EthernetAddress {
35       wire::EthernetAddress { 0: self.0 }
36    }
37 }
```

The following listing shows how to interact with the server to make the HTTP request. The code for this listing is in ch8/ch8-mget/src/http.rs.

Listing 8.22 Manually creating an HTTP request using TCP primitives

```
 1 use std::collections::BTreeMap;
 2 use std::fmt;
 3 use std::net::IpAddr;
 4 use std::os::unix::io::AsRawFd;
 5
 6 use smoltcp::iface::{EthernetInterfaceBuilder, NeighborCache, Routes};
 7 use smoltcp::phy::{wait as phy_wait, TapInterface};
 8 use smoltcp::socket::{SocketSet, TcpSocket, TcpSocketBuffer};
 9 use smoltcp::time::Instant;
10 use smoltcp::wire::{EthernetAddress, IpAddress, IpCidr, Ipv4Address};
11 use url::Url;
12
13 #[derive(Debug)]
14 enum HttpState {
15    Connect,
16    Request,
17    Response,
18 }
19
20 #[derive(Debug)]
21 pub enum UpstreamError {
```

```
22    Network(smoltcp::Error),
23    InvalidUrl,
24    Content(std::str::Utf8Error),
25  }
26
27  impl fmt::Display for UpstreamError {
28    fn fmt(&self, f: &mut fmt::Formatter<'_>) -> fmt::Result {
29      write!(f, "{:?}", self)
30    }
31  }
32
33  impl From<smoltcp::Error> for UpstreamError {
34    fn from(error: smoltcp::Error) -> Self {
35      UpstreamError::Network(error)
36    }
37  }
38
39  impl From<std::str::Utf8Error> for UpstreamError {
40    fn from(error: std::str::Utf8Error) -> Self {
41      UpstreamError::Content(error)
42    }
43  }
44
45  fn random_port() -> u16 {
46    49152 + rand::random::<u16>() % 16384
47  }
48
49  pub fn get(
50    tap: TapInterface,
51    mac: EthernetAddress,
52    addr: IpAddr,
53    url: Url,
54  ) -> Result<(), UpstreamError> {
55    let domain_name = url.host_str().ok_or(UpstreamError::InvalidUrl)?;
56
57    let neighbor_cache = NeighborCache::new(BTreeMap::new());
58
59    let tcp_rx_buffer = TcpSocketBuffer::new(vec![0; 1024]);
60    let tcp_tx_buffer = TcpSocketBuffer::new(vec![0; 1024]);
61    let tcp_socket = TcpSocket::new(tcp_rx_buffer, tcp_tx_buffer);
62
63    let ip_addrs = [IpCidr::new(IpAddress::v4(192, 168, 42, 1), 24)];
64
65    let fd = tap.as_raw_fd();
66    let mut routes = Routes::new(BTreeMap::new());
67    let default_gateway = Ipv4Address::new(192, 168, 42, 100);
68    routes.add_default_ipv4_route(default_gateway).unwrap();
69    let mut iface = EthernetInterfaceBuilder::new(tap)
70      .ethernet_addr(mac)
71      .neighbor_cache(neighbor_cache)
72      .ip_addrs(ip_addrs)
73      .routes(routes)
74      .finalize();
75
76    let mut sockets = SocketSet::new(vec![]);
```

```
77    let tcp_handle = sockets.add(tcp_socket);
78
79    let http_header = format!(
80      "GET {} HTTP/1.0\r\nHost: {}\r\nConnection: close\r\n\r\n",
81      url.path(),
82      domain_name,
83    );
84
85    let mut state = HttpState::Connect;
86    'http: loop {
87      let timestamp = Instant::now();
88      match iface.poll(&mut sockets, timestamp) {
89        Ok(_) => {}
90        Err(smoltcp::Error::Unrecognized) => {}
91        Err(e) => {
92          eprintln!("error: {:?}", e);
93        }
94      }
95
96      {
97        let mut socket = sockets.get::<TcpSocket>(tcp_handle);
98
99        state = match state {
100         HttpState::Connect if !socket.is_active() => {
101           eprintln!("connecting");
102           socket.connect((addr, 80), random_port())?;
103           HttpState::Request
104         }
105
106         HttpState::Request if socket.may_send() => {
107           eprintln!("sending request");
108           socket.send_slice(http_header.as_ref())?;
109           HttpState::Response
110         }
111
112         HttpState::Response if socket.can_recv() => {
113           socket.recv(|raw_data| {
114             let output = String::from_utf8_lossy(raw_data);
115             println!("{}", output);
116             (raw_data.len(), ())
117           })?;
118           HttpState::Response
119         }
120
121         HttpState::Response if !socket.may_recv() => {
122           eprintln!("received complete response");
123           break 'http;
124         }
125         _ => state,
126       }
127     }
128
129     phy_wait(fd, iface.poll_delay(&sockets, timestamp))
130       .expect("wait error");
131   }
```

```
132
133   Ok(())
134 }
```

And finally, the following listing performs the DNS resolution. The source for this listing is in ch8/ch8-mget/src/dns.rs.

Listing 8.23   Creating DNS queries to translate domain names to IP addresses

```
 1 use std::error::Error;
 2 use std::net::{SocketAddr, UdpSocket};
 3 use std::time::Duration;
 4
 5 use trust_dns::op::{Message, MessageType, OpCode, Query};
 6 use trust_dns::proto::error::ProtoError;
 7 use trust_dns::rr::domain::Name;
 8 use trust_dns::rr::record_type::RecordType;
 9 use trust_dns::serialize::binary::*;
10
11 fn message_id() -> u16 {
12   let candidate = rand::random();
13   if candidate == 0 {
14     return message_id();
15   }
16   candidate
17 }
18
19 #[derive(Debug)]
20 pub enum DnsError {
21   ParseDomainName(ProtoError),
22   ParseDnsServerAddress(std::net::AddrParseError),
23   Encoding(ProtoError),
24   Decoding(ProtoError),
25   Network(std::io::Error),
26   Sending(std::io::Error),
27   Receiving(std::io::Error),
28 }
29
30 impl std::fmt::Display for DnsError {
31   fn fmt(&self, f: &mut std::fmt::Formatter) -> std::fmt::Result {
32     write!(f, "{:#?}", self)
33   }
34 }
35
36 impl std::error::Error for DnsError {}        ◁── Falls back to default methods
37
38 pub fn resolve(
39   dns_server_address: &str,
40   domain_name: &str,
41 ) -> Result<Option<std::net::IpAddr>, Box<dyn Error>> {
42   let domain_name =
43     Name::from_ascii(domain_name)
44       .map_err(DnsError::ParseDomainName)?;
45
```

```
46   let dns_server_address =
47     format!("{}:53", dns_server_address);
48   let dns_server: SocketAddr = dns_server_address
49     .parse()
50     .map_err(DnsError::ParseDnsServerAddress)?;
51
52   let mut request_buffer: Vec<u8> =
53     Vec::with_capacity(64);
54   let mut response_buffer: Vec<u8> =
55     vec![0; 512];
56
57   let mut request = Message::new();
58   request.add_query(
59     Query::query(domain_name, RecordType::A)
60   );
61
62   request
63     .set_id(message_id())
64     .set_message_type(MessageType::Query)
65     .set_op_code(OpCode::Query)
66     .set_recursion_desired(true);
67
68   let localhost =
69     UdpSocket::bind("0.0.0.0:0").map_err(DnsError::Network)?;
70
71   let timeout = Duration::from_secs(5);
72   localhost
73     .set_read_timeout(Some(timeout))
74     .map_err(DnsError::Network)?;
75
76   localhost
77     .set_nonblocking(false)
78     .map_err(DnsError::Network)?;
79
80   let mut encoder = BinEncoder::new(&mut request_buffer);
81   request.emit(&mut encoder).map_err(DnsError::Encoding)?;
82
83   let _n_bytes_sent = localhost
84     .send_to(&request_buffer, dns_server)
85     .map_err(DnsError::Sending)?;
86
87   loop {
88     let (_b_bytes_recv, remote_port) = localhost
89       .recv_from(&mut response_buffer)
90       .map_err(DnsError::Receiving)?;
91
92     if remote_port == dns_server {
93       break;
94     }
95   }
96
97   let response =
98     Message::from_vec(&response_buffer)
99       .map_err(DnsError::Decoding)?;
100
```

Attempts to build the internal data structures using the raw text input

Because our DNS request will be small, we only need a little bit of space to hold it.

DNS over UDP uses a maximum packet size of 512 bytes.

DNS messages can hold multiple queries, but here we only use a single one.

Asks the DNS server to make requests on our behalf if it doesn't know the answer

Binding to port 0 asks the OS to allocate a port on our behalf.

There is a small chance another UDP message will be received on our port from some unknown sender. To avoid that, we ignore packets from IP addresses that we don't expect.

```
101  for answer in response.answers() {
102    if answer.record_type() == RecordType::A {
103      let resource = answer.rdata();
104      let server_ip =
105        resource.to_ip_addr().expect("invalid IP address received");
106      return Ok(Some(server_ip));
107    }
108  }
109
110  Ok(None)
111 }
```

mget is an ambitious project. It brings together all the threads from the chapter, is dozens of lines long, and yet is less capable than the request::get(url) call we made in listing 8.2. Hopefully it's revealed several interesting avenues for you to explore. Perhaps, surprisingly, there are several more networking layers to unwrap. Well done for making your way through a lengthy and challenging chapter.

Summary

- Networking is complicated. Standard models such as OSIs are only partially accurate.

- Trait objects allow for runtime polymorphism. Typically, programmers prefer generics because trait objects incur a small runtime cost. However, this situation is not always clear-cut. Using trait objects can reduce space because only a single version of each function needs to be compiled. Fewer functions also benefits cache coherence.

- Networking protocols are particular about which bytes are used. In general, you should prefer using &[u8] literals (b"…") over &str literals ("...") to ensure that you retain full control.

- There are three main strategies for handling multiple upstream error types within a single scope:
  - Create an internal wrapper type and implement From for each of the upstream types
  - Change the return type to make use of a trait object that implements std::error:Error
  - Use .unwrap() and its cousin .expect()

- Finite state machines can be elegantly modeled in Rust with an enum and a loop. At each iteration, indicate the next state by returning the appropriate enum variant.

- To enable two-way communications in UDP, each side of the conversation must be able to act as a client and a server.

Time and timekeeping

9

This chapter covers

- Understanding how a computer keeps time
- How operating systems represent timestamps
- Synchronizing atomic clocks with the Network Time Protocol (NTP)

In this chapter, you'll produce an NTP (Network Time Protocol) client that requests the current time from the world's network of public time servers. It's a fully functioning client that can be included in your own computer's boot process to keep it in sync with the world.

Understanding how time works within computers supports your efforts to build resilient applications. The system clock jumps both backwards and forwards in time. Knowing why this happens allows you to anticipate and prepare for that eventuality.

Your computer also contains multiple physical and virtual clocks. It takes some knowledge to understand the limitations of each and when these are appropriate. Understanding the limitations of each should foster a healthy skepticism about micro benchmarks and other time-sensitive code.

Some of the hardest software engineering involves distributed systems that need to agree on what the time is. If you have the resources of Google, then you're able to maintain a network atomic clock that provides a worldwide time synchronization of 7 ms. The closest open source alternative is CockroachDB (https://www.cockroachlabs.com/). It relies on the NTP, which can have a (worldwide) latency of approximately dozens of milliseconds. But that doesn't make it useless. When deployed within a local network, NTP allows computers to agree on the time to within a few milliseconds or less.

On the Rust side of the equation, this chapter invests lots of time interacting with the OS internals. You'll become more confident with `unsafe` blocks and with using raw pointers. Readers will become familiar with chrono, the de facto standard crate for high-level time and clock operations.

9.1   *Background*

It's easy to think that a day has 86,400 seconds (60 s × 60 min × 24 h = 86,400 s). But the earth's rotation isn't quite that perfect. The length of each day fluctuates due to tidal friction with the moon and other effects such as torque at the boundary of the earth's core and its mantle.

Software does not tolerate these imperfections. Most systems assume that most seconds have an equal duration. The mismatch presents several problems.

In 2012, a large number of services—including high profile sites such as Reddit and Mozilla's Hadoop infrastructure—stopped functioning after a leap second was added to their clocks. And, at times, clocks can go back in time (this chapter does not, however, cover time travel). Few software systems are prepared for the same timestamp to appear twice. That makes it difficult to debug the logs. There are two options for resolving this impasse:

- *Keep the length of each second fixed.* This is good for computers but irritating for humans. Over time, "midday" drifts towards sunset or sunrise.
- *Adjust the length of each year to keep the sun's position relative to noon in the same place from year to year.* This is good for humans but sometimes highly irritating for computers.

In practice, we can chose both options as we do in this chapter. The world's atomic clocks use their own time zone with fixed-length seconds, called TAI. Everything else uses time zones that are periodically adjusted; these are called UTC.

TAI is used by the world's atomic clocks and maintains a fixed-length year. UTC adds leap seconds to TAI about once every 18 months. In 1972, TAI and UTC were 10 seconds apart. By 2016, they had drifted to 36 seconds apart.

In addition to the issues with earth's fickle rotational speed, the physics of your own computer make it challenging to keep accurate time. There are also (at least) two clocks running on your system. One is a battery-powered device, called the *real-time clock*. The other one is known as *system time*. System time increments itself based on hardware interrupts provided by the computer's motherboard. Somewhere in your system, a quartz crystal is oscillating rapidly.

Dealing with hardware platforms without a real-time clock

The Raspberry Pi device does not include a battery-supported, real-time clock. When the computer turns on, the system clock is set to *epoch time*. That it, it is set to the number of elapsed seconds since 1 Jan 1970. During boot, it uses the NTP to identify the current time.

What about situations where there is no network connection? This is the situation faced by the Cacophony Project (https://cacophony.org.nz/), which develops devices to support New Zealand's native bird species by applying computer vision to accurately identify pest species.

The main sensor of the device is a thermal imaging camera. Footage needs to be annotated with accurate timestamps. To enable this, the Cacophony Project team decided to add an additional real-time clock, Raspberry Pi Hat, to their custom board. The following figure shows the internals of the prototype for the Cacophony Project's automated pest detection system.

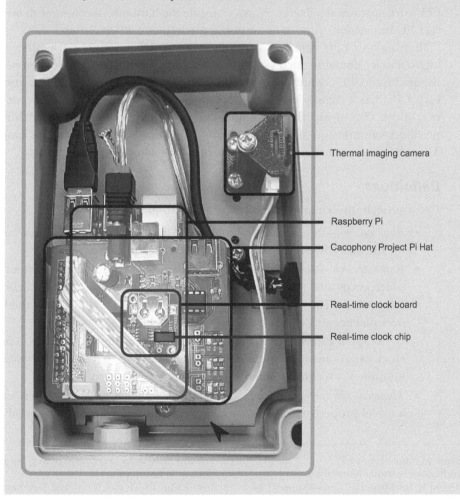

9.2   Sources of time

Computers can't look at the clock on the wall to determine what time it is. They need to figure it out by themselves. To explain how this happens, let's consider how digital clocks operate generally, then how computer systems operate given some difficult constraints, such as operating without power.

Digital clocks consist of two main parts. The first part is some component that ticks at regular intervals. The second part is a pair of counters. One counter increments as ticks occur. The other increments as seconds occur. Determining "now" within digital clocks means comparing the number of seconds against some predetermined starting point. The starting point is known as the *epoch*.

Embedded hardware aside, when your computer is turned off, a small battery-powered clock continues to run. Its electric charge causes a quartz crystal to oscillate rapidly. The clock measures those oscillations and updates its internal counters. In a running computer, the CPU clock frequency becomes the source of regular ticks. A CPU core operates at a fixed frequency.[1] Inside the hardware, a counter can be accessed via CPU instructions and/or by accessing predefined CPU registers.[2]

Relying on a CPU's clock can actually cause problems in niche scientific and other high-accuracy domains, such as profiling an application's behavior. When computers use multiple CPUs, which is especially common in high performance computing, each CPU has a slightly different clock rate. Moreover, CPUs perform out-of-order execution. This means that it's impossible for someone creating a benchmarking/ profiling software suite to know how long a function takes between two timestamps. The CPU instructions requesting the current timestamp may have shifted.

9.3   Definitions

Unfortunately, this chapter needs to introduce some jargon:

- *Absolute time*—Describes the time that you would tell someone if they were to ask for the time. Also referred to as *wall clock time* and *calendar time*.
- *Real-time clock*—A physical clock that's embedded in the computer's motherboard, which keeps time when the power is off. It's also known as the *CMOS clock*.
- *System clock*—The operating system's view of the time. Upon boot, the OS takes over timekeeping duties from the real-time clock.

  All applications derive their idea of time from the system time. The system clock experiences jumps, as it can be manually set to a different position. This jumpiness can confuse some applications.
- *Monotonically increasing*—A clock that never provides the same time twice. This is a useful property for a computer application because, among other advantages,

---

[1] Dynamic adjustments to a CPU's clock speed do occur in many processors to conserve power, but these happen infrequently enough from the point of view of the clock as to be insignificant.

[2] For example, Intel-based processors support the RDTSC instruction, which stands for *Read Time Stamp Counter*.

log messages will never have a repeated timestamp. Unfortunately, preventing time adjustments means being permanently bound to the local clock's skew. Note that the *system clock* is not monotonically increasing.

- *Steady clock*—This clock provides two guarantees: its seconds are all equal length and it is monotonically increasing. Values from steady clocks are unlikely to align with the system clock's time or absolute time. These typically start at 0 when computers boot up, then count upwards as an internal counter progresses. Although potentially useless for knowing the absolute time, these are handy for calculating the duration between two points in time.

- *High accuracy*—A clock is highly accurate if the length of its seconds are regular. The difference between two clocks is known as *skew*. Highly accurate clocks have little skew against the atomic clocks that are humanity's best engineering effort at keeping accurate time.

- *High resolution*—Provides accuracy down to 10 nanoseconds or below. High resolution clocks are typically implemented within CPU chips because there are few devices that can maintain time at such high frequency. CPUs are able to do this. Their units of work are measured in cycles, and cycles have the same duration. A 1 GHz CPU core takes 1 nanosecond to compute one cycle.

- *Fast clock*—A clock that takes little time to read the time. Fast clocks sacrifice accuracy and precision for speed, however.

9.4 Encoding time

There are many ways to represent time within a computer. The typical approach is to use a pair of 32-bit integers. The first counts the number of seconds that have elapsed. The second represents a fraction of a second. The precision of the fractional part depends on the device in question.

The starting point is arbitrary. The most common epoch in UNIX-based systems is 1 Jan 1970 UTC. Alternatives include 1 Jan 1900 (which happens to be used by NTP), 1 Jan 2000 for more recent applications, and 1 Jan 1601 (which is the beginning of the Gregorian calendar). Using fixed-width integers presents two key advantages and two main challenges:

- Advantages include
  - *Simplicity*—It's easy to understand the format.
  - *Efficiency*—Integer arithmetic is the CPU's favorite activity.
- Disadvantages include
  - *Fixed-range*—All fixed-integer types are finite, implying that time eventually wraps around to 0 again.
  - *Imprecise*—Integers are discrete, while time is continuous. Different systems make different trade-offs relating to subsecond accuracy, leading to rounding errors.

It's also important to note that the general approach is inconsistently implemented. Here are some things seen in the wild to represent the seconds component:

- UNIX timestamps, a 32-bit integer, represents milliseconds since epoch (e.g., 1 Jan 1970).
- MS Windows FILETIME structures (since Windows 2000), a 64-bit unsigned integer, represents 100 nanosecond increments since 1 Jan 1601 (UTC).
- Rust community's chronos crate, a 32-bit signed integer, implements NaiveTime alongside an enum to represent time zones where appropriate.[3]
- time_t (meaning *time type* but also called *simple time* or *calendar time*) within the C standard library (libc) varies:
  - Dinkumware's libc provides an unsigned long int (e.g., a 32-bit unsigned integer).
  - GNU's libc includes a long int (e.g., a 32-bit signed integer).
  - AVR's libc uses a 32-bit unsigned integer, and its epoch begins at midnight, 1 January 2000 (UTC).

Fractional parts tend to use the same type as their whole-second counterparts, but this isn't guaranteed. Now, let's take a peek a time zones.

9.4.1 Representing time zones

Time zones are political divisions, rather than technical ones. A soft consensus appears to have been formed around storing another integer that represents the number of seconds offset from UTC.

9.5 clock v0.1.0: Teaching an application how to tell the time

To begin coding our NTP client, let's start by learning how to read time. Figure 9.1 provides a quick overview of how an application does that.

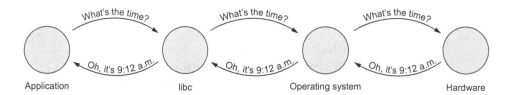

Figure 9.1 An application gets time information from the OS, usually functionally provided by the system's libc implementation.

---

[3] chronos has relatively few quirks, but one of which is sneaking leap seconds into the nanoseconds field.

Listing 9.2, which reads the system time in the local time zone, might almost feel too small to be a full-fledged example. But running the code results in the current timestamp formatted according to the ISO 8601 standard. The following listing provides its configuration. You'll find the source for this listing in ch9/ch9-clock0/Cargo.toml.

Listing 9.1 Crate configuration for listing 9.2

```
[package]
name = "clock"
version = "0.1.0"
authors = ["Tim McNamara <author@rustinaction.com>"]
edition = "2018"

[dependencies]
chrono = "0.4"
```

The following listing reads and prints the system time. You'll find the source code for the listing in ch9/ch9-clock0/src/main.rs.

Listing 9.2 Reading the system time and printing it on the screen

```
1 use chrono::Local;
2
3 fn main() {
4     let now = Local::now();        ⟵  Asks for the time in
5     println!("{}", now);               the system's local
6 }                                      time zone
```

In listing 9.2, there is a lot of complexity hidden by these eight lines of code. Much of it will be peeled away during the course of the chapter. For now, it's enough to know that chrono::Local provides the magic. It returns a typed value, containing a time zone.

> **NOTE** Interacting with timestamps that don't include time zones or performing other forms of illegal time arithmetic results in the program refusing to compile.

9.6 clock v0.1.1: Formatting timestamps to comply with ISO 8601 and email standards

The application that we'll create is called clock, which reports the current time. You'll find the full application in listing 9.7. Throughout the chapter, the application will be incrementally enhanced to support setting the time manually and via NTP. For the moment, however, the following code shows the result of compiling and running the code from listing 9.8 and sending it the --use-standard timestamp flag.

```
$ cd ch9/ch9-clock1

$ cargo run -- --use-standard rfc2822
warning: associated function is never used: `set`
  --> src/main.rs:12:8
```

```
   |
12 |      fn set() -> ! {
   |         ^^^
   |
   |
   = note: `#[warn(dead_code)]` on by default
warning: 1 warning emitted
    Finished dev [unoptimized + debuginfo] target(s) in 0.01s
     Running `target/debug/clock --use-standard rfc2822`
Sat, 20 Feb 2021 15:36:12 +1300
```

9.6.1 *Refactoring the clock v0.1.0 code to support a wider architecture*

It makes sense to spend a short period of time creating a scaffold for the larger application that clock will become. Within the application, we'll first make a small cosmetic change. Rather than using functions to read the time and adjust it, we'll use static methods of a `Clock` struct. The following listing, an excerpt from listing 9.7, shows the change from listing 9.2.

Listing 9.3 Reading the time from the local system clock

```
 2 use chrono::{DateTime};
 3 use chrono::{Local};
 4
 5 struct Clock;
 6
 7 impl Clock {
 8      fn get() -> DateTime<Local> {         DateTime<Local> is a
 9          Local::now()                      DateTime with the Local
10      }                                     time zone information.
11
12      fn set() -> ! {
13          unimplemented!()
14      }
15 }
```

What on earth is the return type of `set()`? The exclamation mark (!) indicates to the compiler that the function never returns (a return value is impossible). It's referred to as the Never type. If the `unimplemented!()` macro (or its shorter cousin `todo!()`) is reached at runtime, then the program panics.

`Clock` is purely acting as a namespace at this stage. Adding a struct now provides some extensibility later on. As the application grows, it might become useful for `Clock` to contain some state between calls or implement some trait to support new functionality.

NOTE A struct with no fields is known as a *zero-sized type* or ZST. It does not occupy any memory in the resulting application and is purely a compile-time construct.

9.6.2 Formatting the time

This section looks at formatting the time as a UNIX timestamp or a formatted string according to ISO 8601, RFC 2822, and RFC 3339 conventions. The following listing, an excerpt from listing 9.7, demonstrates how to produce timestamps using the functionality provided by chrono. The timestamps are then sent to stdout.

> **Listing 9.4 Showing the methods used to format timestamps**

```
48      let now = Clock::get();
49      match std {
50          "timestamp" => println!("{}", now.timestamp()),
51          "rfc2822"   => println!("{}", now.to_rfc2822()),
52          "rfc3339"   => println!("{}", now.to_rfc3339()),
53          _ => unreachable!(),
54      }
```

Our clock application (thanks to chrono) supports three time formats—timestamp, rfc2822, and rfc3339:

- *timestamp*—Formats the number of seconds since the epoch, also known as a *UNIX timestamp*.
- *rfc2822*—Corresponds to RPC 2822 (https://tools.ietf.org/html/rfc2822), which is how time is formatted within email message headers.
- *rfc3339*—Corresponds to RFC 3339 (https://tools.ietf.org/html/rfc3339). RFC 3339 formats time in a way that is more commonly associated with the ISO 8601 standard. However, ISO 8601 is a slightly stricter standard. Every RFC 3339-compliant timestamp is an ISO 8601-compliant timestamp, but the inverse is not true.

9.6.3 Providing a full command-line interface

Command-line arguments are part of the environment provided to an application from its OS when it's established. These are raw strings. Rust provides some support for accessing the raw Vec<String> via std::env::args, but it can be tedious to develop lots of parsing logic for moderately-sized applications.

Our code wants to be able to validate certain input, such that the desired output format is one that the clock app actually supports. But validating input tends to be irritatingly complex. To avoid this frustration, clock makes use of the clap crate.

There are two main types that are useful for getting started: clap::App and clap::Arg. Each clap::Arg represents a command-line argument and the options that it can represent. clap::App collects these into a single application. To support the public API in table 9.1, the code in listing 9.5 uses three Arg structs that are wrapped together within a single App.

Listing 9.5 is an excerpt from listing 9.7. It demonstrates how to implement the API presented in table 9.1 using clap.

Table 9.1   Usage examples for executing the clock application from the command line. Each command needs to be supported by our parser.

Use	Description	Example output
`clock`	Default usage. Prints the current time.	`2018-06-17T11:25:19...`
`clock get`	Provides a `get` action explicitly with default formatting.	`2018-06-17T11:25:19...`
`clock get --use-standard timestamp`	Provides a `get` action and a formatting standard.	`1529191458`
`clock get -s timestamp`	Provides a `get` action and a formatting standard using shorter notation.	`1529191458`
`clock set <datetime>`	Provides a `set` action explicitly with default parsing rules.	
`clock set --use-standard timestamp <datetime>`	Provides a `set` action explicitly and indicates that the input will be a UNIX timestamp.	

Listing 9.5   Using clap to parse command-line arguments

```
18    let app = App::new("clock")
19      .version("0.1")
20      .about("Gets and (aspirationally) sets the time.")
21      .arg(
22       Arg::with_name("action")
23         .takes_value(true)
24         .possible_values(&["get", "set"])
25         .default_value("get"),
26      )
27      .arg(
28       Arg::with_name("std")
29         .short("s")
30         .long("standard")
31         .takes_value(true)
32         .possible_values(&[
33           "rfc2822",
34           "rfc3339",
35           "timestamp",
36         ])
37         .default_value("rfc3339"),
38      )
39      .arg(Arg::with_name("datetime").help(
40       "When <action> is 'set', apply <datetime>. \
41        Otherwise, ignore.",
42      ));
43
44    let args = app.get_matches();
```

The backslash asks Rust to escape the newline and the following indentation.

clap automatically generates some usage documentation for our clock application on your behalf. Using the `--help` option triggers its output.

9.6.4 *clock v0.1.1: Full project*

The following terminal session demonstrates the process of downloading and compiling the clock v0.1.1 project from the public Git repository. It also includes a fragment for accessing the `--help` option that is mentioned in the previous section:

```
$ git clone https://github.com/rust-in-action/code rust-in-action

$ cd rust-in-action/ch9/ch9-clock1

$ cargo build
...
   Compiling clock v0.1.1 (rust-in-action/ch9/ch9-clock1)
warning: associated function is never used: `set`          ◁─────┐  This warning is
  --> src/main.rs:12:6                                            │  eliminated in
   |                                                              │  clock v0.1.2.
12 |     fn set() -> ! {
   |        ^^^
   |
   = note: `#[warn(dead_code)]` on by default

warning: 1 warning emitted
                                         ┌─ Arguments to the right
$ cargo run -- --help          ◁─────────┤  of -- are sent to the
...                                      └─ resulting executable.
clock 0.1
Gets and sets (aspirationally) the time.

USAGE:
    clock.exe [OPTIONS] [ARGS]

FLAGS:
    -h, --help       Prints help information
    -V, --version    Prints version information

OPTIONS:
    -s, --use-standard <std>    [default: rfc3339]
                                [possible values: rfc2822,
                                rfc3339, timestamp]

ARGS:
    <action>      [default: get]  [possible values: get, set]
    <datetime>    When <action> is 'set', apply <datetime>.
                  Otherwise, ignore.       ┌─ Executes the
                                           │  target/debug/clock
$ target/debug/clock           ◁──────────┤  executable directly
2021-04-03T15:48:23.984946724+13:00
```

Creating the project step by step takes slightly more work. As clock v0.1.1 is a project managed by cargo, it follows the standard structure:

```
clock
├── Cargo.toml        ◄──┐   See listing 9.6.
└── src                  │
    └── main.rs       ◄──┘   See listing 9.7.
```

To create it manually, follow these steps:

1 From the command-line, execute these commands:

```
$ cargo new clock
$ cd clock
$ cargo install cargo-edit
$ cargo add clap@2
$ cargo add chrono@0.4
```

2 Compare the contents of your project's Cargo.toml file with listing 9.6. With the
exception of the authors field, these should match.

3 Replace the contents of src/main.rs with listing 9.7.

The next listing is the project's Cargo.toml file. You'll find it at ch9/ch9-clock1/
Cargo.toml. Following that is the project's src/main.rs file, listing 9.7. Its source is in
ch9/ch9-clock1/src/main.rs.

Listing 9.6   Crate configuration for clock v0.1.1

```
[package]
name = "clock"
version = "0.1.1"
authors = ["Tim McNamara <author@rustinaction.com>"]
edition = "2018"

[dependencies]
chrono = "0.4"
clap = "2"
```

Listing 9.7   Producing formatted dates from the command line, clock v0.1.1

```
 1 use chrono::DateTime;
 2 use chrono::Local;
 3 use clap::{App, Arg};
 4
 5 struct Clock;
 6
 7 impl Clock {
 8   fn get() -> DateTime<Local> {
 9     Local::now()
10   }
11
12   fn set() -> ! {
13     unimplemented!()
14   }
15 }
```

```
16
17 fn main() {
18   let app = App::new("clock")
19     .version("0.1")
20     .about("Gets and (aspirationally) sets the time.")
21     .arg(
22       Arg::with_name("action")
23         .takes_value(true)
24         .possible_values(&["get", "set"])
25         .default_value("get"),
26     )
27     .arg(
28       Arg::with_name("std")
29         .short("s")
30         .long("use-standard")
31         .takes_value(true)
32         .possible_values(&[
33           "rfc2822",
34           "rfc3339",
35           "timestamp",
36         ])
37         .default_value("rfc3339"),
38     )
39     .arg(Arg::with_name("datetime").help(
40       "When <action> is 'set', apply <datetime>. \
41        Otherwise, ignore.",
42     ));
43
44   let args = app.get_matches();
45
46   let action = args.value_of("action").unwrap();
47   let std = args.value_of("std").unwrap();
48
49   if action == "set" {
50     unimplemented!()
51   }
52
53   let now = Clock::get();
54   match std {
55     "timestamp" => println!("{}", now.timestamp()),
56     "rfc2822" => println!("{}", now.to_rfc2822()),
57     "rfc3339" => println!("{}", now.to_rfc3339()),
58     _ => unreachable!(),
59   }
60 }
```

> Supplies a default value to each argument via default_value("get") and default_value("rfc3339"). It's safe to call unwrap() on these two lines.

> Aborts early as we're not ready to set the time yet

9.7   *clock v0.1.2: Setting the time*

Setting the time is complicated because each OS has its own mechanism for doing so. This requires that we use OS-specific conditional compilation to create a cross-portable tool.

9.7.1 *Common behavior*

Listing 9.11 provides two implementations of setting the time. These both follow a common pattern:

1 Parsing a command-line argument to create a `DateTime<FixedOffset>` value.

  The `FixedOffset` time zone is provided by chrono as a proxy for "whichever time zone is provided by the user." chrono doesn't know at compile time which time zone will be selected.

2 Converting the `DateTime<FixedOffset>` to a `DateTime<Local>` to enable time zone comparisons.

3 Instantiating an OS-specific struct that's used as an argument for the necessary system call (*system calls* are function calls provided by the OS).

4 Setting the system's time within an `unsafe` block. This block is required because responsibility is delegated to the OS.

5 Printing the updated time.

WARNING This code uses functions to teleport the system's clock to a different time. This jumpiness can cause system instability.

Some applications expect monotonically increasing time. A smarter (but more complex) approach is to adjust the length of a second for *n* seconds until the desired time is reached. Functionality is implemented within the `Clock` struct that was introduced in section 9.6.1.

9.7.2 *Setting the time for operating systems that use libc*

POSIX-compliant operating systems can have their time set via a call to `settimeof-day()`, which is provided by libc. libc is the C Standard Library and has lots of historic connections with UNIX operating systems. The C language, in fact, was developed to write UNIX. Even today, interacting with a UNIX derivative involves using the tools provided by the C language. There are two mental hurdles required for Rust programmers to understanding the code in listing 9.11, which we'll address in the following sections:

- The arcane types provided by libc
- The unfamiliarity of providing arguments as pointers

LIBC TYPE NAMING CONVENTIONS
libc uses conventions for naming types that differ from Rust's. libc does not use Pascal-Case to denote a type, preferring to use lowercase. That is, where Rust would use `TimeVal`, libc uses `timeval`. The convention changes slightly when dealing with type aliases. Within libc, type aliases append an underscore followed by the letter t (`_t`) to the type's name. The next two snippets show some libc imports and the equivalent Rust code for building those types.

On line 64 of listing 9.8, you will encounter this line:

```
libc::{timeval, time_t, suseconds_t};
```

It represents two type aliases and a struct definition. In Rust syntax, these are defined like this:

```
#![allow(non_camel_case_types)]

type time_t = i64;
type suseconds_t = i64;

pub struct timeval {
    pub tv_sec: time_t,
    pub tv_usec: suseconds_t,
}
```

time_t represents the seconds that have elapsed since the epoch. suseconds_t represents the fractional component of the current second.

The types and functions relating to timekeeping involve a lot of indirection. The code is intended to be easy to implement, which means providing local implementors (hardware designers) the opportunity to change aspects as their platforms require. The way this is done is to use type aliases everywhere, rather than sticking to a defined integer type.

NON-WINDOWS CLOCK CODE

The libc library provides a handy function, settimeofday, which we'll use in listing 9.8. The project's Cargo.toml file requires two extra lines to bring libc bindings into the crate for non-Windows platforms:

```
[target.'cfg(not(windows))'.dependencies]
libc = "0.2"
```
You can add these two lines to the end of the file.

The following listing, an extract from listing 9.11, shows how to set the time with C's standard library, libc. In the listing, we use Linux and BSD operating systems or other similar ones.

Listing 9.8 Setting the time in a libc environment

```
62 #[cfg(not(windows))]
63 fn set<Tz: TimeZone>(t: DateTime<Tz>) -> () {
64     use libc::{timeval, time_t, suseconds_t};
65     use libc::{settimeofday, timezone }
66
67     let t = t.with_timezone(&Local);
68     let mut u: timeval = unsafe { zeroed() };
69
70     u.tv_sec = t.timestamp() as time_t;
71     u.tv_usec =
72         t.timestamp_subsec_micros() as suseconds_t;
73
74     unsafe {
75         let mock_tz: *const timezone = std::ptr::null();
76         settimeofday(&u as *const timeval, mock_tz);
77     }
78 }
```

The timezone parameter of settimeofday() appears to be some sort of historic accident. Non-null values generate an error.

t is sourced from the command line and has already been parsed.

Makes OS-specific imports within the function to avoid polluting the global scope. libc::settimeofday is a function that modifies the system clock, and suseconds_t, time_t, timeval, and timezone are all types used to interact with it.

This code cheekily, and probably perilously, avoids checking whether the settime-ofday function is successful. It's quite possible that it isn't. That will be remedied in the next iteration of the clock application.

9.7.3   *Setting the time on MS Windows*

The code for MS Windows is similar to its libc peers. It is somewhat wordier, as the struct that sets the time has more fields than the second and subsecond part. The rough equivalent of the libc library is called kernel32.dll, which is accessible after including the winapi crate.

WINDOWS API INTEGER TYPES

Windows provides its own take on what to call integral types. This code only makes use of the WORD type, but it can be useful to remember the two other common types that have emerged since computers have used 16-bit CPUs. The following table shows how integer types from kernel32.dll correspond to Rust types.

Windows type	Rust type	Remarks
WORD	u16	Refers to the width of a CPU "word" as it was when Windows was initially created
DWORD	u32	Double word
QWORD	u64	Quadruple word
LARGE_INTEGER	i64	A type defined as a crutch to enable 32-bit and 64-bit platforms to share code
ULARGE_INTEGER	u64	An unsigned version of LARGE_INTEGER

REPRESENTING TIME IN WINDOWS

Windows provides multiple time types. Within our clock application, however, we're mostly interested in SYSTEMTIME. Another type that is provided is FILETIME. The following table describes these types to avoid confusion.

Windows type	Rust type	Remarks
SYSTEMTIME	winapi::SYSTEMTIME	Contains fields for the year, month, day of the week, day of the month, hour, minute, second, and millisecond.
FILETIME	winapi::FILETIME	Analogous to libc::timeval. Contains second and millisecond fields. Microsoft's documentation warns that on 64-bit platforms, its use can cause irritating overflow bugs without finicky type casting, which is why it's not employed here.

WINDOWS CLOCK CODE

As the SYSTEMTIME struct contains many fields, generating one takes a little bit longer. The following listing shows this construct.

Listing 9.9 Setting the time using the Windows kernel32.dll API

```
19  #[cfg(windows)]
20  fn set<Tz: TimeZone>(t: DateTime<Tz>) -> () {
21    use chrono::Weekday;
22    use kernel32::SetSystemTime;
23    use winapi::{SYSTEMTIME, WORD};
24
25    let t = t.with_timezone(&Local);
26
27    let mut systime: SYSTEMTIME = unsafe { zeroed() };
28
29    let dow = match t.weekday() {
30      Weekday::Mon => 1,
31      Weekday::Tue => 2,
32      Weekday::Wed => 3,
33      Weekday::Thu => 4,
34      Weekday::Fri => 5,
35      Weekday::Sat => 6,
36      Weekday::Sun => 0,
37    };
38
39    let mut ns = t.nanosecond();
40    let mut leap = 0;
41    let is_leap_second = ns > 1_000_000_000;
42
43    if is_leap_second {
44      ns -= 1_000_000_000;
45      leap += 1;
46    }
47
48    systime.wYear = t.year() as WORD;
49    systime.wMonth = t.month() as WORD;
50    systime.wDayOfWeek = dow as WORD;
51    systime.wDay = t.day() as WORD;
52    systime.wHour = t.hour() as WORD;
53    systime.wMinute = t.minute() as WORD;
54    systime.wSecond = (leap + t.second()) as WORD;
55    systime.wMilliseconds = (ns / 1_000_000) as WORD;
56
57    let systime_ptr = &systime as *const SYSTEMTIME;
58
59    unsafe {
60      SetSystemTime(systime_ptr);
61    }
62  }
```

The chrono::Datelike trait provides the weekday() method. Microsoft's developer documentation provides the conversion table. (lines 29–37)

As an implementation detail, chrono represents leap seconds by adding an extra second within the nanoseconds field. To convert the nanoseconds to milliseconds as required by Windows, we need to account for this. (lines 39–46)

From the perspective of the Rust compiler, giving something else direct access to memory is unsafe. Rust cannot guarantee that the Windows kernel will be well-behaved. (lines 59–61)

9.7.4   *clock v0.1.2: The full code listing*

clock v0.1.2 follows the same project structure as v0.1.1, which is repeated here. To
create platform-specific behavior, some adjustments are required to Cargo.toml.

```
clock
├── Cargo.toml      ◁──┘   See listing 9.10.
└── src
    └── main.rs     ◁──┘   See listing 9.11.
```

Listings 9.10 and 9.11 provide the full source code for the project. These are available
for download from ch9/ch9-clock0/Cargo.toml and ch9/ch9-clock0/src/main.rs,
respectively.

Listing 9.10   Crate configuration for listing 9.11

```toml
[package]
name = "clock"
version = "0.1.2"
authors = ["Tim McNamara <author@rustinaction.com>"]
edition = "2018"

[dependencies]
chrono = "0.4"
clap = "2"

[target.'cfg(windows)'.dependencies]
winapi = "0.2"
kernel32-sys = "0.2"

[target.'cfg(not(windows))'.dependencies]
libc = "0.2"
```

Listing 9.11   Cross-portable code for setting the system time

```rust
 1 #[cfg(windows)]
 2 use kernel32;
 3 #[cfg(not(windows))]
 4 use libc;
 5 #[cfg(windows)]
 6 use winapi;
 7
 8 use chrono::{DateTime, Local, TimeZone};
 9 use clap::{App, Arg};
10 use std::mem::zeroed;
11
12 struct Clock;
13
14 impl Clock {
15   fn get() -> DateTime<Local> {
16     Local::now()
17   }
18
```

```rust
19   #[cfg(windows)]
20   fn set<Tz: TimeZone>(t: DateTime<Tz>) -> () {
21     use chrono::Weekday;
22     use kernel32::SetSystemTime;
23     use winapi::{SYSTEMTIME, WORD};
24
25     let t = t.with_timezone(&Local);
26
27     let mut systime: SYSTEMTIME = unsafe { zeroed() };
28
29     let dow = match t.weekday() {
30       Weekday::Mon => 1,
31       Weekday::Tue => 2,
32       Weekday::Wed => 3,
33       Weekday::Thu => 4,
34       Weekday::Fri => 5,
35       Weekday::Sat => 6,
36       Weekday::Sun => 0,
37     };
38
39     let mut ns = t.nanosecond();
40     let is_leap_second = ns > 1_000_000_000;
41
42     if is_leap_second {
43       ns -= 1_000_000_000;
44     }
45
46     systime.wYear = t.year() as WORD;
47     systime.wMonth = t.month() as WORD;
48     systime.wDayOfWeek = dow as WORD;
49     systime.wDay = t.day() as WORD;
50     systime.wHour = t.hour() as WORD;
51     systime.wMinute = t.minute() as WORD;
52     systime.wSecond = t.second() as WORD;
53     systime.wMilliseconds = (ns / 1_000_000) as WORD;
54
55     let systime_ptr = &systime as *const SYSTEMTIME;
56
57     unsafe {
58       SetSystemTime(systime_ptr);
59     }
60   }
61
62   #[cfg(not(windows))]
63   fn set<Tz: TimeZone>(t: DateTime<Tz>) -> () {
64       use libc::{timeval, time_t, suseconds_t};
65   use libc::{settimeofday, timezone};
66
67     let t = t.with_timezone(&Local);
68     let mut u: timeval = unsafe { zeroed() };
69
70     u.tv_sec = t.timestamp() as time_t;
71     u.tv_usec =
72       t.timestamp_subsec_micros() as suseconds_t;
73
```

```
74      unsafe {
75        let mock_tz: *const timezone = std::ptr::null();
76        settimeofday(&u as *const timeval, mock_tz);
77      }
78    }
79  }
80
81  fn main() {
82    let app = App::new("clock")
83      .version("0.1.2")
84      .about("Gets and (aspirationally) sets the time.")
85      .after_help(
86        "Note: UNIX timestamps are parsed as whole \
87         seconds since 1st January 1970 0:00:00 UTC. \
88         For more accuracy, use another format.",
89      )
90      .arg(
91        Arg::with_name("action")
92          .takes_value(true)
93          .possible_values(&["get", "set"])
94          .default_value("get"),
95      )
96      .arg(
97        Arg::with_name("std")
98          .short("s")
99          .long("use-standard")
100         .takes_value(true)
101         .possible_values(&[
102           "rfc2822",
103           "rfc3339",
104           "timestamp",
105         ])
106         .default_value("rfc3339"),
107     )
108     .arg(Arg::with_name("datetime").help(
109       "When <action> is 'set', apply <datetime>. \
110        Otherwise, ignore.",
111     ));
112
113   let args = app.get_matches();
114
115   let action = args.value_of("action").unwrap();
116   let std = args.value_of("std").unwrap();
117
118   if action == "set" {
119     let t_ = args.value_of("datetime").unwrap();
120
121     let parser = match std {
122       "rfc2822" => DateTime::parse_from_rfc2822,
123       "rfc3339" => DateTime::parse_from_rfc3339,
124       _ => unimplemented!(),
125     };
126
127     let err_msg = format!(
128       "Unable to parse {} according to {}",
```

```
129        t_, std
130      );
131      let t = parser(t_).expect(&err_msg);
132
133      Clock::set(t)
134    }
135
136    let now = Clock::get();
137
138    match std {
139      "timestamp" => println!("{}", now.timestamp()),
140      "rfc2822" => println!("{}", now.to_rfc2822()),
141      "rfc3339" => println!("{}", now.to_rfc3339()),
142      _ => unreachable!(),
143    }
144  }
```

9.8   *Improving error handling*

Those readers who have dealt with operating systems before will probably be dismayed at some of the code in section 9.7. Among other things, it doesn't check to see whether the calls to settimeofday() and SetSystemTime() were actually successful.

There are multiple reasons why setting the time might fail. The most obvious one is that the user who is attempting to set the time lacks permission to do so. The robust approach is to have Clock::set(t) return Result. As that requires modifying two functions that we have already spent some time explaining in depth, let's introduce a workaround that instead makes use of the operating system's error reporting:

```
fn main() {
  // ...
  if action == "set" {
    // ...

    Clock::set(t);                          // Deconstructs maybe_error, a Rust
                                            // type, to convert it into a raw i32
                                            // value that's easy to match
    let maybe_error =
      std::io::Error::last_os_error();   <—
    let os_error_code =
      &maybe_error.raw_os_error();       <—— Matching on a raw integer saves
                                            importing an enum, but sacrifices
                                            type safety. Production-ready code
    match os_error_code {                   shouldn't cheat in this way.
      Some(0) => (),                     <—
      Some(_) => eprintln!("Unable to set the time: {:?}", maybe_error),
      None => (),
    }
  }
}
```

After calls to Clock::set(t), Rust happily talks to the OS via std::io::Error::last _os_error(). Rust checks to see if an error code has been generated.

9.9   *clock v0.1.3: Resolving differences between clocks with the Network Time Protocol (NTP)*

Coming to a consensus about the correct time is known formally as *clock synchronization*. There are multiple international standards for synchronizing clocks. This section focuses on the most prominent one—the Network Time Protocol (NTP).

NTP has existed since the mid-1980s, and it has proven to be very stable. Its on-wire format has not changed in the first four revisions of the protocol, with backwards compatibility retained the entire time. NTP operates in two modes that can loosely be described as *always on* and *request/response*.

The always on mode allows multiple computers to work in a peer-to-peer fashion to converge on an agreed definition of *now*. It requires a software daemon or service to run constantly on each device, but it can achieve tight synchronization within local networks.

The request/response mode is much simpler. Local clients request the time via a single message and then parse the response, keeping track of the elapsed time. The client can then compare the original timestamp with the timestamp sent from the server, alter any delays caused by network latency, and make any necessary adjustments to move the local clock towards the server's time.

Which server should your computer connect to? NTP works by establishing a hierarchy. At the center is a small network of atomic clocks. There are also national pools of servers.

NTP allows clients to request the time from computers that are closer to atomic clocks. But that only gets us part of the way. Let's say that your computer asks 10 computers what they think the time is. Now we have 10 assertions about the time, and the network lag will differ for each source!

9.9.1   *Sending NTP requests and interpreting responses*

Let's consider a client-server situation where your computer wants to correct its own time. For every computer that you check with—let's call these *time servers*—there are two messages:

- The message from your computer to each time server is the *request*.
- The reply is known as the *response*.

These two messages generate four time points. Note that these occur in serial:

- T_1—The client's timestamp for when the request was sent. Referred to as `t1` in code.
- T_2—The time server's timestamp for when the request was received. Referred to as `t2` in code.
- T_3—The time server's timestamp for when it sends its response. Referred to as `t3` in code.
- T_4—The client's timestamp for when the response was received. Referred to as `t4` in code.

The names T_1–T_4 are designated by the RFC 2030 specification. Figure 9.2 shows the timestamps.

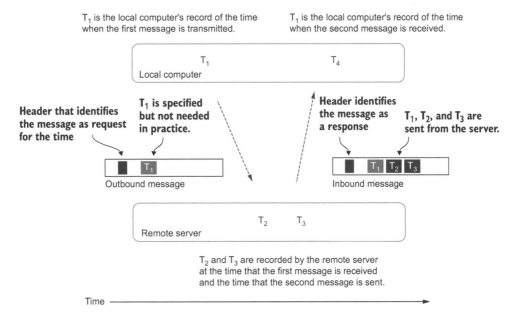

T_1 is the local computer's record of the time when the first message is transmitted.

T_1 is the local computer's record of the time when the second message is received.

Header that identifies the message as request for the time

T_1 is specified but not needed in practice.

Header identifies the message as a response

T_1, T_2, and T_3 are sent from the server.

Outbound message

Inbound message

Local computer

T_1

T_4

Remote server

T_2

T_3

T_2 and T_3 are recorded by the remote server at the time that the first message is received and the time that the second message is sent.

Time

Figure 9.2   Timestamps that are defined within the NTP standard

To see what this means in code, spend a few moments looking through the following listing. Lines 2–12 deal with establishing a connection. Lines 14–21 produce T_1–T_4.

Listing 9.12   Defining a function that sends NTP messages

```
1 fn ntp_roundtrip(
2   host: &str,
3   port: u16,
4 ) -> Result<NTPResult, std::io::Error> {
5   let destination = format!("{}:{}", host, port);
6   let timeout = Duration::from_secs(1);
7
8   let request = NTPMessage::client();
9   let mut response = NTPMessage::new();
10
11   let message = request.data;
12
13   let udp = UdpSocket::bind(LOCAL_ADDR)?;
14   udp.connect(&destination).expect("unable to connect");
15
16   let t1 = Utc::now();
17
```

This code cheats slightly by not encoding t1 in the outbound message. In practice, however, this works perfectly well and requires fractionally less work.

```
18    udp.send(&message)?;                              Sends a request payload (defined
19    udp.set_read_timeout(Some(timeout))?;            elsewhere) to the server
20    udp.recv_from(&mut response.data)?;
21                                                       Blocks the application until
22    let t4 = Utc::now();                               data is ready to be received
23
24    let t2: DateTime<Utc> =
25      response                                         rx_time() stands for received
26        .rx_time()                                     timestamp and is the time
27        .unwrap()                                      that the server received the
28        .into();                                       client's message.
29
30    let t3: DateTime<Utc> =
31      response                                         tx_time() stands for
32        .tx_time()                                     transmitted timestamp
33        .unwrap()                                      and is the time that the
34        .into();                                       server sent the reply.
35
36    Ok(NTPResult {
37      t1: t1,
38      t2: t2,
39      t3: t3,
40      t4: t4,
41    })
42 }
```

T_1–T_4, encapsulated in listing 9.12 as `NTPResult`, are all that's required to judge whether the local time matches the server's time. The protocol contains more related to error handling, but that's avoided here for simplicity. Otherwise, it's a perfectly capable NTP client.

9.9.2 *Adjusting the local time as a result of the server's response*

Given that our client has received at least one (and hopefully a few more) NTP responses, all that's left to do is to calculate the "right" time. But wait, which time is right? All we have are relative timestamps. There is still no universal "truth" that we've been given access to.

> **NOTE** For those readers who don't enjoy Greek letters, feel free to skim or even skip the next few paragraphs.

The NTP documentation provides two equations to help resolve the situation. Our aim is to calculate two values. Table 9.2 shows the calculations.

- *The time offset is what we're ultimately interested in.* It is denoted as θ (theta) by the official documentation. When θ is a positive number, our clock is fast. When it is negative, our clock is slow.
- *The delay caused by network congestion, latency, and other noise.* This is denoted as δ (delta). A large δ implies that the reading is less reliable. Our code uses this value to follow servers that respond quickly.

Table 9.2   How to calculate δ and θ in NTP

$\delta = (T_4 - T_1) - (T_3 - T_2)$	$(T_4 - T_1)$ calculates the total time spent on the client's side. $(T_3 - T_2)$ calculates the total time spent on the server's side.
	The distinction between the two differences (e.g., δ), is an estimate of the difference between the clocks, plus a delay caused by network traffic and processing.
$\theta = ((T_2 - T_1) + (T_4 - T_3)) / 2$	We take the average of the two pairs of timestamps.

The mathematics can be confusing because there is always an innate desire to know what the time *actually is*. That's impossible to know. All we have are assertions.

NTP is designed to operate multiple times per day, with participants nudging their clocks incrementally over time. Given sufficient adjustments, θ tends to 0 while δ remains relatively stable.

The standard is quite prescriptive about the formula to carry out the adjustments. For example, the reference implementation of NTP includes some useful filtering to limit the effect of bad actors and other spurious results. But we're going to cheat. We'll just take a mean of the differences, weighted by $1 / \theta^2$. This aggressively penalizes slow servers. To minimize the likelihood of any negative outcomes:

- *We'll check the time with known "good" actors.* In particular, we'll use time servers hosted by major OS vendors and other reliable sources to minimize the chances of someone sending us a questionable result.
- *No single result will affect the result too much.* We'll provide a cap of 200 ms on any adjustments we make to the local time.

The following listing, an extract from listing 9.15, shows this process for multiple time servers.

Listing 9.13   Adjusting the time according to the responses

```
175 fn check_time() -> Result<f64, std::io::Error> {
176     const NTP_PORT: u16 = 123;
177
178     let servers = [
179         "time.nist.gov",
180         "time.apple.com",
181         "time.euro.apple.com",
182         "time.google.com",
183         "time2.google.com",
184         //"time.windows.com",
185     ];
186
187     let mut times = Vec::with_capacity(servers.len());
188
189     for &server in servers.iter() {
190         print!("{} =>", server);
191
192         let calc = ntp_roundtrip(&server, NTP_PORT);
```

Google's time servers implement leap seconds by expanding the length of a second rather than adding an extra second. Thus, for one day approximately every 18 months, this server reports a different time than the others.

At the time of writing, Microsoft's time server provides a time that's 15 s ahead of its peers.

```
193
194    match calc {
195      Ok(time) => {
196        println!(" {}ms away from local system time", time.offset());
197        times.push(time);
198      }
199      Err(_) => {
200        println!(" ? [response took too long]")
201      }
202    };
203  }
204
205  let mut offsets = Vec::with_capacity(servers.len());
206  let mut offset_weights = Vec::with_capacity(servers.len());
207
208  for time in &times {
209    let offset = time.offset() as f64;
210    let delay = time.delay() as f64;
211
212    let weight = 1_000_000.0 / (delay * delay);        ◁─┐  Penalizes slow servers
213    if weight.is_finite() {                              │  by substantially
214      offsets.push(offset);                              │  decreasing their
215      offset_weights.push(weight);                       │  relative weights
216    }
217  }
218
219  let avg_offset = weighted_mean(&offsets, &offset_weights);
220
221  Ok(avg_offset)
222 }
```

9.9.3 Converting between time representations that use different precisions and epochs

chrono represents the fractional part of a second, down to a nanosecond precision, whereas NTP can represent times that differ by approximately 250 picoseconds. That's roughly four times more precise! The different internal representations used imply that some accuracy is likely to be lost during conversions.

The From trait is the mechanism for telling Rust that two types can be converted. From provides the from() method, which is encountered early on in one's Rust career (in examples such as String::from("Hello, world!")).

The next listing, a combination of three extracts from listing 9.15, provides implementations of the std::convert::From trait. This code enables the .into() calls on lines 28 and 34 of listing 9.13.

Listing 9.14   Converting between chrono::DateTime and NTP timestamps

```
19 const NTP_TO_UNIX_SECONDS: i64 = 2_208_988_800;    ◁─┐
                                                         │
              Number of seconds between 1 Jan 1900       │
        (the NTP epoch) and 1 Jan 1970 (the UNIX epoch)  │
```

```
22 #[derive(Default,Debug,Copy,Clone)]
23 struct NTPTimestamp {
24   seconds: u32,
25   fraction: u32,
26 }
```

> **Our internal type represents an NTP timestamp.**

```
52 impl From<NTPTimestamp> for DateTime<Utc> {
53   fn from(ntp: NTPTimestamp) -> Self {
54     let secs = ntp.seconds as i64 - NTP_TO_UNIX_SECONDS;
55     let mut nanos = ntp.fraction as f64;
56     nanos *= 1e9;
57     nanos /= 2_f64.powi(32);
58
59     Utc.timestamp(secs, nanos as u32)
60   }
61 }
62
63 impl From<DateTime<Utc>> for NTPTimestamp {
64   fn from(utc: DateTime<Utc>) -> Self {
65     let secs = utc.timestamp() + NTP_TO_UNIX_SECONDS;
66     let mut fraction = utc.nanosecond() as f64;
67     fraction *= 2_f64.powi(32);
68     fraction /= 1e9;
69
70     NTPTimestamp {
71       seconds: secs as u32,
72       fraction: fraction as u32,
73     }
74   }
75 }
```

> **You can implement these conversions using bit-shift operations, but at the expense of even less readability.**

From has a reciprocal peer, Into. Implementing From allows Rust to automatically generate an Into implementation on its own, except in advanced cases. In those cases, it's likely that developers already possess the knowledge required to implement Into manually and so probably don't need assistance here.

9.9.4   *clock v0.1.3: The full code listing*

The complete code listing for our clock application is presented in listing 9.15. Taken in its full glory, the whole of the clock application can look quite large and imposing. Hopefully, there is no new Rust syntax to digest within the listing. The source for this listing is in ch9/ch9-clock3/src/main.rs.

Listing 9.15   Full listing for the command-line NTP client, clock

```
1 #[cfg(windows)]
2 use kernel32;
3 #[cfg(not(windows))]
4 use libc;
5 #[cfg(windows)]
6 use winapi;
7
```

```
 8 use byteorder::{BigEndian, ReadBytesExt};
 9 use chrono::{
10   DateTime, Duration as ChronoDuration, TimeZone, Timelike,
11 };
12 use chrono::{Local, Utc};
13 use clap::{App, Arg};
14 use std::mem::zeroed;
15 use std::net::UdpSocket;
16 use std::time::Duration;
17
18 const NTP_MESSAGE_LENGTH: usize = 48;
19 const NTP_TO_UNIX_SECONDS: i64 = 2_208_988_800;
20 const LOCAL_ADDR: &'static str = "0.0.0.0:12300";
21
22 #[derive(Default, Debug, Copy, Clone)]
23 struct NTPTimestamp {
24   seconds: u32,
25   fraction: u32,
26 }
27
28 struct NTPMessage {
29   data: [u8; NTP_MESSAGE_LENGTH],
30 }
31
32 #[derive(Debug)]
33 struct NTPResult {
34   t1: DateTime<Utc>,
35   t2: DateTime<Utc>,
36   t3: DateTime<Utc>,
37   t4: DateTime<Utc>,
38 }
39
40 impl NTPResult {
41   fn offset(&self) -> i64 {
42     let duration = (self.t2 - self.t1) + (self.t4 - self.t3);
43     duration.num_milliseconds() / 2
44   }
45
46   fn delay(&self) -> i64 {
47     let duration = (self.t4 - self.t1) - (self.t3 - self.t2);
48     duration.num_milliseconds()
49   }
50 }
51
52 impl From<NTPTimestamp> for DateTime<Utc> {
53   fn from(ntp: NTPTimestamp) -> Self {
54     let secs = ntp.seconds as i64 - NTP_TO_UNIX_SECONDS;
55     let mut nanos = ntp.fraction as f64;
56     nanos *= 1e9;
57     nanos /= 2_f64.powi(32);
58
59     Utc.timestamp(secs, nanos as u32)
60   }
61 }
62
```

Annotations:

Line 18 — **12 * 4 bytes (the width of 12, 32-bit integers)**

Line 20 — **12300 is the default port for NTP.**

```
63 impl From<DateTime<Utc>> for NTPTimestamp {
64   fn from(utc: DateTime<Utc>) -> Self {
65     let secs = utc.timestamp() + NTP_TO_UNIX_SECONDS;
66     let mut fraction = utc.nanosecond() as f64;
67     fraction *= 2_f64.powi(32);
68     fraction /= 1e9;
69
70     NTPTimestamp {
71       seconds: secs as u32,
72       fraction: fraction as u32,
73     }
74   }
75 }
76
77 impl NTPMessage {
78   fn new() -> Self {
79     NTPMessage {
80       data: [0; NTP_MESSAGE_LENGTH],
81     }
82   }
83
84   fn client() -> Self {
85     const VERSION: u8 = 0b00_011_000;
86     const MODE: u8    = 0b00_000_011;
87
88     let mut msg = NTPMessage::new();
89
90     msg.data[0] |= VERSION;
91     msg.data[0] |= MODE;
92     msg
93   }
94
95   fn parse_timestamp(
96     &self,
97     i: usize,
98   ) -> Result<NTPTimestamp, std::io::Error> {
99     let mut reader = &self.data[i..i + 8];
100    let seconds   = reader.read_u32::<BigEndian>()?;
101    let fraction  = reader.read_u32::<BigEndian>()?;
102
103    Ok(NTPTimestamp {
104      seconds:  seconds,
105      fraction: fraction,
106    })
107  }
108
109  fn rx_time(
110    &self
111  ) -> Result<NTPTimestamp, std::io::Error> {
112    self.parse_timestamp(32)
113  }
114
115  fn tx_time(
116    &self
117  ) -> Result<NTPTimestamp, std::io::Error> {
```

Underscores delimit the NTP fields: leap indicator (2 bits), version (3 bits), and mode (3 bits).

The first byte of every NTP message contains three fields, but we only need to set two of these.

msg.data[0] is now equal to 0001_1011 (27 in decimal).

Takes a slice to the first byte

RX stands for receive.

TX stands for transmit.

```
118        self.parse_timestamp(40)
119    }
120 }
121
122 fn weighted_mean(values: &[f64], weights: &[f64]) -> f64 {
123   let mut result = 0.0;
124   let mut sum_of_weights = 0.0;
125
126   for (v, w) in values.iter().zip(weights) {
127     result += v * w;
128     sum_of_weights += w;
129   }
130
131   result / sum_of_weights
132 }
133
134 fn ntp_roundtrip(
135   host: &str,
136   port: u16,
137 ) -> Result<NTPResult, std::io::Error> {
138   let destination = format!("{}:{}", host, port);
139   let timeout = Duration::from_secs(1);
140
141   let request = NTPMessage::client();
142   let mut response = NTPMessage::new();
143
144   let message = request.data;
145
146   let udp = UdpSocket::bind(LOCAL_ADDR)?;
147   udp.connect(&destination).expect("unable to connect");
148
149   let t1 = Utc::now();
150
151   udp.send(&message)?;
152   udp.set_read_timeout(Some(timeout))?;
153   udp.recv_from(&mut response.data)?;
154   let t4 = Utc::now();
155
156   let t2: DateTime<Utc> =
157     response
158       .rx_time()
159       .unwrap()
160       .into();
161   let t3: DateTime<Utc> =
162     response
163       .tx_time()
164       .unwrap()
165       .into();
166
167   Ok(NTPResult {
168     t1: t1,
169     t2: t2,
170     t3: t3,
171     t4: t4,
172   })
```

```
173  }
174
175  fn check_time() -> Result<f64, std::io::Error> {
176    const NTP_PORT: u16 = 123;
177
178    let servers = [
179      "time.nist.gov",
180      "time.apple.com",
181      "time.euro.apple.com",
182      "time.google.com",
183      "time2.google.com",
184      //"time.windows.com",
185    ];
186
187    let mut times = Vec::with_capacity(servers.len());
188
189    for &server in servers.iter() {
190      print!("{} =>", server);
191
192      let calc = ntp_roundtrip(&server, NTP_PORT);
193
194      match calc {
195        Ok(time) => {
196          println!(" {}ms away from local system time", time.offset());
197          times.push(time);
198        }
199        Err(_) => {
200          println!(" ? [response took too long]")
201        }
202      };
203    }
204
205    let mut offsets = Vec::with_capacity(servers.len());
206    let mut offset_weights = Vec::with_capacity(servers.len());
207
208    for time in &times {
209      let offset = time.offset() as f64;
210      let delay = time.delay() as f64;
211
212      let weight = 1_000_000.0 / (delay * delay);
213      if weight.is_finite() {
214        offsets.push(offset);
215        offset_weights.push(weight);
216      }
217    }
218
219    let avg_offset = weighted_mean(&offsets, &offset_weights);
220
221    Ok(avg_offset)
222  }
223
224  struct Clock;
225
226  impl Clock {
227    fn get() -> DateTime<Local> {
```

```
228    Local::now()
229  }
230
231  #[cfg(windows)]
232  fn set<Tz: TimeZone>(t: DateTime<Tz>) -> () {
233    use chrono::Weekday;
234    use kernel32::SetSystemTime;
235    use winapi::{SYSTEMTIME, WORD};
236
237    let t = t.with_timezone(&Local);
238
239    let mut systime: SYSTEMTIME = unsafe { zeroed() };
240
241    let dow = match t.weekday() {
242      Weekday::Mon => 1,
243      Weekday::Tue => 2,
244      Weekday::Wed => 3,
245      Weekday::Thu => 4,
246      Weekday::Fri => 5,
247      Weekday::Sat => 6,
248      Weekday::Sun => 0,
249    };
250
251    let mut ns = t.nanosecond();
252    let is_leap_second = ns > 1_000_000_000;
253
254    if is_leap_second {
255      ns -= 1_000_000_000;
256    }
257
258    systime.wYear = t.year() as WORD;
259    systime.wMonth = t.month() as WORD;
260    systime.wDayOfWeek = dow as WORD;
261    systime.wDay = t.day() as WORD;
262    systime.wHour = t.hour() as WORD;
263    systime.wMinute = t.minute() as WORD;
264    systime.wSecond = t.second() as WORD;
265    systime.wMilliseconds = (ns / 1_000_000) as WORD;
266
267    let systime_ptr = &systime as *const SYSTEMTIME;
268    unsafe {
269      SetSystemTime(systime_ptr);
270    }
271  }
272
273  #[cfg(not(windows))]
274  fn set<Tz: TimeZone>(t: DateTime<Tz>) -> () {
275    use libc::settimeofday;
276    use libc::{suseconds_t, time_t, timeval, timezone};
277
278    let t = t.with_timezone(&Local);
279    let mut u: timeval = unsafe { zeroed() };
280
281    u.tv_sec = t.timestamp() as time_t;
282    u.tv_usec = t.timestamp_subsec_micros() as suseconds_t;
```

```
283
284     unsafe {
285        let mock_tz: *const timezone = std::ptr::null();
286        settimeofday(&u as *const timeval, mock_tz);
287     }
288   }
289 }
290
291 fn main() {
292   let app = App::new("clock")
293     .version("0.1.3")
294     .about("Gets and sets the time.")
295     .after_help(
296       "Note: UNIX timestamps are parsed as whole seconds since 1st \
297        January 1970 0:00:00 UTC. For more accuracy, use another \
298        format.",
299     )
300     .arg(
301       Arg::with_name("action")
302         .takes_value(true)
303         .possible_values(&["get", "set", "check-ntp"])
304         .default_value("get"),
305     )
306     .arg(
307       Arg::with_name("std")
308         .short("s")
309         .long("use-standard")
310         .takes_value(true)
311         .possible_values(&["rfc2822", "rfc3339", "timestamp"])
312         .default_value("rfc3339"),
313     )
314     .arg(Arg::with_name("datetime").help(
315       "When <action> is 'set', apply <datetime>. Otherwise, ignore.",
316     ));
317
318   let args = app.get_matches();
319
320   let action = args.value_of("action").unwrap();
321   let std = args.value_of("std").unwrap();
322
323   if action == "set" {
324     let t_ = args.value_of("datetime").unwrap();
325
326     let parser = match std {
327       "rfc2822" => DateTime::parse_from_rfc2822,
328       "rfc3339" => DateTime::parse_from_rfc3339,
329       _ => unimplemented!(),
330     };
331
332     let err_msg =
333       format!("Unable to parse {} according to {}", t_, std);
334     let t = parser(t_).expect(&err_msg);
335
336     Clock::set(t);
337
```

```
338    } else if action == "check-ntp" {
339      let offset = check_time().unwrap() as isize;
340
341      let adjust_ms_ = offset.signum() * offset.abs().min(200) / 5;
342      let adjust_ms = ChronoDuration::milliseconds(adjust_ms_ as i64);
343
344      let now: DateTime<Utc> = Utc::now() + adjust_ms;
345
346      Clock::set(now);
347    }
348
349    let maybe_error =
350      std::io::Error::last_os_error();
351    let os_error_code =
352      &maybe_error.raw_os_error();
353
354    match os_error_code {
355      Some(0) => (),
356      Some(_) => eprintln!("Unable to set the time: {:?}", maybe_error),
357      None => (),
358    }
359
360    let now = Clock::get();
361
362    match std {
363      "timestamp" => println!("{}", now.timestamp()),
364      "rfc2822" => println!("{}", now.to_rfc2822()),
365      "rfc3339" => println!("{}", now.to_rfc3339()),
366      _ => unreachable!(),
367    }
368 }
```

Summary

- Keeping track of elapsed time is difficult. Digital clocks ultimately rely on fuzzy signals from analog systems.

- Representing time is difficult. Libraries and standards disagree about how much precision is required and when to start.

- Establishing truth in a distributed system is difficult. Although we continually deceive ourselves otherwise, there is no single arbiter of what time it is. The best we can hope for is that all of the computers in our network are reasonably close to each other.

- A struct with no fields is known as a zero-sized type or ZST. It does not occupy any memory in the resulting application and is purely a compile-time construct.

- Creating cross-portable applications is possible with Rust. Adding platform-specific implementations of functions requires the precise use of the cfg annotation, but it can be done.

- When interfacing with external libraries, such as the API provided by the operating system (OS), a type conversion step is almost always required. Rust's type system does not extend to libraries that it did not create!

- System calls are used to make function calls to the OS. This invokes a complex interaction between the OS, the CPU, and the application.
- The Windows API typically uses verbose PascalCase identifiers, whereas operating systems from the POSIX tradition typically use terse lowercase identifiers.
- Be precise when making assumptions about the meaning of terms such as epoch and time zone. There is often hidden context lurking beneath the surface.
- Time can go backwards. Never write an application that relies on monotonically increasing time without ensuring that it requests a monotonically increasing clock from the OS.

Processes, threads, *10*
and containers

So far this book has almost completely avoided two fundamental terms of systems programming: threads and processes. Instead, the book has used the single term: program. This chapter expands our vocabulary.

Processes, threads, and containers are abstractions created to enable multiple tasks to be carried out at the same time. This enables *concurrency*. Its peer term, *parallelism*, means to make use of multiple physical CPU cores at the same time.

Counterintuitively, it is possible to have a concurrent system on a single CPU core. Because accessing data from memory and I/O take a long time, threads requesting data can be set to a *blocked* state. Blocked threads are rescheduled when their data is available.

Concurrency, or doing multiple things at the same time, is difficult to introduce into a computer program. Employing concurrency effectively involves both new concepts and new syntax.

The aim of this chapter is to give you the confidence to explore more advanced material. You will have a solid understanding of the different tools that are available to you as an applications programmer. This chapter exposes you to the standard library and the well engineered crates crossbeam and rayon. It will enable you to use them, though it won't give you sufficient background to be able to implement your own concurrency crates. The chapter follows the following structure:

- *It introduces you to Rust's closure syntax in section 10.1.* Closures are also known as anonymous functions and lambda functions. The syntax is important because the standard library and many (perhaps all) external crates rely on that syntax to provide support for Rust's concurrency model.
- *It provides a quick lesson on spawning threads in section 10.2.* You'll learn what a thread is and how to create (spawn) those. You'll also encounter a discussion of why programmers are warned against spawning tens of thousands of threads.
- *It distinguishes between functions and closures in section 10.3.* Conflating these two concepts can be a source of confusion for programmers new to Rust as these are often indistinguishable in other languages.
- *It follows with a large project in section 10.4.* You'll implement a multithreaded parser and a code generator using multiple strategies. As a nice aside, you get to create procedural art along the way.
- *The chapter concludes with an overview of other forms of concurrency.* This includes processes and containers.

10.1 Anonymous functions

This chapter is fairly dense, so let's get some points on the board quickly with some basic syntax and practical examples. We'll circle back to fill in a lot of the conceptual and theoretical material.

Threads and other forms of code that can run concurrently use a form of function definition that we've avoided for the bulk of the book. Taking a look at it now, defining a function looks like this:

```
fn add(a: i32, b: i32) -> i32 {
  a + b
}
```

The (loosely) equivalent lambda function is

```
let add = |a,b| { a + b };
```

Lambda functions are denoted by the pair of vertical bars (|...|) followed by curly brackets ({...}). The pair of vertical bars lets you define arguments. Lambda functions in Rust can read variables from within their scope. These are *closures*.

Unlike regular functions, lambda functions cannot be defined in global scope. The following listing gets around this by defining one within its main(). It defines two functions, a regular function and a lambda function, and then checks that these produce the same result.

> **Listing 10.1   Defining two functions and checking the result**

```
fn add(a: i32, b: i32) -> i32 {
  a + b
}

fn main() {
  let lambda_add = |a,b| { a + b };

 assert_eq!(add(4,5), lambda_add(4,5));
}
```

When you run listing 10.1, it executes happily (and silently). Let's now see how to put this functionality to work.

10.2   Spawning threads

Threads are the primary mechanism that operating systems provide for enabling concurrent execution. Modern operating systems ensure that each thread has fair access to the CPU. Understanding how to create threads (often referred to as spawning treads) and understanding their impact are fundamental skills for programmers wanting to make use of multi-core CPUs.

10.2.1   Introduction to closures

To spawn a thread in Rust, we pass an anonymous function to `std::thread::spawn()`. As described in section 10.1, anonymous functions are defined with two vertical bars to provide arguments and then curly brackets for the function's body. Because `spawn()` doesn't take any arguments, you will typically encounter this syntax:

```
thread::spawn(|| {
    // ...
});
```

When the spawned thread wants to access variables that are defined in the parent's scope, called a *capture*, Rust often complains that captures must be moved into the closure. To indicate that you want to move ownership, anonymous functions take a move keyword:

```
thread::spawn(move || {
    // ...
});
```
⟵ **The move keyword allows the anonymous function to access variables from their wider scope.**

Why is move required? Closures spawned in subthreads can potentially outlive their calling scope. As Rust will always ensure that accessing the data is valid, it requires ownership to move to the closure itself. Here are some guidelines for using captures while you gain an understanding of how these work:

- To reduce friction at compile time, implement `Copy`.
- Values originating in outer scopes may need to have a `static` lifetime.
- Spawned subthreads can outlive their parents. That implies that ownership should pass to the subthread with `move`.

10.2.2 Spawning a thread

A simple task waits, sleeping the CPU for 300 ms (milliseconds). If you have a 3 GHz CPU, you're getting it to rest for nearly 1 billion cycles. Those electrons will be very relieved. When executed, listing 10.2 prints the total duration (in "wall clock" time) of both executing threads. Here's the output:

```
300.218594ms
```

Listing 10.2   Sleeping a subthread for 300 ms

```
1 use std::{thread, time};
2
3 fn main() {
4   let start = time::Instant::now();
5
6   let handler = thread::spawn(|| {
7     let pause = time::Duration::from_millis(300);
8     thread::sleep(pause.clone());
9   });
10
11   handler.join().unwrap();
12
13   let finish = time::Instant::now();
14
15   println!("{:02?}", finish.duration_since(start));
16 }
```

If you had encountered multi-threaded programming before, you would have been introduced to `join` on line 11. Using `join` is fairly common, but what does it mean?

`join` is an extension of the thread metaphor. When threads are spawned, these are said to have *forked* from their parent thread. To join threads means to weave these back together again.

In practice, *join* means wait for the other thread to finish. The `join()` function instructs the OS to defer scheduling the calling thread until the other thread finishes.

10.2.3 Effect of spawning a few threads

In ideal settings, adding a second thread doubles the work we can do in the same amount of time. Each thread can gets its work done independently. Reality is not ideal, unfortunately. This has created a myth that threads are slow to create and bulky to maintain. This section aims to dispel that myth. When used as intended, threads perform very well.

Listing 10.3 shows a program that measures the overall time taken for two threads to perform the job that was carried out by a single thread in listing 10.2. If adding threads take a long time, we would expect the duration of listing 10.3's code to be longer.

As you'll notice, there is a negligible impact from creating one or two threads. As with listing 10.2, listing 10.3 prints almost the same output:

```
300.242328ms        ⟵  Versus 300.218594 ms
                       from listing 10.2
```

The difference in these two runs on my computer was 0.24 ms. While by no means a robust benchmark suite, it does indicate that spawning a thread isn't a tremendous performance hit.

Listing 10.3 Creating two subthreads to perform work on our behalf

```
1 use std::{thread, time};
2
3 fn main() {
4   let start = time::Instant::now();
5
6   let handler_1 = thread::spawn(move || {
7     let pause = time::Duration::from_millis(300);
8       thread::sleep(pause.clone());
9   });
10
11   let handler_2 = thread::spawn(move || {
12     let pause = time::Duration::from_millis(300);
13       thread::sleep(pause.clone());
14   });
15
16   handler_1.join().unwrap();
17   handler_2.join().unwrap();
18
19   let finish = time::Instant::now();
20
21   println!("{:?}", finish.duration_since(start));
22 }
```

If you've had any exposure to the field before, you may have heard that threads "don't scale." What does that mean?

Every thread requires its own memory, and by implication, we'll eventually exhaust our system's memory. Before that terminal point, though, thread creation begins to trigger slowdowns in other areas. As the number of threads to schedule increases, the OS scheduler's work increases. When there are many threads to schedule, deciding which thread to schedule next takes more time.

10.2.4 *Effect of spawning many threads*

Spawning threads is not free. It demands memory and CPU time. Switching between threads also invalidates caches.

Figure 10.1 shows the data generated by successive runs of listing 10.4. The variance stays quite tight until about 400 threads per batch. After that, there's almost no knowing how long a 20 ms sleep will take.

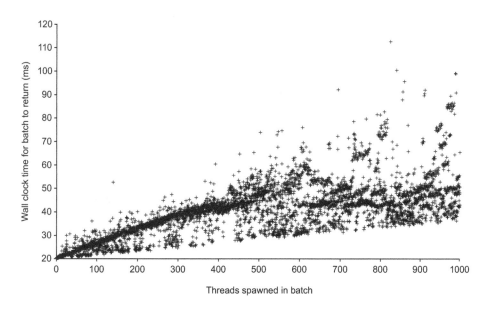

Figure 10.1 Duration needed to wait for threads to sleep 20 ms

And, if you're thinking that sleeping is not a representative workload, figure 10.2 shows the next plot, which is even more telling. It asks each thread to enter a spin loop.

Figure 10.2 provides features that are worth focusing in on briefly. First, for the first seven or so batches, the spin loop version returned closer to 20 ms. The operating system's sleep functionality isn't perfectly accurate, however. If you want to sleep pause a thread for short amounts of time, or if your application is sensitive to timing, use a spin loop.[1]

Second, CPU-intensive multithreading doesn't scale well past the number of physical cores. The benchmarking was performed on a 6-core CPU (the Intel i7-8750H) with hyper-threading disabled. Figure 10.3 shows that as soon as the thread count exceeds the core count, performance degrades quickly.

---

[1] It's also possible to use both: sleep for the bulk of the time and a spin loop towards the end.

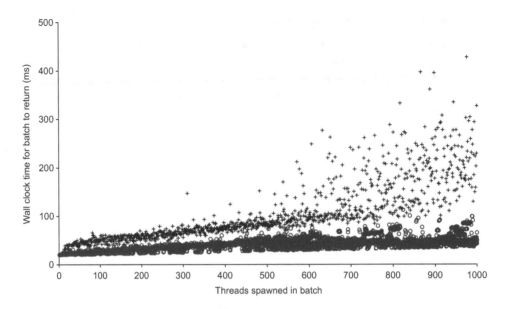

Figure 10.2 Comparing the time taken to wait for 20m using the sleep strategy (circles) versus the spin lock strategy (plus symbols). This chart shows the differences that occur as hundreds of threads compete.

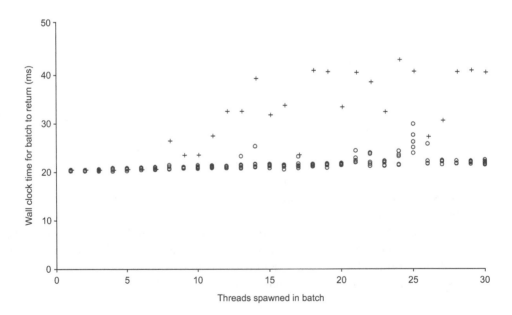

Figure 10.3 Comparing the time taken to wait for 20m using the sleep strategy (circles) versus the spin lock strategy (plus symbols). This chart shows the differences that occur as the number of threads exceeds the number of CPU cores (6).

10.2.5 *Reproducing the results*

Now that we've seen the effects of threading, let's look at the code that generated the input data to the plots in figures 10.1–10.2. You are welcome to reproduce the results. To do so, write the output of listings 10.4 and 10.5 to two files, and then analyze the resulting data.

Listing 10.4, whose source code is available at c10/ch10-multijoin/src/main.rs, suspends threads for 20 ms with a sleep. A *sleep* is a request to the OS that the thread should be suspended until the time has passed. Listing 10.5, whose source code is available at c10/ch10-busythreads/src/main.rs, uses the *busy wait* strategy (also known as *busy loop* and *spin loop*) to pause for 20 ms.

Listing 10.4 Using `thread::sleep` to suspend threads for 20 ms

```
 1 use std::{thread, time};
 2
 3 fn main() {
 4   for n in 1..1001 {
 5     let mut handlers: Vec<thread::JoinHandle<()>> = Vec::with_capacity(n);
 6
 7     let start = time::Instant::now();
 8     for _m in 0..n {
 9       let handle = thread::spawn(|| {
10         let pause = time::Duration::from_millis(20);
11         thread::sleep(pause);
12       });
13       handlers.push(handle);
14     }
15
16     while let Some(handle) = handlers.pop() {
17         handle.join();
18     }
19
20     let finish = time::Instant::now();
21     println!("{}\t{:02?}", n, finish.duration_since(start));
22   }
23 }
```

Listing 10.5 Using a spin loop waiting strategy

```
 1 use std::{thread, time};
 2
 3 fn main() {
 4   for n in 1..1001 {
 5     let mut handlers: Vec<thread::JoinHandle<()>> = Vec::with_capacity(n);
 6
 7     let start = time::Instant::now();
 8     for _m in 0..n {
 9       let handle = thread::spawn(|| {
10         let start = time::Instant::now();
11         let pause = time::Duration::from_millis(20);
```

```
12              while start.elapsed() < pause {
13                  thread::yield_now();
14              }
15          });
16          handlers.push(handle);
17      }
18
19      while let Some(handle) = handlers.pop() {
20          handle.join();
21      }
22
23      let finish = time::Instant::now();
24      println!("{}\t{:02?}", n, finish.duration_since(start));
25   }
26 }
```

The control flow we've chosen for lines 19–21 is slightly odd. Rather than iterating through the handlers vector, we call pop() and then drain it. The following two snippets compare the more familiar for loop (listing 10.6) with the control flow mechanism that is actually employed (listing 10.7).

Listing 10.6   What we would expect to see in listing 10.5

```
19 for handle in &handlers {
20   handle.join();
21 }
```

Listing 10.7   Code that's actually used in listing 10.5

```
19 while let Some(handle) = handlers.pop() {
20   handle.join();
21 }
```

Why use the more complex control flow mechanism? It might help to remember that once we join a thread back to the main thread, it ceases to exist. Rust won't allow us to retain a reference to something that doesn't exist. Therefore, to call join() on a thread handler within handlers, the thread handler must be removed from handlers. That poses a problem. A for loop does not permit modifications to the data being iterated over. Instead, the while loop allows us to repeatedly gain mutable access when calling handlers.pop().

Listing 10.8 provides a broken implementation of the spin loop strategy. It is broken because it uses the more familiar for loop control flow that was avoided in listing 10.5. You'll find the source for this listing in c10/ch10-busythreads-broken/src/main.rs. Its output follows the listing.

Listing 10.8   Using a spin loop waiting strategy

```
1 use std::{thread, time};
2
```

```
 3 fn main() {
 4   for n in 1..1001 {
 5     let mut handlers: Vec<thread::JoinHandle<()>> = Vec::with_capacity(n);
 6
 7     let start = time::Instant::now();
 8     for _m in 0..n {
 9       let handle = thread::spawn(|| {
10         let start = time::Instant::now();
11         let pause = time::Duration::from_millis(20);
12         while start.elapsed() < pause {
13           thread::yield_now();
14         }
15       });
16       handlers.push(handle);
17     }
18
19     for handle in &handlers {
20       handle.join();
21     }
22
23     let finish = time::Instant::now();
24     println!("{}\t{:02?}", n, finish.duration_since(start));
25   }
26 }
```

Here is the output generated when attempting to compile listing 10.8:

```
$ cargo run -q
error[E0507]: cannot move out of `*handle` which is behind a
shared reference
  --> src/main.rs:20:13
   |
20 |             handle.join();
   |             ^^^^^^ move occurs because `*handle` has type
   `std::thread::JoinHandle<()>`, which does not implement the
   `Copy` trait

error: aborting due to previous error

For more information about this error, try `rustc --explain E0507`.
error: Could not compile `ch10-busythreads-broken`.

To learn more, run the command again with --verbose.
```

This error is saying that taking a reference isn't valid here. That's because multiple threads might also be taking their own references to the underlying threads. And those references need to be valid.

Astute readers know that there is actually a simpler way to get around this problem than what was used in listing 10.5. As the following listing shows, simply remove the ampersand.

```
19 for handle in handlers {
20   handle.join();
21 }
```

What we've encountered is one of those rare cases where taking a reference to an object causes more issues than using the object directly. Iterating over `handlers` directly retains ownership. That pushes any concerns about shared access to the side, and we can proceed as intended.

YIELDING CONTROL WITH THREAD::YIELD_NOW()

As a reminder, the busy loop within listing 10.5 includes some unfamiliar code, repeated in the following listing. This section explains its significance.

```
14 while start.elapsed() < pause {
15   thread::yield_now();
16 }
```

`std::thread::yield_now()` is a signal to the OS that the current thread should be unscheduled. This allows other threads to proceed while the current thread is still waiting for the 20 ms to arrive. A downside to yielding is that we don't know if we'll be able to resume at exactly 20 ms.

An alternative to yielding is to use the function `std::sync::atomic::spin_loop _hint()`. `spin_loop_hint()` avoids the OS; instead, it directly signals the CPU. A CPU might use that hint to turn off functionality, thus saving power usage.

> **NOTE** The `spin_loop_hint()` instruction is not present for every CPU. On platforms that don't support it, `spin_loop_hint()` does nothing.

10.2.6 *Shared variables*

In our threading benchmarks, we created pause variables in each thread. If you're not sure what I'm referring to, the following listing provides an excerpt from listing 10.5.

```
 9 let handle = thread::spawn(|| {
10   let start = time::Instant::now();
11   let pause = time::Duration::from_millis(20);     ⟵┐  This variable doesn't
12   while start.elapsed() < pause {                   │  need to be created
13     thread::yield_now();                            │  in each thread.
14   }
15 });
```

We want to be able to write something like the following listing. The source for this listing is ch10/ch10-sharedpause-broken/src/main.rs.

Listing 10.12 Attempting to share a variable in multiple subthreads

```
 1 use std::{thread,time};
 2
 3 fn main() {
 4   let pause = time::Duration::from_millis(20);
 5   let handle1 = thread::spawn(|| {
 6     thread::sleep(pause);
 7   });
 8   let handle2 = thread::spawn(|| {
 9     thread::sleep(pause);
10   });
11
12   handle1.join();
13   handle2.join();
14 }
```

If we run listing 10.12, we'll receive a verbose—and surprisingly helpful—error message:

```
$ cargo run -q
error[E0373]: closure may outlive the current function, but it borrows
`pause`, which is owned by the current function
 --> src/main.rs:5:33
  |
5 |     let handle1 = thread::spawn(|| {
  |                                 ^^ may outlive borrowed value `pause`
6 |         thread::sleep(pause);
  |                       ----- `pause` is borrowed here
  |
note: function requires argument type to outlive `'static`
 --> src/main.rs:5:19
  |
5 |       let handle1 = thread::spawn(|| {
  |  _____^
6 | |         thread::sleep(pause);
7 | |       });
  | |_____^
help: to force the closure to take ownership of `pause` (and any other
references variables), use the `move` keyword
  |
5 |     let handle1 = thread::spawn(move || {
  |                                 ^^^^^^^

error[E0373]: closure may outlive the current function, but it borrows
`pause`, which is owned by the current function
 --> src/main.rs:8:33
  |
8 |     let handle2 = thread::spawn(|| {
  |                                 ^^ may outlive borrowed value `pause`
9 |         thread::sleep(pause);
  |                       ----- `pause` is borrowed here
  |
note: function requires argument type to outlive `'static`
 --> src/main.rs:8:19
```

```
     |
  8  |          let handle2 = thread::spawn(|| {
     |  _____^
  9  | |             thread::sleep(pause);
 10  | |      });
     | |_____^
help: to force the closure to take ownership of `pause` (and any other
referenced variables), use the `move` keyword
     |
  8  |          let handle2 = thread::spawn(move || {
     |                                      ^^^^^^^

error: aborting due to 2 previous errors

For more information about this error, try `rustc --explain E0373`.
error: Could not compile `ch10-sharedpause-broken`.

To learn more, run the command again with --verbose.
```

The fix is to add the move keyword to where the closures are created, as hinted at in section 10.2.1. The following listing adds the move keyword, which switches the closures to use move semantics. That, in turn, relies on Copy.

Listing 10.13   Using a variable defined in a parent scope in multiple closures

```
 1 use std::{thread,time};
 2
 3 fn main() {
 4   let pause = time::Duration::from_millis(20);
 5   let handle1 = thread::spawn(move || {
 6     thread::sleep(pause);
 7   });
 8   let handle2 = thread::spawn(move || {
 9     thread::sleep(pause);
10   });
11
12   handle1.join();
13   handle2.join();
14 }
```

The details of why this works are interesting. Be sure to read the following section to learn those.

10.3 *Differences between closures and functions*

There are some differences between closures (|| {}) and functions (fn). The differences prevent closures and functions from being used interchangeably, which can cause problems for learners.

Closures and functions have different internal representations. Closures are anonymous structs that implement the std::ops::FnOnce trait and potentially std::ops::Fn and `std::ops::FnMut`. Those structs are invisible in source code but contain any variables from the closure's environment that are used inside it.

Functions are implemented as function pointers. A *function pointer* is a pointer that points to code, not data. Code, when used in this sense, is computer memory that has been marked as executable. To complicate matters, closures that do not enclose any variables from their environment are also function pointers.

Forcing the compiler to reveal the type of closure

The concrete type of a Rust closure is inaccessible as source code. The compiler creates it. To retrieve it, force a compiler error like this:

```
1 fn main() {
2   let a = 20;
3
4   let add_to_a = |b| { a + b };
5   add_to_a == ();
6 }
```

Closures are values and can be assigned to a variable.

A quick method to inspect a value's type, this attempts to perform an illegal operation on it. The compiler quickly reports it as an error message.

Among other errors, the compiler produces this one when attempting to compile the snippet as /tmp/a-plus-b.rs:

```
$ rustc /tmp/a-plus-b.rs
error[E0369]: binary operation `==` cannot be applied to type
`[closure@/tmp/a-plus-b.rs:4:20: 4:33]`
  --> /tmp/a-plus-b.rs:6:14
   |
6  |     add_to_a == ();
   |     -------- ^^ -- ()
   |     |
   |     [closure@/tmp/a-plus-b.rs:4:20: 4:33]

error: aborting due to previous error

For more information about this error, try `rustc --explain E0369`.
```

10.4 Procedurally generated avatars from a multithreaded parser and code generator

This section applies the syntax that we learned in section 10.2 to an application. Let's say that we want the users of our app to have unique pictorial avatars by default. One approach for doing this is to take their usernames and the digest of a hash function, and then use those digits as parameter inputs to some procedural generation logic. Using this approach, everyone will have visually similar yet completely distinctive default avatars.

Our application creates parallax lines. It does this by using the characters within the Base 16 alphabet as opcodes for a LOGO-like language.

10.4.1   *How to run render-hex and its intended output*

In this section, we'll produce three variations. These will all be invoked in the same way. The following listing demonstrates this. It also shows the output from invoking our render-hex project (listing 10.18):

```
$ git clone https://github.com/rust-in-action/code rust-in-action
...

$ cd rust-in-action/ch10/ch10-render-hex

$ cargo run -- $(
>    echo 'Rust in Action' |
>    sha1sum |
>    cut -f1 -d' '
> )
$ ls
5deaed72594aaa10edda990c5a5eed868ba8915e.svg  Cargo.toml  target
Cargo.lock                                    src

$ cat 5deaed72594aaa10edda990c5a5eed868ba8915e.svg
<svg height="400" style='style="outline: 5px solid #800000;"'
viewBox="0 0 400 400" width="400" xmlns="http://www.w3.org/2000/svg">
<rect fill="#ffffff" height="400" width="400" x="0" y="0"/>
<path d="M200,200 L200,400 L200,400 L200,400 L200,400 L200,400 L200,
400 L480,400 L120,400 L-80,400 L560,400 L40,400 L40,400 L40,400 L40,
400 L40,360 L200,200 L200,200 L200,200 L200,200 L200,200 L200,560 L200,
-160 L200,200 L200,200 L400,200 L400,200 L400,0 L400,0 L400,0 L400,0 L80,
0 L-160,0 L520,0 L200,0 L200,0 L520,0 L-160,0 L240,0 L440,0 L200,0"
fill="none" stroke="#2f2f2f" stroke-opacity="0.9" stroke-width="5"/>
<rect fill="#ffffff" fill-opacity="0.0" height="400" stroke="#cccccc"
stroke-width="15" width="400" x="0" y="0"/>
</svg>
```

Annotations in the listing:
- **Generates some input from the Base 16 alphabet (e.g., 0-9 and A-F)**
- **The project creates a filename that matches the input data.**
- **Inspects the output**

Any stream of valid Base 16 bytes generates a unique image. The file generated from echo 'Rust in Action' | sha256sum renders as shown in figure 10.4. To render SVG files, open the file in a web browser or a vector image program such as Inkscape (https://inkscape.org/).

10.4.2   *Single-threaded render-hex overview*

The render-hex project converts its input to an SVG file. The SVG file format succinctly describes drawings using mathematical operations. You can view the SVG file in any web browser and many graphics packages. Very little of the program relates to multithreading at this stage, so I'll skip much of the details. The program has a simple pipeline comprised of four steps:

1 Receives input from STDIN
2 Parses the input into operations that describe the movement of a pen across a sheet of paper
3 Converts the movement operations into its SVG equivalent
4 Generates an SVG file

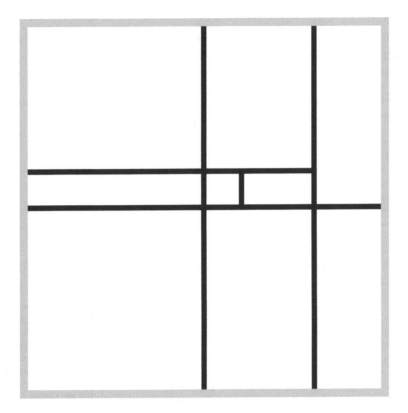

Figure 10.4   The SHA256 digest of *Rust in Action* displayed as a diagram

Why can't we directly create path data from input? Splitting this process into two steps allows for more transformations. This pipeline is managed directly within main().

The following listing shows the main() function for render-hex (listing 10.18). It parses the command-line arguments and manages the SVG generation pipeline. You'll find the source for this listing in ch10/ch10-render-hex/src/main.rs.

Listing 10.14   The main() function of render-hex

```
166 fn main() {
167     let args = env::args().collect::<Vec<String>>();        Command-line
168     let input = args.get(1).unwrap();                       argument
169     let default = format!("{}.svg", input);                 parsing
170     let save_to = args.get(2).unwrap_or(&default);
171
172     let operations = parse(input);
173     let path_data = convert(&operations);                   SVG generation
174     let document = generate_svg(path_data);                 pipeline
175     svg::save(save_to, &document).unwrap();
176 }
```

INPUT PARSING

Our job in this section is to convert hexadecimal digits to instructions for a virtual pen that travels across a canvas. The `Operation` enum, shown in the following code snippet, represents these instructions.

> **NOTE**   The term *operation* is used rather than *instruction* to avoid colliding with the terminology used within the SVG specification for path drawing.

```
21 #[derive(Debug, Clone, Copy)]
22 enum Operation {
23     Forward(isize),
24     TurnLeft,
25     TurnRight,
26     Home,
27     Noop(usize),
28 }
```

To parse this code, we need to treat every byte as an independent instruction. Numerals are converted to distances, and letters change the orientation of the drawing:

```
123 fn parse(input: &str) -> Vec<Operation> {
124    let mut steps = Vec::<Operation>::new();
125    for byte in input.bytes() {
126       let step = match byte {
127         b'0' => Home,
128         b'1'..=b'9' => {
129           let distance = (byte - 0x30) as isize;
130           Forward(distance * (HEIGHT/10))
131         },
132         b'a' | b'b' | b'c' => TurnLeft,
133         b'd' | b'e' | b'f' => TurnRight,
134         _ => Noop(byte),
135       }
136    };
137       steps.push(step);
138    }
139    steps
140 }
```

In ASCII, numerals start at 0x30 (48 in Base 10), so this converts the u8 value of b'2' to 2. Performing this operation on the whole range of u8 could cause a panic, but we're safe here, thanks to the guarantee provided by our pattern matching.

There's plenty of opportunity to add more instructions to produce more elaborate diagrams without increasing the parsing complexity.

Although we don't expect any illegal characters, there may be some in the input stream. Using a Noop operation allows us to decouple parsing from producing output.

INTERPRET INSTRUCTIONS

The `Artist` struct maintains the state of the diagram. Conceptually, the `Artist` is holding a pen at the coordinates x and y and is moving it in the direction of `heading`:

```
49 #[derive(Debug)]
50 struct Artist {
51    x: isize,
52    y: isize,
53    heading: Orientation,
54 }
```

To move, `Artist` implements several methods of the render-hex project, two of which are highlighted in the following listing. Rust's match expressions are used to succinctly refer to and modify internal state. You'll find the source for this listing in ch10-render-hex/src/main.rs.

Listing 10.15 Moving `Artist`

```
70   fn forward(&mut self, distance: isize) {
71     match self.heading {
72       North => self.y += distance,
73       South => self.y -= distance,
74       West  => self.x += distance,
75       East  => self.x -= distance,
76     }
77   }
78
79   fn turn_right(&mut self) {
80     self.heading = match self.heading {
81       North => East,
82       South => West,
83       West  => North,
84       East  => South,
85     }
86   }
```

The `convert()` function in listing 10.16, an extract from the render-hex project (listing 10.18), makes use of the `Artist` struct. Its role is to convert the `Vec<Operation>` from `parse()` to a `Vec<Command>`. That output is used later to generate an SVG. As a nod to the LOGO language, `Artist` is given the local variable name `turtle`. The source for this listing is in ch10-render-hex/src/main.rs.

Listing 10.16 Focusing on the `convert()` function

```
131 fn convert(operations: &Vec<Operation>) -> Vec<Command> {
132   let mut turtle = Artist::new();
133   let mut path_data: Vec<Command> = vec![];
134   let start_at_home = Command::Move(
135     Position::Absolute, (HOME_X, HOME_Y).into()      ◄──┐ To start, positions
136   );                                                      the turtle in the
137   path_data.push(start_at_home);                          center of the
                                                              drawing area
138
139   for op in operations {
140     match *op {
141       Forward(distance) => turtle.forward(distance),   We don't generate a
142       TurnLeft => turtle.turn_left(),                  Command immediately.
143       TurnRight => turtle.turn_right(),                Instead, we modify the
144       Home => turtle.home(),                           internal state of turtle.
145       Noop(byte) => {
146         eprintln!("warning: illegal byte encountered: {:?}", byte)
147       },
148     };
```

```
149        let line = Command::Line(
150            Position::Absolute,
151            (turtle.x, turtle.y).into()
152        );
153        path_data.push(line);
154
155        turtle.wrap();
156    }
157    path_data
158 }
```

Creates a Command::Line (a straight line toward the turtle's current position)

If the turtle is out of bounds, returns it to the center

GENERATING AN SVG

The process of generating the SVG file is rather mechanical. generate_svg() (lines 161–192 of listing 10.18) does the work.

SVG documents look a lot like HTML documents, although the tags and attributes are different. The <path> tag is the most important one for our purposes. It has a d attribute (d is short for data) that describes how the path should be drawn. convert() produces a Vec<Command> that maps directly to the path data.

SOURCE CODE FOR THE SINGLE-THREADED VERSION OF RENDER-HEX

The render-hex project has an orthodox structure. The whole project sits within a (fairly large) main.rs file managed by cargo. To download the project's source code from its public code repository, use the following commands:

```
$ git clone https://github.com/rust-in-action/code rust-in-action
Cloning into 'rust-in-action'...
```

```
$ cd rust-in-action/ch10/ch10-render-hex
```

Otherwise, to create the project by hand, follow the commands in the following snippet, and then copy the code from listing 10.18 into src/main.rs:

```
$ cargo new ch10-render-hex
    Created binary (application) `ch10-render-hex` package
```

```
$ cd ch10-render-hex
```

```
$ cargo install cargo-edit
   Updating crates.io index
 Downloaded cargo-edit v0.7.0
 Downloaded 1 crate (57.6 KB) in 1.35s
 Installing cargo-edit v0.7.0
. . .
```

```
$ cargo add svg@0.6
    Updating 'https://github.com/rust-lang/crates.io-index' index
      Adding svg v0.6 to dependencies
```

The standard project structure, which you can compare against the following snippet, has been created for you:

```
ch10-render-hex/
├── Cargo.toml          ◁──┐  See listing 10.17.
└── src
     └── main.rs        ◁──┐  See listing 10.18.
```

The following listing shows the metadata for our project. You should check that your project's Cargo.toml matches the relevant details. You'll find the source for this listing in ch10/ch10-render-hex/Cargo.toml.

Listing 10.17   Project metadata for render-hex

```
[package]
name = "render-hex"
version = "0.1.0"
authors = ["Tim McNamara <author@rustinaction.com>"]
edition = "2018"

[dependencies]
svg = "0.6"
```

The single-threaded version of render-hex appears in the following listing. You'll find the source for this listing in ch10-render-hex/src/main.rs.

Listing 10.18   Source code for render-hex

```
 1 use std::env;
 2
 3 use svg::node::element::path::{Command, Data, Position};
 4 use svg::node::element::{Path, Rectangle};
 5 use svg::Document;
 6
 7 use crate::Operation::{
 8     Forward,
 9     Home,
10     Noop,
11     TurnLeft,
12     TurnRight
13 };
14 use crate::Orientation::{
15     East,
16     North,
17     South,
18     West
19 };
20
21 const WIDTH: isize = 400;
22 const HEIGHT: isize = WIDTH;
23
24 const HOME_Y: isize = HEIGHT / 2;
25 const HOME_X: isize = WIDTH / 2;
26
27 const STROKE_WIDTH: usize = 5;
28
```

Operation and Orientation enum types are defined later. Including these with the use keyword removes a lot of noise from the source code.

HEIGHT and WIDTH provide the bounds of the drawing.

HOME_Y and HOME_X constants allow us to easily reset where we are drawing from. Here y is the vertical coordinate and x is the horizontal.

STROKE_WIDTH, a parameter for the SVG output, defines the look of each drawn line.

```
29  #[derive(Debug, Clone, Copy)]
30  enum Orientation {
31    North,
32    East,
33    West,
34    South,
35  }
36
37  #[derive(Debug, Clone, Copy)]
38  enum Operation {
39    Forward(isize),
40    TurnLeft,
41    TurnRight,
42    Home,
43    Noop(u8),
44  }
45
46  #[derive(Debug)]
47  struct Artist {
48    x: isize,
49    y: isize,
50    heading: Orientation,
51  }
52
53  impl Artist {
54    fn new() -> Artist {
55      Artist {
56        heading: North,
57        x: HOME_X,
58        y: HOME_Y,
59      }
60    }
61
62    fn home(&mut self) {
63      self.x = HOME_X;
64      self.y = HOME_Y;
65    }
66
67    fn forward(&mut self, distance: isize) {
68      match self.heading {
69        North => self.y += distance,
70        South => self.y -= distance,
71        West => self.x += distance,
72        East => self.x -= distance,
73      }
74    }
75
76    fn turn_right(&mut self) {
77      self.heading = match self.heading {
78        North => East,
79        South => West,
80        West => North,
81        East => South,
82      }
83    }
```

Using descriptions rather than numerical values avoids mathematics.

To produce richer output, extends the operations available to your programs

Using isize lets us extend this example to implement a Reverse operation without adding a new variant.

Uses Noop when we encounter illegal input. To write error messages, we retain the illegal byte.

The Artist struct maintains the current state.

forward() mutates self within the match expression. This contrasts with turn_left() and turn_right(), which mutate self outside of the match expression.

```
84
85   fn turn_left(&mut self) {
86     self.heading = match self.heading {
87       North => West,
88       South => East,
89       West => South,
90       East => North,
91     }
92   }
93
94   fn wrap(&mut self) {
95     if self.x < 0 {
96       self.x = HOME_X;
97       self.heading = West;
98     } else if self.x > WIDTH {
99       self.x = HOME_X;
100      self.heading = East;
101    }
102
103    if self.y < 0 {
104      self.y = HOME_Y;
105      self.heading = North;
106    } else if self.y > HEIGHT {
107      self.y = HOME_Y;
108      self.heading = South;
109    }
110  }
111 }
112
113 fn parse(input: &str) -> Vec<Operation> {
114   let mut steps = Vec::<Operation>::new();
115   for byte in input.bytes() {
116     let step = match byte {
117       b'0' => Home,
118       b'1'..=b'9' => {
119         let distance = (byte - 0x30) as isize;
120         Forward(distance * (HEIGHT / 10))
121       }
122       b'a' | b'b' | b'c' => TurnLeft,
123       b'd' | b'e' | b'f' => TurnRight,
124       _ => Noop(byte),
125     };
126     steps.push(step);
127   }
128   steps
129 }
130
131 fn convert(operations: &Vec<Operation>) -> Vec<Command> {
132   let mut turtle = Artist::new();
133
134   let mut path_data = Vec::<Command>::with_capacity(operations.len());
135   let start_at_home = Command::Move(
136     Position::Absolute, (HOME_X, HOME_Y).into()
137   );
138   path_data.push(start_at_home);
```

> forward() mutates self within the match expression. This contrasts with turn_left() and turn_right(), which mutate self outside of the match expression.

> wrap() ensures that the drawing stays within bounds.

> In ASCII, numerals start at 0x30 (48). byte – 0x30 converts a u8 value of b'2' to 2. Performing this operation on the whole range of u8 could cause a panic, but we're safe here, thanks to the guarantee provided by our pattern matching.

> Although we don't expect any illegal characters, there may be some in the input stream. A Noop operation allows us to decouple parsing from producing output.

```
139
140   for op in operations {
141     match *op {
142       Forward(distance) => turtle.forward(distance),
143       TurnLeft => turtle.turn_left(),
144       TurnRight => turtle.turn_right(),
145       Home => turtle.home(),
146       Noop(byte) => {
147         eprintln!("warning: illegal byte encountered: {:?}", byte);
148       },
149     };
150
151     let path_segment = Command::Line(
152       Position::Absolute, (turtle.x, turtle.y).into()
153     );
154     path_data.push(path_segment);
155
156     turtle.wrap();
157   }
158   path_data
159 }
160
161 fn generate_svg(path_data: Vec<Command>) -> Document {
162   let background = Rectangle::new()
163     .set("x", 0)
164     .set("y", 0)
165     .set("width", WIDTH)
166     .set("height", HEIGHT)
167     .set("fill", "#ffffff");
168
169   let border = background
170     .clone()
171     .set("fill-opacity", "0.0")
172     .set("stroke", "#cccccc")
173     .set("stroke-width", 3 * STROKE_WIDTH);
174
175   let sketch = Path::new()
176     .set("fill", "none")
177     .set("stroke", "#2f2f2f")
178     .set("stroke-width", STROKE_WIDTH)
179     .set("stroke-opacity", "0.9")
180     .set("d", Data::from(path_data));
181
182   let document = Document::new()
183     .set("viewBox", (0, 0, HEIGHT, WIDTH))
184     .set("height", HEIGHT)
185     .set("width", WIDTH)
186     .set("style", "style=\"outline: 5px solid #800000;\"")
187     .add(background)
188     .add(sketch)
189     .add(border);
190
191   document
192 }
193
```

```
194 fn main() {
195   let args = env::args().collect::<Vec<String>>();
196   let input = args.get(1).unwrap();
197   let default_filename = format!("{}.svg", input);
198   let save_to = args.get(2).unwrap_or(&default_filename);
199
200   let operations = parse(input);
201   let path_data = convert(&operations);
202   let document = generate_svg(path_data);
203   svg::save(save_to, &document).unwrap();
204 }
```

10.4.3 Spawning a thread per logical task

Our render-hex project (listing 10.18) also presents several opportunities for parallelism. We'll focus on one of these, the parse() function. To begin, adding parallelism is a two-step process:

1 Refactor code to use a functional style.
2 Use the rayon crate and its par_iter() method.

Using a functional programming style

The first step in adding parallelism is to replace our for. Rather than for, the toolkit for creating a Vec<T> with functional programming constructs includes the map() and collect() methods and higher-order functions, typically created with closures.

To compare the two styles, consider the differences to the parse() function from listing 10.18 (in ch10-render-hex/src/main.rs), repeated in the following listing, and a more functional style in listing 10.20 (in ch10-render-hex-functional/src/main.rs).

Listing 10.19 Implementing `parse()` with imperative programming constructs

```
113 fn parse(input: &str) -> Vec<Operation> {
114   let mut steps = Vec::<Operation>::new();
115   for byte in input.bytes() {
116     let step = match byte {
117       b'0' => Home,
118       b'1'..=b'9' => {
119         let distance = (byte - 0x30) as isize;
120         Forward(distance * (HEIGHT / 10))
121       }
122       b'a' | b'b' | b'c' => TurnLeft,
123       b'd' | b'e' | b'f' => TurnRight,
124       _ => Noop(byte),
125     };
126     steps.push(step);
127   }
128   steps
129 }
```

Listing 10.20   Implementing `parse()` with functional programming constructs

```
 99 fn parse(input: &str) -> Vec<Operation> {
100    input.bytes().map(|byte|{
101      match byte {
102        b'0' => Home,
103        b'1'..=b'9' => {
104          let distance = (byte - 0x30) as isize;
105          Forward(distance * (HEIGHT/10))
106        },
107        b'a' | b'b' | b'c' => TurnLeft,
108        b'd' | b'e' | b'f' => TurnRight,
109        _ => Noop(byte),
110    }}).collect()
111 }
```

Listing 10.20 is shorter, more declarative, and closer to idiomatic Rust. At a surface level, the primary change is that there is no longer a need to create the temporary variable steps. The partnership of `map()` and `collect()` removes the need for that: `map()` applies a function to every element of an iterator, and `collect()` stores the output of an iterator into a `Vec<T>`.

There is also a more fundamental change than eliminating temporary variables in this refactor, though. It has provided more opportunities for the Rust compiler to optimize your code's execution.

In Rust, iterators are an efficient abstraction. Working with their methods directly allows the Rust compiler to create optimal code that takes up minimal memory. As an example, the `map()` method takes a closure and applies it to every element of the iterator. Rust's trick is that `map()` also returns an iterator. This allows many transformations to be chained together. Significantly, although `map()` may appear in multiple places in your source code, Rust often optimizes those function calls away in the compiled binary.

When every step that the program should take is specified, such as when your code uses `for` loops, you restrict the number of places where the compiler can make decisions. Iterators provide an opportunity for you to delegate more work to the compiler. This ability to delegate is what will shortly unlock parallelism.

USING A PARALLEL ITERATOR

We're going to cheat here and make use of a crate from the Rust community: rayon. rayon is explicitly designed to add *data parallelism* to your code. Data parallelism applies the same function (or closure!) on different data (such as a `Vec<T>`).

Assuming that you've already worked with the base render-hex project, add rayon to your crate's dependencies with cargo by executing `cargo add rayon@1`:

> Run cargo install cargo-edit if the cargo add command is unavailable.

```
$ cargo add rayon@1
    Updating 'https://github.com/rust-lang/crates.io-index' index
      Adding rayon v1 to dependencies
```

Ensure that the [dependencies] section of your project's Cargo.toml matches the following listing. You'll find the source for this listing in ch10-render-hex-parallel-iterator/Cargo.toml.

Listing 10.21   Adding rayon as a dependency to Cargo.toml

```
7 [dependencies]
8 svg = "0.6.0"
9 rayon = "1"
```

At the head of the main.rs file, add rayon and its prelude as listing 10.23 shows. prelude brings several traits into the crate's scope. This has the effect of providing a par_bytes() method on string slices and a par_iter() method on byte slices. Those methods enable multiple threads to cooperatively process data. The source for this listing is in ch10-render-hex-parallel-iterator/Cargo.toml.

Listing 10.22   Adding rayon to our render-hex project

```
3 use rayon::prelude::*;

100 fn parse(input: &str) -> Vec<Operation> {
101     input
102         .as_bytes()                      ⟵——  Converts the input string
103         .par_iter()               ⟵             slice into a byte slice
104         .map(|byte| match byte {         Converts the byte slice
105             b'0' => Home,                into a parallel iterator
106             b'1'..=b'9' => {
107                 let distance = (byte - 0x30) as isize;
108                 Forward(distance * (HEIGHT / 10))
109             }
110             b'a' | b'b' | b'c' => TurnLeft,
111             b'd' | b'e' | b'f' => TurnRight,
112             _ => Noop(*byte),      ⟵——  The byte variable has the type &u8,
113         })                              whereas the Operation::Noop(u8)
114         .collect()                      variant requires a dereferenced value.
115 }
```

Using rayon's par_iter() here is a "cheat mode" available to all Rust programmers, thanks to Rust's powerful std::iter::Iterator trait. rayon's par_iter() is guaranteed to never introduce race conditions. But what should you do if you do not have an iterator?

10.4.4   *Using a thread pool and task queue*

Sometimes, we don't have a tidy iterator that we want to apply a function to. Another pattern to consider is the *task queue*. This allows tasks to originate anywhere and for the task processing code to be separated from task creation code. A fleet of worker threads can then pick tasks once these have finished their current one.

There are many approaches to modeling a task queue. We could create a `Vec<Task>` and `Vec<Result>` and share references to these across threads. To prevent each thread from overwriting each other, we would need a data protection strategy.

The most common tool to protect data shared between threads is `Arc<Mutex<T>>`. Fully expanded, that's your value `T` (e.g., `Vec<Task>` or `Vec<Result>` here) protected by a `std::sync::Mutex`, which itself is wrapped within `std::sync::Arc`. A `Mutex` is a mutually-exclusive lock. Mutually exclusive in this context means that no one has special rights. A lock held by any thread prevents all others. Awkwardly, a `Mutex` must itself be protected between threads. So we call in extra support. The `Arc` provides safe multithreaded access to the `Mutex`.

`Mutex` and `Arc` are not unified into a single type to provide programmers with added flexibility. Consider a struct with several fields. You may only need a `Mutex` on a single field, but you could put the `Arc` around the whole struct. This approach provides faster read access to the fields that are not protected by the `Mutex`. A single `Mutex` retains maximum protection for the field that has read-write access. The lock approach, while workable, is cumbersome. Channels offer a simpler alternative.

Channels have two ends: sending and receiving. Programmers don't get access to what is happening inside the channel. But placing data at the sending end means it'll appear at the receiving end at some future stage. Channels can be used as a task queue because multiple items can be sent, even if a receiver is not ready to receive any messages.

Channels are fairly abstract. These hide their internal structure, preferring to delegate access to two helper objects. One can `send()`; the other can `recv()` (receive). Importantly, we don't get access to *how* channels transmit any information sent through the channel.

NOTE By convention, from radio and telegraph operators, the `Sender` is called `tx` (shorthand for *transmission*) and the `Receiver` is called `rx`.

ONE-WAY COMMUNICATION

This section uses the channels implementation from the crossbeam crate rather than from the `std::sync::mpsc` module within the Rust standard library. Both APIs provide the same API, but crossbeam provides greater functionality and flexibility. We'll spend a little time explaining how to use channels. If you would prefer to see them used as a task queue, feel free to skip ahead.

The standard library provides a channels implementation, but we'll make use of the third-party crate, crossbeam. It provides slightly more features. For example, it includes both *bounded queues* and *unbounded queues*. A bounded queue applies *back pressure* under contention, preventing the consumer from becoming overloaded. Bounded queues (of fixed-width types) have deterministic maximum memory usage. These do have one negative characteristic, though. They force queue producers to wait until a space is available. This can make unbounded queues unsuitable for asynchronous messages, which cannot tolerate waiting.

The channels-intro project (listings 10.23 and 10.24) provides a quick example. Here is a console session that demonstrates running the channels-intro project from its public source code repository and providing its expected output:

```
$ git clone https://github.com/rust-in-action/code rust-in-action
Cloning into 'rust-in-action'...

$ cd ch10/ch10-channels-intro

$ cargo run
...
    Compiling ch10-channels-intro v0.1.0 (/ch10/ch10-channels-intro)
     Finished dev [unoptimized + debuginfo] target(s) in 0.34s
      Running `target/debug/ch10-channels-intro`
Ok(42)
```

To create the project by hand, follow these instructions:

1   Enter these commands from the command-line:

```
$ cargo new channels-intro
$ cargo install cargo-edit
$ cd channels-intro
$ cargo add crossbeam@0.7
```

2   Check that the project's Cargo.toml file matches listing 10.23.
3   Replace the contents of src/main.rs with listing 10.24.

The following two listings make up the project. Listing 10.23 shows its Cargo.toml file. Listing 10.24 demonstrates creating a channel for i32 messages from a worker thread.

Listing 10.23   Cargo.toml metadata for channels-intro

```
[package]
name = "channels-intro"
version = "0.1.0"
authors = ["Tim McNamara <author@rustinaction.com>"]
edition = "2018"

[dependencies]
crossbeam = "0.7"
```

Listing 10.24   Creating a channel that receives i32 messages

```
1 #[macro_use]
2 extern crate crossbeam;
3
4 use std::thread;
5 use crossbeam::channel::unbounded;
6
7
8 fn main() {
```

Provides the select! macro, which simplifies receiving messages

```
 9      let (tx, rx) = unbounded();
10
11      thread::spawn(move || {
12          tx.send(42)
13              .unwrap();                      Provides the select!
14      });                                     macro, which simplifies
15                                              receiving messages
16      select!{
17          recv(rx) -> msg => println!("{:?}", msg),    recv(rx) is syntax
18      }                                                defined by the macro.
19 }
```

Some notes about the channels-intro project:

- *Creating a channel with crossbeam involves calling a function that returns* `Sender<T>` *and* `Receiver<T>`*.* Within listing 10.24, the compiler infers the type parameter. `tx` is given the type `Sender<i32>` and `rx` is given the type `Receiver<i32>`.

- *The* `select!` *macro takes its name from other messaging systems like the POSIX sockets API.* It allows the main thread to block and wait for a message.

- *Macros can define their own syntax rules.* That is why the `select!` macro uses syntax (`recv(rx) ->`) that is not legal Rust.

WHAT CAN BE SENT THROUGH A CHANNEL?

Mentally, you might be thinking of a channel like you would envision a network protocol. Over the wire, however, you only have the type `[u8]` available to you. That byte stream needs to be parsed and validated before its contents can be interpreted.

Channels are richer than simply streaming bytes (`[u8]`). A byte stream is opaque and requires parsing to have structure extracted out of it. Channels offer you the full power of Rust's type system. I recommend using an `enum` for messages as it offers exhaustiveness testing for robustness and has a compact internal representation.

TWO-WAY COMMUNICATION

Bi-directional (duplex) communication is awkward to model with a single channel. An approach that's simpler to work with is to create two sets of senders and receivers, one for each direction.

The channels-complex project provides an example of this two channel strategy. channels-complex is implemented in listings 10.25 and 10.26. These are available in ch10/ch10-channels-complex/Cargo.toml and ch10/ch10-channels-complex/src/main.rs, respectively.

When executed, channels-complex produces three lines of output. Here is a session that demonstrates running the project from its public source code repository:

```
$ git clone https://github.com/rust-in-action/code rust-in-action
Cloning into 'rust-in-action'...

$ cd ch10/ch10-channels-complex

$ cargo run
...
```

```
  Compiling ch10-channels-intro v0.1.0 (/ch10/ch10-channels-complex)
   Finished dev [unoptimized + debuginfo] target(s) in 0.34s
    Running `target/debug/ch10-channels-complex`
Ok(Pong)
Ok(Pong)
Ok(Pong)
```

Some learners prefer to type everything out by hand. Here are the instructions to follow if you are one of those people:

1 Enter these commands from the command-line:

```
$ cargo new channels-intro
$ cargo install cargo-edit
$ cd channels-intro
$ cargo add crossbeam@0.7
```

2 Check that the project's Cargo.toml matches listing 10.25.

3 Replace src/main.rs with the contents of listing 10.26.

Listing 10.25   Project metadata for channels-complex

```
[package]
name = "channels-complex"
version = "0.1.0"
authors = ["Tim McNamara <author@rustinaction.com>"]
edition = "2018"

[dependencies]
crossbeam = "0.7"
```

Listing 10.26   Sending messages to and from a spawned thread

```
 1 #[macro_use]
 2 extern crate crossbeam;
 3
 4 use crossbeam::channel::unbounded;
 5 use std::thread;
 6
 7 use crate::ConnectivityCheck::*;
 8
 9 #[derive(Debug)]
10 enum ConnectivityCheck {
11     Ping,
12     Pong,
13     Pang,
14 }
15
16 fn main() {
17     let n_messages = 3;
18     let (requests_tx, requests_rx) = unbounded();
19     let (responses_tx, responses_rx) = unbounded();
20
```

Defining a bespoke message type simplifies interpreting messages later.

```
21   thread::spawn(move || loop {                          ◄─┐   Because all control flow
22     match requests_rx.recv().unwrap() {                      is an expression, Rust
23       Pong => eprintln!("unexpected pong response"),         allows the loop
24       Ping => responses_tx.send(Pong).unwrap(),              keyword here.
25       Pang => return,           ◄─┐
26     }                              The Pang message
27   });                             indicates the thread
28                                   should shut down.
29   for _ in 0..n_messages {
30     requests_tx.send(Ping).unwrap();
31   }
32   requests_tx.send(Pang).unwrap();
33
34   for _ in 0..n_messages {
35     select! {
36       recv(responses_rx) -> msg => println!("{:?}", msg),
37     }
38   }
39 }
```

IMPLEMENTING A TASK QUEUE

After spending some time discussing channels, it's time to apply these to the problem first introduced in listing 10.18. You'll notice that the code that follows shortly in listing 10.28 is quite a bit more complex than the parallel iterator approach seen in listing 10.24.

The following listing displays the metadata for the channel-based task queue implementation of render-hex. The source for this listing is in ch10/ch10-render-hex-threadpool/Cargo.toml.

> **Listing 10.27   The channel-based task queue metadata for render-hex**

```
[package]
name = "render-hex"
version = "0.1.0"
authors = ["Tim McNamara <author@rustinaction.com>"]
edition = "2018"

[dependencies]           The crossbeam crate
svg = "0.6"              is a new dependency
crossbeam = "0.7" #   ◄─┘ for the project.
```

The following listing focuses on the parse() function. The rest of the code is the same as listing 10.18. You'll find the code for the following listing in ch10/ch10-render-hex-threadpool/src/main.rs.

> **Listing 10.28   Partial code for the channel-based task queue for render-hex**

```
1 use std::thread;
2 use std::env;
3
4 use crossbeam::channel::{unbounded};
```

```
 99 enum Work {
100     Task((usize, u8)),
101     Finished,
102 }
103
104 fn parse_byte(byte: u8) -> Operation {
105     match byte {
106         b'0' => Home,
107         b'1'..=b'9' => {
108             let distance = (byte - 0x30) as isize;
109             Forward(distance * (HEIGHT/10))
110         },
111         b'a' | b'b' | b'c' => TurnLeft,
112         b'd' | b'e' | b'f' => TurnRight,
113         _ => Noop(byte),
114     }
115 }
116
117 fn parse(input: &str) -> Vec<Operation> {
118     let n_threads = 2;
119     let (todo_tx, todo_rx) = unbounded();
120     let (results_tx, results_rx) = unbounded();
121     let mut n_bytes = 0;
122     for (i,byte) in input.bytes().enumerate() {
123         todo_tx.send(Work::Task((i,byte))).unwrap();
124         n_bytes += 1;
125     }
126
127     for _ in 0..n_threads {
128         todo_tx.send(Work::Finished).unwrap();
129     }
130
131     for _ in 0..n_threads {
132         let todo = todo_rx.clone();
133         let results = results_tx.clone();
134         thread::spawn(move || {
135             loop {
136                 let task = todo.recv();
137                 let result = match task {
138                     Err(_) => break,
139                     Ok(Work::Finished) => break,
140                     Ok(Work::Task((i, byte))) => (i, parse_byte(byte)),
141                 };
142                 results.send(result).unwrap();
143
144             }
145         });
146     }
147     let mut ops = vec![Noop(0); n_bytes];
148     for _ in 0..n_bytes {
149         let (i, op) = results_rx.recv().unwrap();
150         ops[i] = op;
151     }
152     ops
153 }
```

Creates a type for the messages we send through the channels

The usize field of this tuple indicates the position of the processed byte. This is necessary because these can be returned out of order.

Gives worker threads a marker message to indicate that it's time to shut down

Extracts the functionality that workers will need to carry out to simplify the logic

Creates one channel for tasks to be completed

Creates one channel for the decoded instructions to be returned to

Fills the task queue with work

Keeps track of how many tasks there are to do

Sends each thread a signal that it's time to shut down

When cloned, channels can be shared between threads.

Because results can be returned in arbitrary order, initializes a complete Vec<Command> that will be overwritten by our incoming results. We use a vector rather than an array because that's what's used by the type signature, and we don't want to refactor the whole program to suit this new implementation.

When independent threads are introduced, the order in which tasks are completed becomes non-deterministic. Listing 10.28 includes some additional complexity to handle this.

Previously, we created an empty `Vec<Command>` for the commands that we interpreted from our input. Once parsed, `main()` repeatedly added elements via the vector's `push()` method. Now, at line 147, we fully initialize the vector. Its contents don't matter. It will all be overwritten. Even so, I've chosen to use `Command::Noop` to ensure that a mistake won't result in a corrupt SVG file.

10.5   *Concurrency and task virtualization*

This section explains the difference between models of concurrency. Figure 10.5 displays some of the trade-offs.

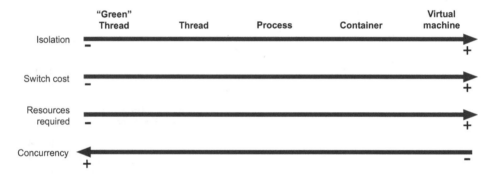

Figure 10.5   Trade-offs relating to different forms of task isolation in computing. In general terms, increasing the isolation level increases the overhead.

The primary benefit of more costly forms of task virtualization is isolation. What is meant by the term *isolation?*

Isolated tasks cannot interfere with each other. Interference comes in many forms. Examples include corrupting memory, saturating the network, and congestion when saving to disk. If a thread is blocked while waiting for the console to print output to the screen, none of the coroutines acting in that thread are able to progress.

Isolated tasks cannot access each other's data without permission. Independent threads in the same process share a memory address space, and all threads have equal access to data within that space. Processes, however, are prohibited from inspecting each other's memory.

Isolated tasks cannot cause another task to crash. A failure in one task should not cascade into other systems. If a process induces a kernel panic, all processes are shut down. By conducting work in virtual machines, tasks can proceed even when other tasks are unstable.

Isolation is a continuum. Complete isolation is impractical. It implies that input and output is impossible. Moreover, isolation is often implemented in software. Running extra software implies taking on extra runtime overhead.

A small glossary of terms relating to concurrency

This subfield is filled with jargon. Here is a brief introduction to some important terms and how we use them:

- *Program*—A program, or application, is a brand name. It's a name that we use to refer to a software package. When we execute a program, the OS creates a process.
- *Executable*—A file that can be loaded into memory and then run. Running an executable means creating a process and a thread for it, then changing the CPU's instruction pointer to the first instruction of the executable.
- *Task*—This chapter uses the term task in an abstract sense. Its meaning shifts as the level of abstraction changes:
  - a When discussing processes, a task is one of the process's threads.
  - b When referring to a thread, a task might be a function call.
  - c When referring to an OS, a task might be a running program, which might be comprised of multiple processes.
- *Process*—Running programs execute as processes. A process has its own virtual address space, at least one thread, and lots of bookkeeping managed by the OS. File descriptors, environment variables, and scheduling priorities are managed per process. A process has a virtual address space, executable code, open handles to system objects, a security context, a unique process identifier, environment variables, a priority class, minimum and maximum working set sizes, and at least one thread of execution.

  Each process is started with a single thread, often called the *primary thread*, but can create additional threads from any of its threads. Running programs begin their life as a single process, but it isn't uncommon to spawn subprocesses to do the work.
- *Thread*—The thread metaphor is used to hint that multiple threads can work together as a whole.
- *Thread of execution*—A sequence of CPU instructions that appear in serial. Multiple threads can run concurrently, but instructions within the sequence are intended to be executed one after another.
- *Coroutine*—Also known as *fibre*, *green thread*, and *lightweight thread*, a coroutine indicates tasks that switch within a thread. Switching between tasks becomes the responsibility of the program itself, rather than the OS. Two theoretical concepts are important to distinguish:
  - a Concurrency, which is multiple tasks of any level of abstraction running at the same time
  - b Parallelism, which is multiple threads executing on multiple CPUs at the same time

(continued)

Outside of the fundamental terminology, there are also interrelated terms that appear frequently: *asynchronous programming* and *non-blocking I/O*. Many operating systems provide non-blocking I/O facilities, where data from multiple sockets is batched into queues and periodically polled as a group. Here are the definitions for these:

- *Non-blocking I/O*—Normally a thread is unscheduled when it asks for data from I/O devices like the network. The thread is marked as *blocked*, while it waits for data to arrive.

  When programming with non-blocking I/O, the thread can continue executing even while it waits for data. But there is a contradiction. How can a thread continue to execute if it doesn't have any input data to process? The answer lies in asynchronous programming.

- *Asynchronous programming*—Asynchronous programming describes programming for cases where the control flow is not predetermined. Instead, events outside the control of the program itself impact the sequence of what is executed. Those events are typically related to I/O, such as a device driver signalling that it is ready, or are related to functions returning in another thread.

  The asynchronous programming model is typically more complicated for the developer, but results in a faster runtime for I/O-heavy workloads. Speed increases because there are fewer system calls. This implies fewer context switches between the user space and the kernel space.

10.5.1   *Threads*

A *thread* is the lowest level of isolation that an OS understands. The OS can schedule threads. Smaller forms of concurrency are invisible to the OS. You may have encountered terms such as coroutines, fibers, and green threads.

Switching between tasks here is managed by the process itself. The OS is ignorant of the fact that a program is processing multiple tasks. For threads and other forms of concurrency, context switching is required.

10.5.2   *What is a context switch?*

Switching between tasks at the same level of virtualization is known as a *context switch*. For threads to switch, CPU registers need to be cleared, CPU caches might need to be flushed, and variables within the OS need to be reset. As isolation increases, so does the cost of the context switch.

CPUs can only execute instructions in serial. To do more than one task, a computer, for example, needs to be able to press the Save Game button, switch to a new task, and resume at that task's saved spot. The CPU is *save scum*.

Why is the CPU constantly switching tasks? Because it has so much time available. Programs often need to access data from memory, disk, or the network. Because waiting for data is incredibly slow, there's often sufficient time to do something else in the meantime.

10.5.3 Processes

Threads exist within a process. The distinguishing characteristic of a process is that its memory is independent from other processes. The OS, in conjunction with the CPU, protects a process's memory from all others.

To share data between processes, Rust channels and data protected by `Arc<Mutex<_>>` won't suffice. You need some support from the OS. For this, reusing network sockets is common. Most operating systems provide specialized forms of interprocess communication (IPC), which are faster, while being less portable.

10.5.4 WebAssembly

WebAssembly (Wasm) is interesting because it is an attempt at isolating tasks within the process boundary itself. It's impossible for tasks running inside a Wasm module to access memory available to other tasks. Originating in web browsers, Wasm treats all code as potentially hostile. If you use third-party dependencies, it's likely that you haven't verified the behavior of all of the code that your process executes.

In a sense, Wasm modules are given access to address spaces within your process's address space. Wasm address spaces are called *linear memory*. Runtime interprets any request for data within linear memory and makes its own request to the actual virtual memory. Code within the Wasm module is unaware of any memory addresses that the process has access to.

10.5.5 Containers

Containers are extensions to processes with further isolation provided by the OS. Processes share the same filesystem, whereas containers have a filesystem created for them. The same is true for other resources, such as the network. Rather than address space, the term used for protections covering these other resources is *namespaces*.

10.5.6 Why use an operating system (OS) at all?

It's possible to run an application as its own OS. Chapter 11 provides one implementation. The general term for an application that runs without an OS is to describe it as *freestanding*—freestanding in the sense that it does not require the support of an OS. Freestanding binaries are used by embedded software developers when there is no OS to rely on.

Using freestanding binaries can involve significant limitations, though. Without an OS, applications no longer have virtual memory or multithreading. All of those concerns become your application's concerns. To reach a middle ground, it is possible to compile a *unikernel*. A unikernel is a minimal OS paired with a single application. The compilation process strips out everything from the OS that isn't used by the application that's being deployed.

Summary

- Closures and functions both feel like they should be the same type, but they aren't identical. If you want to create a function that accepts either a function or a closure as an argument, then make use of the `std::ops::Fn` family of traits.
- A functional style that makes heavy use of higher-order programming and iterators is idiomatic Rust. This approach tends to work better with third-party libraries because `std::iter::Iterator` is such a common trait to support.
- Threads have less impact than you have probably heard, but spawning threads without bounds can cause significant problems.
- To create a byte (`u8`) from a literal, use single quotes (e.g., `b'a'`). Double quotes (e.g., `b"a"`) creates a byte slice (`[u8]`) of length 1.
- To increase the convenience of enums, it can be handy to bring their variants into local scope with `use crate::`.
- Isolation is provided as a spectrum. In general, as isolation between software components increases, performance decreases.

Kernel

Let's build an operating system (OS). By the end of the chapter, you'll be running your own OS (or, at least, a minimal subset of one). Not only that, but you will have compiled your own bootloader, your own kernel, and the Rust language directly for that new target (which doesn't exist yet).

This chapter covers many features of Rust that are important for programming without an OS. Accordingly, the chapter is important for programmers who intend to work with Rust on embedded devices.

11.1 *A fledgling operating system (FledgeOS)*

In this section, we'll implement an OS kernel. The OS kernel performs several important roles, such as interacting with hardware and memory management, and coordinating work. Typically, work is coordinated through processes and threads. We won't be able to cover much of that in this chapter, but we will get off the ground. We'll fledge, so let's call the system we're building *FledgeOS*.

11.1.1   Setting up a development environment for developing an OS kernel

Creating an executable for an OS that doesn't exist yet is a complicated process. For instance, we need to compile the core Rust language for the OS from your current one. But your current environment only understands your current environment. Let's extend that. We need several tools to help us out. Here are several components that you will need to install and/or configure before creating FledgeOS:

- *QEMU*—A virtualization technology. Formally part of a class of software called *virtual machine monitors*," it runs operating systems for any machine on any of its supported hosted architectures. Visit https://www.qemu.org/ for installation instructions.
- *The bootimage crate and some supporting tools*—The bootimage crate does the heavy lifting for our project. Thankfully, installing it and the tools needed to work with it effectively is a lightweight process. To do that, enter the following commands from the command line:

```
$ cargo install cargo-binutils
...
    Installed package `cargo-binutils v0.3.3` (executables `cargo-cov`,
    `cargo-nm`, `cargo-objcopy`, `cargo-objdump`, `cargo-profdata`,
    `cargo-readobj`, `cargo-size`, `cargo-strip`, `rust-ar`, `rust-cov`,
    `rust-ld`, `rust-lld`, `rust-nm`, `rust-objcopy`, `rust-objdump`,
    `rust-profdata`, `rust-readobj`, `rust-size`, `rust-strip`)

$ cargo install bootimage
...
    Installed package `bootimage v0.10.3` (executables `bootimage`,
    `cargo-bootimage`)

$ rustup toolchain install nightly
info: syncing channel updates for 'nightly-x86_64-unknown-linux-gnu'
...

$ rustup default nightly
info: using existing install for 'nightly-x86_64-unknown-linux-gnu'
info: default toolchain set to 'nightly-x86_64-unknown-linux-gnu'
...

$ rustup component add rust-src
info: downloading component 'rust-src'
...

$ rustup component add llvm-tools-preview
info: downloading component 'llvm-tools-preview'
...
```

> **Over time, this may become the llvm-tools component.**

Each of these tools performs an important role:

- *The cargo-binutils crate*—Enables cargo to directly manipulate executable files via subcommands using utilities built with Rust and installed by cargo. Using cargo-binutils rather than installing binutils via another route prevents any potential version mismatches.

- *The bootimage crate*—Enables cargo to build a *boot image*, an executable that can be booted directly on hardware.

- *The nightly toolchain*—Installing the nightly version of the Rust compiler unlocks features that have not yet been marked as stable, and thus constrained by Rust's backward-compatibility guarantees. Some of the compiler internals that we will be accessing in this chapter are unlikely to ever be stabilized.

  We set nightly to be our default toolchain to simplify the build steps for projects in this chapter. To revert the change, use the command `rustup default stable`.

- *The rust-src component*—Downloads the source code for the Rust programming language. This enables Rust to compile a compiler for the new OS.

- *The llvm-tools-preview component*—Installs extensions for the LLVM compiler, which makes up part of the Rust compiler.

11.1.2 Verifying the development environment

To prevent significant frustration later on, it can be useful to double-check that everything is installed correctly. To do that, here's a checklist:

- *QEMU*—The qemu-system-x86_64 utility should be on your PATH. You can check that this is the case by providing the `--version` flag:

```
$ qemu-system-x86_64 --version
QEMU emulator version 4.2.1 (Debian 1:4.2-3ubuntu6.14)
Copyright (c) 2003-2019 Fabrice Bellard and the QEMU Project developers
```

- *The cargo-binutils crate*—As indicated by the output of `cargo install cargo-binutils`, several executables were installed on your system. Executing any of those with the `--help` flag should indicate that all of these are available. For example, to check that `rust-strip` is installed, use this command:

```
$ rust-strip --help
OVERVIEW: llvm-strip tool

USAGE: llvm-strip [options] inputs..
...
```

- *The bootimage crate*—Use the following command to check that all of the pieces are wired together:

```
$ cargo bootimage --help
Creates a bootable disk image from a Rust kernel
...
```

- *The llvm-tools-preview toolchain component*—The LLVM tools are a set of auxiliary utilities for working with LLVM. On Linux and macOS, you can use the following commands to check that these are accessible to rustc:

```
$ export SYSROOT=$(rustc --print sysroot)

$ find "$SYSROOT" -type f -name 'llvm-*' -printf '%f\n' | sort
llvm-ar
llvm-as
llvm-cov
llvm-dis
llvm-nm
llvm-objcopy
llvm-objdump
llvm-profdata
llvm-readobj
llvm-size
llvm-strip
```

On MS Windows, the following commands produce a similar result:

```
C:\> rustc --print sysroot
C:\> cd <sysroot>          ◁─┤  Replace <sysroot> with the
C:\> dir llvm*.exe /s /b        output of the previous command
```

Great, the environment has been set up. If you encounter any problems, try reinstalling the components from scratch.

11.2 Fledgeos-0: Getting something working

FledgeOS requires some patience to fully comprehend. Although the code may be short, it includes many concepts that are probably novel because they are not exposed to programmers who make use of an OS. Before getting started with the code, let's see FledgeOS fly.

11.2.1 First boot

FledgeOS is not the world's most powerful operating system. Truthfully, it doesn't look like much at all. At least it's a graphical environment. As you can see from figure 11.1, it creates a pale blue box in the top-left corner of the screen.

To get fledgeos-0 up and running, execute these commands from a command-line prompt:

```
$ git clone https://github.com/rust-in-action/code rust-in-action
Cloning into 'rust-in-action'...
...

$ cd rust-in-action/ch11/ch11-fledgeos-0

$ cargo +nightly run       ◁─┤  Adding +nightly ensures that
...                             the nightly compiler is used.
Running:  qemu-system-x86_64 -drive
          format=raw,file=target/fledge/debug/bootimage-fledgeos.bin
```

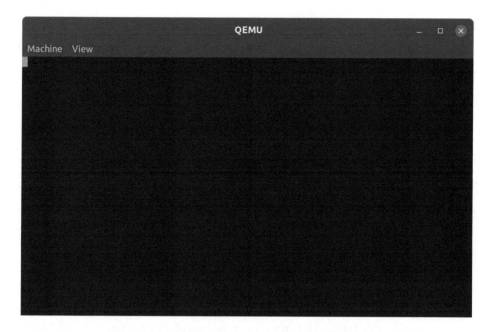

Figure 11.1 Expected output from running fledgeos-0 (listings 11.1–11.4)

Don't worry about *how* the block at the top left changed color. We'll discuss the retro-computing details for that shortly. For now, success is being able to compile your own version of Rust, an OS kernel using that Rust, a bootloader that puts your kernel in the right place, and having these all work together.

Getting this far is a big achievement. As mentioned earlier, creating a program that targets an OS kernel that doesn't exist yet is complicated. Several steps are required:

1. Create a machine-readable definition of the conventions that the OS uses, such as the intended CPU architecture. This is the *target platform*, also known as a *compiler target* or simply *target*. You have seen targets before. Try executing rustup target list for a list that you can compile Rust to.

2. Compile Rust for the target definition to create the new target. We'll suffice with a subset of Rust called *core* that excludes the standard library (crates under std).

3. Compile the OS kernel for the new target using the "new" Rust.

4. Compile a bootloader that can load the new kernel.

5. Execute the bootloader in a virtual environment, which, in turn, runs the kernel.

Thankfully, the bootimage crate does all of this for us. With all of that fully automated, we're able to focus on the interesting pieces.

11.2.2   *Compilation instructions*

To make use of the publicly available source code, follow the steps in section 11.1.3. That is, execute these commands from a command prompt:

```
$ git clone https://github.com/rust-in-action/code rust-in-action
Cloning into 'rust-in-action'...
...
$ cd rust-in-action/ch11/ch11-fledgeos-0
```

To create the project by hand, here is the recommended process:

1 From a command-line prompt, execute these commands:

```
$ cargo new fledgeos-0
$ cargo install cargo-edit
$ cd fledgeos-0
$ mkdir .cargo
$ cargo add bootloader@0.9
$ cargo add x86_64@0.13
```

2 Add the following snippet to the end of project's Cargo.toml file. Compare the result with listing 11.1, which can be downloaded from ch11/ch11-fledgeos-0/Cargo.toml:

```
[package.metadata.bootimage]
build-command = ["build"]

run-command = [
  "qemu-system-x86_64", "-drive", "format=raw,file={}"
]
```

3 Create a new fledge.json file at the root of the project with the contents from listing 11.2. You can download this from the listing in ch11/ch11-fledgeos-0/fledge.json.

4 Create a new .cargo/config.toml file from listing 11.3, which is available in ch11/ch11-fledgeos-0/.cargo/config.toml.

5 Replace the contents of src/main with listing 11.4, which is available in ch11/ch11-fledgeos-0/src/main.rs.

11.2.3   *Source code listings*

The source code for the FledgeOS projects (code/ch11/ch11-fledgeos-*) uses a slightly different structure than most cargo projects. Here is a view of their layout, using fledgeos-0 as a representative example:

```
fledgeos-0
├── Cargo.toml        ◁──┘  See listing 11.1.
├── fledge.json       ◁───  See listing 11.2.
├── .cargo
│   └── config.toml   ◁──┘  See listing 11.3.
```

```
└── src
    └── main.rs          ◁──┘   See listing 11.4.
```

The projects include two extra files:

- *The project root directory contains a fledge.json file.* This is the definition of the compiler target that bootimage and friends will be building.
- *The .cargo/config.toml file provides extra configuration parameters.* These tell cargo that it needs to compile the std::core module itself for this project, rather than relying on it being preinstalled.

The following listing provides the project's Cargo.toml file. It is available in ch11/ch11-fledgeos-0/Cargo.toml.

Listing 11.1   Project metadata for fledgeos-0

```
[package]
name = "fledgeos"
version = "0.1.0"
authors = ["Tim McNamara <author@rustinaction.com>"]
edition = "2018"

[dependencies]
bootloader = "0.9"
x86_64 = "0.13"

[package.metadata.bootimage]          Updates cargo run to invoke a
build-command = ["build"]             QEMU session. The path to the OS
                                      image created during the build
                                      replaces the curly braces ({}).
run-command = [              ◁──┘
  "qemu-system-x86_64", "-drive", "format=raw,file={}"
]
```

The project's Cargo.toml file is slightly unique. It includes a new table, [package .metadata.bootimage], which contains a few directives that are probably confusing. This table provides instructions to the bootimage crate, which is a dependency of bootloader:

- bootimage—Creates a bootable disk image from a Rust kernel
- build-command—Instructs bootimage to use the cargo build command rather than cargo xbuild for cross-compiling
- run_command—Replaces the default behavior of cargo run to use QEMU rather than invoking the executable directly

TIP   See the documentation at https://github.com/rust-osdev/bootimage/ for more information about how to configure bootimage.

The following listing shows our kernel target's definition. It is available from ch11/ch11-fledgeos-0/fledge.json.

Listing 11.2   Kernel definition for FledgeOS

```
{
  "llvm-target": "x86_64-unknown-none",
  "data-layout": "e-m:e-i64:64-f80:128-n8:16:32:64-S128",
  "arch": "x86_64",
  "target-endian": "little",
  "target-pointer-width": "64",
  "target-c-int-width": "32",
  "os": "none",
  "linker": "rust-lld",
  "linker-flavor": "ld.lld",
  "executables": true,
  "features": "-mmx,-sse,+soft-float",
  "disable-redzone": true,
  "panic-strategy": "abort"
}
```

Among other things, the target kernel's definition specifies that it is a 64-bit OS built for x86-64 CPUs. This JSON specification is understood by the Rust compiler.

> **TIP**   Learn more about custom targets from the "Custom Targets" section of the rustc book at https://doc.rust-lang.org/stable/rustc/targets/custom.html.

The following listing, available from ch11/ch11-fledgeos-0/.cargo/config.toml, provides an additional configuration for building FledgeOS. We need to instruct cargo to compile the Rust language for the compiler target that we defined in the previous listing.

Listing 11.3   Extra build-time configuration for cargo

```
[build]
target = "fledge.json"

[unstable]
build-std = ["core", "compiler_builtins"]
build-std-features = ["compiler-builtins-mem"]

[target.'cfg(target_os = "none")']
runner = "bootimage runner"
```

We are finally ready to see the kernel's source code. The next listing, available from ch11/ch11-fledgeos-0/src/main.rs, sets up the boot process, and then writes the value 0x30 to a predefined memory address. You'll read about how this works in section 11.2.5.

Listing 11.4   Creating an OS kernel that paints a block of color

```
1 #![no_std]            Prepares the program for
2 #![no_main]           running without an OS
3 #![feature(core_intrinsics)]
4                                    Unlocks the LLVM compiler's
5 use core::intrinsics;              intrinsic functions
```

```
 6 use core::panic::PanicInfo;
 7
 8 #[panic_handler]
 9 #[no_mangle]
10 pub fn panic(_info: &PanicInfo) -> ! {
11     intrinsics::abort();
12 }
13
14 #[no_mangle]
15 pub extern "C" fn _start() -> ! {
16     let framebuffer = 0xb8000 as *mut u8;
17
18     unsafe {
19         framebuffer
20             .offset(1)
21             .write_volatile(0x30);
22     }
23
24     loop {}
25 }
```

- Line 6 → **Allows the panic handler to inspect where the panic occurred**
- Line 11 → **Crashes the program**
- Lines 19–20 → **Increments the pointer's address by 1 to 0xb8001**
- Line 21 → **Sets the background to cyan**

Listing 11.4 looks very different from the Rust projects that we have seen so far. Here are some of the changes to ordinary programs that are intended to be executed along-side an OS:

- *The central FledgeOS functions never return.* There is no place to return to. There are no other running programs. To indicate this, our functions' return type is the Never type (`!`).

- *If the program crashes, the whole computer crashes.* The only thing that our program can do when an error occurs is terminate. We indicate this by relying on LLVM's `abort()` function. This is explained in more detail in section 11.2.4.

- *We must disable the standard library with `![no_std]`.* As our application cannot rely on an OS to provide dynamic memory allocation, it's important to avoid any code that dynamically allocates memory. The `![no_std]` annotation excludes the Rust standard library from our crate. This has the side effect of preventing many types, such as `Vec<T>`, from being available to our program.

- *We need to unlock the unstable core_intrinsics API with the `#![core_intrinsics]` attribute.* Part of the Rust compiler is provided by LLVM, the compiler produced by the LLVM project. LLVM exposes parts of its internals to Rust, which are known as *intrinsic functions*. As LLVM's internals are not subject to Rust's stability guarantees, there is always a risk that what is offered to Rust will change. Therefore, this implies that we must use the nightly compiler toolchain and explicitly opt into the unstable API in our program.

- *We need to disable the Rust symbol-naming conventions with the `#![no_mangle]` attribute.* Symbol names are strings within the compiled binary. For multiple libraries to coexist at runtime, it's important that these names do not collide. Ordinarily, Rust avoids this by creating symbols via a process called *name mangling*. We need to disable this from occurring in our program; otherwise, the boot process may fail.

- *We should opt into C's calling conventions with* `extern "C"`. An operating system's calling convention relates to the way function arguments are laid out in memory, among other details. Rust does not define its calling convention. By annotating the `_start()` function with `extern "C"`, we instruct Rust to use the C language's calling conventions. Without this, the boot process may fail.

- *Writing directly to memory changes the display.* Traditionally, operating systems used a simplistic model for adjusting the screen's output. A predefined block of memory, known as the *frame buffer,* was monitored by the video hardware. When the frame buffer changed, the display changed to match. One standard, used by our bootloader, is VGA (Video Graphics Array). The bootloader sets up address 0xb8000 as the start of the frame buffer. Changes to its memory are reflected onscreen. This is explained in detail in section 11.2.5.

- *We should disable the inclusion of a* `main()` *function with the* `#![no_main]` *attribute.* The `main()` function is actually quite special because its arguments are provided by a function that is ordinarily included by the compiler (`_start()`), and its return values are interpreted before the program exits. The behavior of `main()` is part of the Rust runtime. Read section 11.2.6 for more details.

Where to go to learn more about OS development

The `cargo bootimage` command takes care of lots of nuisances and irritation. It provides a simple interface—a single command—to a complicated process. But if you're a tinkerer, you might like to know what's happening beneath the surface. In that case, you should search Philipp Oppermann's blog, "Writing an OS in Rust," at https://os .phil-opp.com/ and look into the small ecosystem of tools that has emerged from it at https://github.com/rust-osdev/.

Now that our first kernel is live, let's learn a little bit about how it works. First, let's look at panic handling.

11.2.4 *Panic handling*

Rust won't allow you to compile a program that doesn't have a mechanism to deal with panics. Normally, it inserts panic handling itself. This is one of the actions of the Rust runtime, but we started our code with `#[no_std]`. Avoiding the standard library is useful in that it greatly simplifies compilation, but manual panic handling is one of its costs. The following listing is an excerpt from listing 11.4. It introduces our panic-handling functionality.

Listing 11.5   Focusing on panic handling for FledgeOS

```
1 #![no_std]
2 #![no_main]
```

```
 3 #![feature(core_intrinsics)]
 4
 5 use core::intrinsics;
 6 use core::panic::PanicInfo;
 7
 8 #[panic_handler]
 9 #[no_mangle]
10 pub fn panic(_info: &PanicInfo) -> ! {
11   unsafe {
12     intrinsics::abort();
13   }
14 }
```

There is an alternative to `intrinsics::abort()`. We could use an infinite loop as the panic handler, shown in the following listing. The disadvantage of that approach is that any errors in the program trigger the CPU core to run at 100% until it is shut down manually.

> **Listing 11.6   Using an infinite loop as a panic handler**

```
#[panic_handler]
#[no_mangle]
pub fn panic(_info: &PanicInfo) -> ! {
  loop { }
}
```

The `PanicInfo` struct provides information about where the panic originates. This information includes the filename and line number of the source code. It'll come in handy when we implement proper panic handling.

11.2.5 *Writing to the screen with VGA-compatible text mode*

The bootloader sets some magic bytes with raw assembly code in boot mode. At startup, the bytes are interpreted by the hardware. The hardware switches its display to an 80x25 grid. It also sets up a fixed-memory buffer that is interpreted by the hardware for printing to the screen.

VGA-compatible text mode in 20 seconds

Normally, the display is split into an 80x25 grid of cells. Each cell is represented in memory by 2 bytes. In Rust-like syntax, those bytes include several fields. The following code snippet shows the fields:

```
struct VGACell {
    is_blinking: u1,
    background_color: u3,
    is_bright: u1,
    character_color: u3,
    character: u8,
}
```

These four fields occupy a single byte in memory.

Available characters are drawn from the code page 437 encoding, which is (approximately) an extension of ASCII.

(continued)

VGA text mode has a 16-color palette, where 3 bits make up the main 8 colors. Foreground colors also have an additional bright variant, shown in the following:

```
#[repr(u8)]
enum Color {
    Black = 0,      White = 8,
    Blue = 1,       BrightBlue = 9,
    Green = 2,      BrightGreen = 10,
    Cyan = 3,       BrightCyan = 11,
    Red = 4,        BrightRed = 12,
    Magenta = 5,    BrightMagenta = 13,
    Brown = 6,      Yellow = 14,
    Gray = 7,       DarkGray = 15,
}
```

This initialization at boot time makes it easy to display things onscreen. Each of the points in the 80x25 grid are mapped to locations in memory. This area of memory is called the *frame buffer*.

Our bootloader designates 0xb8000 as the start of a 4,000 byte frame buffer. To actually set the value, our code uses two new methods, offset() and write_volatile(), that you haven't encountered before. The following listing, an excerpt from listing 11.4, shows how these are used.

Listing 11.7 Focusing on modifying the VGA frame buffer

```
18    let mut framebuffer = 0xb8000 as *mut u8;
19    unsafe {
20        framebuffer
21            .offset(1)
22            .write_volatile(0x30);
23    }
```

Here is a short explanation of the two new methods:

- *Moving through an address space with* offset()—A pointer type's offset() method moves through the address space in increments that align to the size of the pointer. For example, calling .offset(1) on a *mut u8 (mutable pointer to a u8) adds 1 to its address. When that same call is made to a *mut u32 (mutable pointer to a u32), the pointer's address moves by 4 bytes.
- *Forcing a value to be written to memory with* write_volatile()—Pointers provide a write_volatile() method that issues a "volatile" write. Volatile prevents the compiler's optimizer from optimizing away the write instruction. A smart compiler might simply notice that we are using lots of constants everywhere and initialize the program such that the memory is simply set to the value that we want it to be.

The following listing shows another way to write framebuffer.offset(1).write_volatile(0x30). Here we use the dereference operator (*) and manually set the memory to 0x30.

> **Listing 11.8 Manually incrementing a pointer**

```
18    let mut framebuffer = 0xb8000 as *mut u8;
19    unsafe {
20        *(framebuffer + 1) = 0x30;      ◁───  Sets the memory location
21    }                                          0xb8001 to 0x30
```

The coding style from listing 11.8 may be more familiar to programmers who have worked heavily with pointers before. Using this style requires diligence. Without the aid of type safety provided by offset(), it's easy for a typo to cause memory corruption. The verbose coding style used in listing 11.7 is also friendlier to programmers with less experience performing pointer arithmetic. It declares its own intent.

11.2.6 _start(): The main() function for FledgeOS

An OS kernel does not include the concept of a main() function, in the sense that you're used to. For one thing, an OS kernel's main loop never returns. Where would it return to? By convention, programs return an error code when they exit to an OS. But operating systems don't have an OS to provide an exit code to. Secondly, starting a program at main() is also a convention. But that convention also doesn't exist for OS kernels. To start an OS kernel, we require some software to talk directly to the CPU. The software is called a *bootloader*.

The linker expects to see one symbol defined, _start, which is the program's *entry point*. It links _start to a function that's defined by your source code.

In an ordinary environment, the _start() function has three jobs. Its first is to reset the system. On an embedded system, for example, _start() might clear registers and reset memory to 0. Its second job is to call main(). Its third is to call _exit(), which cleans up after main(). Our _start() function doesn't perform the last two jobs. Job two is unnecessary as the application's functionality is simple enough to keep within _start(). Job three is unnecessary, as is main(). If it were to be called, it would never return.

11.3 fledgeos-1: Avoiding a busy loop

Now that the foundations are in place, we can begin to add features to FledgeOS.

11.3.1 Being power conscious by interacting with the CPU directly

Before proceeding, FledgeOS needs to address one major shortcoming: it is extremely power hungry. The _start() function from listing 11.4 actually runs a CPU core at 100%. It's possible to avoid this by issuing the halt instruction (hlt) to the CPU.

The halt instruction, referred to as HLT in the technical literature, notifies the CPU that there's no more work to be done. The CPU resumes operating when an interrupt triggers new action. As listing 11.9 shows, making use of the x84_64 crate allows us to issue instructions directly to the CPU. The listing, an excerpt of listing 11.10, makes use of the x86_64 crate to access the hlt instruction. It is passed to the CPU during the main loop of _start() to prevent excessive power consumption.

Listing 11.9   Using the hlt instruction

```
7 use x86_64::instructions::{hlt};


17 #[no_mangle]
18 pub extern "C" fn _start() -> ! {
19   let mut framebuffer = 0xb8000 as *mut u8;
20   unsafe {
21     framebuffer
22       .offset(1)
23       .write_volatile(0x30);
24   }
25   loop {
26     hlt();        ⟵──┐  This saves
27   }                  │  electricity.
28 }
```

The alternative to using hlt is for the CPU to run at 100% utilization, performing no work. This turns your computer into a very expensive space heater.

11.3.2   *fledgeos-1 source code*

fledgeos-1 is mostly the same as fledgeos-0, except that its src/main.rs file includes the additions from the previous section. The new file is presented in the following listing and is available to download from code/ch11/ch11-fledgeos-1/src/main.rs. To compile the project, repeat the instructions in section 11.2.1, replacing references to fledgeos-0 with fledgeos-1.

Listing 11.10   Project source code for fledgeos-1

```
 1 #![no_std]
 2 #![no_main]
 3 #![feature(core_intrinsics)]
 4
 5 use core::intrinsics;
 6 use core::panic::PanicInfo;
 7 use x86_64::instructions::{hlt};
 8
 9 #[panic_handler]
10 #[no_mangle]
11 pub fn panic(_info: &PanicInfo) -> ! {
12   unsafe {
13     intrinsics::abort();
14   }
15 }
16
17 #[no_mangle]
```

```
18 pub extern "C" fn _start() -> ! {
19   let mut framebuffer = 0xb8000 as *mut u8;
20   unsafe {
21    framebuffer
22     .offset(1)
23     .write_volatile(0x30);
24   }
25   loop {
26     hlt();
27   }
28 }
```

The x86_64 crate provided us with the ability to inject assembly instructions into our code. Another approach to explore is to use *inline assembly*. The latter approach is demonstrated briefly in section 12.3.

11.4 *fledgeos-2: Custom exception handling*

The next iteration of FledgeOS improves on its error-handling capabilities. FledgeOS still crashes when an error is triggered, but we now have a framework for building something more sophisticated.

11.4.1 *Handling exceptions properly, almost*

FledgeOS cannot manage any exceptions generated from the CPU when it detects an abnormal operation. To handle exceptions, our program needs to define an exception-handling personality function.

Personality functions are called on each stack frame as the stack is unwound after an exception. This means the call stack is traversed, invoking the personality function at each stage. The personality function's role is to determine whether the current stack frame is able to handle the exception. Exception handling is also known as *catching an exception*.

> **NOTE** What is *stack unwinding*? When functions are called, stack frames accumulate. Traversing the stack in reverse is called *unwinding*. Eventually, unwinding the stack will hit _start().

Because handling exceptions in a rigorous way is not necessary for FledgeOS, we'll implement only the bare minimum. Listing 11.11, an excerpt from listing 11.12, provides a snippet of code with the minimal handler. Inject it into main.rs. An empty function implies that any exception is fatal because none will be marked as the handler. When an exception occurs, we don't need to do anything.

> Listing 11.11 Minimalist exception-handling personality routine

```
4 #![feature(lang_items)]

18 #[lang = "eh_personality"]
19 #[no_mangle]
20 pub extern "C" fn eh_personality() { }
```

NOTE What is a *language item*? Language items are elements of Rust implemented as libraries outside of the compiler itself. As we strip away the standard library with #[no_std], we'll need to implement some of its functionality ourselves.

Admittedly, that's a lot of work to do nothing. But at least we can be comforted knowing that we are doing nothing in the right way.

11.4.2 fledgeos-2 source code

fledgeos-2 builds on fledgeos-0 and fledgeos-1. Its src/main.rs file includes the additions from the previous listing. The new file is presented in the following listing and is available to download from code/ch11/ch11-fledgeos-2/src/main.rs. To compile the project, repeat the instructions in section 11.2.1, replacing references to fledgeos-0 with fledgeos-2.

Listing 11.12   Source code for fledgeos-2

```
 1 #![no_std]
 2 #![no_main]
 3 #![feature(core_intrinsics)]
 4 #![feature(lang_items)]
 5
 6 use core::intrinsics;
 7 use core::panic::PanicInfo;
 8 use x86_64::instructions::{hlt};
 9
10 #[panic_handler]
11 #[no_mangle]
12 pub fn panic(_info: &PanicInfo) -> ! {
13    unsafe {
14       intrinsics::abort();
15    }
16 }
17
18 #[lang = "eh_personality"]
19 #[no_mangle]
20 pub extern "C" fn eh_personality() { }
21
22 #[no_mangle]
23 pub extern "C" fn _start() -> ! {
24    let framebuffer = 0xb8000 as *mut u8;
25
26    unsafe {
27       framebuffer
28          .offset(1)
29          .write_volatile(0x30);
30    }
31
32    loop {
33       hlt();
34    }
```

11.5 *fledgeos-3: Text output*

Let's write some text to the screen. That way, if we really do encounter a panic, we can report it properly. This section explains the process of sending text to the frame buffer in more detail. Figure 11.2 shows the output from running fledgeos-3.

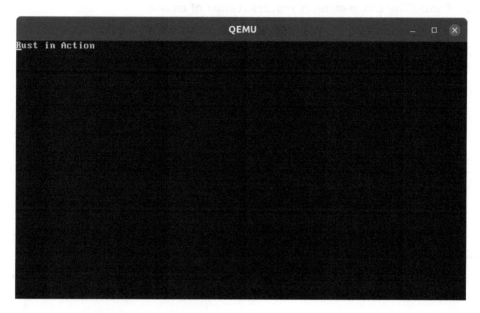

Figure 11.2   Output produced by fledgeos-3

11.5.1 *Writing colored text to the screen*

To start, we'll create a type for the color numeric constants that are used later in listing 11.16. Using an enum rather than defining a series of const values provides enhanced type safety. In some sense, it adds a semantic relationship between the values. These are all treated as members of the same group.

The following listing defines an enum that represents the VGA-compatible text mode color palette. The mapping between bit patterns and colors is defined by the VGA standard, and our code should comply with it.

Listing 11.13   Representing related numeric constants as an enum

```
 9 #[allow(unused)]
10 #[derive(Clone,Copy)]
11 #[repr(u8)]
12 enum Color {
13    Black = 0x0,    White = 0xF,
14    Blue = 0x1,     BrightBlue = 0x9,
15    Green = 0x2,    BrightGreen = 0xA,
16    Cyan = 0x3,     BrightCyan = 0xB,
```

> We won't be using every color variant in our code, so we can silence warnings.

> Opts into copy semantics

> Instructs the compiler to use a single byte to represent the values

```
17    Red = 0x4,      BrightRed = 0xC,
18    Magenta = 0x5,  BrightMagenta = 0xD,
19    Brown = 0x6,    Yellow = 0xE,
20    Gray = 0x7,     DarkGray = 0x8
21  }
```

11.5.2 *Controlling the in-memory representation of enums*

We've been content to allow the compiler to determine how an enum is represented. But there are times when we need to pull in the reins. External systems often demand that our data matches their requirements.

Listing 11.13 provides an example of fitting the colors from the VGA-compatible text mode palette enum into a single u8. It removes any discretion from the compiler about which bit pattern (formally called the *discriminant*) to associate with particular variants. To prescribe a representation, add the repr attribute. You are then able to specify any integer type (i32, u8, i16, u16,...), as well as some special cases.

Using a prescribed representation has some disadvantages. In particular, it reduces your flexibility. It also prevents Rust from making space optimizations. Some enums, those with a single variant, require no representation. These appear in source code but occupy zero space in the running program.

11.5.3 *Why use enums?*

You could model colors differently. For instance, it's possible to create numeric constants that look identical in memory. The following shows one such possibility:

```
const BLACK: u8 = 0x0;
const BLUE: u8 = 0x1;
// ...
```

Using an enum adds an extra guard. It becomes much more difficult to use an illegal value in our code than if we were using an u8 directly. You will see this demonstrated when the Cursor struct is introduced in listing 11.17.

11.5.4 *Creating a type that can print to the VGA frame buffer*

To print to the screen, we'll use a Cursor struct that handles the raw memory manipulation and can convert between our Color type and what is expected by VGA. As the following listing shows, this type manages the interface between our code and the VGA frame buffer. This listing is another excerpt from listing 11.16.

> **Listing 11.14   Definition and methods for `Cursor`**

```
25 struct Cursor {
26   position: isize,
27   foreground: Color,
28   background: Color,
29 }
30
```

```
31 impl Cursor {
32   fn color(&self) -> u8 {
33     let fg = self.foreground as u8;
34     let bg = (self.background as u8) << 4;
35     fg | bg
36   }
37
38   fn print(&mut self, text: &[u8]) {
39     let color = self.color();
40
41     let framebuffer = 0xb8000 as *mut u8;
42
43     for &character in text {
44       unsafe {
45         framebuffer.offset(self.position).write_volatile(character);
46         framebuffer.offset(self.position + 1).write_volatile(color);
47       }
48       self.position += 2;
49     }
50   }
51 }
```

Lines 32–36: **Uses the foreground color as a base, which occupies the lower 4 bits. Shift the background color left to occupy the higher bits, then merge these together.**

Line 38: **For expediency, the input uses a raw byte stream rather than a type that guarantees the correct encoding.**

11.5.5 Printing to the screen

Making use of Cursor involves setting its position and then sending a reference to Cursor.print(). The following listing, an excerpt from listing 11.16, expands the _start() function to also print to the screen.

Listing 11.15 Demonstrating printing to the screen

```
67 #[no_mangle]
68 pub extern "C" fn _start() -> ! {
69   let text = b"Rust in Action";
70
71   let mut cursor = Cursor {
72     position: 0,
73     foreground: Color::BrightCyan,
74     background: Color::Black,
75   };
76   cursor.print(text);
77
78   loop {
79     hlt();
80   }
81 }
```

11.5.6 fledgeos-3 source code

fledgeos-3 continues to build on fledgeos-0, fledgeos-1, and fledgeos-2. Its src/main.rs file includes the additions from the this section. The complete file is presented in the following listing and is available to download from code/ch11/ch11-fledgeos-3/src/main.rs. To compile the project, repeat the instructions in section 11.2.1, replacing references to fledgeos-0 with fledgeos-3.

Listing 11.16   FledgeOS now prints text to the screen

```
1 #![feature(core_intrinsics)]
2 #![feature(lang_items)]
3 #![no_std]
4 #![no_main]
5
6 use core::intrinsics;
7 use core::panic::PanicInfo;
8
9 use x86_64::instructions::{hlt};
10
11 #[allow(unused)]
12 #[derive(Clone,Copy)]
13 #[repr(u8)]
14 enum Color {
15   Black = 0x0,     White = 0xF,
16   Blue = 0x1,      BrightBlue = 0x9,
17   Green = 0x2,     BrightGreen = 0xA,
18   Cyan = 0x3,      BrightCyan = 0xB,
19   Red = 0x4,       BrightRed = 0xC,
20   Magenta = 0x5,   BrightMagenta = 0xD,
21   Brown = 0x6,     Yellow = 0xE,
22   Gray = 0x7,      DarkGray = 0x8
23 }
24
25 struct Cursor {
26   position: isize,
27   foreground: Color,
28   background: Color,
29 }
30
31 impl Cursor {
32   fn color(&self) -> u8 {
33     let fg = self.foreground as u8;
34     let bg = (self.background as u8) << 4;
35     fg | bg
36   }
37
38   fn print(&mut self, text: &[u8]) {
39     let color = self.color();
40
41     let framebuffer = 0xb8000 as *mut u8;
42
43     for &character in text {
44       unsafe {
45         framebuffer.offset(self.position).write_volatile(character);
46         framebuffer.offset(self.position + 1).write_volatile(color);
47       }
48       self.position += 2;
49     }
50   }
51 }
52
53 #[panic_handler]
```

```
54 #[no_mangle]
55 pub fn panic(_info: &PanicInfo) -> ! {
56   unsafe {
57     intrinsics::abort();
58   }
59 }
60
61 #[lang = "eh_personality"]
62 #[no_mangle]
63 pub extern "C" fn eh_personality() { }
64
65 #[no_mangle]
66 pub extern "C" fn _start() -> ! {
67   let text = b"Rust in Action";
68
69   let mut cursor = Cursor {
70     position: 0,
71     foreground: Color::BrightCyan,
72     background: Color::Black,
73   };
74   cursor.print(text);
75
76   loop {
77     hlt();
78   }
79 }
```

11.6 *fledgeos-4: Custom panic handling*

Our panic handler, repeated in the following snippet, calls `core::intrinsics::abort()`. This shuts down the computer immediately, without providing any further input:

```
#[panic_handler]
#[no_mangle]
pub fn panic(_info: &PanicInfo) -> ! {
  unsafe {
    intrinsics::abort();
  }
}
```

11.6.1 *Implementing a panic handler that reports the error to the user*

For the benefit of anyone doing embedded development or wanting to execute Rust on microcontrollers, it's important to learn how to report where a panic occurs. A good place to start is with `core::fmt::Write`. That trait can be associated with the panic handler to display a message, as figure 11.3 shows.

11.6.2 *Reimplementing panic() by making use of core::fmt::Write*

The output shown by figure 11.3 is produced by listing 11.17. `panic()` now goes through a two-stage process. In the first stage, `panic()` clears the screen. The second stage involves the `core::write!` macro. `core::write!` takes a destination object as its

Figure 11.3 Displaying a message when a panic occurs

first argument (cursor), which implements the core::fmt::Write trait. The following listing, an excerpt from listing 11.19, provides a panic handler that reports that an error has occurred using this process.

Listing 11.17 Clearing the screen and printing the message

```
61 pub fn panic(info: &PanicInfo) -> ! {
62   let mut cursor = Cursor {
63     position: 0,
64     foreground: Color::White,
65     background: Color::Red,
66   };
67   for _ in 0..(80*25) {          Clears the screen by
68     cursor.print(b" ");         filling it with red
69   }
70   cursor.position = 0;                           Resets the position
71   write!(cursor, "{}", info).unwrap();           of the cursor
72
73   loop {}      Spins in an infinite loop, allowing    Prints PanicInfo
74 }              the user to read the message and       to the screen
                  restart the machine manually
```

11.6.3 *Implementing core::fmt::Write*

Implementing core::fmt::Write involves calling one method: write_str(). The trait defines several others, but the compiler can autogenerate these once an implementation of write_str() is available. The implementation in the following listing

reuses the print() method and converts the UTF-8 encoded &str into & [u8] with the
to_bytes() method. The code for this listing is in ch11/ch11-fledgeos-4/src/main.rs.

Listing 11.18   Implementing `core::fmt::Write` **for the** `Cursor` **type**

```
54 impl fmt::Write for Cursor {
55   fn write_str(&mut self, s: &str) -> fmt::Result {
56     self.print(s.as_bytes());
57     Ok(())
58   }
59 }
```

11.6.4 fledge-4 source code

The following listing shows the user-friendly panic-handling code for FledgeOS. You'll
find the source for this listing in ch11/ch11-fledgeos-4/src/main.rs. As with earlier
versions, to compile the project, repeat the instructions at section 11.2.1 but replace
references to fledgeos-0 with fledgeos-4.

Listing 11.19   Full code listing of FledgeOS with complete panic handling

```
 1 #![feature(core_intrinsics)]
 2 #![feature(lang_items)]
 3 #![no_std]
 4 #![no_main]
 5
 6 use core::fmt;
 7 use core::panic::PanicInfo;
 8 use core::fmt::Write;
 9
10 use x86_64::instructions::{hlt};
11
12 #[allow(unused)]
13 #[derive(Copy, Clone)]
14 #[repr(u8)]
15 enum Color {
16   Black = 0x0,    White = 0xF,
17   Blue = 0x1,     BrightBlue = 0x9,
18   Green = 0x2,    BrightGreen = 0xA,
19   Cyan = 0x3,     BrightCyan = 0xB,
20   Red = 0x4,      BrightRed = 0xC,
21   Magenta = 0x5,  BrightMagenta = 0xD,
22   Brown = 0x6,    Yellow = 0xE,
23   Gray = 0x7,     DarkGray = 0x8
24 }
25
26 struct Cursor {
27   position: isize,
28   foreground: Color,
29   background: Color,
30 }
31
32 impl Cursor {
```

```
33    fn color(&self) -> u8 {
34      let fg = self.foreground as u8;
35      let bg = (self.background as u8) << 4;
36      fg | bg
37    }
38
39    fn print(&mut self, text: &[u8]) {
40      let color = self.color();
41
42      let framebuffer = 0xb8000 as *mut u8;
43
44      for &character in text {
45        unsafe {
46          framebuffer.offset(self.position).write_volatile(character);
47          framebuffer.offset(self.position + 1).write_volatile(color);
48        }
49        self.position += 2;
50      }
51    }
52  }
53
54  impl fmt::Write for Cursor {
55    fn write_str(&mut self, s: &str) -> fmt::Result {
56      self.print(s.as_bytes());
57      Ok(())
58    }
59  }
60
61  #[panic_handler]
62  #[no_mangle]
63  pub fn panic(info: &PanicInfo) -> ! {
64    let mut cursor = Cursor {
65      position: 0,
66      foreground: Color::White,
67      background: Color::Red,
68    };
69    for _ in 0..(80*25) {
70      cursor.print(b" ");
71    }
72    cursor.position = 0;
73    write!(cursor, "{}", info).unwrap();
74
75    loop { unsafe { hlt(); }}
76  }
77
78  #[lang = "eh_personality"]
79  #[no_mangle]
80  pub extern "C" fn eh_personality() { }
81
82  #[no_mangle]
83  pub extern "C" fn _start() -> ! {
84    panic!("help!");
85  }
```

Summary

- Writing a program that is intended to run without an operating system can feel like programming in a barren desert. Functionality that you take for granted, such as dynamic memory or multithreading, is not available to you.

- In environments such as embedded systems that do not have dynamic memory management, you will need to avoid the Rust standard library with the #![no_std] annotation.

- When interfacing with external components, naming symbols becomes significant. To opt out of Rust's name-mangling facilities, use the #![no_mangle] attribute.

- Rust's internal representations can be controlled through annotations. For example, annotating an enum with #![repr(u8)] forces the values to be packed into a single byte. If this doesn't work, Rust refuses to compile the program.

- Raw pointer manipulation is available to you, but type-safe alternatives exist. When it's practical to do so, use the offset() method to correctly calculate the number of bytes to traverse through the address space.

- The compiler's internals are always accessible to you at the cost of requiring a nightly compiler. Access compiler intrinsics like intrinsics::abort() to provide functionality to the program that's ordinarily inaccessible.

- cargo should be thought of as an extensible tool. It sits at the center of the Rust programmer's workflow, but its standard behavior can be changed when necessary.

- To access raw machine instructions, such as HTL, you can use helper crates like x86_64 or rely on inline assembly.

- Don't be afraid to experiment. With modern tools like QEMU, the worst that can happen is that your tiny OS crashes, and you'll need to run it again instantly.

Signals, interrupts, and exceptions

12

This chapter covers

- What interrupts, exceptions, traps, and faults are
- How device drivers inform applications that data is ready
- How to transmit signals between running applications

This chapter describes the process by which the outside world communicates with your operating system (OS). The network constantly interrupts program execution when bytes are ready to be delivered. This means that after connecting to a database (or at any other time), the OS can demand that your application deal with a message. This chapter describes this process and how to prepare your programs for it.

In chapter 9, you learned that a digital clock periodically notifies the OS that time has progressed. This chapter explains how those notifications occur. It also introduces the concept of multiple applications running at the same time via the concept of signals. Signals emerged as part of the UNIX OS tradition. These can be used to send messages between different running programs.

We'll address both concepts—signals and interrupts—together, as the programming models are similar. But it's simpler to start with signals. Although this chapter focuses on the Linux OS running on x86 CPUs, that's not to say that users of other operating systems won't be able to follow along.

12.1 Glossary

Learning how CPUs, device drivers, applications, and operating systems interact is difficult. There is a lot of jargon to take in. To make matters worse, the terms all look similar, and it certainly does not help that these are often used interchangeably. Here are some examples of the jargon that is used in this chapter. Figure 12.1 illustrates how these interrelate:

- *Abort*—An unrecoverable exception. If an application triggers an abort, the application terminates.
- *Fault*—A recoverable exception that is expected in routine operations such as a *page fault*. Page faults occur when a memory address is not available and data must be fetched from the main memory chip(s). This process is known as *virtual memory* and is explained in section 4 of chapter 6.
- *Exception*—Exception is an umbrella term that incudes aborts, faults, and traps. Formally referred to as *synchronous interrupts*, exceptions are sometimes described as a form of an interrupt.
- *Hardware interrupt*—An interrupt generated by a device such as a keyboard or hard disk controller. Typically used by devices to notify the CPU that data is available to be read from the device.
- *Interrupt*—A hardware-level term that is used in two senses. It can refer only to *synchronous interrupts*, which include hardware and software interrupts. Depending on context, it can also include exceptions. Interrupts are usually handled by the OS.
- *Signal*—An OS-level term for interruptions to an application's control flow. Signals are handled by applications.
- *Software interrupt*—An interrupt generated by a program. Within Intel's x86 CPU family, programs can trigger an interrupt with the INT instruction. Among other uses of this facility, debuggers use software interrupts to set breakpoints.
- *Trap*—A recoverable exception such as an integer overflow detected by the CPU. Integer overflow is explained in section 5.2.

NOTE The meaning of the term *exception* may differ from your previous programming experience. Programming languages often use the term exception to refer to any error, whereas the term has a specialized meaning when referring to CPUs.

12.1.1 Signals vs. interrupts

The two concepts that are most important to distinguish between are signals and interrupts. A *signal* is a software-level abstraction that is associated with an OS. An *interrupt* is a CPU-related abstraction that is closely associated with the system's hardware.

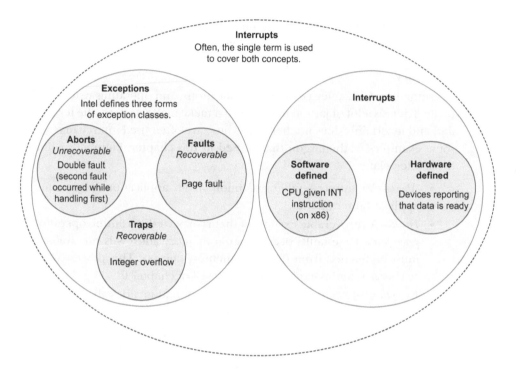

Figure 12.1   A visual taxonomy of how the terms interrupt, exception, trap, and fault interact within Intel's x86 family of CPUs. Note that signals do not appear within this figure. Signals are not interrupts.

Signals are a form of limited interprocess communication. They don't contain content, but their presence indicates something. They're analogous to a physical, audible buzzer. The buzzer doesn't provide content, but the person who presses it still knows what's intended as it makes a very jarring sound. To add confusion to the mix, signals are often described as software interrupts. This chapter, however, avoids the use of the term interrupt when referring to a signal.

There are two forms of interrupts, which differ in their origin. One form of interrupt occurs within the CPU during its processing. This is the result of attempting to process illegal instructions and trying to access invalid memory addresses. This first form is known technically as a *synchronous interrupt*, but you may have heard it referred to by its more common name, *exception*.

The second form of interrupt is generated by hardware devices like keyboards and accelerometers. This is what's commonly implied by the term interrupt. This can occur at any time and is formally known as an *asynchronous interrupt*. Like signals, this can also be generated within software.

Interrupts can be specialized. A *trap* is an error detected by the CPU, so it gives the OS a chance to recover. A *fault* is another form of a recoverable problem. If the CPU is given a memory address that it can't read from, it notifies the OS and asks for an updated address.

Interrupts force an application's control flow to change, whereas many signals can be ignored if desired. Upon receiving an interrupt, the CPU jumps to handler code, irrespective of the current state of the program. The location of the handler code is predefined by the BIOS and OS during a system's bootup process.

Treating signals as interrupts

Handling interrupts directly means manipulating the OS kernel. Because we would prefer not to do that in a learning environment, we'll play fast and loose with the terminology. The rest of this chapter, therefore, treats signals as interrupts.

Why simplify things? Writing OS components involves tweaking the kernel. Breaking things there means that our system could become completely unresponsive without a clear way to fix anything. From a more pragmatic perspective, avoiding tweaks to the kernel means that we'll avoid learning a whole new compiler toolchain.

To our advantage, code that handles signals looks similar to code that handles interrupts. Practicing with signals allows us to keep any errors within our code constrained to our application rather than risk bringing the whole system down. The general pattern is as follows:

1. Model your application's standard control flow.
2. Model the interrupted control flow and identify resources that need to be cleanly shut down, if required.
3. Write the interrupt/signal handler to update some state and return quickly.
4. You will typically delegate time-consuming operations by only modifying a global variable that is regularly checked by the main loop of the program.
5. Modify your application's standard control flow to look for the GO/NO GO flag that a signal handler may have changed.

12.2 How interrupts affect applications

Let's work through this challenge by considering a small code example. The following listing shows a simple calculation that sums two integers.

Listing 12.1 A program that calculates the sum of two integers

```
1 fn add(a: i32, b:i32) -> i32 {
2   a + b
3 }
4
5 fn main() {
6   let a = 5;
7   let b = 6;
8   let c = add(a,b);
9 }
```

Irrespective of the number of hardware interrupts, c is always calculated. But the program's wall clock time becomes nondeterministic because the CPU performs different tasks every time it runs.

When an interrupt occurs, the CPU immediately halts execution of the program and jumps to the interrupt handler. The next listing (illustrated in figure 12.2) details what happens when an interrupt occurs between lines 7 and 8 in listing 12.1.

Listing 12.2   Depicting the flow of listing 12.1 as it handles an interrupt

```
 1 #[allow(unused)]
 2 fn interrupt_handler() {
 3   // ..
 4 }
 5
 6 fn add(a: i32, b:i32) -> i32 {
 7   a + b
 8 }
 9
10 fn main() {
11   let a = 5;
12   let b = 6;
13
14   // Key pressed on keyboard!
15   interrupt_handler()
16
17   let c = add(a,b);
18 }
```

Although presented in this listing as an extra function, the interrupt handler is typically defined by the OS.

Normal program execution
Control flow in the normal case operates in a linear sequence of instructions. Function calls and return statements do jump a CPU around in memory, but the order of events can be predetermined.

Interrupted program execution
When a hardware interrupt occurs, the program is not unaffected directly, although there may be a negligible performance impact as the operating system must deal with the hardware.

Dashes mark the CPU's progression through the program.

```
main()
    let a = 5;
    let b = 6;
    .... add(a,b)
    let c = ...
```

```
main()
    let a = 5;
    let b = 6;
    .... add(a,b)
    let c = ...
```

?

Program is unaware of what the CPU is doing. Once it is finished with other tasks, execution proceeds as normal.

```
add(a: i32, b: i32) -> i32
    a + b
    RETURN
```

```
add(a: i32, b: i32) -> i32
    a + b
    RETURN
```

Return instruction is implicit in Rust.

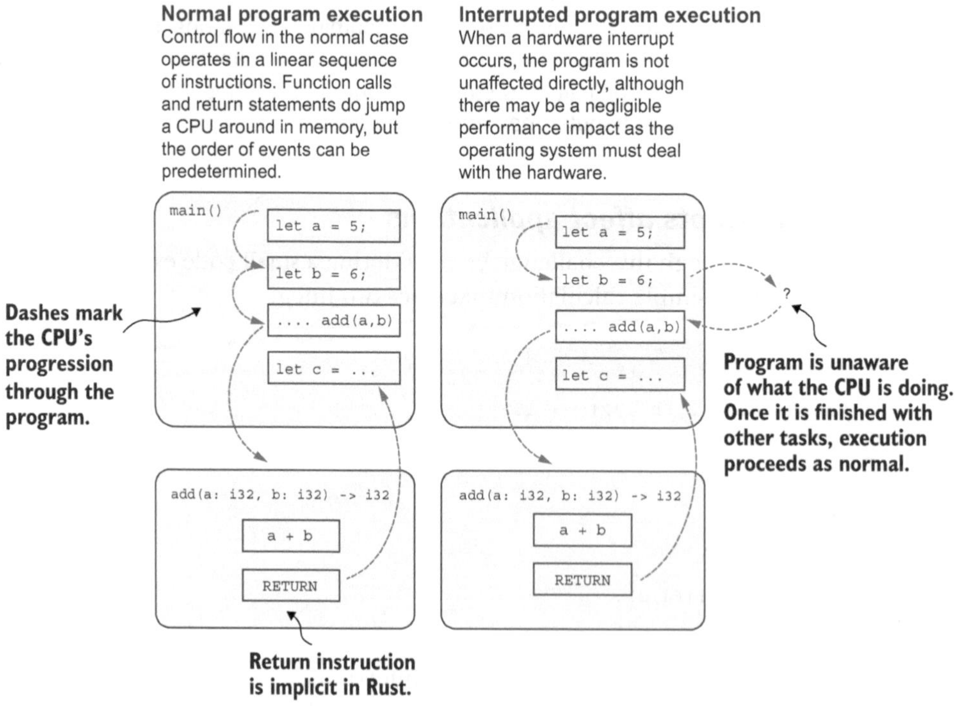

Figure 12.2   Using addition to demonstrate control flow for handling signals

One important point to remember is that, from the program's perspective, little changes. It isn't aware that its control flow has been interrupted. Listing 12.1 is still an accurate representation of the program.

12.3 Software interrupts

Software interrupts are generated by programs sending specific instructions to the CPU. To do this in Rust, you can invoke the asm! macro. The following code, available at ch12/asm.rs, provides a brief view of the syntax:

```
#![feature(asm)]              ◁─┐  Enables an
                                 │  unstable feature
use std::asm;

fn main() {
    unsafe {
        asm!("int 42");
    }
}
```

Running the compiled executable presents the following error from the OS:

```
$ rustc +nightly asm.rs
$ ./asm
Segmentation fault (core dumped)
```

As of Rust 1.50, the asm! macro is unstable and requires that you execute the nightly Rust compiler. To install the nightly compiler, use rustup:

```
$ rustup install nightly
```

12.4 Hardware interrupts

Hardware interrupts have a special flow. Devices interface with a specialized chip, known as the *Programmable Interrupt Controller (PIC)*, to notify the CPU. Figure 12.3 provides a view of how interrupts flow from hardware devices to an application.

12.5 Signal handling

Signals require immediate attention. Failing to handling a signal typically results in the application being terminated.

12.5.1 Default behavior

Sometimes the best approach is to let the system's defaults do the work. Code that you don't need to write is code that's free from bugs that you inadvertently cause.

The default behavior for most signals is shutting down the application. When an application does not provide a special handler function (we'll learn how to do that in this chapter), the OS considers the signal to be an *abnormal* condition. When an OS detects an abnormal condition within an application, things don't end well for the application—it terminates the application. Figure 12.4 depicts this scenario.

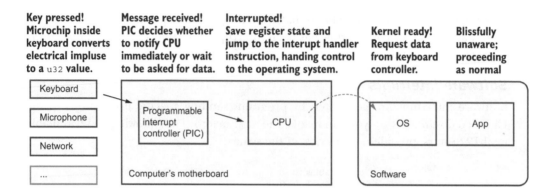

Key pressed!
Microchip inside keyboard converts electrical impulse to a `u32` value.

Message received!
PIC decides whether to notify CPU immediately or wait to be asked for data.

Interrupted!
Save register state and jump to the interrupt handler instruction, handing control to the operating system.

Kernel ready!
Request data from keyboard controller.

Blissfully unaware;
proceeding as normal

Figure 12.3   **How applications are notified of an interrupt generated from a hardware device. Once the OS has been notified that data is ready, it then directly communicates with the device (in this case, the keyboard) to read the data into its own memory.**

Figure 12.4   **An application defending itself from marauding hoards of unwanted signals. Signal handlers are the friendly giants of the computing world. They generally stay out of the way but are there when your application needs to defend its castle. Although not part of everyday control flow, signal handlers are extremely useful when the time is right. Not all signals can be handled. `SIGKILL` is particularly vicious.**

Your application can receive three common signals. The following lists them and their intended actions:

- `SIGINT`—Terminates the program (usually generated by a person)
- `SIGTERM`—Terminates the program (usually generated by another program)
- `SIGKILL`—Immediately terminates the program without the ability to recover

You'll find many other less common signals. For your convenience, a fuller list is provided in table 12.2.

You may have noticed that the three examples listed here are heavily associated with terminating a running program. But that's not necessarily the case.

12.5.2 *Suspend and resume a program's operation*

There are two special signals worth mentioning: SIGSTOP and SIGCONT. SIGSTOP halts the program's execution, and it remains suspended until it receives SIGCONT. UNIX systems use this signal for job control. It's also useful to know about if you want to manually intervene and halt a running application but would like the ability to recover at some time in the future.

The following snippet shows the structure for the sixty project that we'll develop in this chapter. To download the project, enter these commands in the console:

```
$ git clone https://github.com/rust-in-action/code rust-in-action
$ cd rust-in-action/ch12/ch12-sixty
```

To create the project manually, set up a directory structure that resembles the following and populate its contents from listings 12.3 and 12.4:

```
ch12-sixty
├── src             See listing 12.4.
│   └── main.rs  ◁──┤
└── Cargo.toml   ◁──┘ See listing 12.3.
```

The following listing shows the initial crate metadata for the sixty project. The source code for this listing is in the ch12/ch12-sixty/ directory.

Listing 12.3 Crate metadata for the sixty project

```
[package]
name = "sixty"
version = "0.1.0"
authors = ["Tim McNamara <author@rustinaction.com>"]

[dependencies]
```

The next listing provides the code to build a basic application that lives for 60 seconds and prints its progress along the way. You'll find the source for this listing in ch12/ch12-sixty/src/main.rs.

Listing 12.4 A basic application that receives SIGSTOP and SIGCONT

```
 1 use std::time;
 2 use std::process;
 3 use std::thread::{sleep};
 4
 5 fn main() {
 6     let delay = time::Duration::from_secs(1);
 7
 8     let pid = process::id();
 9     println!("{}", pid);
10
11     for i in 1..=60 {
12         sleep(delay);
```

```
13          println!(". {}", i);
14     }
15 }
```

Once the code from listing 12.4 is saved to disk, two consoles open. In the first, execute cargo run. A 3–5 digit number appears, followed by a counter that increments by the second. The first line number is the *PID* or *process ID*. Table 12.1 shows the operation and expected output.

Table 12.1   How processes can be suspended and resumed with SIGSTOP and SIGCONT

Step	Console 1	Console 2
	Executes application	Sends signals
1	`$ cd ch12/ch12-sixty`	
2	`$ cargo run` 23221 . 1 . 2 . 3 . 4	
3		`$ kill -SIGSTOP 23221`
4	`[1]+  Stopped      cargo run` `$`	
5		`$ kill -SIGCONT 23221`
6	. 5 . 6 . 7 . 8 ⋮ . 60	

The program flow in table 12.1 follows:

1 In console 1, move to the project directory (created from listings 12.3 and 12.4).

2 Compile and run the project.

   cargo provides debugging output that is omitted here. When running, the sixty program prints the PID, and then prints some numbers to the console every second. Because it was the PID for this invocation, 23221 appears as output in the table.

3 In console 2, execute the kill command, specifying -SIGSTOP.

   If you are unfamiliar with the shell command kill, its role is to send signals. It's named after its most common role, terminating programs with either SIGKILL or SIGTERM. The numeric argument (23221) must match the PID provided in step 2.

4 Console 1 returns to the command prompt as there is no longer anything running in the foreground.

5 Resume the program by sending SIGCONT to the PID provided in step 2.

6 The program resumes counting. It terminates when it hits 60, unless interrupted by Ctrl-C (SIGINT).

SIGSTOP and SIGCONT are interesting special cases. Let's continue by investigating more typical signal behavior.

12.5.3 Listing all signals supported by the OS

What are the other signals and what are their default handlers? To find the answer, we can ask the kill command to provide that information:

```
$ kill -l          ⟵⎦  -l stands for list.
 1) SIGHUP       2) SIGINT       3) SIGQUIT      4) SIGILL       5) SIGTRAP
 6) SIGABRT      7) SIGEMT       8) SIGFPE       9) SIGKILL     10) SIGBUS
11) SIGSEGV     12) SIGSYS      13) SIGPIPE     14) SIGALRM     15) SIGTERM
16) SIGURG      17) SIGSTOP     18) SIGTSTP     19) SIGCONT     20) SIGCHLD
21) SIGTTIN     22) SIGTTOU     23) SIGIO       24) SIGXCPU     25) SIGXFSZ
26) SIGVTALRM   27) SIGPROF     28) SIGWINCH    29) SIGPWR      30) SIGUSR1
31) SIGUSR2     32) SIGRTMAX
```

That's a lot, Linux! To make matters worse, few signals have standardized behavior. Thankfully, most applications don't need to worry about setting handlers for many of these signals (if any). Table 12.1 shows a much tighter list of signals. These are more likely to be encountered in day-to-day programming.

Table 12.2 List of common signals, their default actions, and shortcuts for sending them from the command line

Signal	Read as	Default action	Comment	Shortcut
SIGHUP	Hung up	Terminate	Originally from telephone-based digital communications. Now often sent to background applications (daemons/services) to request that these reread their configuration files. Sent to running programs when you log out from a shell.	Ctrl-D
SIGINT	Interrupt (or perhaps interactive)	Terminate	User-generated signal to terminate a running application.	Ctrl-C
SIGTERM	Terminate	Terminate	Asks application to gracefully terminate.	

Table 12.2 List of common signals, their default actions, and shortcuts for sending them from the command line (continued)

Signal	Read as	Default action	Comment	Shortcut
SIGKILL	Kill	Terminate	This action is unstoppable.	
SIGQUIT	Quit		Writes memory to disk as a core dump, then terminates.	Ctrl-\
SIGTSTP	Terminal stop	Pause execution	The terminal requests the application to stop.	Ctrl-Z
SIGSTOP	Stop	Pause execution	This action is unstoppable.	
SIGCONT	Continue	Resume execution when paused		

NOTE SIGKILL and SIGSTOP have special status: these cannot be handled or blocked by the application. Programs can avoid the others.

12.6 *Handling signals with custom actions*

The default actions for signals are fairly limited. By default, receiving a signal tends to end badly for applications. For example, if external resources such as database connections are left open, they might not be cleaned up properly when the application ends.

The most common use case for signal handlers is to allow an application to shut down cleanly. Some common tasks that might be necessary when an application shuts down include

- Flushing the hard disk drive to ensure that pending data is written to disk
- Closing any network connections
- Deregistering from any distributed scheduler or work queue

To stop the current workload and shut down, a signal handler is required. To set up a signal handler, we need to create a function with the signature f(i32) -> (). That is, the function needs to accept an i32 integer as its sole argument and returns no value.

This poses some software engineering issues. The signal handler isn't able to access any information from the application except which signal was sent. Therefore, because it doesn't know what state anything is in, it doesn't know what needs shutting down beforehand.

There are some additional restrictions in addition to the architectural one. Signal handlers are constrained in time and scope. These must also act quickly within a subset of functionality available to general code for these reasons:

- Signal handlers can block other signals of the same type from being handled.
- Moving fast reduces the likelihood of operating alongside another signal handler of a different type.

Signal handlers have reduced scope in what they're permitted to do. For example, they must avoid executing any code that might itself generate signals.

To wriggle out of this constrained environment, the ordinary approach is to use a Boolean flag as a global variable that is regularly checked during a program's execution. If the flag is set, then you can call a function to shutdown the application cleanly within the context of the application. For this pattern to work, there are two requirements:

- The signal handler's sole responsibility is to mutate the flag.
- The application must regularly check the flag to detect whether the flag has been modified.

To avoid race conditions caused by multiple signal handlers running at the same time, signal handlers typically do little. A common pattern is to set a flag via a global variable.

12.6.1 *Global variables in Rust*

Rust facilitates *global variables* (variables accessible anywhere within the program) by declaring a variable with the `static` keyword in global scope. Suppose we want to create a global value SHUT_DOWN that we can set to `true` when a signal handler believes it's time to urgently shut down. We can use this declaration:

```
static mut SHUT_DOWN: bool = false;
```

> **NOTE** `static mut` is read as *mutable static*, irrespective of how grammatically contorted that is.

Global variables present an issue for Rust programmers. Accessing these (even just for reading) is unsafe. This means that the code can become quite cluttered if it's wrapped in `unsafe` blocks. This ugliness is a signal to wary programmers—avoid global state whenever possible.

Listing 12.6 presents a example of a `static mut` variable that reads from line 12 and writes to lines 7–9. The call to `rand::random()` on line 8 produces Boolean values. Output is a series of dots. About 50% of the time, you'll receive output that looks like what's shown in the following console session:[1]

```
$ git clone https://github.com/rust-in-action/code rust-in-action
$ cd rust-in-action/ch12/ch2-toy-global
$ cargo run -q
.
```

The following listing provides the metadata for listing 12.6. You can access its source code in ch12/ch12-toy-global/Cargo.toml.

---

[1] Output assumes a fair random number generator, which Rust uses by default. This assumption holds as long as you trust your operating system's random number generator.

Listing 12.5   Crate metadata for listing 12.6

```
[package]
name = "ch12-toy-global"
version = "0.1.0"
authors = ["Tim McNamara <author@rustinaction.com>"]
edition = "2018"

[dependencies]
rand = "0.6"
```

The following listing presents our toy example. Its source code is in ch12/ch12-toy-global/src/main.rs.

Listing 12.6   Accessing global variables (mutable statics) in Rust

```
 1 use rand;
 2
 3 static mut SHUT_DOWN: bool = false;
 4
 5 fn main() {
 6   loop {
 7     unsafe {
 8       SHUT_DOWN = rand::random();
 9     }
10     print!(".");
11
12     if unsafe { SHUT_DOWN } {
13       break
14     };
15   }
16   println!()
17 }
```

Reading from and writing to a static mut variable requires an unsafe block.

rand::random() is a shortcut that calls rand::thread_rng().gen() to produce a random value. The required type is inferred from the type of SHUT_DOWN.

12.6.2 Using a global variable to indicate that shutdown has been initiated

Given that signal handlers must be quick and simple, we'll do the minimal amount of possible work. In the next example, we'll set a variable to indicate that the program needs to shut down. This technique is demonstrated by listing 12.8, which is structured into these three functions:

- `register_signal_handlers()`—Communicates to the OS via libc, the signal handler for each signal. This function makes use of a function pointer, which treats a function as data. Function pointers are explained in section 11.7.1.
- `handle_signals()`—Handles incoming signals. This function is agnostic as to which signal is sent, although we'll only deal with SIGTERM.
- `main()`—Initializes the program and iterates through a main loop.

When run, the resulting executable produces a trace of where it is. The following console session shows the trace:

```
$ git clone https://github.com/rust-in-action/code rust-in-action
$ cd rust-in-action/ch12/ch12-basic-handler
$ cargo run -q
1
SIGUSR1
2
SIGUSR1
3
SIGTERM
4
*
```

> I hope that you will forgive the cheap ASCII art explosion.

NOTE If the signal handler is not correctly registered, `Terminated` may appear in the output. Make sure that you add a call to `register_signal_handler()` early within `main()`. Listing 12.8 does this on line 38.

The following listing shows the package and dependency for listing 12.8. You can view the source for this listing in ch12/ch12-basic-handler/Cargo.toml.

Listing 12.7 Crate setup for listing 12.10

```
[package]
name = "ch12-handler"
version = "0.1.0"
authors = ["Tim McNamara <author@rustinaction.com>"]
edition = "2018"

[dependencies]
libc = "0.2"
```

When executed, the following listing uses a signal handler to modify a global variable. The source for this listing is in ch12/ch12-basic-handler/src/main.rs.

Listing 12.8 Creating a signal handler that modifies a global variable

```
1  #![cfg(not(windows))]
2
3  use std::time::{Duration};
4  use std::thread::{sleep};
5  use libc::{SIGTERM, SIGUSR1};
6
7  static mut SHUT_DOWN: bool = false;
8
9  fn main() {
10   register_signal_handlers();
11
12   let delay = Duration::from_secs(1);
13
14   for i in 1_usize.. {
15     println!("{}", i);
16     unsafe {
17       if SHUT_DOWN {
18         println!("*");
```

Line 1 — Indicates that this code won't run on Windows

Line 10 — Must occur as soon as possible; otherwise signals will be incorrectly handled

Line 16 — Accessing a mutable static is unsafe.

```
19        return;
20      }
21    }
22
23    sleep(delay);
24
25    let signal = if i > 2 {
26      SIGTERM
27    } else {
28      SIGUSR1
29    };
30
31    unsafe {
32      libc::raise(signal);
33    }
34  }
35  unreachable!();
36 }
37
38 fn register_signal_handlers() {
39   unsafe {
40     libc::signal(SIGTERM, handle_sigterm as usize);
41     libc::signal(SIGUSR1, handle_sigusr1 as usize);
42   }
43 }
44
45 #[allow(dead_code)]
46 fn handle_sigterm(_signal: i32) {
47   register_signal_handlers();
48
49   println!("SIGTERM");
50
51   unsafe {
52     SHUT_DOWN = true;
53   }
54 }
55
56 #[allow(dead_code)]
57 fn handle_sigusr1(_signal: i32) {
58   register_signal_handlers();
59
60   println!("SIGUSR1");
61 }
```

Calling libc functions is unsafe; their effects are outside of Rust's control.

Without this attribute, rustc warns that these functions are never called.

Modifying a mutable static is unsafe.

Reregisters signals as soon as possible to minimize signal changes affecting the signal handler itself

In the preceding listing, there is something special about the calls to libc::signal()
on lines 40 and 41. libc::signal takes a signal name (which is actually an integer)
and an untyped function pointer (known in C parlance as a *void function pointer*) as
arguments and associates the signal with the function. Rust's fn keyword creates function pointers. handle_sigterm() and handle_sigusr1() both have the type fn(i32)
-> (). We need to cast these as usize values to erase any type information. Function
pointers are explained in more detail in section 12.7.1.

> ## Understanding the difference between `const` and `static`
>
> Static and constant seem similar. Here is the main difference between them:
>
> - `static` values appear in a single location in memory.
> - `const` values can be duplicated in locations where they are accessed.
>
> Duplicating `const` values can be a CPU-friendly optimization. It allows for data locality and improved cache performance.
>
> Why use confusingly similar names for two different things? It could be considered a historical accident. The word `static` refers to the segment of the address space that the variables live in. `static` values live outside the stack space, within the region where string literals are held, near the bottom of the address space. That means accessing a `static` variable almost certainly implies dereferencing a pointer.
>
> The constant in `const` values refers to the value itself. When accessed from code, the data might get duplicated to every location that it's needed if the compiler believes that this will result in faster access.

12.7 Sending application-defined signals

Signals can be used as a limited form of messaging. Within your business rules, you can create definitions for `SIGUSR1` and `SIGUSR2`. These are unallocated by design. In listing 12.8, we used `SIGUSR1` to do a small task. It simply prints the string `SIGUSR1`. A more realistic use of custom signals is to notify a peer application that some data is ready for further processing.

12.7.1 Understanding function pointers and their syntax

Listing 12.8 includes some syntax that might be confusing. For example, on line 40 `handle_sigterm as usize` appears to cast a function as an integer.

What is happening here? The address where the function is stored is being converted to an integer. In Rust, the `fn` keyword creates a function pointer.

Readers who have worked through chapter 5 will understand that functions are just data. That is to say, functions are sequences of bytes that make sense to the CPU. A *function pointer* is a pointer to the start of that sequence. Refer back to chapter 5, especially section 5.7, for a refresher.

A *pointer* is a data type that acts as a stand-in for its referent. Within an application's source code, pointers contain both the address of the value referred to as well as its type. The type information is something that's stripped away in the compiled binary. The internal representation for pointers is an integer of `usize`. That makes pointers very economical to pass around. In C, making use of function pointers can feel like arcane magic. In Rust, they hide in plain sight.

Every `fn` declaration is actually declaring a function pointer. That means that listing 12.9 is legal code and should print something similar to the following line:

```
$ rustc ch12/fn-ptr-demo-1.rs && ./fn-ptr-demo-1
noop as usize: 0x5620bb4af530
```

> **NOTE**   In the output, `0x5620bb4af530` is the memory address (in hexadecimal notation) of the start of the `noop()` function. This number will be different on your machine.

The following listing, available at ch12/noop.rs, shows how to cast a function to `usize`. This demonstrates how `usize` can be used as a function pointer.

Listing 12.9   Casting a function to `usize`

```
fn noop() {}

fn main() {
    let fn_ptr = noop as usize;

    println!("noop as usize: 0x{:x}", fn_ptr);
}
```

But what is the type of the function pointer created from `fn noop()`? To describe function pointers, Rust reuses its function signature syntax. In the case of `fn noop()`, the type is `*const fn() -> ()`. This type is read as "a const pointer to a function that takes no arguments and returns `unit`." A const pointer is immutable. A `unit` is Rust's stand-in value for "nothingness."

Listing 12.10 casts a function pointer to `usize` and then back again. Its output, shown in the following snippet, should show two lines that are nearly identical:

```
$ rustc ch12/fn-ptr-demo-2.rs && ./fn-ptr-demo-2
noop as usize:    0x55ab3fdb05c0
noop as *const T: 0x55ab3fdb05c0
```

> **NOTE**   These two numbers will be different on your machine, but the two numbers will match each other.

Listing 12.10   Casting a function to `usize`

```
fn noop() {}

fn main() {
  let fn_ptr = noop as usize;
  let typed_fn_ptr = noop as *const fn() -> ();

  println!("noop as usize:    0x{:x}", fn_ptr);
  println!("noop as *const T: {:p}", typed_fn_ptr);    ◁────  Note the use of the
}                                                              pointer format
                                                               modifier, {:p}.
```

12.8 Ignoring signals

As noted in table 12.2, most signals terminate the running program by default. This can be somewhat disheartening for the running program attempting to get its work done. (Sometimes the application knows best!) For those cases, many signals can be ignored.

SIGSTOP and SIGKILL aside, the constant SIG_IGN can be provided to libc::signal() instead of a function pointer. An example of its usage is provided by the ignore project. Listing 12.11 shows its Cargo.toml file, and listing 12.12 shows src/main.rs. These are both available from the ch12/ch12-ignore project directory. When executed, the project prints the following line to the console:

```
$ cd ch12/ch12-ignore
$ cargo run -q
ok
```

The ignore project demonstrates how to ignore selected signals. On line 6 of listing 12.12, libc::SIG_IGN (short for *sig*nal *ign*ore) is provided as the signal handler to libc::signal(). The default behavior is reset on line 13. libc::signal() is called again, this time with SIG_DFL (short for *sig*nal *default*) as the signal handler.

Listing 12.11 Project metadata for ignore project

```
[package]
name = "ignore"
version = "0.1.0"
authors = ["Tim McNamara <author@rustinaction.com>"]
edition = "2018"

[dependencies]
libc = "0.2"
```

Listing 12.12 Ignoring signals with libc::SIG_IGN

```
1 use libc::{signal,raise};
2 use libc::{SIG_DFL, SIG_IGN, SIGTERM};      Requires an unsafe block
3                                             because Rust does not control
4 fn main() {                                 what happens beyond the
5   unsafe {                                  function boundaries
6     signal(SIGTERM, SIG_IGN);        Ignores the
7     raise(SIGTERM);                  SIGTERM signal
8   }
9                           libc::raise() allows code
10   println!("ok");        to make a signal; in this
11                          case, to itself.
12   unsafe {
13     signal(SIGTERM, SIG_DFL);          Resets SIGTERM
14     raise(SIGTERM);                    to its default
15   }                      Terminates
16                          the program
```

```
17  println!("not ok");
18 }
```

This code is never reached, and therefore, this string is never printed.

12.9   *Shutting down from deeply nested call stacks*

What if our program is deep in the middle of a call stack and can't afford to unwind? When receiving a signal, the program might want to execute some cleanup code before terminating (or being forcefully terminated). This is sometimes referred to as *nonlocal control transfer*. UNIX-based operating systems provide some tools to enable you to make use of that machinery via two system calls—setjmp and longjmp:

- setjmp sets a marker location.
- longjmp jumps back to the previously marked location.

Why bother with such programming gymnastics? Sometimes using low-level techniques like these is the only way out of a tight spot. These approach the "Dark Arts" of systems programming. To quote the manpage:

> *"setjmp() and longjmp() are useful for dealing with errors and interrupts encountered in a low-level subroutine of a program."*
>
> —Linux Documentation Project: setjmp(3)

These two tools circumvent normal control flow and allow programs to teleport themselves through the code. Occasionally an error occurs deep within a call stack. If our program takes too long to respond to the error, the OS may simply abort the program, and the program's data may be left in an inconsistent state. To avoid this, you can use longjmp to shift control directly to the error-handling code.

To understand the significance of this, consider what happens in an ordinary program's call stack during several calls to a recursive function as produced by the code in listing 12.13. Each call to dive() adds another place that control eventually returns to. See the left-hand side of table 12.3. The longjmp system call, used by listing 12.17, bypasses several layers of the call stack. Its effect on the call stack is visible on the right-hand side of table 12.3.

Table 12.3   Comparing the intended output from listing 12.13 and listing 12.17

Listing 12.13 produces a symmetrical pattern. Each level is caused by a nested call to dive(), which is removed when the calls return.	Listing 12.17 produces a much different pattern. After a few calls to dive(), control teleports back to main() without returning the calls to dive().
```\n#\n##\n###\n####\n#####\n###\n##\n#\n```	```\n#\n##\n###\nearly return!\nfinishing!\n```

On the left side of table 12.3, the call stack grows one step as functions are called, then shrinks by one as each function returns. On the right side, the code jumps directly from the third call to the top to the call stack.

The following listing depicts how the call stack operates by printing its progress as the program executes. The code for this listing is in ch10/ch10-callstack/src/main.rs.

Listing 12.13   Illustrating how the call stack operates

```
 1 fn print_depth(depth:usize) {
 2     for _ in 0..depth {
 3         print!("#");
 4     }
 5     println!("");
 6 }
 7
 8 fn dive(depth: usize, max_depth: usize) {
 9     print_depth(depth);
10     if depth >= max_depth {
11         return;
12
13     } else {
14         dive(depth+1, max_depth);
15     }
16     print_depth(depth);
17 }
18
19 fn main() {
20     dive(0, 5);
21 }
```

There's a lot of work to do to make this happen. The Rust language itself doesn't have the tools to enable this control-flow trickery. It needs to access some provided by its compiler's toolchain. Compilers provide special functions known as *intrinsics* to application programs. Using an intrinsic function with Rust takes some ceremony to set up, but that operates as a standard function once the set-up is in place.

12.9.1 *Introducing the sjlj project*

The sjlj project demonstrates contorting the normal control flow of a function. With the help of some assistance from the OS and the compiler, it's actually possible to create a situation where a function can move to anywhere in the program. Listing 12.17 uses that functionality to bypass several layers of the call stack, creating the output from the right side of table 12.3. Figure 12.5 shows the control flow for the sjlj project.

12.9.2 *Setting up intrinsics in a program*

Listing 12.17 uses two intrinsics, setjmp() and longjmp(). To enable these in our programs, the crate must be annotated with the attribute provided. The following listing provides this documentation.

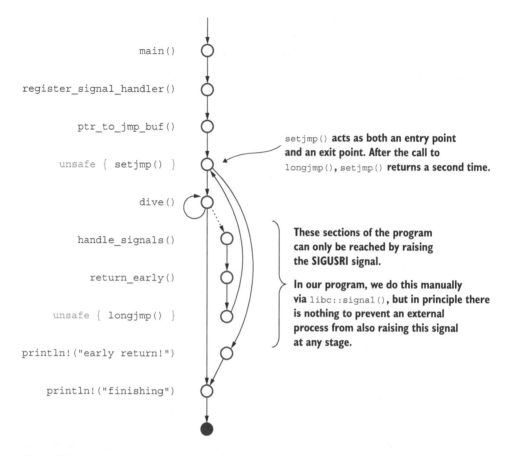

main()

register_signal_handler()

ptr_to_jmp_buf()

unsafe { setjmp() }

setjmp() **acts as both an entry point and an exit point. After the call to** longjmp(), setjmp() **returns a second time.**

dive()

handle_signals()

These sections of the program can only be reached by raising the SIGUSRI signal.

return_early()

In our program, we do this manually via libc::signal(), **but in principle there is nothing to prevent an external process from also raising this signal at any stage.**

unsafe { longjmp() }

println!("early return!")

println!("finishing")

Figure 12.5   Control flow of the sjlj project. The program's control flow can be intercepted via a signal and then resumed from the point of setjmp().

Listing 12.14   Crate-level attribute required in main.rs

```
#![feature(link_llvm_intrinsics)]
```

This raises two immediate questions. We'll answer the following shortly:

- What is an intrinsic function?
- What is LLVM?

Additionally, we need to tell Rust about the functions that are being provided by LLVM. Rust won't know anything about them, apart from their type signatures, which means that any use of these must occur within an unsafe block. The following listing shows how to inform Rust about the LLVM functions. The source for this listing is in ch12/ch12-sjlj/src/main.rs.

Listing 12.15   Declaring the LLVM intrinsic functions within listing 12.17

```
extern "C" {
  #[link_name = "llvm.eh.sjlj.setjmp"]
  pub fn setjmp(_: *mut i8) -> i32;

  #[link_name = "llvm.eh.sjlj.longjmp"]
  pub fn longjmp(_: *mut i8);
}
```

Provides specific instructions to the linker about where it should look to find the function definitions

As we're not using the argument's name, uses an underscore (_) to make that explicit

This small section of code contains a fair amount of complexity. For example

- `extern "C"` means "This block of code should obey C's conventions rather than Rust's."
- The `link_name` attribute tells the linker where to find the two functions that we're declaring.
- The `eh` in `llvm.eh.sjlj.setjmp` stands for exception handling, and the `sjlj` stands for `setjmp/longjmp`.
- `*mut i8` is a pointer to a signed byte. For those with C programming experience, you might recognize this as the pointer to the beginning of a string (e.g., a `*char` type).

WHAT IS AN INTRINSIC FUNCTION?

Intrinsic functions, generally referred to as *intrinsics*, are functions made available via the compiler rather than as part of the language. Whereas Rust is largely target-agnostic, the compiler has access to the target environment. This access can facilitate extra functionality. For example, a compiler understands the characteristics of the CPU that the to-be-compiled program will run on. The compiler can make that CPU's instructions available to the program via intrinsics. Some examples of intrinsic functions include

- *Atomic operations*—Many CPUs provide specialist instructions to optimize certain workloads. For example, the CPU might guarantee that updating an integer is an atomic operation. Atomic here is meant in the sense of being indivisible. This can be extremely important when dealing with concurrent code.
- *Exception handling*—The facilities provided by CPUs for managing exceptions differ. These facilities can be used by programming language designers to create custom control flow. The `setjmp` and `longjmp` intrinsics, introduced later in this chapter, fall into this camp.

WHAT IS LLVM?

From the point of view of Rust programmers, LLVM can be considered as a subcomponent of rustc, the Rust compiler. LLVM is an external tool that's bundled with rustc. Rust programmers can draw from the tools it provides. One set of tools that LLVM provides is intrinsic functions.

LLVM is itself a compiler. Its role is illustrated in figure 12.6.

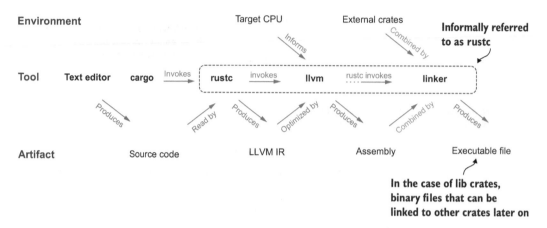

Figure 12.6   Some of the major steps required to generate an executable from Rust source code. LLVM is an essential part of the process but not one that is user-facing.

LLVM translates code produced by rustc, which produces LLVM IR (intermediate language) into machine-readable assembly language. To make matters more complicated, another tool, called a linker, is required to stitch multiple crates together. On Windows, Rust uses link.exe, a program provided by Microsoft as its linker. On other operating systems, the GNU linker ld is used.

Understanding more detail about LLVM implies learning more about rustc and compilation in general. Like many things, getting closer to the truth requires exploring through a fractal-like domain. Learning every subsystem seems to require learning about another set of subsystems. Explaining more here would be a fascinating, but ultimately distracting diversion.

12.9.3   *Casting a pointer to another type*

One of the more arcane parts of Rust's syntax is how to cast between pointer types. You'll encounter this as you make your way through listing 12.17. But problems can arise because of the type signatures of setjmp() and longjmp(). In this code snippet, extracted from listing 12.17, you can see that both functions take a *mut i8 pointer as an argument:

```
extern "C" {
  #[link_name = "llvm.eh.sjlj.setjmp"]
  pub fn setjmp(_: *mut i8) -> i32;

  #[link_name = "llvm.eh.sjlj.longjmp"]
  pub fn longjmp(_: *mut i8);
}
```

Requiring a *mut i8 as an input argument is a problem because our Rust code only has a reference to a *jump buffer* (e.g., &jmp_buf).[2] The next few paragraphs work through the process of resolving this conflict. The jmp_buf type is defined like this:

```
const JMP_BUF_WIDTH: usize =
  mem::size_of::<usize>() * 8;
type jmp_buf = [i8; JMP_BUF_WIDTH];
```

This constant is 64 bits wide (8 × 8 bytes) in 64-bit machines and 32 bits wide (8 × 4 bytes) on 32-bit machines.

The jmp_buf type is a type alias for an array of i8 that is as wide as 8 usize integers. The role of jmp_buf is to store the state of the program, such that the CPU's registers can be repopulated when needed. There is only one jmp_buf value within listing 12.17, a global mutable static called RETURN_HERE, defined on line 14. The following example shows how jmp_buf is initialized:

```
static mut RETURN_HERE: jmp_buf = [0; JMP_BUF_WIDTH];
```

How do we treat RETURN_HERE as a pointer? Within the Rust code, we refer to RETURN_HERE as a reference (&RETURN_HERE). LLVM expects those bytes to be presented as a *mut i8. To perform the conversion, we apply four steps, which are all packed into a single line:

```
unsafe { &RETURN_HERE as *const i8 as *mut i8 }
```

Let's explain what those four steps are:

1 Start with &RETURN_HERE, a read-only reference to a global static variable of type [i8; 8] on 64-bit machines or [i8; 4] on 32-bit machines.
2 Convert that reference to a *const i8. Casting between pointer types is considered safe Rust, but deferencing that pointer requires an unsafe block.
3 Convert the *const i8 to a *mut i8. This declares the memory as mutable (read/write).
4 Wrap the conversion in an unsafe block because it deals with accessing a global variable.

Why not use something like &mut RETURN_HERE as *mut i8? The Rust compiler becomes quite concerned about giving LLVM access to its data. The approach provided here, starting with a read-only reference, puts Rust at ease.

12.9.4 Compiling the sjlj project

We're now in a position where possible points of confusion about listing 12.17 should be minor. The following snippet again shows the behavior we're attempting to replicate:

---

[2] jmp_buf is the conventional name for this buffer, which might be useful for any readers who want to dive deeper themselves.

```
$ git clone https://github.com/rust-in-action/code rust-in-action
$ cd rust-in-action/ch12/ch12-sjlj
$ cargo run -q
#
#
early return!
finishing!
```

One final note: to compile correctly, the sjlj project requires that rustc is on the nightly channel. If you encounter the error "#![feature] may not be used on the stable release channel," use rustup install nightly to install it. You can then make use of the nightly compiler by adding the +nightly argument to cargo. The following console output demonstrates encountering that error and recovering from it:

```
$ cargo run -q
error[E0554]: #![feature] may not be used on the stable release channel
 --> src/main.rs:1:1
  |
1 | #![feature(link_llvm_intrinsics)]
  | ^^^^^^^^^^^^^^^^^^^^^^^^^^^^^^^^^^

error: aborting due to previous error

For more information about this error, try `rustc --explain E0554`.

$ rustup toolchain install nightly
...

$ cargo +nightly run -q
#
##
###
early return!
finishing!
```

12.9.5 *sjlj project source code*

The following listing employs LLVM's compiler to access the operating system's long-jmp facilities. longjmp allows programs to escape their stack frame and jump anywhere within their address space. The code for listing 12.6 is in ch12/ch12-sjlj/Cargo.toml and listing 12.17 is in ch12/ch12-sjlj/src/main.rs.

Listing 12.16 Project metadata for sjlj

```
[package]
name = "sjlj"
version = "0.1.0"
authors = ["Tim McNamara <code@timmcnamara.co.nz>"]
edition = "2018"

[dependencies]
libc = "0.2"
```

Listing 12.17 Using LLVM's internal compiler machinery (intrinsics)

```
 1 #![feature(link_llvm_intrinsics)]
 2 #![allow(non_camel_case_types)]
 3 #![cfg(not(windows))]                       Only compile
 4                                             on supported
 5 use libc::{                                 platforms.
 6   SIGALRM, SIGHUP, SIGQUIT, SIGTERM, SIGUSR1,
 7 };
 8 use std::mem;
 9
10 const JMP_BUF_WIDTH: usize =
11   mem::size_of::<usize>() * 8;
12 type jmp_buf = [i8; JMP_BUF_WIDTH];          When true, the
13                                              program exits.
14 static mut SHUT_DOWN: bool = false;
15 static mut RETURN_HERE: jmp_buf = [0; JMP_BUF_WIDTH];
16 const MOCK_SIGNAL_AT: usize = 3;
17                                              Allows a recursion
18 extern "C" {                                 depth of 3
19   #[link_name = "llvm.eh.sjlj.setjmp"]
20   pub fn setjmp(_: *mut i8) -> i32;
21
22   #[link_name = "llvm.eh.sjlj.longjmp"]
23   pub fn longjmp(_: *mut i8);
24 }
25
26 #[inline]
27 fn ptr_to_jmp_buf() -> *mut i8 {
28   unsafe { &RETURN_HERE as *const i8 as *mut i8 }
29 }
30
31 #[inline]
32 fn return_early() {
33   let franken_pointer = ptr_to_jmp_buf();
34   unsafe { longjmp(franken_pointer) };
35 }
36
37 fn register_signal_handler() {
38   unsafe {
39     libc::signal(SIGUSR1, handle_signals as usize);
40   }
41 }
42
43 #[allow(dead_code)]
44 fn handle_signals(sig: i32) {
45   register_signal_handler();
46
47   let should_shut_down = match sig {
48     SIGHUP => false,
49     SIGALRM => false,
50     SIGTERM => true,
51     SIGQUIT => true,
52     SIGUSR1 => true,
```

An #[inline] attribute marks the function as being available for inlining, which is a compiler optimization technique for eliminating the cost of function calls.

This is unsafe because Rust cannot guarantee what LLVM does with the memory at RETURN_HERE.

Asks libc to associate handle_signals with the SIGUSRI signal

```
53      _ => false,
54    };
55
56    unsafe {
57      SHUT_DOWN = should_shut_down;
58    }
59
60    return_early();
61  }
62
63  fn print_depth(depth: usize) {
64    for _ in 0..depth {
65      print!("#");
66    }
67    println!();
68  }
69
70  fn dive(depth: usize, max_depth: usize) {
71    unsafe {
72      if SHUT_DOWN {
73        println!("!");
74        return;
75      }
76    }
77    print_depth(depth);
78
79    if depth >= max_depth {
80      return;
81    } else if depth == MOCK_SIGNAL_AT {
82      unsafe {
83        libc::raise(SIGUSR1);
84      }
85    } else {
86      dive(depth + 1, max_depth);
87    }
88    print_depth(depth);
89  }
90
91  fn main() {
92    const JUMP_SET: i32 = 0;
93
94    register_signal_handler();
95
96    let return_point = ptr_to_jmp_buf();
97    let rc = unsafe { setjmp(return_point) };
98    if rc == JUMP_SET {
99      dive(0, 10);
100   } else {
101     println!("early return!");
102   }
103
104   println!("finishing!")
105 }
```

12.10 *A note on applying these techniques to platforms without signals*

Signals are a "UNIX-ism." On other platforms, messages from the OS are handled differently. On MS Windows, for example, command-line applications need to provide a handler function to the kernel via SetConsoleCtrlHandler. That handler function is then invoked when a signal is sent to the application.

Regardless of the specific mechanism, the high-level approach demonstrated in this chapter should be fairly portable. Here is the pattern:

- Your CPU generates interrupts that require the OS to respond.
- Operating systems often delegate responsibility for handling interrupts via some sort of callback system.
- A callback system means creating a function pointer.

12.11 *Revising exceptions*

At the start of the chapter, we discussed the distinction between signals, interrupts, and exceptions. There was little coverage of exceptions, directly. We have treated these as a special class of interrupts. Interrupts themselves have been modeled as signals.

To wrap up this chapter (and the book), we explored some of the features available in rustc and LLVM. The bulk of this chapter utilized these features to work with signals. Within Linux, signals are the main mechanism that the OS uses to communicate with applications. On the Rust side, we have spent lots of time interacting with libc and unsafe blocks, unpacking function pointers, and tweaking global variables.

Summary

- Hardware devices, such as the computer's network card, notify applications about data that is ready to be processed by sending an interrupt to the CPU.
- Function pointers are pointers that point to executable code rather than to data. These are denoted in Rust by the fn keyword.
- Unix operating systems manage job control with two signals: SIGSTOP and SIGCONT.
- Signal handlers do the least amount of work possible to mitigate the risk of triggering race conditions caused when multiple signal handlers operate concurrently. A typical pattern is to set a flag with a global variable. That flag is periodically checked within the program's main loop.
- To create a global variable in Rust, create a "mutable static." Accessing mutable statics requires an unsafe block.
- The OS, signals, and the compiler can be utilized to implement exception handling in programming languages via the setjmp and longjmp syscalls.
- Without the unsafe keyword, Rust programs would not be able to interface effectively with the OS and other third-party components.

index

419